The Aztec Economic World

This study explores the organization, scale, complexity, and integration of Aztec commerce across Mesoamerica at Spanish contact. The aims of the book are threefold. The first is to construct an in-depth understanding of the economic organization of precolumbian Aztec society and how it developed in the way that it did. The second is to explore the livelihoods of the individuals who bought, sold, and moved goods across a cultural landscape that lacked both navigable rivers and animal transport. Finally, this study models Aztec economy in a way that facilitates its comparison to other ancient and premodern societies around the world. What makes the Aztec economy unique is that it developed one of the most sophisticated market economies in the ancient world in a society with one of the worse transportation systems. This is the first book to provide an updated and comprehensive view of the Aztec economy in thirty years.

KENNETH G. HIRTH is Professor of Anthropology at Penn State University. His research focuses on the origin and development of ranked and state-level societies in the New World. He is especially interested in political economy and how forms of resource control lead to the development of structural inequalities within society.

The Aztec Economic World

Merchants and Markets in Ancient Mesoamerica

KENNETH G. HIRTH

Department of Anthropology
Penn State University

CAMBRIDGE
UNIVERSITY PRESS

One Liberty Plaza, 20th Floor, New York, NY 10006, USA

Cambridge University Press is part of the University of Cambridge.

It furthers the University's mission by disseminating knowledge in the pursuit of
education, learning and research at the highest international levels of excellence.

www.cambridge.org
Information on this title: www.cambridge.org/9781107142770

First published 2016

Printed in the United States of America by Sheridan Books, Inc.

A catalogue record for this publication is available from the British Library

Library of Congress Cataloging in Publication Data
Hirth, Kenn.
The Aztec economic world : merchants and markets in ancient Mesoamerica / by Kenneth
G. Hirth, Department of Anthropology, Penn State University.
pages cm
Includes bibliographical references and index.
ISBN 978-1-107-14277-0 (Hardback)
1. Aztecs–Economic conditions. 2. Aztecs–Commerce. 3. Merchants–Mexico–History–To
1500. 4. Indians of Mexico–Economic conditions. 5. Indians of Mexico–Commerce–
History–To 1500. I. Title. II. Title: Merchants and markets in ancient Mesoamerica.
F1219.76.E36H57 2016
972–dc23 2015034786

ISBN 978-1-107-14277-0 Hardback

Contents

Figures

Tables

Preface

This volume has grown out of my long-term interests in precolumbian Mesoamerican and the cross-cultural study of ancient economy. As an Economic Anthropologist I have always felt that New World societies are poorly understood and rarely incorporated into a systematic comparative discussion of economic complexity of ancient societies. Interest in the industrial revolution together within the broad theoretical framework of World Systems Theory has led to the impression that the indigenous societies incorporated into European colonial systems were simple suppliers of raw materials for the more complex Euro-centric economies of the Old World. The result is that the economic complexity of indigenous New World societies is often overlooked or underplayed. Furthermore as a Mesoamerican archaeologist, I feel that many students and colleagues have an incomplete understanding of how the precolumbian economy was organized. Archaeologists in Mesoamerica, like those in other areas of the ancient world, are keenly interested in the origin and development of complex society. While investigators have placed a great deal of attention on reconstructing the scale and organization of political structure, the complexity of the economic infrastructure that supported it is either not addressed or under studied.

The development of an evolutionary approach for studying complex society requires a comprehensive understanding of the society's socio-economic structures and how they changed over time. Understanding the structure of the Aztec economy is the goal of this study. In the process I hope to take a step closer to identifying the structure and the complexity of highland Nahua economies at the time of the Spanish conquest. Only then can the Mesoamerican economy be compared in terms of scale, level of trade, and forms of production to that found in other state level societies of the ancient world. The development of a comprehensive picture of economic activity both here and by future investigators will bring us one step closer to incorporating this important region into a broader cross-cultural and comparative study of ancient economy.

The structure of the Aztec economic world is examined using the ethnohistoric and early colonial written sources. A small amount of archaeology information is used but only as supplemental data. Although I have worked in Mesoamerica as an archaeologist my entire career, my goal was to focus on the written sources and construct a model of Aztec economic structure that could be tested systematically using archaeological data. Had I incorporated all of the available archaeological data into the discussion it would have produced a very different type of volume. Instead, I have chosen to push the historic sources to their interpretable limit with the goal of developing as complete and comprehensive model of prehispanic economic behavior as realistically possible. This avoids the problem of equifinality in archaeology where it is difficult to identify specific forms of behavior and organization because of an incompletely preserved material record. The focus on historic sources has made it possible to produce what I feel is an archaeologically informed model of Nahua economy that can be directly evaluated in future research using the direct historical approach.

A short note on presentation format used in this volume is in order. The volume employs Cambridge University Press guidelines. A glossary is included at the end of the volume to assist readers who are unfamiliar with Nahuatl and colonial Spanish terminology. Following format guidelines all glossary terms are placed in italic typeface along with other foreign words that are defined where they occur within the text. The exceptions to this practice are words of Nahuatl origin that refer to the names of precolumbian rulers, modern states and regions in Mexico, archaeological sites and contact period towns which are located on maps within the volume. Italicized words in English are generally for emphasis only. Finally, a detailed Index is presented at the end of the volume to assist readers in finding topical information specifically related to their individual interests.

I want to thank a number of individuals who have directly or indirectly contributed to the completion of this volume. Mark Christensen of Assumption College was my primary *consigliere* for Nahuatl orthography, grammar, and philology; Mark, it would have been impossible to develop an understanding of the Nahuatl view of economic gain and profit without your help. I appreciate the patience of my students in my Ancient Economy seminar for our productive discussions of different aspects of domestic and institutional economy. I especially want to thank the students in my lab for help on different aspects of the volume: Sarah Imfeld for paleographic work in both sixteenth-century Spanish and Nahuatl from the *Matrícula de Huexotzinco*, Sean Carr and Tara Mazurczky for maps and GIS work, and Karin Dennison and Mary Vinciguerra for preparing line drawings, photography, and illustrations. My greatest debt of gratitude goes to my family, especially my wife Susan for reading endless drafts and tolerating all of my eccentricities. Finally I especially want to thank Frances Berdan and Gerardo Gutierrez for reviewing the final draft of the manuscript. Over the years I have benefited from numerous conversations with both of them on different aspects of Aztec economy. I took all of their helpful comments into account to the best of my ability. The errors and inconsistencies that remain are a testimony to where my ability to address them fell short.

The initial sparks that fired my interest in cross-cultural economic comparisons can be traced to the diversity of books that I've read on ancient and premodern economies over the past two decades out of curiosity and for leisure. Penn State University supplied the sabbatical leave that allowed me to read extensively on the cross-cultural practices of merchants. Anastasia Graf and the editorial staff of Cambridge University Press have been very helpful guiding me through all the steps of preparing the final draft for publication. Finally, I want to thank Bridget Gazzo and all of the staff at Dumbarton Oaks for access to their outstanding library. There is no better place in the world to conduct research on Mesoamerican archaeology and ethnohistory and I am fortunate to have spent a summer in residence there as a senior fellow during 2010.

Abbreviations

CIESAS	Centro de Investigaciones y Estudios Superiores en Antropologia Social
BAR	British Archaeological Reports
INAH	Instituto Nacional de Antropología e Historia
UCLA	University of California Los Angeles
UNAM	Universidad Nacional Autónoma de México

Introduction to the Aztec economic world

In the modern world, international commerce provides more links between the people of different nations than *all* the political, religious, and humanitarian delegations combined. Every day, millions of goods are produced, shipped, bought, and sold by over seven billion people around the world. People pay little attention to where these goods come from. Instead, they simply expect them to appear on the shelves of their local grocery stores or in the public marketplace. The ingredients for even a simple lunch can come from many different places around the world, the result of modern commercial networks and how efficiently they mobilize the products we consume. These networks, of course, are not new. The movement of resources from producers to consumers in rural and urban settings has been an indispensable part of large-scale societies throughout human history. Two important questions for the study of ancient economy, of course, are what types of goods moved through regional networks during preindustrial times, and in what volume?

The way goods are transferred from producers to consumers takes many different forms. In the modern world, goods and money move through multiple channels as wages, gifts, grants, and taxes to name a few, each representing a different sphere of distribution and exchange. The same was true for the distant past; goods and resources moved through multiple economic and social channels in large-scale ancient societies. One of the challenges of social historians is to reconstruct the economic organization of ancient societies where information is limited or of uneven quality. As societies grew in size the goods needed to provision them often had to move over further and further distances. One of the solutions to this problem in many places around the world was the appearance of merchants and merchant groups who were the agents that bridged the gap between producers and consumers.

The merchant, whether male or female, is an exchange and transportation specialist. They procure goods or resources and move them over space to their final consumers. Whether merchants link producers directly with consumers or form part of a network through which consumables flow is simply a matter of scale. Their function remains the same: they provide a provisioning function from which they obtain a portion of their livelihood.

This book is about the indigenous merchants and commercial behavior found in prehispanic Mexico at the moment of Spanish contact. When Hernando Cortés landed his expeditionary force of 600 men on the coast of Veracruz, Mexico in 1519 he expected to find a native population organized as relatively small *cacicazgos* or chiefdom societies like those encountered on Hispaniola and elsewhere throughout the Caribbean. Instead, he encountered the densely populated and powerful Aztec empire that was organized for conquest at a continental scale. What ensued was one of the great adventure stories of all time. Cortés and his intrepid force of Spaniards conquered the Aztecs in a two-year period through a series of both planned and unplanned events. Conflict, disease, and political intrigue were the tools of the conquest and Cortés would never have defeated the Aztecs without the tens of thousands of soldiers provided by the Tlaxcalans and other indigenous native kingdoms that were long-standing enemies of the Aztecs.

The Spaniards marveled at the scale and structure of native societies. They were large, well-organized kingdoms with impressive urban centers and complex economies. Two dimensions of the Aztec economy especially impressed the Spanish conquistadors: the wealth of the Aztec tribute network and the size and richness of their indigenous marketplaces. While the tribute system maintained the Aztec state, the marketplaces supported a rich commercial society where the greater population bought and sold the staples of everyday life. These marketplaces were identical in function to the *suqs* and market bazaars that the conquistadors had seen in Spain and other parts of the Old World. What was different was their size. The Spanish were astonished by the number of people who frequented them, the variety of goods sold, and the well-ordered manner in which marketplaces operated. This amazement is captured in many of the first-hand accounts of the Tlatelolco marketplace in the Aztec capital of Tenochtitlan (Cortés 1962; Díaz del Castillo 1956). Bernal Díaz del Castillo writes,

When we arrived at the great market place, called Tlaltelolco, we were astounded at the number of people and the quantity of merchandise that it contained, and at the good order and control that was maintained, for we had never seen such a thing before

(Díaz del Castillo 1956:215).

The Spanish understood commercial society. The Mediterranean world of the fifteenth and sixteenth centuries was in the midst of a mercantile revolution. The Portugese explorations in Africa, India, and Indonesia brought a multitude of new exotic products and riches into the market-places of the western Mediterranean. Many of the conquistadors were well traveled and they were not easily impressed by native institutions given their ethnocentric biases against non-Christian societies. It is within this context that their comments must be understood. While they had seen large markets at Salamanca and Cordoba, they were still impressed with the level of commercial activity found across the Mexican highlands.

This study explores the organization, scale, and complexity of indigenous commercial behavior across the Central and Southern Mexican highlands, an area I refer to as the Aztec economic world. The term Aztec is commonly used to refer to the Late Postclassic (AD 1200–1520) Nahua people of Central Mexico (Evans and Webster 2001:59) and I follow that convention here. The specific population that formed the core of the Aztec empire resided on the island of Tenochtitlan and referred to themselves as the Culhua-Mexica.[1] They are best known for the conquest of a large area of Mesoamerica and its integration into a tribute empire between AD 1428 and 1519 (Figures 1.1 and 1.2). This is the empire that Hernando Cortés and the Spanish conquistadors encountered in 1519 and which represents the greater part of the Aztec world. While many different ethnic groups[2] resided within the empire, they shared similar forms of domestic and institutional economic organization.

The Aztec empire covered an area of between 160,000 and 165,000 sq. km that extended from just south of the Isthmus of Tehuantepec to 150 km north of Mexico City, and from the Gulf of Mexico to the Pacific coast (Figure 1.2). The inception of the Aztec empire can be traced to the formation of the Triple Alliance in AD 1428 when the three city-states of Tenochtitlan, Texcoco, and Tlacopan came together to overthrow the rule of the Tepanec state. From that point on, these three city-states worked together to conquer and shape the tribute empire with the Aztecs playing an increasingly dominant role over its span of growth between AD 1428 and 1519. The empire was composed of many small independent or

FIGURE 1.1 Western Mesoamerica: Major communities and *altepeme* centers mentioned in the text

semi-independent city-states centered on a principal town or confederation of towns from which they derived their name. These small political entities were called *altepeme* (sing. *altepetl*) in the Nahuatl language and were the action entities for political and local economic interaction both before and after Aztec conquest.[3] Examples of some of these *altepeme* polities include Cholula, Coixtlahuaca, Tenochtitlan, Tepeaca, and Texcoco to name a few (Figures 1.1 and 1.3).

THE NATURAL ENVIRONMENT FOR COMMERCE

The core of the Aztec empire was the central and southern Mexican highlands north and west of the Isthmus of Tehuantec. I refer to the area west of the Isthmus of Tehuantec as western Mesoamerica throughout this volume (Figure 1.1) to distinguish it from the greater region of Maya and related Mesoamerican cultures located further to the east. The Aztec empire extended from the Atlantic to the Pacific coasts, incorporating environments extending from sea level to the tops of Mexico's highest

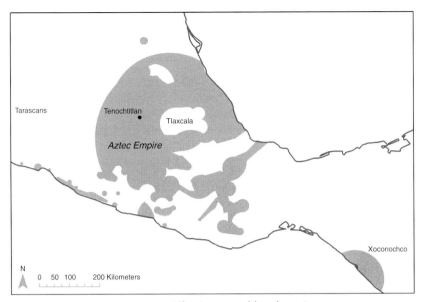

FIGURE I.2 The Aztec world and empire

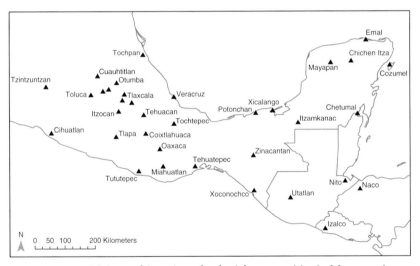

FIGURE I.3 Major prehispanic and colonial communities in Mesoamerica

mountain peaks over 5,000 m in elevation.[4] The highland core of the empire is a dissected environment of several large valley and basin areas (e.g. the Basin of Mexico and the Valleys of Morelos, Oaxaca, Puebla, and Toluca) separated by mountain ridges. Elevation differences within the

FIGURE 1.4 Tierra Fria and Tierra Helada environment of the Iztaccihuatl volcano in Central Mexico

highlands have produced an environment that juxtaposes differing ecological zones in close proximity to one another. These differences are most noticeable during the rainy season when perennial flora spring to life.

Differences in elevation create a mosaic of five differing climatic-vegetation zones that define Mesoamerica's complex resource ecology. These are: 1) the Atlantic and Pacific coasts where marine resources including fish and salt are available; 2) the *tierra caliente* or hot lands below 1,000 m msl where tropical commodities such as fruits, cotton, cacao, and other tropical flora and fauna are found; 3) the frost-free *tierra templada* or temperate lands between 1,000 and 2,000 m msl that maintain an average temperature of around 60 degrees F. throughout the year and are well suited for agriculture; 4) the forested *tierra fria* or cold lands from 2,000–2,800 m msl where temperatures during the coldest months can drop below freezing creating problems for agriculture; and, 5) the *tierra helada* or frozen lands above 2,800 m msl which can receive snowfall during winter months and include the snow covered peaks of Mexico's highest mountains (Figure 1.4). Figure 1.5 illustrates the distribution of these climatic-vegetation zones across western Mesoamerica which represents the area between Lake Cuitzeo and the Isthmus of Tehuantepec. Figures 1.6 and 1.7 show some of the ecological variation found over Mesoamerica ranging from mangrove swamps along the Pacific coast near Xoconochco to thorn forests in the Tehuacan Valley.

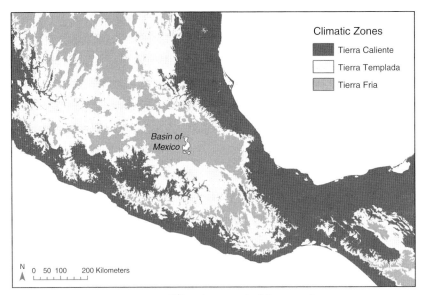

FIGURE 1.5 Climatic zones in Mesoamerica

FIGURE 1.6 Mangrove swamp along the Pacific coast of Xoconochco

What is important about western Mesoamerican cultural geography is that every area within this region is within 90 km of a different resource zone. This was significant for prehispanic trade because it meant that the vast majority of indigenous communities across this area were located

FIGURE 1.7 Thorn Forest in the Tehuacan Valley, Puebla, Mexico

within 1–3 *jornadas*, a normal day's walking journey of 30 km, to a different ecological zone from the one they lived in.[5] This sharp juxtaposition of environmental resources was succinctly summarized by Francisco Hernández in the middle sixteenth century where he states,

It is amazing that in a distance of as little as three miles one encounters so many variations in temperature: here you freeze and there you boil, not because of the weather, but because of the topography of the valleys ... All of this means that these areas produce two harvests a year, nearly three, because at the time that one is extremely cold, another is predominantly hot

(Varey 2000:73).

Figure 1.8 illustrates the portion of western Mesoamerica that is within 30 km of another resource zone of at least 1 sq. km in size. This figure shows that if settlements were randomly distributed across Central Mexico, fully 86.6% of all towns and villages would be within one day's walk or less from another major resource zone (Hirth 2013b). The percentage actually is much higher since the Basin of Mexico and the adjoining areas of the valleys of Toluca and Puebla-Tlaxcala were studded with small fresh water lakes and/or seasonal marshes that provided their own unique set of exploitable waterfowl, fish, and insect resources

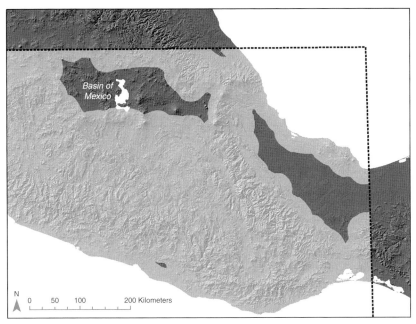

FIGURE 1.8 Areas of the Mexican highlands within 30 km of another ecological interface

(e.g. Parsons 1996, 2001, 2008) that added to regional resource diversity.[6] When these highland lacustrine zones are taken into account virtually all of the western highlands is within a normal day's journey of a different resource zone.

Archaeologists and historians have long recognized that resource diversity was an engine behind trade and commerce (Braudel 1986). William Sanders (1956, 1962; Sanders and Price 1968) was one of the first investigators to argue for the importance of ecological diversity in stimulating economic interaction throughout Central Mexico. While Sanders was concerned with the origin of political complexity, he recognized that economic diversity stimulated economic interaction at multiple levels.[7] The close spacing of different resource zones, and the desire for the different resources and agricultural products available from them, led to a high degree of symbiotic interaction between communities and households located in different ecological zones.

This close juxtaposition of different resources meant that different zones could be exploited by households without much difficulty. It created multiple intersecting distribution spheres that moved different resources over distances of 20–40 km. This is the distance range that commoner households could easily navigate to engage in trade. Differences in elevation and variable rainfall patterns created different agricultural cycles and levels of crop risk across the highlands. Exchange was one way to mediate these risks and to provision households with resources they did not produce. A review of indigenous trade during the sixteenth century reveals that the movement and trade of perishable and imperishable commodities was commonplace over distances of 50–150 km (Hirth 2013b).

The dissected highland topography created a landscape of small polities with strong local ethnic identities that fiercely sought to maintain their independence from one another. This makes discussing general economic practices across the Aztec economic world challenging because it requires generalizing about groups that saw themselves as unique and ethnically distinct. This is complicated by the fact that the largest body of historic information comes from the Basin of Mexico which was the center of the Aztec empire. The marketplace was the central economic institution in all highland societies which enabled all individuals to be involved in commerce to differing degrees. Nevertheless, many of the same economic structures were shared by Tarascan groups to the west, and Maya groups to the east. Juan de Grijalva's initial exploration of the coast of Mexico in 1517 reported bustling markets, port towns, and wealthy merchants along the entire Gulf Coast all the way to Yucatán (Bernal Díaz 1956:6). In one case the Spanish referred to the town of Ecab in northeastern Yucatán as the "Great Cairo" because of its size and apparent commercial prosperity.[8]

Ancient Mexico possessed a rich commercial economy that in the early sixteenth century was as complex as any the Spanish had seen in the Mediterranean world. Understanding the structure of this economy is important for the comparative study of ancient economic systems because it developed under a different set of conditions than those in the Old World. One of its most distinctive differences is that it lacked an effective system of transportation (Hassig 1985). The precolumbian societies of ancient Mexico did not have wheeled vehicles, beasts of burden, or a system of large-scale maritime commerce like that found in the Old World. All the goods moving across the Mexican and Guatemalan highlands were carried on the backs of human porters (*tlameme*) (Figure 1.9). Elsewhere small dugout canoes were important for moving goods across freshwater lakes and along navigable rivers (Figure 1.10). Lake transportation was very important in the economic integration of the Basin of Mexico. Canoes moved agricultural goods from different areas of the lake

FIGURE 1.9 *Tlameme* porters

system and fostered the development of marketplaces in Tenochtitlan, Tlatelolco, and other lakeside cities (Hassig 1985). The nature of maritime and riverine transportation is less well known. Large maritime canoes may have transported goods along the Atlantic and Pacific coasts (Thompson 1949) although it is difficult to know what the frequency and scale of this maritime commerce was.[9]

While several modes of transportation existed in Mesoamerica, the overwhelming majority of goods moved within and between regions on the backs of human porters. This level of transportation technology stands in sharp contrast to that found in the Mediterranean world where the ability to transport items cheaply and regularly by both land and sea was instrumental in enabling or limiting the level of regional and inter-regional

FIGURE 1.10 Canoe transportation in the Aztec world

economic interaction (Braudel 1986; Casson 1991; Landers 2003). Given these differences it would be no surprise to find that the indigenous economies of ancient Mexico were organized differently than the commercial systems found throughout the Old World.

THE IMPORTANCE OF INDIGENOUS NEW WORLD ECONOMIC SYSTEMS

This volume has three fundamental goals. First, it develops a model of the precolumbian highland economy from the perspective of economic anthropology that is relevant for the comparative study of ancient and premodern commercial behavior across the pre-industrial world. The perspective taken here is that all premodern commercial behavior is instructive for understanding the long-term processes of modern market development. The cross-cultural perspective in anthropology assumes that while societies may differ from one another in many ways, there are commonalities in the way humans adapt to their natural and cultural environments that permit making useful inter-societal comparisons about economic organization. Research suggests that many of the commercial behaviors identified in early states (Abu-Loghod 1989; Garraty and Stark

2010; Grassby 1999; Moore and Lewis 1999; Silver 1995) were present in the earlier and simpler societies that preceded them. That similar commercial behaviors may have developed independently in the Old and New Worlds with very different transportation systems is an important topic for the comparative study of ancient economy.

Most discussions of the ancient and premodern economy have focused on Old World societies in the Mediterranean, Near East, and Europe (Braudel 1982, 1986; Finley 1985; Holleran 2012; Marx 1964; Pirenne 1939; Weber 1976; Young 2001). One reason for this is the greater availability of written sources on Mediterranean trade and the role that western merchants played in the formation of modern market systems.[10] It is here that the principal building blocks of the modern economy were laid including the invention of coinage, banking and lending systems, maritime commerce and insurance, the privatization of property, the development of the joint stock company, and the industrial revolution.[11] Conversely Asia, Africa, and the Americas are less frequently discussed or are considered marginal to the discussion of ancient economy. I believe the reason for this is that they are considered to be outside the commercial lineage that led to the development of today's modern capitalistic system.

The emergence of World Systems Theory (Wallerstein 1976) as a way to study globalization and the effects of world capitalism also has impacted the comparative study of economic systems by giving primacy to European economic development. Areas that were embraced by European colonialism or that lay on the periphery of the European World System were viewed as underdeveloped or outside the sphere of emerging European capitalism (Frank 1976, 1981; Wolf 1982). As a result, areas of the New World, East Asia, and Africa have received less economic study despite possessing lively market economies and active commercial systems (Garraty 2010).

Non-western economic systems have been neglected as subjects of study for four reasons. First, they lie outside of the direct historical tradition of western Europe where the industrial revolution took place. While they are important in their own right, they do not provide much direct insight into the development of industrial capitalism. Second, information on the economic structure of non-western societies is often sparse. In many cases non-western economies either lacked writing, did not use it for economic purposes, or have few preserved documents available for scholarly examination. Third, these societies often operated on non-capitalistic principles with different forms of production and distribution from those found in Europe. While true, it did not make these societies any less commercial than some of their European counterparts, an important point that is often overlooked. Fourth and finally, colonialism resulted in both the intentional and unintentional destruction of indigenous systems of trade and commerce minimizing what can be deduced from historic documents about pre-colonial economic structures (Murphy and Steward 1956; A. Smith 1991). The discussion that follows attempts to reconstruct the prehispanic economy of ancient Mexico so that it can be compared to other premodern societies around the world. As such it seeks a broad comparative, rather than a regionally particularistic, view of ancient Aztec economy.

A second goal of this volume is to explore the role and scope of individuals who bought, moved, and sold goods as part of their precolumbian livelihood. It addresses the question of who was involved in commercial activities for profit and/or subsistence provisioning in a system where human porters were the primary vehicle for moving goods over space. It examines the question of *who qualifies as a merchant* within this context. Was it only full-time professionals involved in medium- and long-distance trade, or should it include part-time participants who also sold goods for profit? Professional, full-time merchants were a dynamic component of the commercial landscape in all ancient complex societies where there is evidence of long-distance trade. The issue rarely addressed is the degree that commoner households also engaged in commercial dealings on a part-time basis. This question is addressed to the extent possible using the qualitative information on the economic activities available in the early colonial sources.[12]

Merchants, whether they operate on a full- or part-time basis, are economic agents. They act on their own behalf and move goods over the landscape to the individuals who ultimately purchase them. The investigation of economic strategies, motivations, and the scale of operation of merchants is a contribution to agency theory in that it deals with the outcomes of intentional commercial acts (Dobres and Robb 2000; Flannery 1999). While it is not possible to examine the activities of specific individuals in the context of this study, understanding the level of commercial behavior that they engaged in helps to establish the scope and framework of merchant behavior. More generally, it provides insight into how the collective action of numerous independent commercial decisions can shape a society's economic landscape.

Third and finally, this volume presents a structural model of precolumbian economic organization that describes levels of economic interaction found across the Aztec economic world. It is more concerned with characterizing *how* the precolumbian economy operated than it is adhering to any specific theoretical view of the economy. It presents commercial interaction as the product of individually motivated economic desires designed to enhance household and individual economic well-being. In this regard the approach follows individual maximization principles and recognizes the importance of transaction costs in governing human behavior. It follows formalist and neoclassical economic principles as they are applied to understanding individual decision making, risk minimization, and the creation of wealth (Garraty 2010; Netting 1990; North 1981, 1997). At the same time it recognizes that the valuation criteria involved in individual decision making is established by the society in which individuals reside. Culture sets the parameters of economic interaction which are embedded in existing social networks rather than being a free-standing feature of the society where they are found (Granovetter 1985; Gudeman 2001).

A central objective is to develop a more comprehensive understanding of the modes of organization for both production and exchange. That is, how were labor and resources brought together to produce or procure the resources necessary to support, not only the state apparatus of society, but also the domestic households that supported it. Understanding the structure of economic organization is fundamental for identifying the causes for how it changed over time. The discussion that follows develops a bottom-up view of how individuals in the precolumbian world constructed or used their social networks to improve their economic well-being through commercial interaction.

EXPLORING COMMERCIAL BEHAVIOR

The chapters that follow examine different aspects of economic behavior practiced across the Aztec economic world. I explore the structure of the Aztec economy using ethnohistoric and early colonial written sources. The reason for using a historic rather than an archaeological approach for this investigation is twofold. First, the historic sources while limited in number contain information on a broader range of economic behavior than can be obtained from archaeology. Second, while archaeology can provide useful data on prehispanic production and exchange, the problem of equifinality often makes it difficult to identify the specific economic behavior that produced the patterning of material remains recovered in the archaeological record. What I have chosen to do is push the historic sources to the limits of interpretation to extract as much information from them as reasonably possible. While caution always needs to be maintained when "reading the sources" my goal is to construct a model of Aztec economic organization that can be examined and tested in future research using archaeological data.

The first three chapters provide information on the structure of indigenous economic systems derived from a combination of contact period accounts and archaeological information. Chapter 2 constructs a general model of the precolumbian economy that is germane to understanding both Aztec and earlier economic systems. It subdivides the economy into its two fundamental components, the *domestic economy* organized to support individual family units, and the *institutional economy* operating above the level of individual households (Hirth 2012a). The institutional economy was composed of both formal and informal economic relationships and was much broader in structure than what is often referred to simply as political economy. *Informal institutions* were the principles and customs that operated between households often on a voluntary basis to provide inter-household support and to mobilize labor or resources when needed. *Formal institutions* were the special-purpose organizations that operated at the level of the whole society to integrate multifaceted groups into a cohesive state. This framework provides the context for discussing a range of topics including Aztec land tenure, taxation, tribute, craft production, and prebendal estates. The chapter summarizes how resources were produced and mobilized in each of these different but overlapping domestic and institutional spheres.

Chapter 3 focuses on the structure and operation of the precolumbian marketplace. The marketplace was the center of economic life in highland Mesoamerica. It was the primary conduit through which households provisioned themselves with the resources that they did not produce. It also was the institution through which surpluses were mobilized, made available to the broader population, and perishable goods were converted to storable wealth. Understanding the role and structure of the marketplace is fundamental for modeling the level of commercial development found in Mesoamerica at the time of the conquest. The marketplace was the arena where strangers could meet to exchange goods, enduring business relations could be fostered, and individuals involved in commerce could make a profit to support themselves and their families. Moreover, the marketplace provided economic opportunities for farmers and craftsmen to sell the fruits of their labor for economic gain. The opportunities offered by the marketplace over the course of its development shaped the Aztec economy encountered by the Spanish in the early sixteenth century.

Commerce, as the term implies, is trade and exchange for purposes of making a profit. Anthropologists studying indigenous societies have long recognized that many exchanges are not motivated by profit or even the desire to improve economic well-being. Instead, they may be used to establish and maintain social relationships fundamental to the operation of society (Dalton 1977; Drucker and Heizer 1967; Malinowski 1922; Mauss 1990). Chapter 4, therefore, examines the question of who was engaged in commerce and whether the concept of profit was a motivating force for exchange and is appropriate for exploring the economic relationships in the precolumbian world. It identifies and discusses the three broad categories of commercial practitioners found in the Nahuatl sources: the household producer-seller (*tlachiuhqui*), the general merchandiser and market vender (*tlanamacac*), and the commercial retailer (*tlanecuilo*). The discussion examines what prehispanic merchants did and how their activities affected prehispanic economy.

Chapters 5, 6, and 7 explore the different levels of commercial activity found in the Aztec world at the time of the conquest. Chapter 5 examines the part-time domestic producer-seller whose principal venue was sale in the marketplace. Like many other ancient societies, this group of small-scale producers generated most of the commercial activity in Mesoamerica. They account for the majority of transactions performed, the volume of the goods exchanged, and the number of individuals involved in commerce on a full- or part-time basis. One hundred and twenty four different producer-sellers are identified in the sources, most of who resided in commoner households that produced most of the food, fiber, and craft goods consumed in Mesoamerica. Finally it explores the role of household self-sufficiency and how domestic entrepreneurship led to diversification in household activities.

In contrast to small-scale producer-sellers, Chapters 6 and 7 examine professional merchants who engaged in commerce on a full-time basis. Professional merchants fall into two categories. Chapter 6 discusses those individuals who can be classified as merchant retailers. They worked at a regional and inter-regional scale selling both finished goods and raw materials bought from other individuals. Retail merchants are identified in the historic sources from the terminology used to describe them, the diversity of goods they sold, and, when apparent, from evidence that they sold imported goods from distant lands. The discussion examines the commercial areas where retailing occurred, the role of women in commerce, and the existence of several economic specialists including itinerant peddlers, bankers, and exchange specialists.

Chapter 7 examines the highly specialized long-distant merchants that dealt primarily in luxury goods. Referred to as the *pochteca* and/or *oztomeca*, these merchants criss-crossed Mesoamerica moving a range of high-value goods both within and between regions. These merchants were private entrepreneurs in every sense of the word. Their goal was the procurement of wealth in the form of feathers, textiles, jade, cacao, and other goods that they bought and sold in the marketplace. While economically independent, these long-distant merchants served the state as commercial agents, political envoys, and foreign spies. The size and structure of merchant communities are examined along with a discussion of the ritual life of merchants. The activities of long-distance merchants are relatively well understood because of the rich body of information compiled by Sahagún (1959; Garibay 1961) from his Tlatelolco-Tenochtitlan informants who were some of the last surviving members of prehispanic merchant groups.

The two concluding chapters move the discussion to a broader consideration of prehispanic commercial activity across Mesoamerica. Chapter 8 examines the tools employed in these commercial dealings. It explores the moral economy as well as the commercial structures used to facilitate the movement of goods over space under the constraints of a prehispanic transportation system where most goods moved on the backs of human porters. Forms of precolumbian money are discussed along with the role that barter as a traditional means of trade may have been used to facilitate exchange. Finally, it examines the extent to which commercial practices like loans, credit, and the use of agents found throughout the Old World, were parallel developments in Mesoamerica. The concluding chapter provides a discussion of the main features of the Aztec economy and how it compares to premodern societies elsewhere around the world.

The Aztec economic world was the most highly commercialized indigenous system to develop in the New World. Aztec society lacked price responsive markets in land, labor, and capital. Nevertheless, it has an interesting mix of commercial and non-commercial forms of production in a setting without wage labor, private property, formal currencies, credit and lending institutions, and efficient forms of transportation. Despite these limitations, the network of regionally integrated marketplaces that developed across the Aztec world was among the most sophisticated market systems ever to appear in the ancient world. Understanding the scale, complexity, and integration of this system is important because it provides a uniquely New World perspective on how commercial activity was organized in a different place and moment in time.

2

The structure of Mesoamerican economy

Any meaningful discussion of ancient commerce requires a comprehensive understanding of the prehispanic economy in which it occurred. The reason for this is simple: the economy is broader than the sum of the commercial transactions that it contains.[1] Indeed, small-scale economies may lack commercial exchange relationships entirely, and may be organized primarily around gifting, mobilized transfers, and redistribution mechanisms. While commercial transactions were an important component of all Mesoamerican societies, many resources moved through non-commercial transfers at the household, community, and state levels. It is important, therefore, to situate commerce within the broader systems of production and distribution that define the economy.

Karl Polanyi (1957; Polanyi et al. 1957) emphasized the social dimension of premodern economies and how the production and movement of resources were embedded within larger social networks. From Polanyi's perspective, economic activities were not ends in themselves, but subordinate pursuits to achieve more important social, religious, and political goals. From a structural point of view Polanyi felt that simple forms of exchange could not take place apart from, and outside of, a variety of mediating social institutions that structured economic relationships. While he was correct in drawing attention to the diversity of ways that commercial exchange could be structured, he was incorrect in asserting that individual self-benefit and profit were not motives for trade and exchange. Individuals regularly engaged in exchange transactions across Mesoamerica to enhance their material well-being just as they did in other areas of the ancient world.

Mesoamerican economy is often described either in functional terms or from the perspective of its political economy. The functional perspective views economic behavior in terms of the production, distribution, and consumption of resources (Nash 1967). This approach sorts economic behavior into the key activities that individuals use to support themselves socially and to reproduce themselves biologically. Researchers following this approach in Mesoamerican studies have produced excellent economic studies on agriculture (Luna 2014; Rojas Rabiela 1983), craft production (Clark and Bryant 1997; Feinman and Nicholas 1993; Hirth 2008b; Muñera Bermudez 1985; Pastrana 1998; Sheets 1975), and trade (Dreiss and Brown 1989; Minc 2006; Stark and Garraty 2010). While a functional approach is useful for defining domains of economic behavior, it does not provide a synthetic understanding of the whole economy and how these economic sectors were integrated with one another.

In contrast, the political economy perspective is more interested in how the production and mobilization of resources contributed to the development and support of complex social stratification. Scholars following this approach have focused on the structure of tribute systems, the operation of market systems, and organization of long-distance trade (Berdan and Anawalt 1992; Blanton and Feinman 1984; Blanton and Hodge 1996; Brumfiel 1987; Carrasco 1978; Chapman 1957a, 1957b; M. Smith 2004). Although this provides insight into the creation and maintenance of specific political institutions, it does not provide a comprehensive view of the organization and integration of economic behavior. What is needed is an approach that incorporates functional components of the economy with a holistic discussion of its scale, organizational complexity, and segmental specialization and integration.

This chapter provides a more nuanced view of prehispanic Mesoamerican economy by combining both the structural and distributional aspects of economic activity. These perspectives examine different dimensions of economic behavior. The *structural dimension* examines economic organization and the ways in which people and resources were brought together and integrated in the production, distribution, and consumption of resources and commodities. Here social organization, technology, and ideology all play a role in determining how economic activities were organized across the cultural landscape. The *distributional dimension* of the economy examines the movement of resources from their points of production to their end-points of consumption (Hirth 1998, 2010; Stark and Garraty 2010). This is a resource and commodity focused level of analysis that reconstructs how goods moved within and between different levels of society. Examination of the distribution of specific commodities is a fundamental step in the archaeological reconstruction of prehistoric economic behavior. Although the structure and distributional perspectives are closely related, they provide complementary but contrasting views of an economy's organization and how products flowed between its different sectors.

DOMESTIC AND INSTITUTIONAL ECONOMY

The value of the structural perspective is that it focuses attention on how economic activity was organized in social terms. In this discussion the economy is divided into the domestic and institutional sectors which facilitate examining the multi-faceted modes of production and distribution that operated in Mesoamerica. All societies have this dual, two-part division in economic structure (Hirth 2010, 2012a). The *domestic economy* as mentioned in the introduction refers to the many ways that households access resources individually or jointly to meet their biological and social needs. The domestic economy is organized at the level of the family, household, or minimal domestic unit found in society. Its function is to meet the needs and wants of its members and applies equally well to both commoner and high-status households even if they are organized differently to meet these ends. It deals with the production, procurement, and consumption of food, clothing, housing, knowledge, and technology necessary for life and reproduction (Johnson and Earle 1987:11). While relatively unglamorous in terms of the types of activities that households engaged in, the domestic economy supported the greatest number of people and accounted for the greatest volume of goods produced and consumed in *all* ancient societies. The domestic economy was the foundation on which all other economic activity was based because the majority of the available labor in ancient societies resided in commoner households.

The *institutional economy* refers to the way that social, political, and religious activities are funded and organized above the level of the household. Institutions can be characterized as *informal* or *formal* depending on how economic interaction was structured between domestic contexts. *Formal institutions* refer to the specially constructed organizational structures that provide social, political, and religious functions for the society as a whole. They require resources to operate which they either extract from the households they serve or produce on their own in contexts that they directly control. They also include the ways that members of elite households produce or extract resources from society for their support. When elite households provide services for other domestic units within society and receive support to carry them out they are a component of the institutional economy even though they use a portion of these resources to meet their biological and social needs.

Informal institutions are the special rules, customs, expectations, and economic arrangements that operate on a quasi-voluntary basis and often without directed oversight to assist individual households in their economic and social pursuits. Informal institutions normally operate at the lineage or community levels to support households on a regular basis or in times of need. The domestic and institutional realms of economic activity are fundamental to societies at all levels of cultural complexity and are illustrated in Figure 2.1. What this illustration shows is that while formal

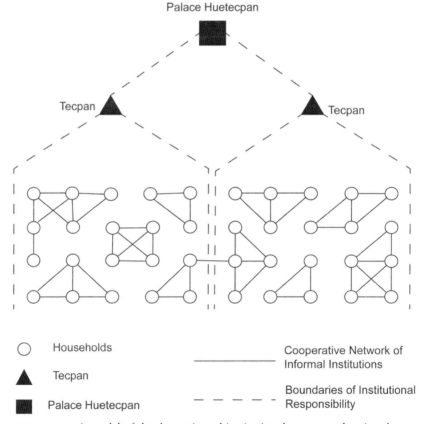

FIGURE 2.1 A model of the domestic and institutional economy showing the interaction of households through informal and formal institutions

institutions embrace all households in society, informal institutions operate on an inter-household basis and the networks they form vary with the initiatives of the households that draw upon them.

The distributional perspective shifts our attention from the way people are organized to the resources and commodities involved in different aspects of economic activity (Hirth 1998). For example, the resources produced and/or consumed in institutional contexts may differ in type and quantity from those moving through domestic contexts. Likewise, there may be different norms of resource use, consumption, or ownership in institutional contexts from those found in households. In our modern society the domestic economy is integrated primarily through commercial interaction while the institutional economy is organized through one-way economic transfers (i.e. taxes, tithes, tariffs, philanthropic donations, etc.) for which there is often variable or questionable reciprocal return (Pryor 1977). Understanding how production and distribution mechanisms affected the movement and flow of resources within and between the domestic and institutional sectors is fundamental to modeling commercial and non-commercial relationships within society.

While the domestic and institutional economy are convenient analytical categories for modeling economic organization, they were not mutually exclusive realms of behavior. Overlapping and/or conflicting demands forced individual households to adjust their domestic time budgets to fulfil institutional obligations for both labor and material goods. It is within this context that the marketplace emerged as an important institution in Mesoamerican society. While the marketplace grew organically out of its fundamental role of provisioning households (Blanton 1983), it eventually became the point of intersection between the domestic and institutional economies. It was here that surplus food produced on elite estates was sold to the broader commoner population to procure wealth goods to support elite and institutional consumption.

It would be naive to assume that all areas of Mesoamerica were organized in exactly the same way and no such assumption is made here. Important differences existed in how economies were structured in highland and lowland areas, within regions of high and low population density, and between areas organized as chiefdoms or states. Nevertheless, archaeological and ethnohistoric research has demonstrated a number of similarities in the production and distribution of resources in domestic and institutional contexts. These common patterns are modeled here. The goal is to provide a backdrop for viewing the diversity and complexity of commercial relationships. It does not, however, represent an economic model that is applicable to all areas of Mesoamerica at all points in time. Prehispanic economies evolved at different rates and with them came differences in structure at both the domestic and institutional levels.

MESOAMERICAN SOCIAL CLASSES

Mesoamerican society was a rich mosaic of differing ethnicities, linguistic communities, and cultural affiliations. Nevertheless, the Aztecs like all Mesoamerican societies were divided into three main social strata (elite lords, commoners, and slaves) which were internally subdivided on the basis of privilege and rank. At the top of Aztec society were nobles or *pipiltin* (plural of *pilli*) who held their positions of privilege as hereditary lords. These elite composed the noble families from which rulers, priests, judges, and chief administrators were selected. While their position in society could change over time, the basis for elite status originally resided in their role as the respected leaders of internally stratified corporate groups called *calpultin* (plural of *calpulli*). The elite married both within their class and across ethnic and community boundaries to enhance their wealth, power, and political influence. Their social status and prestige fluctuated from generation to generation with the individual and collective success of their respective groups. The economic well-being of elites depended on the amount of labor able to work their landed estates, which in turn dictated the size of their households.

Commoners comprised the bulk of the population and included all the farmers and the majority of the craftsmen, merchants, and soldiers in *Nahua* society. Where commoner households differed from one another was in the economic opportunities available to them and their ability to accumulate wealth. Professional merchants (*pochteca*) had the opportunity to amass considerable material wealth which gained them the animosity and jealousy of the elite. Among the Aztecs, successful citizen soldiers could receive ample economic rewards and live a comfortable life if they achieved the distinction of becoming warrior knights. Craftsmen could also prosper, especially those involved in the manufacture of high-value goods. Most commoners, however, were farmers and other primary producers who differed in status depending on their relative rights to land and other resources.

In Central Mexico commoners were divided into two general sub-classes (*macehualli and mayeque*) based on their rights to land and corresponding fealty obligations to their native lords (Hicks 1976).

Macehualtin (the plural of *macehualli*) were members of corporate *calpulli* groups that were the fundamental building blocks of prehispanic society. *Calpultin* were internally stratified social segments with their own elite (*calpuleque*) organized around a common group identity based on ethnicity, hereditary land holdings, and/or a common profession (e.g. farming, crafting, fishing, etc.). *Macehualtin* were expected to provide rotating labor and military support to their lords. *Mayeque* also called *tlalmaitec* were commoners who accessed land for their support through specific fealty and service obligations to elite households (Hicks 1974; Zorita 1994:182). They are referred to in colonial documents as *terrasguerros* or renters because they were granted access to land in return for greater service and/or tribute obligations (López and Hirth 2012). Because of greater labor obligations they normally did not provide military service or labor for public work projects as *macehualtin* did (Berdan 2014). Their lower social position is reflected in the name *mayeque* which is the plural of *mayé*, derived from the *Nahuatl* word for arm or hand (*maitl*) reflecting their role to serve noble households (Gibson 1964:505).

The third and lowest social category in society was the *tlacohtli*. These individuals were referred to as slaves (*tlacohtin*) in colonial documents but more properly should be thought of as indentured individuals who had pawned their labor to another, usually wealthy individual for economic support. They often entered into their indentured status as a result of individual or family hardship. Although this status was not hereditary it was a common punishment for crimes involving financial loss. Because of the nature of *tlacohtin* relationships, these individuals commonly were attached to, and resided in, the households where they owed their service obligations. In urban environments *tlacohtin* often were used as household servants. They also could be used to farm, although their use in agriculture was limited.[2] One instance of their use as agricultural labor is documented for Texcoco and Tenochtitlan where rulers gave slaves to artisans so that they could increase their level of craft production (Katz 1966:52). The important point is that slaves normally were incorporated into the domestic tasks of the households to which they were attached. *Tlacohtin* could further the economic well being of these households by being rented as porters in the marketplace, leased to traveling merchants as porters (Motolinia 1971:371–372; Rojas 1995:116), or rented out to weave textiles for domestic use or sale (Rojas 1995:152).

Among the Aztec as in all *Nahua* societies, the principal economic unit was the household which varied in size and composition based on social position and access to resources. Like other ancient societies, the vast majority of the population across Mesoamerica resided in domestic units of related kinsmen that produced and procured resources to support their members. The Aztecs were a military society with the ranks of their armies drawn from a citizen soldiery. Even garrisons in frontier zones were organized as residential enclaves of relocated colonists and citizen soldiers (Durán 1994:344–348; Silverstein 2001). Instances where individuals did not live in normal family groups included the living arrangements of priests in religious complexes, youths at school, and long-distance *pochteca* merchants in distant trade enclaves. While little is known about how *pochteca* enclave communities were structured, it is unlikely that they married into local communities as was common for merchant enclaves elsewhere in the ancient world.[3] The temporary nature of these living arrangements and the norms of Aztec morality prohibited commoners from taking multiple wives. Aztec males attended formal schools for several years; youths of elite families attended the *calmecac* while commoner youths went to the *telpochcalli*, school of their residential ward (Berdan 2014). In both cases youths lived at their schools and supplied the labor for its maintenance and support.

THE DOMESTIC ECONOMY

Households are the most important social units in human society. They are the settings in which most individuals are created, socialized, and raised. Family settings are where individuals are enculturated and receive many of their core psychological, social, and economic values (Gudeman 2001). Households vary widely in size and composition across cultures which demonstrate their ability to adapt to a wide array of social and environmental conditions. Households also vary in status. Whereas non-elite households supported themselves, elite households in ancient societies normally did not. Instead, the role of elite in the leadership and administrative activities of their societies resulted in their being supported by non-elite households as part of the institutional economy (see the following, this chapter). The domestic economy for the most part, therefore, encompasses all of the economic strategies that non-elite households engaged in to support their social and biological reproduction.

Although the functional features of households are discussed in detail in Chapter 5, several features stand out that are important to understand the structure of the domestic economy. First and foremost, households are the primary units of individual and group survival. Survival is their business and as a result, the majority of their economic activities are oriented to self-maintenance. They are in business for themselves and households employ a range of economic strategies that can be characterized as conservative or entrepreneurial, traditional or innovative, and specialized or diversified (Hirth 2009a). Second, households are the basic unit of both production and consumption in ancient societies. In the aggregate the domestic economy was always the largest economic sector in society. As the primary production units households always fought to maintain access to the primary resources needed for their subsistence. Third, households normally favor sustainable and predictable production strategies over more productive but riskier ones. Households are conservative, stable, and adaptive social units that can intensify their production strategies when needed to enhance their overall economic well-being.

The domestic economy was and still is the armature on which the rest of the economy pivots. Except for special circumstances it provided all, or the majority of the labor used in production tasks. Forms of cooperation learned in the home served as organizational models for social interaction and work outside the household. The domestic economy was not just the foundation on which institutional structures were built, it provided the models and rationales that created and shaped the society's formal and informal institutions.

The *Nahua* domestic economy conformed to all of the household characteristics described earlier. Commoner *macehualli* and *mayeque* households averaged between 4 and 7 persons in size and were often multi-generational in structure (Carrasco 1964; Sanders 1970; M. Smith 1992; Williams and Harvey 1997; Williams and Hicks 2011). They supported themselves with the fruits of their labor and failure to do so resulted in deprivation. Most commoner households were engaged in agriculture as the production of food was essential for feeding their members. Agriculture, however, was not their only subsistence activity. Many households employed a diversified economic strategy that enabled them to minimize risk by investing their labor in a range of different production activities.[4] This involved using labor in non-agricultural seasons and along age and gender lines to generate income and support the household (Hirth 2009a, 2009c; see also Hagstrum 2001). Analysis of household field sizes from the community of Tlanchiuhca in the Texcoco region suggests that voluntary diversification was not an option. Using average maize yields, Barbara Williams (1994) calculated that in normal agricultural years 20% of households did not produce enough maize to meet their needs. In poor agricultural years fully 50% of the households might not produce enough food to feed themselves. In these situations part-time crafting would have been an important auxiliary subsistence activity.

It is not an exaggeration to say that most of the craft goods consumed in prehispanic highland societies were produced by artisans working in their households (see Chapter 5). Very little craft production occurred outside the household, and where it did, was usually restricted to state-defined consumption goals. While the scale of craft production was small, its contribution to a household's normal annual subsistence regime may have been significant. In the aggregate, the volume of craft goods produced by households was enormous; household crafting specialized in products that utilized local resources and supported the development of a lively system of regional commerce.

Textile production was a very important domestic activity. Women spun thread and wove it into textiles on backstrap looms in the confines of their houses alongside child rearing, food preparation, and their other domestic tasks that included buying and selling goods in the marketplace.[5] Textiles were woven from cotton, maguey, and palm fiber and could be painted, or adorned with colored thread, feathers, or rabbit fur that often were the products of other specialized producers (Berdan 2014). Woven textiles were indispensable items for clothing because of the limited availability of materials for garments such as animal skins.

Besides being used for clothing, textiles also entered into the economy in two important ways. First, plain cotton textiles called *quachtli* were a form of commodity money (see Chapter 8) that was used in the marketplace to buy both subsistence and high-value goods. As a result, spinning and weaving provided important contributions to household maintenance.[6] Second, textiles were also important tribute items. A total of 278,400 cotton and maguey fiber textiles were paid annually to the Aztec state, all of which were produced by women throughout the empire (Berdan 1987:241). Although the sources are mute on how tribute goods were produced, the majority of these textiles were probably manufactured in domestic contexts as part of the household's service (*tequitl*) obligation to the state.

The importance of diversified subsistence strategies for household survival is well illustrated in Aztec history beginning with the founding of Tenochtitlan when the population on the island lacked sufficient agricultural land to support itself. Several of its responses are well known: the Aztecs foraged lake products and constructed small *chinampas* plots where they could across the lake floor (Parsons 1991, 1996). But they also used the marketplace on the neighboring island of Tlatelolco to exchange prepared food and craft goods for food (Minc 2006; also see Chapter 5).

The Aztecs rose to political prominence during their early years serving as mercenaries for the lord of Azcapotzalco (Durán 1994). It is likely that the economic rewards received for this military service were important contributions to supporting commoner families during the early years of Aztec settlement on Tenochtitlan when a diversified economy was essential for household existence.

It is difficult to reconstruct the distributional dimension of the domestic economy and the volume of goods that circulated between households without problem focused archaeological research. Colonial sources are generally mute on household commercial activity except for what can be squeezed from testimonial records (Cline and León-Portilla 1984; Kellogg 1986; Kellogg and Restall 1998). Detailed archaeological studies of household consumption patterns have not been conducted (but see De Lucia 2011; M. Smith 1992). Nevertheless, some parameters are clear. First, as mentioned earlier, there was a high level of domestic craft specialization in Aztec society and most of the craft goods recovered from Aztec period households were purchased in the marketplace (Minc 2006). It was this dimension of the domestic economy that led to the high degree of commercial activity throughout *Nahua* society. Second, the majority of the food consumed in *Nahua* society was produced by the domestic economy. Although this is difficult to quantify we know that between 85 and 90% of the land cultivated in the Tepeaca region of the eastern valley of Puebla was used to support domestic units; by extension this probably represented 85–90% of the food produced in this region (López Corral and Hirth 2012:85).[7]

It is important to remember that the majority of the food and craft goods that households produced were used for household maintenance. Very few resources left the household as a tax on domestic production. Instead, most of the tax and tribute needed to support formal institutions were met by forms of production organized in contexts *outside* the household (Hirth 1996). Formal institutions in *Nahua* society were organized to support themselves using corvee labor and provided little economic help for its commoner population except under dire circumstances. When the domestic economy failed the survival of the household depended primarily on the informal institutions organized along kinship and community lines.

THE INFORMAL INSTITUTIONAL ECONOMY

Institutions are forms of organization and modes of operation created by groups to accomplish specific ends (Acheson 1994). Two types of institutions make up the institutional economy: *informal institutions* that operate at the local and community level and *formal institutions* oriented to the society as a whole. Informal economic institutions are norms of behavior that operate through custom and often without formal oversight to provide assistance for households. They are informal in the sense that support comes from other households, participation is voluntary, and is provided either on a regular or *ad hoc* basis as needs arise and means permit. The informal institutions of relevance here are those that came to the aid of households when they failed to meet their subsistence needs.

Corporate land holding groups provide security for their members by guaranteeing access to land for cultivation through usufruct rights. Membership in corporate land holding groups creates a sentiment of group ownership that makes it difficult for households to deny claims for assistance from other members of the community (Gregory 1980, 1982). It is for this reason that group land ownership has continued in many societies around the world after private property became the norm.[8] The most enduring form of corporate organization in *Nahua* societies was the *calpulli*. In rural areas, *calpultin* functioned as corporate land holding units right up to the Spanish conquest (Carrasco 1971; Dycherhoff and Prem 1976). This provided a community based assistant network for its members. When land was needed *calpultin* functioned as collective action groups to rent it from neighboring communities (Carrasco 1971). Likewise, when economic shortfall occurred it provided a network for assistance from more fortunate member households.[9]

As in all societies, the first line of assistance for individuals was kinsmen and family members in other households. Besides accessing food, family networks enabled individuals to move and incorporate themselves into the households of their relatives if they could be supported. In one account Nezahacoyotl, who later became the ruler of Texcoco, fled to live with relatives in the city of Huexotzinco after his attempted assassination (Durán 1994:71; M. Smith 2012c:50). Family assistance, however, was not automatic, especially if it would disrupt relations within the household. In a *Nahuatl* document dating to 1583 a petition is made by a woman named Ana for her husband and son to live with her older brother (Juan Miguel) in the town of Tocuillan near Texcoco. In that petition she makes clear that she will be respectful of her brother and submit to his authority. With this stipulation made the families merged and later Ana petitioned the town elders for permission to establish her own separate family residence within the community (Lockhart 1992:86).

There was a clear sense of intra-family responsibilities to take care of the destitute in *Nahua* society. Orphaned children were taken in by family members in other households. The same was true for widows and it appears that the expectation for custodial assistance fell to the eldest male as the representative family head (Lockhart 1992:90). It is possible that the number of large conjoint households reported throughout Central Mexico in the sixteenth century was a result of systematic intra-family domestic assistance (Carrasco 1964; Williams and Harvey 1997; Williams and Hicks 2011). The large epidemics known as the *cocoliztli*[10] killed millions of people between 1545 and 1576 disrupting virtually every household in Central Mexico (Acuna-Soto et al. 2002; Cook and Simpson 1948). The result would have been the realignment of household composition across all of Central Mexico like that reported for the Black Death and the other great plagues in Europe (Gibson 1964; Gottfried 1983; Horrox 1994).

Of course there were instances where family assistance wasn't available and the plight of the household was dire. In this case people would resort to begging.[11] Adults, particularly women would wander through the town begging on the streets and in plazas as Tariacuri's mother did in the Chronicle of Michoacan (Craine and Reindrop 1970). Children and orphans would beg in the marketplace, collecting kernels of maize and eating what else they found on the ground including half chewed roots and carob beans. In the Chronicle of Michoacan, the destitute nephews of Tariacuri would approach those who were eating in the marketplace and quietly gather the crumbs that were left behind (Craine and Reindrop 1970:170). Here we are told that people would intentionally drop food for them to gather. The assistance given to beggars and orphans was clearly voluntary and based on the compassion of those they encountered.

Collecting what was dropped on the floor of the marketplace is reminiscent of the practice of gleaning in the Old World.[12] Gleaning also was practiced in *Nahua* society but only as a secondary activity since maize ears were covered by external husks, making it easy to harvest all the seeds leaving little for gleaners to obtain for their efforts. Nevertheless gleaning was practiced when households were destitute as Sahagún reports in his discussion of farming practices,

And some walked about as gleaners. They gleaned, gathered, and searched for themselves the forgotten ears of maize, or the small, undeveloped ones, which the harvesters had not gathered. They hurried to all places [and went from field to field] and went everywhere, feeling with their feet among the dry maize stalks, the leaves, and the husks, in order to place their gleanings in the fold of their capes

(Sahagún 1979:129).

According to Ixtlilxóchitl (1891:233–234), begging was not allowed in the province of Texcoco. Here it was the responsibility of the *tlatoani* to take care of widows, orphans, the sick, and those men injured in war. He tells us that overseers were assigned to make sure that these individuals were clothed and given food to eat if they needed it. Nezahualcoyotl the famous Texcocan *tlatoani* is said to have watched over the common people who sold goods in the marketplace. According to Ixtlilxóchitl, this *tlatoani*

ordinarily went out to a place overlooking the plaza to see the poor people that sold there ... and seeing that they couldn't sell [he] would not sit down to eat until his stewards would go to purchase all that they sold at double the price that it was worth so as to give it to others because he had special care in feeding and clothing the old, the sick, and those injured in war and the widows and orphans

(Ixtlilxóchitl 1891:233–234).

The sentiment expressed here is that the ruler was responsible for the well being of the common people. The extent to which rulers in other towns followed this practice as carefully as Nezahualcoyotl remains to be seen.

A corollary strategy followed by commoner households instead of begging was the intensive exploitation of famine foods, those marginal or low productivity resources that were only consumed when agricultural resources failed. This involves a reversion to resources that often formed the basis of earlier foraging economies prior to the development of food production. In hard times,

Nothing was thrown away; all then was saved–wild seeds not commonly eaten; musty maize; corn silk; corn tassels; pulp scraped from maguey, tappings, tuna cactus flowers; cooked maguey leaves; heated maguey sap. Everything was taken into account: [with] amaranth, even the weeds were threshed; ... they satisfied and quickened themselves [with] bird seed, bitter amaranth or bright red amaranth, and *yacacolli* maize[13]

(Sahagún 1953:23).

Archaeologists have identified the use of wild seeds and cooked maguey as food sources as early as the Archaic period (Callen 1970; Scheffler et al. 2012; C. E. Smith 1967:238, 1986:266). The reference to tappings may refer to resins collected from a range of different plant species.

When begging, gleaning, and intensive collecting did not suffice, the last resort was to sell yourself into slavery. Slavery could be the outcome of several unfortunate conditions in addition to impoverishment. These included: not meeting your tribute obligation (Berdan 1975:61), as a punishment for small-scale theft,[14] breaking a business agreement, or not repaying a personal debt or that of your father's (Alba 1949:21–22, 46). Gamblers in moments of desperation were known to become slaves by making themselves part of the wager. The normal price of selling yourself into slavery was 20 large *quachtli* worth 2,000 cacao beans (Durand-Forest 1967:179). It is significant that this is the same estimated value for what it took to support a person over the course of a year (Durand-Forest 1971:116–117; Rojas 1995:215).

The best recorded instance of destitute families selling their children into slavery comes from Durán's (1994) account of the great famine from AD 1452 to 1455.[15] In the Basin of Mexico the famine was so severe that the Aztec king Moctezuma Ilhuicamina resorted to eventually feeding the people in Tenochtitlan from state granaries. Unfortunately, state food supplies ran out before the famine ended and Durán records the people's response to the elite during these trying times:

We know that you can do no more. Therefore, we kiss your royal hands and accept the liberty you give us to seek a remedy for our misery and hunger. We shall sell our sons and daughters to those who can feed them so that they do not starve to death.

Weeping bitterly they began to leave the city in different directions where they hope help would be available. Many of them found relief in certain places where the inhabitants were wealthy. There, in those towns, they sold their sons and daughters to merchants or to noblemen who could maintain them. A mother or father would trade a child for a small basket of maize, and the new owner was obliged to house and feed the infant while the famine lasted. If the parents wished to ransom him later, they would have to pay for all his maintenance.

(Durán 1994:240).

The Totonac people from the Gulf Coast took advantage of the famine and brought loads of maize to the Basin of Mexico where they bought both children and adults for manual service (Chimalpahin Cuauhtlehua-nitzin 1965:200–201).[16]

Households recognized the precarious nature of survival and the risks that they faced. While Moctezuma Ilhuicamina emptied state granaries to help starving families this did not occur until well into the famine after their informal networks had failed (Durán 1994:239). Help from state institutions and elites was appreciated when it occurred, but was not anticipated as a first line of household assistance. Rainfall fluctuation could be highly localized within the highlands creating pockets of drought and poor harvests. The Aztec *tlatoani*, therefore, dealt with crop failure on a region by region basis within the empire when it was reported to him by native lords or his tribute collectors. The following quote from the sixteenth century by Alonso de Zorita summarizes how things worked,

> In the time of pestilence or crop failure, these inferior lords, or the majordomos, reported the occurrence to the supreme and universal lord, but only if they were certain of it, for otherwise they would never dare mention it to him. He would then order that the tribute should not be collected that year from the towns so afflicted. If the crop failure and shortage were very great, he would also order that aid be given for the support of such towns, and seeds for next year's sowing, for it was the ruler's object to relieve his vassals as much as possible
>
> (Zorita 1994:194).

This citation almost certainly summarizes how drought was handled outside the Basin of Mexico since the Aztec *tlatoani* would have been aware of drought in his own region. Alonso de Zorita collected a great deal of his information on highland society when he served as Judge of the Indies in Mexico from 1556 to 1566 (Ahrndt 2001; Keen 1994). In the Puebla-Tlaxcala region tribute fields were dispersed alongside individual fields and the suspension of tribute made whatever maize that field produced available for consumption by the family that cultivated it.

Although groups could not predict the severity of multiple year droughts, households recognized the fertility of their land and how productivity could vary between good and marginal years. As a result households were always looking for better land to cultivate. One way to obtain better land and to decrease risk was to negotiate directly with the nobles that controlled it. This was usually done collectively by the people of *calpultin* willing to move to a new area. This came with a cost. It involved taking on additional service obligations for their new lords and it was the way that the broad class of *mayeque* was formed in many areas of Central Mexico (Hicks 1976).

THE FORMAL INSTITUTIONAL ECONOMY

Formal institutions are constituted entities organized to provide political, economic, and religious functions for the society as a whole. They represent the "bricks and mortar" organizations in our own society. Examples of these organizations in antiquity included the military, temples and religious superstructures, palaces, theaters and sports arenas, marketplaces, judicial courts, and offices of political administration or economic regulation. The scope of activities for these institutions often requires resources, personnel, and built facilities to operate effectively. The need for resources fosters the creation of both the ideological rationales and the physical apparatus to procure them. Obtaining the resources to support formal institutions is usually met in one of two ways. They are either produced in the contexts where they are consumed under the supervision of institutional personnel, or they are mobilized and extracted from the households that the institutions serve. The more institutions use the first approach, the less they will intrude on the household economy to fulfil their needs. The second approach represents direct taxation of individual households which reduces the net economic benefit of the subsistence effort a household can engage in.

Most ancient societies used a combination of means to fund formal institutions. Nevertheless, those societies where institutions produced the resource that they used were less intrusive on the domestic economy than societies that employed direct taxation (Hirth 1996). Throughout this volume I use the term tribute rather than tax to describe the mobilization of resources to support formal institutions. While M. Smith (2014, n.d.) prefers the term tax, I retain the traditional term of tribute because it is important for economic purposes to recognize that the resources extracted within society to meet institutional needs were produced in different ways.

Tax, as I use the term, is a levy placed on a physical product. For it to be a tax the good has to be produced and available for alternative uses including exchange or auto-consumption. Taxes are levied on finished or realized goods. Examples of taxes in our own society include income tax, inheritance tax, sales tax, as well as tolls, duties, and tariffs on goods that move over space.[17] This makes it distinct from something like corvee labor which is an input to production. Formal institutions in most Mesoamerican societies were organized primarily to support themselves and did not intrude significantly into the domestic economy. Direct taxation on households existed but it was limited in both scope and importance.[18] Institutional resources in Mesoamerica were largely produced *ex domesticus*, that is, outside the household. This has important evolutionary implications for the formation of institutional economies. Formal institutions that produce goods for their support without having to draw on household resources through some form of direct taxation can more easily obtain cooperation from the supporting community. This suggests that it is likely that less intrusive forms of exploitation predate more intrusive forms because of the difficulty of developing the extractive rationales to obtain community participation.

Most of the resources used by formal institutions came from tribute collected across their empire and from prebendal and private estates under elite control. A prebend is a subsistence allowance or allotment of resources granted for the support of a particular task or individual.[19] In Aztec society prebends consisted of an allotment of land assigned to support a specific institution or institutional functionary. The labor to cultivate the estate was drawn from commoner households as a rotational labor draft referred to as *coatequitl*. Periodic labor, not physical goods, is what households most often donated to support the institutional superstructure. Although some scholars have casually characterized corvee labor as a labor tax, it should not be lumped together with taxes on household goods. A tax on goods is a *net tax* drawn on household income after incurring all costs of production. In contrast, the use of corvee labor in an institutional setting represents a production input or variable cost for a short period of time. Since agricultural cycles are flexible with regard to when field preparation and planting can begin, short-term rotational labor drafts can be drawn from communities without negatively impacting the productive capacity of their member households.

The goods produced on prebendal and elite estates resulted in a resource flow of staple food (e.g. D'Altroy and Earle 1985). Table 2.1 lists the different types of prebendal lands and how they were assigned to meet specific institutional needs. The private estates (e.g. *huehuetlalli*, *pillalli*, etc.) consisted of hereditary lands assigned to support elite families. Spanish sources occasionally refer to these lands as private property because they were held in perpetuity by elite families. This changed as the Aztec empire expanded and the cost of state institutions was increasingly covered by the inflow of tribute goods. While some of the food produced on prebendal land would have been consumed within institutional contexts, it is likely that most was exchanged for other resources in the marketplace.[20]

Prebendal lands include the communal holdings of *calpultin* (*calpullalli*) as well as those lands assigned to the *tecpan* (*tecpantlalli*). The *tecpan* or "lord place" was both the residence of an elite household and the center of political administration that ranged from the *huetecpan* of the Aztec imperial capital to the multiple small *tecpan* located within each city-state. The *tecpan* palace was a multi-purpose structure used for both political and social functions (Sheehy 1996). Evans (2004:10) estimates that there were well over 500 *tecpan* in the Basin of Mexico at Spanish conquest that supported a range of *tlatoque* rulers, their families, and other functionaries referred to generally as *tecpanpouhque*. There were five to ten times that number in the many small towns and villages

TABLE 2.1: *Nahuatl terms for types of land in Central Mexico*

Nahuatl term	Type of land
altepetlalli	Land of the *altepetl*
cacalomilli	Land for military supplies
calpullalli	Land of the *calpulli*
cihuatlalli	Woman's land, possible dowry
huehuetlalli	Inherited land, ancestral land, patrimonial land
mexicatlalli	Land of the Mexica
milchimalli	Land for military supplies
pillalli	Private land of indigenous lords
tlalcohualli	Purchased land
tecpantlalli	Land of the *tecpan*
tecpillalli	Ancient land of nobles
teopantlalli	Temple land
teotlalli	Sacred lands, land of the temple and the gods
tequitlalli	Tribute land, tribute field
teuctlalli	Land of the lord, ruler
tlatocatlalli, *tlatocamilli*	Ruler's office lands, ruler's land attached to the office of the *tlatoani*
yaotlalli	War land

scattered across Central Mexico that were supported by production on *tecpantlalli* land.[21]

Land also was assigned to religious institutions (*teopantlalli, teotlalli*) to maintain temple facilities and cover costs of operation. The military needed campaign provisions and land was set aside in all towns as *milchimalli* or *cacalomilli* to produce war supplies (Hassig 1988:61). The *tlatocatlalli* were lands assigned to the *tlatoani* to cover the costs of the central palace (*huetecpan*) and operating the imperial government. Lesser officials who fulfilled the positions of judges, military commanders, tribute collectors, and warrior knights were also assigned lands to support their families and to fund the institutions that they oversaw.

Some of these lands were acquired or expropriated from other groups through conquest (*mexicatlalli, tequitlalli*). The *yaotlalli* were lands in conquered areas that were set aside to support the warrior knights and leaders of society as a reward for their involvement in military campaigns.[22] The land to support the *calpultin* leaders were allocations of land from their own corporate holdings (*calpullalli*). Ixtlilxóchitl (1891:2:170) indicates that the *calpullalli* comprised the majority of the land in all of the towns and cities and it could not be transferred or sold, but could only be inherited by the children of the commoner *macehualtin* that worked it. The resources needed to support the youths attending the *calmecac* or the *telpochcalli* schools came from lands worked by the youths themselves. Mention is also occasionally made to individual land holdings including women's land (*cihuatlalli*) and purchased land (*tlalcohualli*) (Cline 1993:69). *Cihuatlalli* appears to be individual dowry land that a woman brought to a marriage between elite families.

The question of land control and the degree of ownership is an important one since it relates to the overall issue of private property in the precolumbian world. Certain types of *pillalli* land could be sold between elites and possibly to merchants (Carrasco 1981:63; Offner 1981a, 1983). Land sales were protected by law and unjust land expropriation could be punished by death (Offner 1981b:47). This allowed elite families to build their individual estates based on their respective desires and financial resources. What remains unclear, however, is how frequent land sales were in prehispanic society. Free labor did not exist and the use of slaves as agricultural workers was relatively rare. The primary way that elites could obtain new labor to farm land was through the migration and relocation of groups who were willing to enter into client relationships as renters (*terrazguerros*) with the elites who controlled it. *Tlalcohualli*, or purchased land, was a prehispanic land category that increased in both breadth and frequency with the growing real estate market during the colonial period. Nevertheless, it very likely existed as a relatively minor land type within the society as a whole that increased rapidly after the conquest with the adoption of Spanish norms of private property.

Production on all these assigned lands depended upon having labor to cultivate them. In *Nahua* society labor regularly was mobilized as rotational corvee work assignments from *macehualli* and *mayeque* households. The obligation (*coatequitl*) to work public lands was seen as part of the normal *tequitl* or duty obligation that all individuals had to serve society and the gods (Figure 2.2). Labor was apportioned in two ways depending on how estate land was distributed. Some of largest estates were large contiguous fields that ranged from 20 to 120 ha in size. These fields were assigned to support rulers and palaces and were cultivated by corvee labor that worked in shifts on a rotating basis, beginning with planting and continuing to harvest and storage (Hicks 1984).

A different land allocation was used in places in the Valley of Puebla. In the Tepeaca-Acatzingo region of the eastern Valley of Puebla, all institutional lands assigned to individuals who rented land from their lords (*terrasguerros*) were small holdings 100 by 6 brazas in size (Martínez 1984:85). Conversion of these fields to metric equivalents indicates that

FIGURE 2.2 Example of *coatequitl* labor illustrating the digging stick used in corvee labor

they were only 0.167 ha in size.[23] Each household was allocated one such parcel to farm as a state obligation that was located alongside 5–8 similarly sized parcels cultivated for their own support. The result was a dispersed landscape of institutional fields attached to the commoner labor pool that cultivated it. The size of elite estates was directly proportional to the number of dependent households that worked the land. Documentation from five elite households from Tepeaca and Acatzingo, Puebla indicates that total elite land holdings from all these small parcels ranged from 16 to 269 ha in size.[24]

Operation of a large prebendal estate

An example of how production on prebendal land was organized is represented by the elite estate in Acatetelco in the Basin of Mexico which was organized differently from elite holdings in eastern Puebla. These were *tlatocatlalli* lands assigned to support the palace of Texcoco. In a litigation document of 1573–1575 commoners from the community of Atenco said they farmed a large plot 500 x 500 brazas in size (110–121 ha) (Hicks 1978).[25] According to testimony, the Atenco community provided an array of resources on a daily basis during its seventy days of palace service. The tribute taken daily to the palace was reported as 25 *tlacopintlis* (31 fanegas, 3 almudes) of maize, 3 *tlacopintlis* of beans, 400,000 tortillas,[26] 4 *xiquipiles* of cacao (32,000 beans), 100 turkeys, 20 measures of salt, 20 baskets of chile hancho, 20 baskets of chile menudo, 10 baskets of tomatoes, and 10 baskets of squash seeds (Hicks 1978:132; Ixtlilxóchitl 1977:2:90). The litigants are clear in stating that the grain cultivated on the Acatetelco field was used to fulfil these tribute obligations and was stored in three large granaries until it had to be taken to the palace (Hirth 2012b).

Several observations emerge from this litigation. First, this field was cultivated on a rotational basis by corvee labor. Second, while this field provided the service tribute paid to the palace, not all of the food items turned into the palace could have been grown on the field. Turkeys, for example, were raised locally but could not be stored like maize. One possibility is that they were raised and fed in Atenco households with small allotments of maize from the three Acatetelco granaries. Cacao and salt provide different problems. Cacao did not grow locally and was imported into the Basin of Mexico from tropical areas. Salt was produced in the Basin of Mexico, but like cacao, had to be procured in the marketplace since it could not be produced in the Acatetelco field. Similarly, while chile and squash seeds store well, tomatoes do not and probably also were procured as fresh produce in the marketplace depending on when the 70 tribute days fell within the calendar year. If Atenco paid its tribute during the winter it could have sold stored grain, chile, or squash seeds in the marketplace and used the receipts to buy fresh tomatoes raised in *chinampas* plots in the southern lake region (Parsons 1991).

The corvee labor assigned to the Acatetelco field probably harvested its crops and stored them in granaries located in or near the field. If this was the case, the labor supervisor for Atenco would have been responsible for converting stored products in the marketplace for all the required items including cacao and salt. The Atenco commoners would have then transported the listed items to the palace over the seventy-day period. Support of the palace came from its assigned fields, but only after some of the stored products would have been converted in the marketplace into other goods.

Mobilizing labor was how work got done. Male labor was used to farm fields, repair buildings, engage in public construction projects, and to transport food and firewood to where it was needed. Female labor was mobilized through the same system to provide elite households with cooking, cleaning, spinning, and weaving services. Labor obligations probably varied from circumstance to circumstance as did the amount of time required to carry them out. What is fairly consistent across Central Mexico was the organization of the corvee labor system in cadres of twenty households, with each cadre having a supervisor known as a *centecpanpixqui* to make sure that work assignments were completed.

How much labor was drawn from each household to complete corvee work remains unclear. The operating principle of the rotational corvee system was that "many hands make light work." The problem with this system is that it didn't work particularly well when there were large-scale reductions in regional population. In prehispanic times a reduction in the male population sometimes occurred as a result of Aztec conquests like that recorded for the war with of Oztoman and Alahuiztlan in the modern state of Guerrero (Durán 1994:344). Prehispanic population reductions, however, were minor in comparison to those that occurred after the Spanish conquest as a result of the introduction of European endemic disease (Cook and Borah 1971–1979; Cook and Simpson 1948). The amount of work that the Spanish demanded remained the same throughout the sixteenth century while the number of households to fulfil it continued to decline. It was this unfortunate trend that led to the overexploitation of native labor by the Spanish which accelerated the population decline and impoverished the commoner population (Gibson 1964).

Careful analysis of colonial documents from Tepeaca allows a preliminary estimate of the labor-time households gave in domestic service to five elite households in 1571. According to Martínez (1984:99, cuadro 15) men spent between 5.5 and 8.6 days/year in personal service to their lords in addition to the time spent cultivating the 0.167 ha plot assigned to them for elite support. When the effective labor expended to cultivate elite plots is calculated it represents only 11–17% of the total household labor involved in farming.[27] Women also provided domestic service to their lords as well as weaving. This consisted of between 4 and 6 days of domestic service (cooking, cleaning, etc.) as well as 20 days of spinning yarn or weaving textiles. Textile labor was probably done in their own homes, and is an average figure. Women in the households attached to elite estates were given a quantity of raw cotton to spin and weave which then was divided among them: half of the households spun the cotton into thread and then the other half wove it into finished goods.

The production of durable goods for institutional use

While the system of prebendal and private land was the foundation for supporting both elite families and the society's formal institutions, it could not provide all of the durable goods needed for their maintenance and operation. One solution to this mentioned earlier was to exchange food and other farm products in the marketplace for durable goods that they did not produce as was the case for the prebendal estate of Acatetelco. An equally feasible solution was to call upon the craftsmen to supply the goods that they produced as a way of meeting their *tequitl* labor obligation (Zorita 1994:181, 187). Elite households required the same domestic tool assemblages as commoners to prepare food, store items, and furnish the household. These assemblages included milling stones to grind maize, ceramic vessels to cook, store, and serve food, baskets for storage, obsidian for cutting tools, mats to cover floors, and an array of textiles for clothing and blankets. How elite households procured these goods certainly varied although it is likely that a large percentage were produced by local craftsmen as part of their normal service obligations.

The extent of this type of craft provisioning remains unclear. That craft products could be mobilized to meet institutional needs is strongly implied by the way corvee labor cadres were organized. In the *Matrícula de Huexotzinxco* from the Valley of Puebla, heads of households were carefully registered by professions (e.g. farmers, carpenters, doctors, etc.) within their corvee labor groups of twenty households (Carrasco 1974; Prem 1974). Tribute documents from Tepeaca also list the number of artisans and merchants attached to elite households (Martínez 1984:98). In the *Relación de Michoacán* craftsmen (potters, obsidian workers, mat makers, metal workers, etc.) and other individuals with specific service abilities or professions (spies, messengers, and hunters) were grouped together in their own corvee tribute cadres (de Alcalá 2013:173–181) implying that they fulfilled part of their service obligation with the goods or services they supplied.

In Tepeaca some craftsmen paid tribute to their lord every eighty days in the goods they produced. This included three *petate* mats from each *petate* maker, one hundred tobacco tubes from a tobacconist, and four pairs of sandals from a sandal maker (Carrasco 1963:98–99). The payment of tribute in usable goods by artisans is called *tlacalaquilli* (Gutiérrez 2013:143). This arrangement was adjusted if the goods artisans worked were not in high demand by the elite houses to whom they were attached.

Two carpenters and one scribe in Tecalli, Puebla each were required to tribute one hundred cacao beans in lieu of their goods (Olivera 1984:166). Merchants in Tepeaca also paid their tribute in cacao as did feather workers (Martínez 1984:117). Other craftsmen split their tribute demands between partial payment in cacao beans and working small agricultural plots for their lords (Martínez 1984). Examples from Tepeaca include stone workers, metal workers, and masons. In one case four masons split their tribute demands between turning in fifty cacao beans and working a small field (Carrasco 1963:98–99). Splitting labor obligations probably varied with the type of craft good that artisans could provide and the regularity that it was needed. The *pillalli* fields that Tepeaca artisans cultivated ranged from 0.056 to 0.067 ha in size (Martínez 1984:118), roughly one-third to 40% the size of those regularly cultivated by commoner farmers.[28]

A pertinent question given the distinction between tax and tribute used here is whether payment of tribute in goods or cacao represents the equivalent of a household tax. A case could be made that it does, but it would be a poor one. Placement of artisan specializations within the *centecpantin* tribute cadres of twenty individuals indicates that tribute-in-kind was thought of in the same way as rotational corvee labor. It was from these lists that craftsmen specializing in the construction trades (e.g. stone workers, masons, carpenters, etc.) were drawn for periodic public work projects that included building temples and administrative structures (Molina 1977; Zavala 1984–1989). *Coatequitl* also involved the periodic manufacture of goods by artisans in an institutional context. One such activity involved the manufacture of military armaments in the community armory called the *tlacochcalco* (house of darts) (Díaz del Castillo (1956:211–212). Each *calpulli* was responsible for their own armaments (Isaac 1986:322) and Hassig (1988:61) believes that many such armories existed in the *tecpan* of towns to equip local militias. In this type of labor, artisans would assemble at the armory to produce the weaponry used by the military. These goods were produced periodically by the local craftsmen with the skills to do so (Carballo 2013:131; Hirth 2006a:181–182).

A second way that goods were procured for institutional use was through forms of managed production organized along a formalized version of the patron-client model (Clark and Parry 1990; Costin 1991, 2000). In this type of system the central institution directly funded the artisans involved in institutional production. This could be on a full-time basis as clients of the institution, or on a part-time basis through periodic project consignments for which artisans were compensated. Although both forms of institutional production were found in *Nahua* society, they were relatively rare and occurred only under special circumstances.

The best example of managed production among the Aztecs was the special workshop facility known as the *totocalli*, located in the pleasure garden of Moctezuma Xocoyotzin's palace in Tenochtitlan (Evans 2007). A wide array of exotic birds and other animals were kept in the *totocalli* gardens to delight the ruler and to entertain his guests. It also contained buildings where highly skilled craftsmen produced prestige goods for Moctezuma Xocoyotzin. The prestige goods produced here were given as gifts in annual celebrations to both his supporters and his enemies. The *totocalli* as described by Sahagún is where Moctezuma Xocoyotzin:

> housed separately, those who were his feather workers, who pertained to him. He gave them a house of their own. The feather artisans of Tenochtitlan and Tlatelolco mingled with one another. And these specialized only in making the array of Uitzilopochtli, which they called the divine cape ... And they made the array which was Moctezuma's own, which he gave, with which he showed favor to his guests, the rulers over cities, wherefore [the craftsmen] were called, were named, feather workers of the palace, artisans of the ruler. And some were known as feather workers of the treasury store house; their domain was everything which was in Moctezuma's treasury store house. They made that which was the dance array of Moctezuma.
>
> (Sahagún 1959:91).

Several important points emerge from Sahagún's description of the *totocalli*. First, it was a special workshop that produced specific prestige goods for Moctezuma Xocoyotzin (Figure 2.3). Second, the artisans who worked there were his clients. Their dependency status is clear because Sahagún (1981b:2:308) states that these artisans were fed from the palace kitchens. Third, the goods produced were signature pieces that carried the imagery of the *tlatoani*'s office. They were part of an elaborate gift economy that operated between rulers and had important geopolitical implications within the Aztec empire. Sahagún and Durán tell us that the feather workers who worked in the *totocalli* had access to everything in Moctezuma Xocoyotzin's treasury store house (Figure 2.4) known as the palace *petlacalco*.[29] The *totocalli* produced goods equivalent to brand label items whose distribution was controlled through Moctezuma's palace.

But the *totocalli* workshops housed more than just the esteemed feather workers. Sahagún clarifies that the *totocalli* contained a variety of different crafts:

FIGURE 2.3 The array of high-value items made for warriors in one of the *totocalli* workshops

there majordomos kept all the various birds ... (a)nd there all the various artisans did their work: the gold and silver-smiths, copper-smiths, the feather workers, painters, cutters of stones, workers in green stone mosaic, carvers of wood. Caretakers of wild animals, majordomos, there guarded all the wild animals: ocelots, bears, mountain lions, and mountain cats

(Sahagún 1979b:45).

Seven different craft specializations are mentioned, all associated with the production of high-value prestige goods (Calnek 1978:109; Carrasco 1978:34; Katz 1966:53). Furthermore, the linkage between space and function was direct. The bird and animal garden probably supplied some of the materials used in craft production. Feathers presumably also were collected for use in craft production as birds molted and furs and skins could have been used when felines and other exotic animals died. This would have been a small supplement to the large quantity of exotic resources available through tribute levies.

FIGURE 2.4 Feather workers, like those who worked feathers in the *totocalli*

What makes the *totocalli* workshops uniquely important is that they represent a case of managed production within the institution that designed and consumed the goods that they produced. How artisans were supported remains unclear. The most likely scenario is that artisans resided in their own households and came to the *totocalli* workshop on a daily basis.[30] The Tenochtitlan palace kitchens fed thousands of people who worked in the palace and these artisans certainly would have received food since it was the custom to feed corvee labor involved in public labor projects. Alternatively, these artisans and their families may have been supported by plots of land set aside and worked for them by corvee labor as was done for warrior knights. State support for artisans is mentioned by Hernán Cortés in a letter to the Consejo de Indias in 1538 where he states that some urban barrios provided tribute support to a variety of craft specialists who resided there (Katz 1966:53).

FIGURE 2.5 Woman weaving on a backstrap loom

Elite households that were involved in governance did not support themselves. Instead they drew their support from *tecpantalli* and *pillalli* lands cultivated for them by corvee labor. This notwithstanding, elite households were far from idle and could engage in alternative forms of production as a result of having institutional support. The way elite households did this was by expanding the size of their domestic labor force.

Plain and embroidered textiles were high-value goods that were produced on backstrap looms by women in all *Nahua* households (Figure 2.5). A direct way to increase the wealth of the household was to increase the number of women in it who were skilled weavers. The practice of polygyny by elite households allowed them to support multiple wives who were skilled in the spinning and weaving arts. Monogamous marriage was the norm in non-elite households because of the cost of supporting their offspring. This was not a problem in elite families. The addition of multiple wives to elite households allowed them to produce a significant amount of high-value textiles that could be stored or exchanged for other goods in the marketplace (Evans 2008).

Two other ways that elite could individually intensify production was to add slaves to their households or to train their offspring as craftsmen to produce high-value goods. Since all women learned to weave at an early age, female slaves were occasionally purchased in the marketplace and employed as weavers in elite households. These slave women often served as subordinate wives, the most famous example of which was the Tepanec slave woman from Azcapotzalco who was the mother of Itzcoatl an Aztec *tlatoani* (Durán 1994). Young girls learned how to spin thread as early as four years of age and by fourteen were accomplished weavers (Berdan and Anawalt 1992; Evans 2008:223). Fathers admonished their daughters to learn these important skills so that they could secure a respectable marriage. A discourse of Aztec lords to their elite born daughters was recorded by Sahagún where they say,

apply thyself well to the really womanly task, the spindle whorl, the weaving stick. Open thine eyes well as to how to be an artisan, how to be a feather worker; the manner of making designs by embroidering; how to judge colors; how to apply color

(Sahagún 1969:96).

This discourse implies that young women were involved in high-value textile production within noble households. Young elite men were also encouraged to take up an artistic craft. The Aztec *tlatoani* Moctezuma Ilhuicamina told his male and female children to become apprentices to artisans so they might live a productive life (Carrasco 1971:373). Texcoco elite families practiced a variety of arts and crafts for recreation and presumably material reward. The crafts they practiced included painting, wood working, metal working, lapidary, stone carving, and carpentry (Acuña 1986:86).

The imperial tribute system

The best known dimension of the institutional economy was the tribute paid by conquered provinces of the empire (Berdan 1996). The Aztec empire was the product of joint military operations carried out by three primary city-states in the Basin of Mexico: the Culhua-Mexica city of Tenochtitlan, the Acolhua city of Texcoco, and the Tepanec city of Tlacopan. These three cities formed an alliance in Tenochtitlan's rebellion against Maxtla, the *tlatoani* of Azcapotzalco who they defeated in AD 1428. The Triple Alliance of Tenochtitlan, Texcoco, and Tlacopan continued in operation until the Spanish conquest although Tenochtitlan quickly took the lead and the other two partners participated to variable degrees in subsequent operations. The first conquests of the alliance were within the Basin of Mexico to integrate the former domain of Azcapotzalco. Subsequent military operations led by Tenochtitlan expanded conquests to neighboring regions creating an extensive tribute domain that extended from the Atlantic to Pacific oceans (Figure 1.2).[31]

By 1519, the imperial empire covered somewhere between 160,000 and 165,000 sq km and contained fifty-five individual tax provinces and client states (M. Smith 2012: table 7.1). The reason for the empire was a simple one, to collect wealth goods in the form of tribute to support state institutions. The *Nahua* military as mentioned earlier was a non-professional citizen-soldiery reinforced by experienced warrior knights. The knights were highly distinguished soldiers who were rewarded for their service with increased social prestige, gifts of textiles and warriors' costumes, and the assignment of land for their family's support. Although all male members of the population were required to participate in warfare, the size of Aztec armies in a given campaign depended on the expected level of resistance (Hassig 1988:59).

Campaigns were waged for a variety of reasons that included real or fabricated insults to Aztec citizens, failure to pay tribute demands, or the need for a military campaign after the installation of a new *tlatoani*. War was never a surprise. It was preceded by formal overtures by Aztec ambassadors who requested that targeted groups join the empire and pay tribute. Failure to do so resulted in conquest. Conquest provided resources for the growing number of Aztec elite, rewards for the soldiers who went to war, and funding for the ever increasing public festivals and large-scale building projects within Tenochtitlan (Durán 1994). The captives taken in battle were sacrificed to *Huitzilopochtli* and the broader pantheon of gods whose existence depended upon receiving nourishment from the blood and hearts of human victims (Matos Moctezuma 1988; Nicholson 1971).

State empires have been classified as either territorial or hegemonic organizations depending on the strength of their administrative structure. Territorial empires were tightly integrated domains where rulers used standing armies and directly supervised the conquered provinces. Hegemonic empires were more loosely integrated domains ruled through indirect control and a combination of force, persuasion, and intimidation of subject groups (M. Smith 2012:164). The Aztec empire was a hegemonic kingdom. They extracted tribute but did not drastically reshape conquered provinces to do so. The Aztecs usually did not install foreign governors in conquered provinces (Berdan 1980:37; Durán 1994; Silver-stein 2001). Instead, they often left native rulers in place as long as they submitted to the Aztecs and met their tribute demands. The advantage of this system was that it kept administrative costs low. The disadvantage of hegemonic structures was that local rulers could rebel when the oppor-tunity arose. This was not seen as a disadvantage before the arrival of the Spanish since revolt and reconquest resulted in the imposition of higher tribute demands.

The tribute system was organized by placing a supervisor called a *calpixqui* in each conquered province to coordinate the collection of tribute from local populations. The *calpixqui* usually was a member of an Aztec elite family who received the required tribute goods or their equivalents at specified intervals from the local population. The goods demanded in tribute were diverse and changed over time with the needs of the Aztec state. These goods were obtained in two different ways. The first and most fundamental way was to collect or manufacture tribute goods from locally available resources.[32] Local goods that were included in the tribute lists included cacao, cotton, natural rubber, paper; specific min-erals such as copper, gold, amber, turquoise, and jade; and products that come from specific habitats such as seashells, jaguar skins, and exotic feathers from the quetzal and cotinga bird species (Berdan and Anawalt 1992).

When not all tribute demands could be met with local resources populations would resort to trade. Cotton textiles were often demanded in tribute even where cotton was not available locally. In one case the people of Papaloticpac traveled over 100 km to the Rio Alvarado to procure raw cotton that they used to weave textiles to pay their tribute (Acuña 1984b:39). These kinds of commercial linkages for procuring cotton were common (Hirth 2013b:figure 4.6) and are illustrated in Figure 2.6. Tepeaca got the cotton it used to weave textiles by importing it over distances of up to 120 km from areas of Morelos, Puebla, and coastal Veracruz (Acuña 1985:256; Berdan 1980:39). Once cotton was procured local female labor was used to spin the thread and weave the textiles paid in tribute.

Trade was also used to procure tribute goods from merchants. The recognition that trade was important in this regard may be the reason that marketplaces were sometimes established as part of tribute demands. This is exactly what happened with the conquest of Tepeaca which was required to expand their marketplace to include more exotic goods, take care of merchants trading there, and to supply porters to help transport

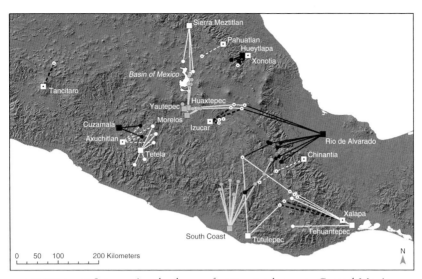

FIGURE 2.6 Inter-regional spheres of cotton trade across Central Mexico

goods (Durán 1994:155, 158–159; Hassig 1986:135). These kinds of arrangements benefitted *pochteca* merchants and one has to wonder whether these stipulations were engineered by the state's *pochteca* advisors to benefit their own involvement in inter-regional commerce[33] (see Chapter 7).

There are numerous examples illustrating the use of trade to obtain non-local goods to meet tribute obligations. Tepeaca offered to pay part of their tribute in salt (Durán 1994:155) even though all its salt was imported from the Tehuacan, Zapotitlan, and Ixtapa salt sources in southern Puebla (Hirth 2013b). The people of Tonameca who were subjects of Tututepec on the coast of Oaxaca had to travel to the high-lands to procure the copper, textiles, and cochineal that they had to pay the Aztecs in tribute (Acuña 1984a:198). Likewise, the town of Guatulco procured gold from the highlands to pay their tribute (Acuña 1984a:191). Puchtla, also subjects of Tututepec, bought the copper they were required to pay in tribute from merchants who sold it in their town, probably in exchange for locally grown cotton (Acuña 1984a:196). The province of Coixtlahuaca needed to pay a portion of its tribute in both feathers and greenstone which had to be procured through trade (Berdan and Anawalt 1992:2:104). The people of Itztepexic, Oaxaca paid tribute in non-local goods (gold, feathers, etc.) that they obtained by selling their labor to the individuals who could supply their needs. Specifically, they served as porters to *pochteca* merchants or traveled over 140 km to Tehuantepec, Xoconochco, and Guatemala to work as laborers on elite estates for up to six months to obtain tribute items[34] (Acuña 1984a:255; Carrasco 1999:232).

In all cases, the imposition of tribute obligations brought about changes in existing *tequitl* and service relations in conquered areas. Instead of redirecting local labor and resources toward meeting tribute demands, local elites most likely just increased labor demands on the local population. This would be the result of leaving local lords in governance positions within conquered provinces. In some cases local elites may even have benefitted from the imposition of new tribute demands. After its conquest, Tepeaca was designated as an area where outsiders could settle which expanded the labor supply and enriched the elite households to which they were assigned (Martínez 1984). Furthermore, Tepeaca was required to expand its marketplace giving local elite more access to the local and foreign merchants who frequented it (Durán 1994:159).

Tribute goods shipped to Tenochtitlan were taken to the palace where they were tabulated, stored, or forwarded to Texcoco and Tlacopan by the *petlacalcatl*, the high steward in charge of the *petlacalco* storage facility (Carrasco 1999:4). The goods that moved into state treasuries ranged from staple foods and utilitarian items, to exotic raw materials and finished goods (Berdan and Anawalt 1992). Staple foods were tabulated as large granaries of maize, beans, *chia*, and amaranth and were the bulkiest items collected for tribute; as a rule they did not move over distances greater than 100 km (Berdan 1992b:1:map 9). High-value raw materials (e.g. feathers, gold bars, amber, jade, turquoise, etc.) and finished goods (e.g. warriors' costumes, labrets, jade beads, etc.) moved over longer distances from the periphery of the empire (Berdan 1992b:1:maps 12–14). For the most part the further the tribute province was from Tenochtitlan, the higher the value of goods demanded that could absorb the cost of long-distance transportation.

Frances Berdan (1992a) has itemized the tribute in the *Codex Mendoza*, one of the main tribute lists for Tenochtitlan. An abbreviated summary of this tribute is presented in Table 2.2. One of the most important items moving through the tribute system were finished textiles which functioned as a form of commodity money, a medium of exchange, and a form of stored wealth. Berdan (1992a) estimates that anywhere from 128,000 to 255,360 textiles entered Tenochtitlan as tribute every year which are conservative estimates in contrast to those made by other scholars.[35] Textiles moved across the empire irrespective of distances

TABLE 2.2: *Annual tribute paid to* Tenochtitlan *listed in the Codex Mendoza*

Tribute items	Quantity
Manta cloths	
Plain white	68,000
Decorated and quilted	52,000
Richly decorated	8,000
Total manta cloths	128,000
Clothing	
Men's loincloths	7,200
Women's shirts and tunics	12,000
Warrior's costumes and shields	665
Food	
Bins of foodstuffs	88
Loads of chile	1,600
Jars of honey and syrup	3,800
Loaves of salt	4,000
Baskets of *pinolli* (war rations)	160
Cacao, loads and baskets	840
Miscellaneous items	
Loads of raw cotton	4,400
Loads of lime	16,800
Bags of cochineal	65
Beams and planks	14,400
Carrying frames	800
Loads of firewood	4,800
Reed mats and seats	16,000
Sheets of paper	32,000
Canes	48,000
Smoking canes	32,000
Gourd bowls	17,600
Pottery bowls	2,400
Rubber balls	16,000
Copal, balls and baskets	67,200
Pans of yellow ochre	40
Exotic goods	
Seashells	1,600
Live eagles	2 or more
Live enemy warriors	Unspecified
Deerskins	3,200
Jaguar skins	40
Liquidambar, jars and cakes	16,100
Lip plugs	82
Amber ornamental items	2

(*continued*)

TABLE 2.2: (*continued*)

Tribute items	Quantity
Turquoise ornamental items	15
Jade ornamental items	22
Copper bells	80
Copper axes	560
Gold, bowls, bars, and disks	130
Gold ornamental items	5
Feathers	
Quetzal feathers	2,480
Blue and red cotinga feathers	17,600
Green and yellow feathers	9,600
Green and yellow bunches	4
Feather ornamental items	3
Bags of feather down	20
Bird skins	160

and only two provinces (Tepeaca and Xoconochco) did not pay tribute in textiles (Berdan 1992b:map 3). They provided an unparalleled wealth base to support the expanding infrastructure and to build local clientages and political relationships across Mesoamerica. Tribute goods in the form of woven textiles, clothing, labrets, and warrior's costumes were given as gifts to political dignitaries at Aztec festivals as well as to warrior knights who were the backbone of the imperial army (Anawalt 1992; Sahagún 1979b:76).

One of the interesting anomalies found in the tribute documents is that differences exist between the goods turned in for tribute at the local level and those received at Tenochtitlan as recorded in the *Codex Mendoza* and the *Matrícula de Tributos*. Litvak King (1971:96–97) in an analysis of tribute documents from Cihuatlan and Tepequacuilco, Guerrero observed that a broader array of goods were turned in at the local level than ever reached Tenochtitlan. Gutiérrez (2013) observes the same phenomena for the neighboring province of Tlapa. Here, however, a detailed pictorial manuscript exists for the tribute paid quarterly by the Tlapa population to Aztec *calpixque* over a thirty-six-year period from 1486 to 1522. Table 2.3 compares the items turned in by local tribute payers recorded in the *Tribute Record of Tlapa* to the three imperial tribute documents that record the goals received at Tenochtitlan for the last year of the Aztec empire.[36]

TABLE 2.3: *Record of the annual tribute paid by Tlapa to the Aztec Empire from four tribute sources*

Tribute item	Tribute record of Tlapa	Codex Mendoza	Matrícula de Tributos	Información de 1554
Huipiles (women's tunics)	o	800	1,600	o
Cloth mantas with stripes	o	800	1,600	o
Plain white mantas	6,400	1,600	3,200	3,200
Warrior's costumes with shields	o	2	2	2
Gold bars	38	10	10	10
Gourds of gold dust	24	20	20	20
Gourd bowls for drinking cacao	o	1,600	800	400
Cakes of rubber	o	o	o	2,000
Human figures of rubber	o	o	o	400

Note: Information is summarized from Berdan and Anawalt (1992:2:85–87); Gutierrez (2013: 151–154, tables 6.1–6.2); Reyes (1997); Scholes and Adams (1957).

Each of the tribute documents tells a slightly different story. The *Codex Mendoza* and the *Matrícula de Tributos* are quite close in content recording different quantities of textile and gourd tribute based on whether they were paid twice or four times per year. The tribute listed in the *Información de 1554* is very similar to these other two except that it lists two tribute items from Tlapa not included elsewhere: cakes and human effigies made of rubber. The greatest deviation, however, is found in the very detailed list of tribute items recorded in the *Tribute Record of Tlapa* paid to the Aztec *calpixqui* (Gutiérrez et al. 2009a, 2009b). Here only three items were listed as paid for the year 2 Movement (1520–1521): plain cotton textiles, gold bars, and gourds of gold dust (Table 2.3).

Three important points emerge from Gutiérrez's (2013) comparison of local and imperial tribute records. First, the amount of tribute changed over time. The initial tribute demand of Tlapa during the first year of tribute payments was low consisting of only four gourds of gold dust and 8.4 gold bars. Although decorated textiles are listed in both the *Codex*

Mendoza and the *Matrícula de Tributos*, they are only registered as part of Tlapa's tribute between 1511 and 1514. After that point only plain white textiles are turned in at Tlapa (Gutiérrez 2013:153–154).

Second, the difference between local records and imperial records does not seem to be the result of inaccurate record keeping, but reflects the operation of an economic valuation system that permitted a considerable degree of negotiation and substitution of goods to meet tribute demands. Tlapa was one of the main provinces in the empire that paid tribute in gold according to the *Codex Mendoza*[37] and its overpayment in this commodity appears to have been both intentional and acceptable to the Aztec *calpixqui*. Tlapa paid its tribute demands in plain white textiles (*quachtli*) and two forms of gold, one of which, quills filled with gold dust, served as a form of commodity money within *Nahua* society. The *Información de 1554* provides value equivalents in Spanish pesos for all items listed. While this document reflects the early colonial value system, the payment of all of Tlapa's prehispanic tribute in textile and gold equivalents indicates the operation of a prehispanic valuation system that allowed considerable flexibility in how local groups could meet their obligations. Early tribute documents from Morelos suggest similar substitutions with earlier obligations in food tribute being paid in textiles by AD 1521 (Cline 1993:95).

The unresolved question is whether the Tlapa *calpixqui* only turned in the gold bars, gold dust, and white mantas to the *petlacalcatl* in Tenochtitlan, or whether he was responsible for converting these goods into all specified items listed in the tribute records. If the imperial tribute lists are viewed as a system of fixed demand, then the Tlapa *calpixqui* would have been responsible for procuring the items not turned in by the local population. This could have been structured either by procuring stipulated items through the merchant *pochteca*, or by trading gold and tribute mantas in the Tlatelolco marketplace (or other marketplaces) for all of the requisite tribute goods. That relationships existed between *calpixque* and merchant *pochteca* is documented in the *Codex of Tepeucila* where rulers and the tribute steward of that town repeatedly borrowed money from merchant *pochteca* to pay their tribute between 1535 and 1540 (Herrera Meza and Ruíz Medrano 1997). Future research needs to examine the flexibility of tribute systems and the role that local *calpixque* (plural of *calpixqui*) played in meeting tribute demands.

Finally, the *Información de 1554* makes it possible to compare the relative value of what was paid in local tribute items to the Tlapa *calpix-qui*, to what was turned in at Tenochtitlan. Again a discrepancy is noted.

The value of the tribute in plain textiles paid by the Tlapa population is 13–14% higher than what is demanded in any of the imperial tribute documents.[38] Gutiérrez (2013:157) notes that this is close to the 10% that the *tepantlato* (litigant attorney) was given from tribute levies for his performance in the native court system. In practical terms this overpayment by the Tlapa population may represent the commission paid by the local population to support the imperial *calpixqui*.

INTERFACING CONCLUSIONS

While ancient societies varied greatly in size and complexity, they all shared a number of structural similarities that are useful starting points for examining the internal organization of their respective economies. These were identified as the domestic and institutional economy, the former of which was the foundation for both ancient and modern societies. While variability can be found in how households are organized from society to society, they are responsible for the support and reproduction of their respective members. In prehispanic Mesoamerica it was the largest sector of the economy and the locale where most resources were produced, stored, and consumed. Relations within the household were intimate and direct. From the perspective of society as a whole, it was in commoner households that the vast majority of available labor was found and mobilized through an ideology of social obligation for public and privately directed work.

At the other end of the spectrum from households are the formal institutions that provide the framework for large-scale interaction across society (Figure 2.1). These institutions comprise the greater array of socially authorized corporate organizations within society. The integration and organization of these institutions enable societies to grow, mediate their internal disputes, and regulate inter-household relationships within both homogenous and heterogenous populations. Formal institutions define what is often referred to as social complexity. In ancient Mesoamerica these institutions encompassed everything from the organs of local governance found in all small villages and hamlets (*calpultin*), to the conquest empire of the Triple Alliance and the social and religious structures that supported it. All formal institutions need resources to carry out their tasks. In Mesoamerica the majority of these resources were produced by mobilizing domestic labor for work on assigned lands.

While formal institutions depended on domestic labor for their support, they were not responsible for the well-being of households except in a very general sense. Households were expected to be auto-sufficient and maintain themselves through their own efforts and the informal relationships forged at the community level. These inter-household relations represent what were discussed earlier as informal institutions. Some operated on a continual basis between households, while others were activated on an "as-needs" basis to provide support for households to meet consumption needs. It was the array of informal institutions that households relied on to minimize risk during times of famine, drought, and pestilence.

Maintaining access to the resources necessary to maintain life was the *raison d'etre* of ancient economies. As a result, informal institutions often evolved into formal institutions to ensure resource availability either through the intentional sponsorship of community leaders, or the regular undirected interactions of community members. This occurred in Mesoamerica with the development of the marketplace. The marketplace represents a formal institution in Mesoamerica that enhanced the ability of households to provision and support themselves in both good times and bad. Not only was it where households could sell the small surpluses that they produced, but it provided a framework through which they could also engage in specialized economic activities as part of their annual subsistence regime.

The marketplace was the fulcrum on which highland Mesoamerican economy pivoted and was the place where the domestic and institutional economies intersected. Because of its importance for shaping the structure and organization of Mesoamerican economy, the marketplace is discussed separately in Chapter 3.

3

The Mesoamerican marketplace

When we arrived at the great market place, called Tlaltelolco, we were astounded at the number of people and the quantity of merchandise that it contained, for we had never seen such a thing before
(Díaz del Castillo 1956:215).

The marketplace was the center of economic life across much of Mesoamerica. It was a creative, enabling force that more than any royal edict, military conquest, or religious tenant shaped the structure and organization of prehispanic society. It impacted the way that households organized their provisioning strategies, how elites converted food surpluses from their estates into storable wealth, and how imperial tribute was converted into the goods needed to operate the state bureaucracy. Marketplaces were where formalized trade took place and where the majority of goods moving in society changed hands. It was also the center of social life in Nahua society and where people of different social classes interacted with one another. It was where friends met, gossip was exchanged, economic livelihoods were defined, and the news of the day was shared and spread. In short, the marketplace was both a unique social institution and a macrocosm of the societies where it was found.

The marketplace was a formal institution. As discussed in Chapter 2, formal institutions are corporate organizations designed to provide specific functions for the society as a whole. Its primary economic function was to mobilize resources enabling households to procure what they needed and to dispose of any surplus that they produced. Without the marketplace highland Mesoamerica would not have had the commercial economic structure that it had. Like all formal institutions the marketplace required resources to operate in an efficient manner. Moreover, the marketplace could not operate without the development of a special ideology and place-specific mode of behavior.

This chapter discusses the importance of the marketplace in highland Mesoamerican society. It begins with clarifying what the marketplace is and what it is not. It then examines prehispanic marketplaces as they are known from the eyewitness accounts of the Spaniards who first saw them. Although the marketplace was a prominent institution, most everything known about its prehispanic organization and operation comes from accounts written during the early colonial period. Until archaeologists identify and excavate one in its entirety, these accounts remain the primary guide about their structure (see Hirth 1998, 2009b; Shaw 2012). The discussion then shifts to how the marketplace was organized and funded. Central to this discussion is the market tax and whether it was intended primarily to support the operation of the marketplace or the nobles who had jurisdiction over it. The economic advantages of marketplaces are then examined and the chapter concludes with an evaluation of prehispanic market systems, how they were structured, and the effect they had on inter-regional interaction.

THE MARKET, MARKET EXCHANGE, MARKET ECONOMY, AND THE MARKETPLACE

Terminology is important to clarify meaning and avoid confusion. The term market needs clarification so that its meaning in today's capitalistic system is not applied to a discussion of preindustrial and ancient economies. Market in the modern economic vernacular is used to refer to both a place where goods are bought and sold, and a demand stream for specific products within a market economy. Market is used in this first sense throughout this book. It is also important to clarify the differences implied by the terms market exchange, marketplace, market system, and market economy because they all bear upon the discussion of market function.

Market exchange refers to the balanced exchange or purchase of goods where the forces of supply and demand are visible between two or more interacting parties (Pryor 1977:104). They are commercial exchanges where value and price are determined through active negotiation.[1] Most often the exchange of goods is immediate, although delayed exchanges involving credit or commissioning the procurement of an object may also occur. The primary aspect of market exchange is the reciprocal negotiation of value; nothing is implied about the location of the transaction. Market exchanges can occur in a retail shop, on a street corner, or in someone's private residence. They can occur in multiple dispersed locations across society or concentrated in a centralized locale. As a form of economic interaction, market exchange is balanced and occurs in all societies from hunters and gatherers to complex states.[2]

The *marketplace* is a specialized locale where a large number of market exchanges take place on a regular or periodic basis (Plattner 1989b). Marketplaces make exchange activity more efficient by concentrating potential buyers and sellers in a centralized location. They develop as separate institutions because marketplaces do not presume existing social relationships between interacting parties. It is a locale where parties negotiate the value of goods and exchanges as economic equals, without regard to the social status of the participants involved. Establishing equality for purposes of negotiation is important when interaction occurs between individuals of sharply differing social status. For a marketplace to operate effectively social status must be removed or deconstructed temporarily for purposes of exchange. Marketplaces are liminal places according to Richard Blanton (2013:29) where existing social identities have to be suspended or ignored for purposes of transacting exchange (see also Hutson 2000). Markets need a special social rationality to operate (Weber 1946:333–336) so that offers between individuals can be negotiated and accepted or rejected on the basis of perceived value without the fear of social reprisal.

Marketplaces require a special set of conditions be met if they are to operate efficiently and without conflict. As a result they are often constituted as formal institutions where they are found. They have their own rules of operation, are convened on a regular schedule, and usually have administrators that oversee the organization and honesty of transactions. As a result it has been argued that marketplaces depended on strong elite sponsorship (Dyer 2005:20; Hicks 1987; Polanyi 1957) despite instances where political supervision is weak or absent (Benet 1957; Blanton 2013). Alternative approaches see the development of marketplaces as piggyback events at religious and political gatherings (Abbott 2010; Blanton 2013:30; Burger 2013) or as a response to urban food needs and agricultural specialization (Appleby 1976; Blanton 1983; C. Smith 1974).

While marketplaces may occur as isolated places, they often are part of larger economic networks at the regional and inter-regional levels. These networks of marketplaces are referred to as *market systems* and are an important feature of mature economic landscapes often associated with state societies (Garraty 2010:10). The articulation of marketplaces at the regional level can take many forms depending on the density of regional population and constraints to transportation (C. Smith 1976, 1983; G. Skinner 1964). Moreover, the scheduling of when marketplaces are convened can create a hierarchy of places in terms of size and the types of goods they contain. It is characterizing the variation within market systems that has created a diversity of names for types of marketplaces that include border markets, peripheral markets, central place markets, restricted markets, barter markets, price-making markets, and periodic fairs (Abu-Lughod 1989; Blanton 2013; Kurtz 1974; Stanish and Coben 2013).

Market economy is a system of economic interaction where the production of goods and services is strongly determined by demand, competition, and price. The price of goods and services influences the production decisions of those who make them and vice versa. While suitable for discussing modern economic systems, this concept is inappropriate for discussing ancient economies for two reasons. First, market economies are not simply economies with marketplaces; instead they have active supply and demand sectors for land, labor, and capital. Mesoamerica supported complex market systems but it lacked large, active markets in land and labor both of which were accessed through the social system rather than through free market negotiation. Second, for a market economy to operate through the interplay of supply and demand, there needs to be good communication between the production and distribution sectors. Ancient economies had imperfect systems of communication with multiple year delays under conditions of long-distance trade. As a result units of production remained small, focused on quality over quantity, and resistant to innovation (Homans 1974; Silver 1981).

EYEWITNESS ACCOUNTS OF PREHISPANIC MARKETPLACES

The Spanish conquistadors marveled at the richness of the Aztec world. Bernal Díaz del Castillo captures the awe of the conquistadors as they looked down from the mountain passes leading into the eastern side of the Basin of Mexico,

> Gazing on such wonderful sights, we did not know what to say, or whether what appeared before us was real, for on one side, on the land, there were great cities, and in the lake ever so many more ... and in front of us stood the great City of Mexico
>
> (Díaz del Castillo 1956:192).

FIGURE 3.1 Prehispanic marketplace in Michoacan*

The marketplace (Figure 3.1) was a vital part of every large city providing fresh food and other goods to the urban population. This was especially important for the residents of the Aztec capital of Tenochtitlan which, because of its location in the center of the lake, lacked agricultural land and relied on the importation of food from *chinampas* fields in the southern lakes region. The presence of marketplaces in other large cities is clarified by the Spanish conquistador Francisco López de Gomara:

> The market place is called a *tianquiztli*. Each district and parish has its square for the exchange of merchandise, Mexico and Tlatelolco, the largest districts, having vast ones, especially the latter, where markets are held on most weekdays. [In the rest,] one every five days is customary, and I believe, in the whole kingdom and territory of Moctezuma.
>
> (López de Gomara 1966:160).

All cities that were the center of a city-state known as an *altepetl* had a marketplace. The size of the marketplace and the number of people who visited it varied with the size and provisioning needs of the city. The two largest and most important cities in the Basin of Mexico were the imperial cities of Tenochtitlan-Tlatelolco and Texcoco. Their markets were the only ones in the Basin held daily; the markets of other large cities were held every five days. Not only were these marketplaces large, but they teemed with a vast array of finished goods and raw materials that entered the region both through exchange networks and the imperial tribute system.

Although all cities had marketplaces, the largest market in the Basin was located at Tlatelolco on the west side of Tenochtitlan island. This is the market referred to in the epigram at the beginning of the chapter. The two things that impressed the Spanish conquistadors who visited the Tlatelolco marketplace were its size and the quantity of goods that it contained. Although Tlatelolco was the largest marketplace in the Basin, Cortés indicates that there were multiple marketplaces in Tenochtitlan that serviced its resident population. One can imagine that these market-places varied in the types of products offered for sale. In his second letter to the king of Spain, Cortés identified that the Tlatelolco market was twice the size of the largest market he had ever seen in his travels throughout the western Mediterranean.

The city has many open squares in which markets are continuously held and the general business of buying and selling proceeds. One square in particular is twice as big as that of Salamanca and completely surrounded by arcades where there are daily more than sixty thousand folk buying and selling

(Cortés 1962:87).

Cortés' estimate of the number of people frequenting the Tlatelolco marketplace was either his impressionistic estimate or an average figure provided by the native guides who took him there. I believe the estimate of 60,000 people was likely supplied by native guides since they would have been well aware of the level of market traffic. The Anonymous Conqueror (1971:392) indicates that market populations were cyclical with 20,000–25,000 people in this market on a daily basis which surged to 40,000–50,000 persons every fifth day (Berdan 1975:197). The daily market at Tlaxcala also was large and regularly had over 30,000 persons attending it (Zorita 1994:152). The largest estimate of market goers is from López de Gomara where he states:

The market place of Mexico is wide and long, surrounded on all sides by an arcade; so large is it, indeed, that it will hold seventy thousand or even one hundred thousand people, who go about buying and selling, for it is, so to speak, the capital of the whole country, to which people come, not only from the vicinity, but from farther

(López de Gomara 1966:160).

The number of individuals who frequented the Tlatelolco and Tenoch-titlan marketplaces were not all residents of the city. Instead it attracted people from the neighboring towns who entered the city both on foot and by dugout canoes that plied the surrounding lake.[3] According to López de Gomara,

> Upon these lakes float some two hundred thousand small boats, called by the natives *acalli* ... I am understanding, rather than exaggerating the number of these *acalli*, for some affirm that in Mexico alone there are commonly some fifty thousand of them, used for bringing in provisions and transporting people. So the canals are covered with them to a great distance beyond the city, especially on market days
>
> (López de Gomara 1966:159–160).

The abundance and variety of items offered for sale within the Tlatelolco marketplace overwhelmed the conquistadors. While they were especially interested in the gold and high-value goods, they also noted the variety of goods used to meet the needs of everyday life:

> There is nothing to be found in all the land which is not sold in these markets ... that on account of their very number and the fact that I do not know their names, I cannot now detail them
>
> (Cortés 1962:89).

> The kinds of foodstuffs sold are numberless. They will eat virtually anything that lives
>
> (López de Gomara 1966:162).

> Every kind of merchandise ... met with in every land is for sale there, whether of food and victuals, or ornaments of gold and silver, or lead, brass, copper, tin, precious stones, bones, shells, snails and feathers
>
> (Cortés 1962:87).

The abundance of items found in marketplaces was combined with good organization. Marketplaces were organized by the class of items sold. In the words of Bernal Díaz del Castillo (1956:215), "each kind of merchandise was kept by itself and had its fixed place marked out." Foods were grouped together as were utilitarian and high-value goods. This made it easier for potential buyers to find and compare goods offered for sale. Grouping similar items together also made it easier for market administrators to check the price of goods and supervise the dealings of the individuals who sold them.

The central market was reserved for staples and light to moderate sized goods that could be moved relatively easily into and out of the main square. Bulky items such as building materials were located on the peripheries of the Tlatelolco marketplace presumably along the canals that criss-crossed the city. The result was that bulky items did not take up space in the central marketplace and could be easily loaded and unloaded into canoes for movement to their designated places of use.

Each trade and each kind of merchandise has its own place reserved for it, which no one else can take or occupy – which shows no little regard for public order – and because such a multitude of people and quantity of goods cannot be accommodated in the great square, the goods are spread out over the nearest streets, especially the more bulky materials, such stone, lumber, lime, bricks, adobes and all building materials, both rough and finished

(López de Gomara 1966:160).

The marketplace was an orderly place laid out much like the city itself in a series of parallel aisles and streets. As Cortés observes,

Each kind of merchandise is sold in its own particular street and no other kind may be sold there: this rule is very well enforced. All is sold by number and measure, but up till now no weighting by balance has been observed

(Cortés 1962:89).

While Cortés does not describe every aisle that he walked down, he does provide several examples that illustrate the diversity of things found along them. For example,

There is a street of game where they sell all manner of birds that are to be found in their country, including hens, partridges, quails, wild duck, fly-cachers, widgeon, turtle doves, pigeons, little birds in round nests made of grass, parrots, owls, eagles, vulcans, sparrow-hawks, and kestrels

(Cortés 1962:87).

In another example,

There is a street of herb-sellers where there are all manner of roots and medicinal plants that are found

(Cortés 1962:87).

If variety is the spice of life, then the Tlatelolco marketplace was where commercial life found its fullest flavor. The Spanish marveled at its diversity, but it is next to impossible to estimate the complete range of products offered for sale. Sahagún attempts to represent this variability in his illustration of the goods sold in the marketplace (Figure 3.2). He depicts both male and female sellers seated in the marketplace with the goods offered for sale between them and the individual on the right offering to purchase them. These products range from high-value goods (feathers,

FIGURE 3.2 Goods sold in the marketplace. Note the glyph for the marketplace in the lower left hand corner of the illustration

embroidered capes, jade beads, etc.) to everyday items (ceramic vessels, salt, fruit, etc.) and prepared food represented by a goblet of chocolate and a bowl with food inside. The glyph for the marketplace is the circle with footprints inside of it located at the lower left corner of the figure.

Because of its location at the center of the empire it is reasonable to imagine that the Tlatelolco market contained a more diverse array of products than any other marketplace in Mesoamerica at the time. In the past, like today, preference, quality, price, and novelty all affected the purchasing decisions of market goers. Retailers today measure the diversity of retail inventories in terms of stock keeping units (SKUs) that are offered for sale in commercial establishments (Beinhocker 2006:9). The SKU is a qualitative measurement of the number of *categories* of items offered for sale in large establishments at any given time.[4]

Table 3.1 summarizes the different types of items included in Sahagún's (1961) discussion of the goods offered for sale within the Tlatelolco marketplace. A total of 705 categorically distinct SKUs are listed which certainly is only a fraction of the items sold. Even if it represents only 1% of the goods available it provides a glimpse of the richness of the Tlatelolco marketplace that the Spanish encountered. While Tlatelolco was a unique market in terms of its size, many of the same trade items were also sold in other large regional marketplaces across Central Mexico. The richness of the Tlatelolco market was a product of its operation as a daily market allowing venders to build up diverse inventories, possibly even storing them in or near the marketplace for daily retrieval and display.

Table 3.1 groups the categories of goods sold into seven categories: food products, prepared food products, raw materials, craft goods, textiles, high-value items, and herbs and medicines. The provisioning function of the marketplace is evident in the goods sold. Food, both in unprepared form and as ready-to-eat dishes make up 41% (n=290) of the items listed for sale. What is interesting is that the dividing line between whether venders sold prepared or unprepared food is not completely clear. Some venders only sold unprepared staples such as maize, beans, or tomatoes. Venders who sold fruit, fish, and meat products, however, dealt in both prepared and unprepared foods possibly as a function of spoilage or to prolong their use-life by cooking. Of course the market has always been a place to buy a hot meal and this also was the case during prehispanic times. The list of hot dishes includes a rich array of tamales, *atoles,* and savory meat dishes in a variety of sauces. Foods prepared and served cold include cacao and a range of different *atole* drinks.

Other utilitarian goods sold include raw materials (n=74), finished craft goods (n=173), and herbs and medicines (n=42). These three non-food utilitarian goods (n=289) represent another 41% of the SKUs listed in the sources. The individuals selling these goods are a mixture of retail venders who bought herbs, dyes, baskets, and ceramic and gourd containers for resale, as well as the craftsmen who only sold the goods that they made.

TABLE 3.1: *A partial list of diversity of items (SKUs) offered for sale by venders in the Tlatelolco market*

Merchant category	No. of items sold	Merchant category	No. of items sold
Food sellers		**Craft goods**	
Amaranth sellers	10	Basket sellers	23
Bean sellers	11	Broom sellers	5
Chia sellers	8	Candle sellers (colonial)	3
Maize sellers	8	Footwear sellers	14
Wheat sellers (colonial)	5	Gourd bowl sellers	29
Cacao dealers	7	Needle sellers	11
Chili sellers	16	Paper sellers	3
Fruit sellers*	52	Peddlers	9
Maguey syrup sellers	2	Potters	22
Tomato sellers	7	Reed mat sellers	15
Fish sellers*	34	Tobacconists	11
Meat sellers*	18	Wood products	28
Poultry products	10	Subtotal miscellaneous products	173
Subtotal food sellers	188		
Prepared Food Sellers		**Textiles**	
Atole sellers	16	Bag and sash sellers	8
Chocolate-drink sellers	10	Cotton cape sellers	24
Food/tortilla sellers	68	Maguey cape sellers	14
Gourd seed sellers	7	Palm cape sellers	10
Subtotal prepared foods	102	Rabbit-hair sellers	13
		Subtotal textiles	69
Raw materials			
Bitumen sellers	2	**High-value items**	
Cotton sellers	3	Metal object sellers	3
Dye sellers	4	Feather sellers	17
Glue sellers	2	Gold dealers	3
Lime sellers	6	Green stone sellers	8
Obsidian sellers	8	Mirror stone sellers	5
Pigment sellers	30	Jewelry sellers	18
Resin sellers	5	Slave dealers	3
Rubber sellers	4	Subtotal high-value items	57
Salt sellers	4		
Saltpeter and chalk sellers	6	**Herbs and medicines**	
Subtotal raw materials	74	Herb sellers	21
		Pharmacists	21
		Subtotal medicines	42
Total SKUs			705

* These venders sell both prepared and unprepared foods

Note: The sources used are from Sahagún (1961, 1979b:67–68). Itemization is a qualitative assessment following the principle of retail Stock Keeping Units (SKUs)

High-value goods such as textiles or items manufactured using feathers, gold, copper, or jade have significant levels of invested labor. Textiles are well represented in the list with sixty-nine different products offered for sale. Included in this category are cotton, maguey, and palm capes, as well as finished sashes and bags. The rabbit-hair vender probably sold dyed and processed rabbit hair used in the manufacture of textiles rather than a finished good. Feathers were important in the manufacture of both capes and emblematic devices used to indicate social rank (Berdan 2014). The finished jewelry offered for sale represented many unique pieces cast from gold, silver, copper, or bronze which incorporated different types of precious stones (n=18). While high-value goods were offered for sale in the Tlatelolco marketplace, they were in a minority (18.3%) compared to the many utilitarian goods sold there.

It is easy to envision the marketplace as the location where finished goods were sold. The sources are clear on that. What is often overlooked is that marketplaces also were the location where some craft goods were made and services were sold. The best case of market craft production was the manufacture of obsidian blades which were the primary cutting implements in this society (see Hirth 2009b). Obsidian blades were razor sharp knives that were produced on demand for individuals who needed cutting edge.[5] Numerous Spanish chroniclers observed these craftsmen at work (Clark 1989; Sahagún 1961:148). Bernal Díaz del Castillo was one of them, who as an afterthought about his visit to the Tlatelolco marketplace remarked, "I am forgetting those who sell salt, and those who make the stone knives, and how they split them off the stone itself (Díaz del Castillo 1956:216–217)."

Other products that probably were made or modified within the marketplace include flower arrangements, fiber-sandals, baskets, reed-mats, herbal concoctions, blends of tobacco, and small items of apparel such as bags and sashes (Hirth 2006a:182, 2009b). These are items that could be fabricated by craftsmen "in-between" sales, needed individual adjustments, or were made to the preference of the consumer. Modern flower workers who produce wreaths and displays for special events still work in the marketplace where fresh flowers are available on a daily basis (Hirth 2009b; G. Rojas 1927:167; J. Rojas 1995:148). The marketplace was also a place to contract labor or arrange the consignment of special projects. As Cortés (1962:93) relates, "Every day in all the markets and public places of the city there are a number of workmen and masters of all manner of crafts waiting to be hired by the day."

The picture of marketplaces across Central Mexico is one of open air emporia with few permanent installations or shops, paralleling what is reported for ethnographic marketplaces. This differed sharply from markets and emporia in the Old World where permanent installations were common and marketplaces often evolved into sectors of retail shops and small craft workshops (Davis 1966; De Ligt 1993:26; Shiba 1977:411; Starr 1977:86). Permanent installations in Central Mexico were limited because most large marketplaces met on a rotating five-day cycle requiring merchants to travel between them with their goods in tow (see later). This made it impractical and unprofitable to leave large quantities of goods in fixed locations. Daily markets were an exception to this practice and as a result a few small shops were present within the Tlatelolco marketplace. As Cortés observed during his visit,

There are houses as it were of apothecaries where they sell medicines made from these herbs, both for drinking and for use as ointments and salves. There are barbers' shops where you may have your hair washed and cut. There are other shops where you may obtain food and drink. There are street porters such as we have in Spain to carry packages

(Cortés 1962:87–88).

Cortés (1962:50–52) observed similar facilities at the daily marketplace at Ocotelulco, Tlaxcala. He noted the presence of shops and booths where jewelers sold finished featherwork and where barbers washed people's hair and gave them a shave. López de Gómara (1966:120) noted a public bath, probably a *temazcalli* in the Ocotelulco marketplace.[6] What is notable about Ocotelulco is that Cortés implies that there were shops in other parts of the city outside of the marketplace. If this was the case it would imply a slightly different form of selling in Tlaxcala than we assume was present elsewhere in Central Mexico.[7] In his own words,

There is a market in this city in which more than thirty thousand people daily are occupied in buying and selling, and this in addition to other similar shops which there are in all parts of the city

(Cortés 1962:50).

The conquistadors were products of a European feudal society with a strong commercial base. Items were bought and sold with regularity in shops, marketplaces, and craftsmen's workshops. It is significant, therefore, that the Spanish quickly identified *Nahua* economy as a commercial one, where things were regularly bought and sold with commodity money and through barter. According to López de Gomara,

Buying and selling consisted merely of exchanging one thing for another: this man offers a turkey for a sheaf of maize; that one, mantles for salt or money (rather, for cacao beans, which circulate as money throughout the country), and in this fashion their trading is done. They kept accounts: so many cacao beans for a mantle or a turkey, and they used a string for measuring things like maize and feathers; pots for other things, such as honey and wine

(López de Gomara 1966:163).

The Spanish were particularly interested in gold and silver since these were their standards of value for judging wealth. It is no surprise, therefore, that they took special notice of gold and how it was used as a form of currency. Cacao beans and plain cotton textiles known as *quachtli* were the fundamental commodity money used in market exchange across the highlands. In both the preceding account and the one that follows it is clear that the conquistadors understood how cacao and cotton textiles were used in commercial transactions even if they did not completely understand the structure of the monetary system. It is likely that what Díaz del Castillo describes in the following passage is what Sahagún (1961:61–62) referred to as an "exchange dealer" (*tlapatlac, teucuitlapatlac*) who functioned as a banker and money changer within the marketplace (see Chapter 6).

There were many more merchants, who, as I was told brought gold for sale in grains, just as it is taken from the mines. The gold is placed in thin quills of the geese of the country, white quills, so that the gold can be seen through, and according to the length and thickness of the quills they arrange their accounts with one another, how much so many mantles or so many gourds full of cacao were worth, or how many slaves, or whatever other things they were exchanging

(Díaz del Castillo 1956:217).

THE MARKETPLACE AS A FORMAL INSTITUTION

The marketplace was the central social and economic institution in *Nahua* society (Figure 3.1). Although it provided many social functions, its *raison d'être* was to promote economic exchange. It was a centralized locale where surpluses were mobilized and converted to alternative goods. The marketplace and the types of goods it contained was the pride of the ruler who oversaw it. It also was the mechanism through which commoner households provisioned themselves independent of elite control.

While individual participation in the marketplace was voluntary, it operated as a permanent and predictable fixture within society. Like other formal institutions the marketplace required labor and resources to carry out business and to ensure that transactions were conducted in an open and fair way. The need for institutional infrastructure in the form of special architectural constructions was minimal. While it is true that the market of Tlatelolco was surrounded by an arcade wall (Cortés 1962:87; López de Gomara 1966:160), this was because it was a daily market. Most other large markets in Central of Mexico operated on a five-day schedule[8] (Hassig 1982a) and did not have permanent facilities, but were held in plazas that were multi-functional assembly areas.[9]

Nevertheless, two architectural constructions were an integral part of market operations and were always constructed within the marketplace. The first was the market shrine (*momoztli*) that housed the god of the marketplace (Figure 3.3). While Durán mentions this in the singular, it is possible that there were multiple such shrines in the marketplace depending on its size. This shrine was important for two reasons. First, it designated the marketplace as a special reverential place even when it was held in plazas surrounding by other administrative and religious structures (Kurtz 1974:697). Second, it was a place where venders could place offerings to the market god. As Durán observed it was here that people "offered ears of corn, chili, tomatoes, fruit, and other vegetables, seeds, and breads–in sum, everything sold in the *tianguiz* (Durán 1971:276)." In addition to providing merchants with good fortune, these offerings supplied a material base for the support of the marketplace. An example of a market shrine with side altars to receive offerings has been excavated in a marketplace at Xochicalco, Morelos (Hirth 2009b).

The second architectural facility associated with the largest market-places was a dais or audience chamber that housed market magistrates. These administrators served as judges to evaluate cases of fraud and theft within the marketplace.[10] The judges often were *pochtecatlatoque*, esteemed professional merchants who understood commercial dealings (Berdan 1975: 206). Both Díaz del Castillo (1956:216) and Cortés observed the centrally located audience chamber where market magis-trates were located,[11]

a very fine building in the great square serves as a kind of audience chamber where ten or a dozen persons are always seated, as judges who deliberate on all cases arising in the market and pass sentence on evildoers

(Cortés 1962:89).

The judicial function of the marketplace extended to the broader soci-ety. These magistrates also passed sentences on crimes committed outside the marketplace. The reason they did so was to broadcast the penalty for

FIGURE 3.3 The marketplace represented as a circle. Notice the circular market shrine in the center of the marketplace

committing crimes to the broader public. In one case, a man who stole gold from a Spaniard in Tlaxcala fled to Cholula where he was later apprehended and brought back to Tlaxcala where they,

> took him with a public crier, who proclaimed his offense, leading him through the great marketplace, where they put him at the foot of a building like a theater which stands in the middle of that market square. The public crier … ascended the platforms and in a loud voice again proclaimed the man's guilt. All having looked upon him, they beat him on the head with sticks until they killed him
>
> (Zorita 1994:154–155).

In many respects this execution resembles the public hangings of societies in Europe whose purpose was to underscore publically the punishment for breaking the law.

Resources were needed for the marketplace to operate, but not many. Some resources were necessary to support its supervisory personnel. This included the judges mentioned earlier and the commercial inspectors (*tianquizpan tlayacaque*) who circulated through the marketplace. These inspectors checked merchandise and oversaw commercial transactions to insure that fraud was not committed intentionally or accidentally (Durand-Forest 1971, 1994:175) (see Chapter 7). Senior members of the knight societies also patrolled the marketplace to prevent disputes. According to López de Gomara (1966:163), "If anyone gave short weight, he was fined and his measures were broken." In a fuller description Cortés reports,

there are officials who continually walk amongst the people inspecting goods exposed for sale and the measures by which they are sold, on certain occasions I have seen them destroy measures which were false

(Cortés 1962:89).

The individuals in these supervisory roles took their responsibilities seriously. If they did not, they either lost their job and/or were exiled. When judges failed to exercise good judgement they could be put to death (Alba 1949:15). The implication here is that this was more than volunteer service. Rather, market supervisors most likely received institutional support to enable them to carry out their duties. The question is where would these resources have come from? The logical place was through a market tax.

INSTITUTIONAL FINANCE AND THE MARKET TAX

The costs of the marketplace could have been financed in different ways. The construction of market architecture and the post-market cleanup could have been covered through *coatequitl* labor rotations. Important administrative personnel most likely were supported by prebendal land assigned to that purpose (Carrasco 1978). Rojas (1995:109) believes that judges were supported with the products grown on *tecpantlalli* land. A second source of income was the market tax that was a tax-in-kind placed on sellers in the marketplace. Two accounts report the collection of this tax. López de Gomara was specific in this regard:

The vendors paid the king something for their place, either for the right to sell or for protection against thieves, for which purpose certain men like policemen were always walking about the market place

(López de Gomara 1966:163).

Cortés also reports the existence of a market tax where he states,

At all entrances to the city and at those parts where canoes are unloaded, which is
where the greatest amount of provisions enters the city, certain huts have been
built, where there are official guards to exact so much on everything that enters.
I know not whether this goes to the lord or to the city itself, and have not yet been
able to ascertain, but I think that it is to the ruler, since in the markets of several
other towns we have seen such a tax exacted on behalf of the ruler

(Cortés 1962:93).

The important question that needs to be answered is how large was the
market tax and what was it used for? Blanton (1996:82) believes that the
market tax was an important source of revenue for elite families and for
this reason ruling dynasties attempted to expand the marketplace that
they controlled. Blanton argues that market taxes were a lucrative 20%
sales tax on the items sold. If this was true then rulers would have indeed
benefitted by increasing the size of the marketplace since the larger the
market, "the more revenue that could be earned (Blanton 1996:82)."
A 20% tax rate combined with Cortés' (1962:93) description of what
sounds like toll or tax booths at city entrances suggests a formidable level
of control over the resources entering the city. Unfortunately I do not
believe this is what the sources indicate. Instead, Blanton has confused a
special conquest tribute levy resulting from an attack on the Aztecs as a
market tax. The basis for a 20% market tax comes from a passage in
Durán where he states,

King Axayacatl decreed that the Tlatelolco market and square that constituted the
land won by the Tenochca Aztecs (for the Tlatelolcas possessed no more land than
this) be divided into lots among the different Aztec lords, and that the Tlatelolco
merchants who occupied space here were to pay a tax amounting to one part for
every five. In this way the marketplace was divided up among all the merchants,
and the tax was collected from each one according to what he had sold

(Durán 1994:262).

There are three reasons for why a 20% tax was not a standard market
tax. First, Central Mexico had a thriving network of marketplaces and the
imposition of a 20% market tax every time a vender came to the marketplace as the Cortés and López de Gomara accounts suggest, would have
stifled if not eliminated market participation. Most large markets were
held every five days with merchants traveling from market to market with
the goods they offered for sale. Now imagine a merchant setting out with
one hundred gourd vessels to sell in five separate periodic marketplaces
over a five day period. If no items were sold over that period, but a 20%

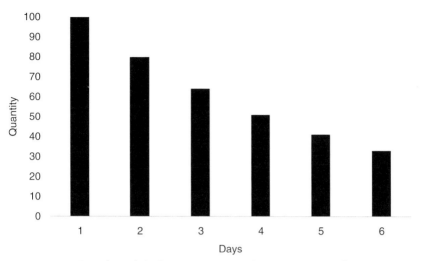

FIGURE 3.4 Hypothetical decline in inventory of an itinerant merchant over a
five day period if a 20% market tax was paid each day at a marketplace

market tax was charged at each market he entered, the merchant would
lose fully two-thirds of his stock to tax in those five days! Figure 3.4
illustrates the theoretical drop in salable stock over his five day circuit.
A 20% market tax on individuals entering marketplaces would have
depressed market participation and made market selling unfeasible.
Moreover, this level of taxation would have fostered the distribution of
resources through informal, less centralized forms of distribution which is
not what occurred.

Second, the percentage cited by Durán's account is exactly the same as
the Spanish imperial tax known as the royal fifth. This similarity makes
the information suspect especially considering the fact that ethnographically market sellers pay a small fixed amount for the right to sell in the
marketplace (Gerardo Gutierrez, personal communication 2015). That
this was also likely the case during both the prehispanic and early colonial
periods is evident in the tax records of Coyoacan (see later).

The third reason for doubting the 20% tax rate is that the levy cited by
Durán (1994:262) was not a market tax; it was a tribute levy laid on the
population of Tlatelolco after its conquest in AD 1473. Like the Aztecs of
Tenochtitlan, the people of Tlatelolco lacked sufficient agricultural land
for all their needs[12] and benefitted economically from their participation
in commerce. The result was that after their conquest the Aztecs levied a
tribute tax on the stocks of merchandise that Tlatelolco merchants had in

the marketplace. If Durán's account is taken at face value, that levy was a full 20%. Durán further explains that this tribute had to be paid every eighty days, not in the goods sold in the marketplace, but at least initially in slaves that were to be bought with the goods collected. What is clear is that Durán is describing a special conquest levy that was the result from Tlatelolco's attack on the Aztecs.[13] In a similar manner Tlatelolco merchants were also charged with supplying war rations for Aztec military campaigns (Isaac 1986:341; Sahagún 1979b:69).

The position taken here is that sellers indeed paid a market tax, but it did *not* provide a significant revenue stream for elite support. Instead, I believe that the market tax was a relatively modest surcharge much like the modest amount of labor time required to cultivate institutional land (see Chapter 2). A market tax was collected to cover the cost of maintaining the marketplace but it did not provide a significant income for the dynastic elite charged with its operation. Documents from the sixteenth-century market at Coyoacan indicate that the market tax provided revenue for at least one judge who worked there (Berdan 1975:208) as well as the elite who oversaw the marketplace (Berdan 1975:46: Carrasco and Monjarás-Ruiz 1978:41–42). What is significant, however, is that this market tax was very small. Testimonies given by two Coyoacan market supervisors indicate that payment of the market tax was voluntary, only paid if something was sold, or was so small that it was a token payment only.[14]

Table 3.2 summarizes the information available from the four market tax documents from Coyoacan. The average total market tax was 9 pesos and 4½ tomines.[15] According to Berdan (1988:646) the Coyoacan market levy most likely covered a full year's attendance at the marketplace.[16]

TABLE 3.2: *Recorded market tax from the Coyoacan market during the sixteenth century*

Coyoacan document	Total tax
Document 1*	8 pesos, 6½ tomines
Document 2*	9 pesos, 5½ tomines
Document 3**	10 pesos, 4½ tomines
Document 4***	9 pesos, 5 tomines
Average tax	9 pesos, 4½ tomines

Note: Information is from Anderson, Berdan, and Lockhart (1976).
  * Document specifies no time period for tax payment
  ** Document specifies tax was paid once a year
  *** Document specifies tax was paid every thirty days

Did this tax represent a significant income for the indigenous lord who collected it in Coyoacan? Conversion of the 9 pesos, 4½ tomines to its 1560 purchasing power in maize reveals that it is enough to purchase 897 kg of grain; this is a good amount, but in terms of total calories needed is barely enough to support a family of five for a year.[17] The market tax, however, was insignificant compared to the 1,386 pesos and 6 tomines paid by the Coyoacan population during the same period to fulfil its *tequitl* service obligation to their lord.[18] The difference between market tax income and the return from normal service to lords would have been even greater in Coyoacan prior to Spanish contact because, while market activity continued unabated into the colonial era, the native population providing service tribute drastically declined (Cook and Simpson 1948; Gibson 1964). The conclusion drawn from this comparison is that market tax was *not* a significant source of income for indigenous elite especially in those marketplaces that trafficked primarily in utilitarian goods.[19]

Finally, it is important to note that there was considerable variation in the structure of market taxes across the Mexican highlands. While it was an aspect of market operations in *Nahua* markets in the central highlands, it was less important and possibly absent in the southern highlands in the Mixteca and the Valley of Oaxaca. For example, an attempt by Spanish administrators to tax market activity throughout the Mixteca during the sixteenth century resulted in considerable resistance by local populations.[20] An initiative to charge a mere 2% market tax on non-Spanish goods brought sharp resistance and protests from local populations (Terraciano 2001:249). Given the level of these protests it is possible that a prehispanic market tax was not charged anywhere throughout the southern highlands (Blanton 2013:34).

The marketplace was important but how it was funded seemed to have varied significantly across Mesoamerica. In the central highlands a market tax was used to cover the administrative costs of its operation. The marketplace was a source of prestige but not a significant source of income for the royal dynasties that controlled it. In the southern highlands market tax appears to be absent, or so small that it wasn't mentioned in colonial documents. Under these circumstances the marketplace would have been supported by elite patronage, *coatequitl* service, and the resources offered at its market shrines. In both cases the market levy was not a means for elite to accumulate significant wealth in comparison to their other sources of income.

FIVE ECONOMIC FUNCTIONS OF THE MARKETPLACE

The presence of marketplaces creates an environment that fosters economic interaction and development not possible without them. One of the most important dimensions of the marketplace facilitated household provisioning. Although prehispanic households produced goods that they consumed they rarely met all their resource needs. Instead they produced what they could and engaged in exchange to procure the rest. The marketplace made household provisioning both more efficient and more economical. It provided access to a wide array of goods and allowed households to make more informed decisions about how to utilize their labor in alternative production tasks.

The role of household provisioning shaped the development of marketplaces in many ancient and preindustrial societies around the world. Food and staple markets were a ubiquitous feature of virtually all chiefdom and state level societies (e.g. Kurtz 1974). In chiefdoms the marketplace supplied the population with staple goods while prestige goods moved through other forms of exchange (Bohannan and Dalton 1965). In the Roman empire, the presence of marketplaces in rural areas reduced the time and distance that commoners had to travel to obtain the agricultural tools, textiles, and footwear produced in urban areas. Rural marketplaces facilitated the exchange of goods between town and country (De Ligt 1993:140–143). Many marketplaces were established on rural estates by land owners to help provision their tenants. This was not an altruistic gesture, but one intended to avoid having tenant households lose work time by traveling to urban markets (De Ligt 1993:155, 178).

A second function of the marketplace is to mobilize surplus. In marketless societies where production is oriented to auto-consumption, food is stored within the household and is mobilized through inter-personal kinship and community relationships. A surplus is difficult to mobilize under these circumstances (e.g. Harris 1959) unless there is the demand for goods to meet institutional taxes, rents, tribute, or religious tithes (Hirth 1996; M. Smith 2004:87). The marketplace works to mobilize surpluses from households on a voluntary basis. The mobilization of these resources helps to mediate subsistence risk in two ways. It concentrates food and other staples in a central locale on a predictable schedule, and it increases the number of inter-personal contacts through which resources can move. The size and periodicity of staple marketplaces correlates directly with the size of the household surplus able to be mobilized. Small periodic marketplaces are found in areas of low population density where the aggregate surplus is small, while large marketplaces are found where production surpluses are large.

A third feature of the marketplaces is that it provides agricultural households with the opportunity to utilize seasonally available labor in economically rewarding craft activities (Hagstrum 2001). This was important for the emergence of craft specialization in Mesoamerica where the majority of craft production occurred in domestic contexts (Feinman 1999; Hirth 2009a). Robert Netting has argued that the marketplace enabled households to intensify production activities on multiple levels. It provided an outlet for marketing craft goods, specialized agricultural crops, normal surpluses, and local resources that households might otherwise not exploit (Netting 1981, 1989, 1993). It was the harnessing of household labor through the putting-out system in rural England that was the forerunner of more complex forms of textile production at the advent of the industrial revolution (Abu-Lughod 1989:54; Braudel 1986:298, 316; Dyer 2005; Shiba 1977:412; Smith 1991).

The marketplace provides an opportunity for households to flex their entrepreneurial imagination and skill. Not all do so, but those that do use the marketplace as an additional source of income. This has both an upside and a potential downside for households who use the marketplace in this way. The upside is that it enables households to broaden and diversify their subsistence base. This can be important for reducing risk even if it contributes a relatively small percentage of resources to the household's total needs. It may, for example, enable households to meet all their outside purchases through the sales of craft goods without having to sell their agricultural production. The downside of market involvement is that it can draw households out of subsistence pursuits into more specialized production of cash crops or more lucrative craft goods. This is exactly what happened during the sixteenth century across highland Mexico as households specialized in the production of cochineal dye (*grana*) for export.[21] The economic return from cochineal production was so lucrative that many households gave up farming food crops and legislation had to be enacted by the colonial government to enforce maize agriculture (Gibson 1967:149; Lockhart et al. 1986:79).

A fourth benefit of the marketplace is that it increases the distribution and circulation of commodities by reducing transportation costs to both buyers and sellers. By concentrating economic transactions in a central locale households are able to minimize overall procurement costs. Instead of making trips to multiple locations to procure different types of goods, the marketplace enables households to combine multiple procurement activities into a single trip. Economizing transportation costs is also what enables professional merchants to bring goods to rural marketplaces and/or use them as collection points to buy commodities for resale elsewhere. It is the reduction in overall transportation costs that enabled commerce to develop in an area like Mesoamerica where goods had to move by human porters.

Finally, the marketplace plays a key role in the conversion of goods into alternative commodities. This conversion capacity made the marketplace, rather than the palace or the temple, the central node in the economic system. It was where different production sectors intersected and goods from individual holdings, tax and tribute levies, merchant accumulations, and agricultural surpluses from prebendal lands could be exchanged and converted into alternative commodities. This certainly was the role that the marketplace took during the seventy-five years prior to the Spanish conquest as tribute goods entered the marketplace from across the Aztec empire (Carrasco 1978). The conversion function of the marketplace facilitated the adoption of wealth-based economic strategies on multiple levels of society. It was where wealth goods entering through the tribute system were converted into staple foods for use within the palace or during special festivals. It also allowed households to convert perishable agricultural products into storable wealth (e.g. cacao, textiles, etc.) that could be reconverted into food should the need arise. The large quantity of different goods offered in the marketplace and their ready convertibility into *cacao*, *quachtli*, or other goods made it possible for individuals to use this conversion strategy. It also helped merchants to transport "accumulated value" over space. In Mesoamerica some forms of itinerant crafting like obsidian blade production could result in large profits that could not be realized in subsistence products (e.g. maize and other foods) to support the households of craftsmen unless they can be transported over space in an efficient form (Hirth 2013b). The conversion of staples to higher value goods such as *quachtli* for purposes of transportation, and their reconversion to staples in their home market was a means by which commerce could be carried out in an area with unusually high costs of moving bulk goods over space.

MARKET SYSTEMS

Markets can exist in isolation as single entities, but when they do they have much less of a transformative effect on the regions where they occur than when they are part of an integrated network of marketplaces. The growth of cities with large resident populations created marketplaces to help meet the food needs of their residents (Appleby 1976; Fall et al. 2002; C. Smith 1983; Zeder 1988). Isolated marketplaces can also be found in commercial cities located along frontier zones or trade routes (Abu-Lughod 1989; Blanton 2013; Lattimore 1995:22; Vance 1970). Marketplaces along trade routes are often poorly integrated into the surrounding hinterland and operate largely to serve the needs of passing merchant caravans.[22] Conversely, it is the development of regional market systems that transformed the organization of prehispanic societies in highland Mesoamerica.

The appearance and growth of marketplaces is a benchmark in the development of commercial societies (Plattner 1989a 1989b; C. Smith 1974). Marketplaces shape the distribution of resources within the landscapes where they occur. The structure of these systems has been studied from the vantage point of central place theory to understand the variables involved in the location of markets and how they operated (Blanton 1996; Christaller 1966; Losch 1938; Santley and Alexander 1992; G. Skinner 1964; C. Smith 1976; M. Smith 1979). From this perspective the commercial integration of regions is a function of three primary variables: the spacing of marketplaces on the landscape, their frequency of operation, and the size and degree of involvement of the population in market transactions. All three of these variables are inter-related and they are affected by the configuration of the natural landscape, the ease of transportation across it, the level of disposable surplus that can move through the marketplace, and the simultaneous operation of non-commercial forms of distribution within society. Nevertheless, market participation grows as marketplaces provide opportunities and solutions to the problems of economic provisioning.

While several good studies have been conducted of the market system in the Basin of Mexico (Blanton 1996; M. Smith 1979), the structure of prehispanic market networks elsewhere in Mesoamerica remains largely unstudied. The highest concentration of marketplaces appears to have been in the Basin of Mexico and northern Morelos where three factors fostered their development (Figure 3.5). First, the presence of over one million people within the Basin at the time of the conquest was the highest population density in Mesoamerica (Sanders et al. 1979). This together with limited agricultural land led households in some communities to augment their subsistence budgets with increased participation in the marketplace. Second, the presence of the central lake system created an efficient means of transporting large cargos via canoes across the Basin.

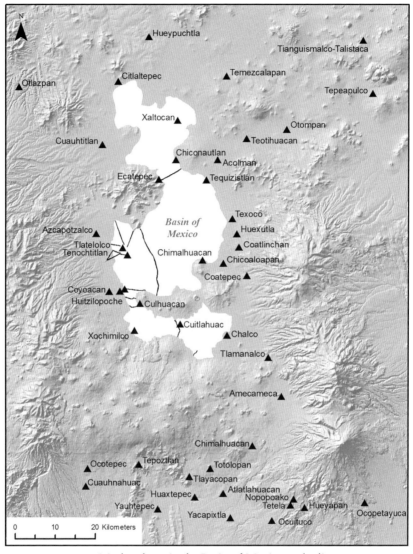

FIGURE 3.5 Marketplaces in the Basin of Mexico and adjacent areas

This helped to integrate communities and facilitated the movement of both goods and people between them (Hassig 1982b). Third and finally, the emergence of Tlatelolco as the largest marketplace in the Basin was the combined result of its location in the center of the lake system, its active merchant community involved in both regional and long-distance

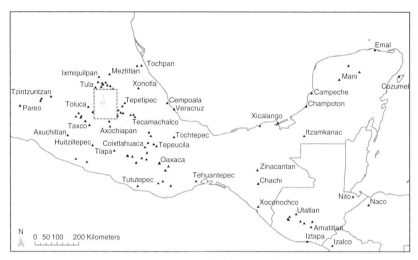

FIGURE 3.6 Documented marketplaces in Mesoamerica in the early sixteenth century

trade, and the high demand for goods by the urban population of Tlatelolco and Tenochtitlan.

At the time of Spanish conquest a network of rotating marketplaces extended across the Mexican highlands south into the Isthmus of Tehuantepec and beyond (Figure 3.6). Most of these marketplaces operated on a rotating schedule. The largest marketplaces at Tenochtitlan–Tlatelolco, Texcoco, and Tlaxcala operated daily. The remainder of marketplaces operated on a 5-, 8-, 9-, 13-, or 20-day rotation based on the prehispanic calendar system (Hassig 1982a). The 5-day rotation was the norm and the sequence most commonly associated with marketplaces in large communities. Markets could be convened on any day within the rotational sequence although adjacent communities normally had marketplaces on alternative days (Hassig 1985:80). Depending on community spacing this complementary scheduling provided multiple sources of market supply for populations in their regions. Lower level marketplaces on longer marketplace rotations (e.g. 13-day, 20-day, etc.) were held on schedules that dovetailed rather than competed with large markets on a five-day rotation.[23] This system provided good spatial access to market services and gave buyers access to the greatest number of sellers, and vice versa. Perpetual access of all individuals to a market somewhere in their region is succinctly emphasized by Clavijero (1974:235) where he states that a market could be found every day of the year across the Aztec empire.

This network of coordinated marketplaces is a reflection of a well integrated commercial system. Indigenous participants recognized the advantages of prehispanic market scheduling. In 1575 the community of Coixtlahuaca petitioned the Spanish government to return its market, which the Spanish had placed on a 7-day rotation, back to its prehispanic 5-day rotation so that it would not conflict with neighboring markets (Terraciano 2001:249). Aztec periodic marketplaces in the Basin of Mexico were spaced between 8 and 12 km apart, providing the regional population with round-trip access to a marketplace in a single day's travel (Figure 3.5).

Integration of the market system at the regional and inter-regional levels is evident in the presence of markets that specialized in assembling and selling certain types of goods. These marketplaces were bulking points for locally available goods and were specialized centers out of custom or political designation. Examples of specialized markets within the Basin of Mexico included: the turkey markets at Tepeapulco, Otumba and Acapetlayocan (Berdan 1985:559; Blanton and Hodge 1996; Motolinia 1971), the market for wood products at Coyoacan (Berdan 1980:39), the Texcoco market for cloth, ceramics, and fine gourd containers (Berdan 1975:197–198), the dog market at Acolman, and the slave market at Azcapotzalco moved from Cuauhtitlan after its conquest by the Tepanecs (Anales de Cuauhtitlan 1975:42–43). Prominent markets elsewhere in Central Mexico included: the slave market at Itzocan (M. Smith 2012:112), the market at Cholula for jewels, precious stones and fine featherwork (Berdan 1975:197–198; M. Smith 2012:112), the Ocopetlayuca market near Cholula for chile and maguey honey, the market at Tepeaca for agricultural products and textiles (Berdan 1980:39), and the salt market in the Mixteca at Miahuatlan (Berdan 1988:647) (Figure 3.6).

The existence of regionally integrated market systems facilitated access to, and the mobilization of resources both within and across regions. Ecological variation and the different natural resources and crop complexes associated with different environmental zones were important factors in both the location of marketplaces and synchronizing market cycles (Bromley and Symanski 1974; Symanski and Webber 1974:211). Sanders (1956) argued that ecological variation was an early stimulus for the exchange of products across different environmental zones within Central Mexico. Figure 1.8 reveals that over 85% of all the towns between the Basin of Mexico and the Isthmus of Tehuantepec were within 30 km (one day's journey on foot) from another major resource zone. This environmental variability stimulated small-scale inter-regional exchange for natural and agricultural products that grew in different zones and matured at different times throughout the year. The location of periodic marketplaces within these zones created a network that permitted small-scale traders to traffic in goods from neighboring regions. The line of markets in northern Morelos near the interface between the *tierra templada* and the *tierra fria* of the Basin of Mexico is an example of this locational advantage (Figure 3.5)

The scheduling of periodic markets on alternative days gave professional merchants and small traders a choice about where they could go to buy and sell goods. Market periodicity enabled traders to move across the landscape traveling from marketplace to marketplace. Bromley and Symanski (1974:20) observe that itinerant market traders often travel between two or more regional markets. Conditions of resource availability, safety, and economic opportunity can affect the circuits that merchants follow. While regional traders may not have traveled very far, professional merchants like the Aztec *pochteca* followed the circuit of rotating marketplaces from region to region over hundreds of kilometers (see Chapter 7). That this was a normal practice is evident in the words of Clavijero who states that,

> many were the merchants who rotated from market to market throughout all the imperial provinces, obtaining goods in one place in order to exchange them for profit in another. They acquired in some places (raw) cotton, untanned hides, precious stones and other materials. Carrying them to Mexico [Tenochtitlan] they expended all the labor and favor of which they were capable in their manufacture, in order to make new and profitable exchanges
>
> (Clavijero 1974:235).[24]

His mention of a utilitarian commodity such as untanned hides alongside raw cotton and precious stones implies that this was not a practice restricted only to long-distance merchants trafficking in high-value goods.

CONCLUSIONS

Mackinder's dictum (1921:78) states that "no human settlement is more difficult to supplant than an established market (Bird 1958:464; Bromley et al. 1975:531)." The reason for this is not because it is mandated by administrative edict or religious fervor. The durability of marketplaces is because of the indispensable socioeconomic services that they provide for society. The conquest did little to change or modify the structure of indigenous marketplaces in Mesoamerica during the first century of Spanish rule (Berdan 1980:37; Carmack 1965:293; Gibson

1964:352–353; Lockhart 1992:188). Perhaps the only significant change that the Spanish implemented after the conquest was shifting indigenous markets to the seven-day week. Native *pochteca* merchants continued to travel, procuring cacao, feathers, and a range of other products throughout the sixteenth century. Indigenous people continued to dominate the marketplace up through 1560 when slowly but surely non-native peoples became involved in its commercial operation (Lockhart 1992:191; Szewczyk 1976:140).

The marketplace was the central most important economic institution in prehispanic society. It was where food and other staple goods were mobilized from the households that produced them. Although prehispanic societies sought to obtain tribute through conquest, the marketplace remained the conduit through which staple goods flowed. The marketplace provided several economic opportunities for commoner households. First, it was the avenue that households used to provision themselves with the goods they could not produce. Second, the marketplace permitted commoner households to supplement their domestic subsistence activities by collecting, producing, and selling a range of natural resources, specialized agricultural products, and craft goods. Participation of commoner households in the marketplace was an avenue to enhanced economic well-being for both women and men. It made economic provisioning and commercial ventures more efficient and it served as society's central clearing house for converting staples to wealth goods and wealth goods to food. It was where the systems of wealth finance and staple finance converged and it operated efficiently as individuals acted in their own self interest and in the interests of the institutions that they represented.

Without question the marketplace had important social and political functions. After all, the marketplace was where people socialized, news was spread, and where foreign spies could assess both the power and sentiment of the people toward their rulers. It was the nerve center of communication in prehispanic society. Rulers were the patrons of their marketplaces. They took pride in the size and diversity of products offered and were responsible for their smooth and honest operation (Hicks 1987:94). Marketplaces also played a role in the broader political arena and the state tinkered with the market system when it was in their advantage to do so. The establishment of new marketplaces was relatively rare and when the state stipulated a change in market practice it was to influence local flows of resources. Within the Basin of Mexico marketplaces fostered the mobilization of food and other resources from rural producers on which urban growth and political activities depended (Blanton 1996:52, 83). But the state did not drastically reshape existing market systems. The "new market" the Aztecs commanded to be built at Tepeaca, Puebla (Durán 1994:158–159) was actually an expansion of the old marketplace to include a wider range of exotic goods. I believe that the Aztecs commanded the expansion of this marketplace to siphon off the important array of goods (e.g. salt, cotton, textiles, etc.) moving into the large daily market of Tlaxcala, the Aztec's primary political competitor[25] (Cortés 1962:50–51).

While the marketplace was many things to many people, it remained the setting in which most economic interactions took place. It was also the cauldron in which economic relationships were forged and economic opportunities were conceived. Marketplaces shaped the face of highland Mesoamerican society. The origin of the marketplace remains obscure, but the information available suggests that they were present across Mesoamerica for 2000 years before the Spanish conquest.[26] The most important effect of the marketplace in Central Mexico was that it created an environment where all members of society regardless of gender, status, or ethnicity could "truck and barter" not only with the goal of meeting subsistence needs but also to increase their economic well-being. What emerged over time was a network of marketplaces where individuals could become petty merchants by selling their own production, or by acquiring goods from neighboring areas in marketplaces within a day or so travel from their home community. The marketplace created a diverse economic landscape that included a diversity of local hawkers and professional merchants. It is this entrepreneurial behavior that is examined next.

4

Merchants, profit, and the precolumbian world

It is often said that money makes the world go around.[1] This also was true for the precolumbian world and merchants were the individuals who applied the grease to make it spin. The native economies of the Aztec realm were a complex web of production and distribution relationships fueled by both political and commercial agendas. Professional and semi-professional merchants moved goods over the landscape both for individual gain and as agents of the Aztec state. These individuals stocked the marketplaces with food and luxury goods and supplied urban centers with the resources needed for daily life. It was through merchants that gold smiths, copper smiths, lapidaries, and feather workers obtained the raw materials to make the luxury goods consumed by the state and its social elite. These individuals moved goods over space, a formidable task in a tumpline economy.[2] Long-distance trade was especially risky and the merchants who undertook it often lost their lives and merchandise to attacks by hostile groups along the routes they traveled.

Despite their importance, merchants throughout history have rarely received the treatment necessary to understand their role in the societies where they operated. There are several reasons for this. The first is that the success of merchants throughout the ancient world was based on the possession of "trade secrets." These secrets encompassed knowledge of the routes to travel, where to get goods at low prices, and how to establish the social contacts to obtain merchandise. Whether merchants operated in groups or as individuals, knowing where goods could be profitably bought and sold was the key to commercial prosperity. The formula for success involved keeping this information to yourself or only sharing it with family members or close associates. The result is that a great deal more information exists about what goods moved over space than is known about the organization of trade and how merchants operated on a daily basis. Even in the Old World where there are written records of economic transactions, important information is lacking on prices, the structure of inter-ethnic commercial relations, logistic arrangements, and the cross-cultural economic institutions established to facilitate trade.

Social status is another factor influencing our understanding of the role that merchants played in ancient societies. When merchants were members of the social elite there is a higher probability that information about their activities was recorded in the historic record. Commercial diaries, correspondence, and manuals of operation have been preserved in the Old World (Goitein 1963, 1967; Khachikian 1966; Pegolotti 1936) that convey some information about premodern commercial procedures. However, when merchants were members of tribal groups or lower social strata, these records may be non-existent or intentionally suppressed (Habib 1999; Harding 1967; Levi 1994). In China and Japan merchants occupied the lowest level of society and were held in general disdain despite their wealth (Lee-fang Chien 2004; Milton 2002; Morris-Suzuki 1989:7). Wealth was no guarantee of security in these circumstances and merchants often were the target of exploitation by nobles in need of loans and ready cash. When merchants were commoners it was often in their best interest to suppress all information about the scale of their economic activities and their wealth.

Our knowledge of precolumbian merchants in the New World is hampered by the absence of a written record of their economic activities. While forms of pictorial writing existed in the precolumbian world they were used primarily to record religious information, narrative histories, and tribute information.[3] Writing was not used for commercial purposes and forms of business accounting have not been found in ancient Mesoamerica.[4] We know that merchants had simple maps that recorded roads and trade routes because Cortés used one drawn on cotton cloth during his trip to Honduras (Cortés 1866:396–397; Scholes and Roys 1968:93). Unfortunately none of these *lienzos* or travel maps has survived to the present day. Instead, the bulk of the information on merchant activities comes from Spanish accounts or the wills and testaments of indigenous merchants during the early colonial period. While few in number, these documents provide a glimpse of how indigenous merchants continued to carry out their economic activities after the Spanish conquest (Cline and León-Portilla 1984; Horn 1998; Kellogg and Restall 1998).

It is easy to talk about precolumbian merchants if the discussion is restricted to the full-time professionals who specialized in procuring high-value goods for elite consumption (Acosta Saignes 1945; Berdan 1980, 1982; Bittmann Simons and Sullivan 1978; Garibay 1961; Nichols 2013; Rojas 1995; Sahagún 1959). The problem in doing this is that it excludes the majority of individuals who trafficked in staple goods on a regular basis within regional settings. Hernando Cortés (1962:87) reports that over 60,000 individuals frequented the Aztec market of Tlatelolco on a daily basis. The vast majority of these individuals were urban consumers who purchased food and other staple goods from small-scale producer-sellers, artisans, and merchant retailers who sold or transported goods in small quantities in pursuit of their individual livelihoods. While they may have desired to amass significant wealth, their fundamental goal was to support themselves and their families. These are the individuals who get lost or ignored in most discussions of traditional economic systems.

The challenge here is to define what a merchant is in a way that captures the breadth of commercial behavior found in prehispanic society. The task is not easy. When, for example, does a farmer become a merchant in our own society? Is it when he sells his produce to a grain elevator, or when he uses direct marketing to sell his fruits and vegetables at a weekly farmer's market or in a permanent roadside stand?[5] Likewise, did Aztec farmers in the Basin of Mexico only sell food in the marketplace when they had a surplus beyond their immediate needs, or did they produce goods specifically for resale in urban marketplaces on a regular basis as was observed throughout the colonial period? Farmers can be labeled as subsistence provisioners when they sell extra maize that they don't consume to obtain things that they need. However, when they raise crops specifically for trade that they do not intend to consume, then their actions have moved them into a merchant-like category. It is important to widen the definition to include all individuals involved in commercial activities if we want to understand the prehispanic economy. Once this is done, defining and discussing the types of merchants and how they operated becomes an empirical problem of identifying different levels of commercial involvement (e.g. full-time, part-time, wholesale, retail, local, regional, etc.). This is important for the Aztec world because a large number of individuals were involved in small-scale commerce at multiple levels of the society.

DEFINING THE PRECOLUMBIAN MERCHANT

If there is one thing that archaeology and history have demonstrated beyond a shadow of a doubt it is that merchants played an important role in just about every large, state level society throughout the history of the world. It is more of a challenge to find state level societies where merchants did *not* play an important role in resource distribution networks.[6] Even in China and Japan where Confucian principles relegated merchants to the lowest social strata, they still distributed resources for the state and the society at large[7] (Lee-fang Chien 2004). Whether they procured wealth items for the elite or staple commodities for urban centers, merchants moved goods from the places where they were produced to the populations that consumed them.

Websters New World Dictionary (1968) defines the merchant as an individual involved in "buying and selling goods for profit." This definition is simple, to the point, and emphasizes the merchant's function as a purveyor of goods for economic gain. It is a good place to initiate the discussion of what constitutes a merchant because it highlights three fundamental characteristics: the merchant as agent, the merchant as profiteer, and the merchant as trade intermediary.

The first of these three features is that merchants are specialized *exchange agents* who operate as individuals in the true sense of the word. Commodities do not appear on their own. They have to be found or produced, processed into usable forms, and taken to the marketplace for sale. Merchants make the decisions to buy and sell goods, and take the associated risks largely as individuals.[8] While they may be organized into guilds and share information through formal associations, the decisions to invest, trade, buy, and sell were often made individually at the point of purchase. This was especially the case in antiquity where information on supply and demand was very limited. Like shoppers in a modern supermarket or a trader on Wall Street, sale and purchase decisions are based on information, timing, experience, and expectations of future returns or losses. It is here that we can talk about merchant skill when decisions are good, and commercial risk when decisions are bad.

The second important feature of Webster's definition of a merchant is that it is someone "who profits" from the exchanges made. The concepts of *profit* and *profit motivation* are controversial topics within Anthropology. Not only are they difficult to define and measure, but there are many social reasons why individuals engage in exchange beyond simple economic ones. I follow Gudeman (2001) who views profit simply as the creation of value.[9] While Gudeman restricts the term profit to market settings where gains in value can be measured in monetary terms, value also is created at the level of individual households through production and exchange activities.

Profit is defined here as gains in the economic base. At the household and community levels, these gains may be reflected by an increase in durable resources. In societies that employ formal currencies they may be reflected *either* in monetary terms *or* in the material goods added to the economic base. In both cases the gains in value are the result of products and services that individuals create to improve their overall economic well-being (Gudeman 2001:102). Agency and entrepreneurial activity are central to creating these gains in value. In non-monetized economies they lead to the accumulation of resources that may be consumed, saved, or invested, while in monetized situations they create and expand monetary capital.[10]

The third and final dimension of merchants is that they are trade intermediaries. They provide the links through which goods move from their place of origin to the point of final consumption. In this sense merchants are exchange specialists who supply the intermediary connection between production and consumption. What is implied here is that the merchant is an autonomous intermediary who buys goods for resale rather than producing them him or herself, a distinction which is conceptually useful, but potentially misleading depending on how the goods are obtained or processed for sale.

A merchant's viability depended on obtaining reliable stocks of goods for sale at a reasonable price. How these inventories were obtained could take many paths. In premodern societies goods often moved through the durable social relationships that venders established with suppliers and consumers (Heider 1969; Mintz 1964).[11] Eric Wolf (1982) has demonstrated how the changing demand for goods brought about significant changes in the role of merchants in the organization of production during the fifteenth to nineteenth centuries. In some cases merchants became directly involved in the production of the goods just to guarantee access to sufficient quantities of goods to sell. In Africa merchants who sold palm oil and kola nuts were eventually forced to produce them (Dike and Ekejiuba 1990:215, 235). Similarly, in colonial North America rural shop keepers often had to exchange goods for items that required processing before they could be resold.[12] Moreover merchants in England created the *putting out* system during the fifteenth century using the domestic labor of women to create textiles that were collected and sold. The putting out system represents a proto-industrialization scale of production created by merchants to produce stocks of textiles for both local consumption and export[13] (Dyer 2005:230).

It would be wrong to assume that artisans were not also merchants. Throughout the European middle ages craft guilds controlled the production of goods, regulated prices, and controlled the labor market so that local craftsmen could produce and sell products from the storefronts of their shops. The guilds and their craftsmen controlled the markets for their products (Epstein 1991). During the embargo on British goods during the American Revolution, urban craftsmen organized themselves into groups to produce and market products that could no longer be obtained from England. The result was a market revolution that was a side product of the American drive for independence (Cuddy 2008:8). The dividing line between producer and trade intermediary often narrowed or completely disappeared depending on the commodity sold.

PROFILING PRECOLUMBIAN COMMERCIAL ACTIVITY

Two questions need to be considered if we hope to broaden our cross-cultural understanding of economic activity in the precolumbian world. First, can western concepts of agent, trade intermediary, and profit be meaningfully applied to prehispanic economic behavior, and if so, under what circumstances? Second, what do the sources indicate about the types of people who engaged in buying and selling and can they justifiably be included in any discussion of merchants?

One of the best sources on prehispanic society is the *Florentine Codex* compiled by Fray Bernardino Sahagún between 1547 and 1562. The purpose of Sahagún's work was to gain a comprehensive understanding of *Nahua* society to aid the Franciscan friars in the conversion of the indigenous population to Christianity. In his words,

It was ordered me as holy obedience to my superior prelate to write in the Mexican tongue what I thought would be useful for the doctrine, culture, and subsistence of the Christianity of these natives of this New Spain, and for the aid of the workers and ministers who indoctrinate them

(López Austin 1974:112).

Three things were unique and innovative about Sahagún's work: his systematic use of expert native informants, the use of an interview – question and answer format, and the direct recording of informant responses in their native language (*Nahuatl*). This is good ethnographic technique for obtaining accurate information about indigenous society. The fact that responses were recorded in *Nahuatl* allows us to hear indigenous culture described in the words of the people who practiced it. Sahagún always used expert witnesses to obtain informed observations about different aspects of indigenous society. The twelve volumes of the *Florentine Codex* in many respects represents the first encyclopedia on precolumbian *Nahua* society and is an indispensable source for examining indigenous economic structure.

For information on economics, commerce, and the marketplace Sahagún used the merchants of Tlatelolco as his key informants. The word for merchant in *Nahuatl* is *pochtecatl*, and when he asked them what a merchant was, this is what they told him,

> The merchant is a seller, a merchandiser, a retailer; [he is] one who profits, who gains; who has reached an agreement on prices; who secures increase, who multiplies [his possessions]. The good merchant [is] a follower of the routes, a traveler [with merchandise; he is] one who sets correct prices, who gives equal value

> (Sahagún 1961:42–43).

The attributes of the merchant as an agent and trade intermediary are clearly evident in this description. The good merchant is described as an individual who engages in a variety of tasks. He follows routes, sets prices, makes decisions, and by giving equal value acts in a morally correct way. The merchant is described in the masculine voice in the above citation by Sahagún's English translators because, although *Nahuatl* is a gender neutral language, the pictures accompanying Sahagún's narrative of traveling vanguard merchants depict men (Figure 4.1). Women normally did not participate in long-distance trade-journeys, but they were actively involved in a wide range of commercial activities within the marketplace. Clearly the decision making activities needed for commercial dealing pertained to both men and women. The merchant's role of trade intermediary is also clear from tasks described. Merchants were sellers, merchandisers, and retailers who negotiated prices and made a profit. This short description is a thoughtful characterization about indigenous commerce. As a generalization it provides an umbrella that covers the great diversity of economic activity explored in the chapters to follow.

A key element in this description is the merchant's desire to make a profit. An important question is whether the concept of profit-making was widely shared across society and the foundation for commercial activity. If it was, then Mesoamerican commercial activity can be discussed in the same way that merchants and mercantile activities are examined in other premodern societies around the world. If it was not, then the social and political structures need to be examined from a more substantive perspective to reconstruct economic interaction (e.g. Dalton 1961; Polanyi 1957). Resolving this issue is the starting point for evaluating and placing Aztec economic systems in their proper cross-cultural perspective.

The information from Sahagún and other sources make it clear that profit seeking was indeed the motive underlying a great deal of economic activity. In the preceding quotation the *Nahuatl* terms for "to profit" and

FIGURE 4.1 Merchants on the road

"to gain" are *tlaixtlapanqui* and *tlaixtlapanani*.[14] According to Molina (1977) the root word meaning to gain or turn a profit is *tlaixtlapana*. The etymology of the word is *tla-ix-tlapan(a)*, where *tla* is the indefinate object prefix meaning "something", *ix* is from *ixtli* meaning face, and *tlapan(a)* is the verb meaning to split or divide something. Molina (1977) translates *ixtlapana* as "to split wood or a similar thing, or to put out money at usury, that is profit *(dar alogro)*." Put them together and you create the whole concept of making profit by dividing things, (i.e. goods or money) in a face-to-face setting through some form of reciprocal exchange like that found in the marketplace.[15] Profit and profit-making appear to be prehispanic concepts and motives for economic interaction. That merchants engaged in trade with the specific intent of making a profit is clear from another statement from Sahagún that characterizes the goal in life for the long distant *pochteca* merchant.

somewhere some of the wealth of the master, our lord, hath been shown me. Somewhere I shall make use of it; I shall cast it into the water; I shall reap a *profit*. With this you are content

(Sahagún 1959:55).

This passage is important in two respects. First, it shows that profit is the goal of the merchant. He has resources and by taking a risk (casting it

into the water) he reaps a profit. Second and perhaps even more important, it shows that profit is a respectable goal for its own sake. In the
making of profit, the merchant is satisfied. From a merchant's point of
view, there is no loftier goal of social recognition to achieve. Instead,
profit alone makes you content. That does not mean that wealth was not
used for social, religious, or political purposes because it clearly was. But
profit was good in its own right because it was seen as a blessing from
their god *Huitzilopochtli* who is referred to in this passage as the master
and lord to whom all material wealth belongs. The idea that wealth was a
personal blessing from *Huitzilopochtli* is both a rationalization of, and a
justification for, the pursuit of individual wealth. It is a feature of commercialized groups and societies around the world. It was, for example, a
pronounced feature of Puritan beliefs in seventeenth-century North America where the level of individual prosperity was seen as a direct measure of
an individual's goodness and God's blessing upon them.

The goal of making a profit can be viewed in two different ways. It can
represent abstract material gain and the accumulation of wealth (capital),
or it can simply represent the use of commerce to accumulate the material
goods to support one's family. Both are probably correct for *Nahua*
society depending on the economic objectives of the individuals involved.
The marketplace was the central venue for commerce in Mesoamerica
and it is here that the majority of individuals bought and sold the goods
needed for everyday life. That most members of society understood
commercial principles is supported by how quickly Spanish currency
norms were integrated with the native monetary system into daily economic activities.[16]

It is also clear that profit making could be abused. Fair value and profit
was acceptable, but unfair profit was seen as an abuse in both indigenous
and Spanish colonial society. It is not surprising, therefore, to find the idea
of unfair profit, cheating, and charging unfair prices, repeated frequently
in the sixteenth century *Nahuatl* confessional manuals used by the Spanish friars to confess the sins of native people.[17] In an example of probing
for unfair pricing among market venders, Molina's confessional manual
asks, "And when you sell . . . do you set the same price for those well made
and those not well made? Did you not take the right (price) (Christiansen
2011; Molina 1984:ff. 37v–38r)?" The fact that commercial cheating is
included in a general confessional manual suggests that commerce was
widely practiced by a large number of individuals across society.

Merchants operate by buying and selling goods, and whether these
transactions occur in private houses, shops, the marketplace, or a

combination of all three go a long way in defining the structure of commercial economy. The marketplace was the center of the *Nahua* economy and it is within this context that indigenous and Spanish writers describe the types of commercial transactions that occurred there. As was discussed in Chapter 3 many different types of sellers operated within the marketplace.

The informants of Sahagún were very precise when they described the people selling goods in the Tlatelolco marketplace and this precision provides a great deal of insight into how the commercial system was structured. Three different *Nahuatl* terms are used to describe economic status of the individuals engaged in trade.[18] These three terms refer to venders who were producer-sellers, merchant retailers, and a generic category of venders that combined the other two.[19]

The *Nahuatl* words for these three categories are *tlachiuhqui*, a class of nouns used to describe makers or producer-sellers, *tlanamacac* a general term used for generic sellers, and *tlanecuilo* a specific term for merchant retailers. Venders within the market descriptions are distinguished from one another by the word for the good they sold with the appropriate suffix indicating the type of vender that they represent. For example, a person who sold shelled corn (*tlaolli*) would be called a *tlaolnamacac*, a corn seller. Conversely a craftsperson who sold the reed mats (*petlatl*) that they made would be called a *petlachiuhqui*. The suffix *chiuhqui* is a specific referent to a person who sells what they produce, and may even refer to a craftsperson who practiced their trade in the marketplace. Based on the terminological categories supplied by Sahagún's informants it is clear that artisan merchants or producer-sellers were an important component of the commercial landscape. While their merchandising activities could have been cyclical, varied in intensity, and limited in geographic extent, producer-sellers appear to have accounted for a significant amount, if not the majority of goods sold in regional markets.

The suffix *namacac* is a less specific, generic term that lumps producer-sellers with retailers into the same category. Thus a seller of reed mats may be called a *petlachiuhqui* in one source and a *petlanamacac* in another. Unfortunately the words are used situationally rather than in a categorically consistent fashion. It is clear, however, that the suffix for a vender or seller of things (*namacac*) is often used to identify both producer-sellers and retailers where they occur together. In this regard Sahagún's informants characterized the shelled corn seller as,

The seller of maize grains [is] a worker of the fields, a worker of the land, or a retailer

(Sahagún 1961:65).

In this passage the term for the seller of maize grains is *tlaolnamacac*.[20] This term is used to refer to both the regular farmers who produced maize for sale in the marketplace, as well as the larger scale retailers who bought it for resale. Clearly the farmer who sells the corn that he grows is a producer-seller in the same sense as the reed mat maker (*petlachiuhqui*), but here the generic suffix *namacac* also is used to include persons with different commercial orientations selling the same good.

The category *tlanecuilo* refers specifically to a merchant reseller. This term is usually translated, as in the above passage, as retailers to clarify that they do not produce the goods that are sold, but bought them for resale either in the marketplace or as mobile peddlers. The term is used to cover the range of retailers, shop keepers, and retail dealers mentioned in the historic sources. These merchant resellers bought and sold for profit. They would have been sensitive to the geography of price differentials since it was the basis of their income. They would actively have sought to obtain the lowest price at the point of production (or supply) and the highest price at the point of greatest demand. Vance (1970:16) identifies the geographical separation of production and sale as the foundation for profit seeking behavior. The presence of these individuals in the marketplace indicates that complex chains of commercial relationships existed within Aztec society, with retail dealers buying directly from producers, and/or intermediary wholesale agents. The nature of these individuals and the commercial networks that they represent are discussed more fully in Chapter 6.

What the terminology indicates is that an array of individuals participated in commercial transactions at different levels of intensity in the prehispanic world. What is generally missing from these commercial descriptions is any discussion about the scale of business operations. We assume that the merchant retailers operated at a larger scale, and on a more continuous basis than small-scale producer-sellers, but the degree of difference is by no means clear. Neither is it clear how *tlanecuiloque* (plural of *tlanecuilo*) retailers organized their activities or pursued their professional endeavors. Were they full-time merchant professionals, or did they divide their time between a range of different economic pursuits within their households? The long-distance merchants known as the *pochteca* are most often discussed as examples of full-time specialized merchant professionals (Acosta Saignes 1945; Berdan 1982). But they were not "specialized" in the strict sense of modern business theory in that they *only* engaged in commercial pursuits through trade (Vance 1970). Instead, the sources indicate that some *pochteca* also owned land, farmed it, and consumed the food that it produced (Katz 1966; Léon-Portilla 1962:35; Martinez 1984).

MERCHANTS BIG AND SMALL

Webster's definition of a merchant presented in this chapter as a person who makes a profit is a useful starting point for exploring the nature of commerce in the prehispanic world. Precolumbian merchants were motivated by profit and moved goods over space selling them to interested consumers. When we think of who precolumbian merchants were, we naturally think of those intrepid individuals who traveled long distances and underwent the dangers of the road to bring back high-value goods. These merchants were trade intermediaries and commercial middle-men in ways that we can understand them today. But in precolumbian thinking merchants were *all* those individuals who worked to gain a profit though buying and or selling. The category included more than just commercial middle-men. They also included a broad array of small-scale and part-time merchandisers who made things in their homes for sale in the marketplace. Small-scale commercial activity was an important component of the domestic economy. It was an avenue for individual households to improve their economic well-being by small increments alongside farming their agricultural fields. According to Sahagún, the essential features that defined who a merchant was involved establishing prices, selling goods for a profit, and traveling with them to secure an increase (Sahagún 1961:42–43). These are the activities of *both* specialized long-distance merchants and small-scale artisans who produced goods to sell in the marketplace. Small-scale commercial activity was an integral part of the domestic economy and it is the structure and diversity of domestic artisans and other producer-sellers that is explored in Chapter 5.

5

Often invisible

Domestic entrepreneurs in Mesoamerican commerce

> *people who only eat black bread and drink water would like to eat wheaten bread and drink wine; people who never have eaten meat would like to do so; people with poor clothes would like better ones; people without wood to warm themselves by would like to buy it, and so on.*
> (François Quesnay on domestic consumption, 1766)[1]

It is taken for granted in most discussions of the ancient economy that non-elite domestic consumption played little to no role in stimulating trade and commerce at the regional and inter-regional levels. Instead, the stimulus for inter-regional trade often is credited to long-distance trade in high-value goods.[2] The reasons for emphasizing the importance of wealth goods over staple goods are varied and include: the impoverished conditions of peasants in ancient society, the self-sufficient orientation of domestic production, the high cost and limited ability of transporting bulk commodities over space, and the lack of historic evidence for the domestic consumption of non-local products on any significant scale in premodern societies.[3] Furthermore, low population densities in rural areas made it difficult for merchants to locate the demand for imported goods across the countryside. The result has been to discount the importance of the rural market and to focus on the sources of special, concentrated demand as the stimuli behind ancient commerce. These include the political and religious institutions, the nobility and their appetite for high-value goods, and, of course, urban communities which contained a mixture of demand from their nucleated population and their corresponding elite and institutional consumers.[4]

If there ever was a place where this characterization should fit it is Mesoamerica. The agricultural technology was not complex by western standards, restricted to simple hand tools, and constrained by a transportation system where most goods moved on the backs of human porters. Furthermore, as discussed in Chapter 2, support for the institutional economy was based on labor service rather than a head tax or tax-in-kind on domestic production. This provided households with greater autonomy and reduced their need to sell goods to meet any type of annual tax obligation. Although these conditions fostered insularity, very few households in Mesoamerica were ever completely self-sufficient for all the domestic items used in everyday life. Even simple goods like ceramic cooking and serving vessels were bought from part-time specialists rather than produced within the households that used them (Beals 1975:21–22). Although the level of domestic self-sufficiency varied from region to region, domestic consumption was not the moribund economic force that it has sometimes been made out to be in the Old World.

How domestic production and consumption were linked to commercial networks in ancient and premodern economies is an empirical question that needs to be addressed with problem-oriented research. Adam Smith (1937) believed that the drive for individual gain was the principle behind economic interaction within society. He called it the principle of the invisible hand and saw it as the motivating force behind the growth of economic networks. If we ignore his concern with "free markets," the invisible hand can be linked with the fundamental responsibility that households have for their individual security and well-being. Were farmers in Mesoamerica actively involved in the commercial economy, or has their participation in it been rendered invisible by the research strategies that investigators have used to study them? François Quesnay was an eighteenth-century contemporary of Adam Smith whose epigram at the beginning of this chapter summarizes his views on the power of the invisible hand and how agriculture and rural household consumption were engines behind economic growth at both the local and national level.

This chapter explores the role of households in commercial transactions in prehispanic Mesoamerica. It approaches this question by examining the opportunities and range of commercial activities that households could engage in if they chose to do so. There are several ways that domestic commercial involvement can be examined. The first is to identify the types of production activities and quantity of goods that households produced for exchange and/or sale as part of their overall subsistence strategies. This can be a difficult task even when studying contemporary households because of the way they diversify work or pool resources over the course of their developmental cycle (Chayanov 1966;

M. G. Smith 1955). Another approach is to measure the quantity of goods that entered households from exchange or other forms of household interaction. In both cases what is needed is quantitative archaeological information that often is not available. Historic sources rarely discuss household production and consumption in quantitative terms.[5] Although the archaeological record can provide quantitative information on both production and consumption, it has not addressed economic questions as successfully as it might because of problems of equifinality and limited sample size.[6]

A third alternative method is to explore the options and opportunities for participation in extra-household commercial activities. This opportunity cost approach is qualitative in the sense that it seeks to identify the range of commercial behaviors that households could and did engage in. If the range of commercial behaviors is narrow, then either the commercial economy was a minor portion of the overall economy or households were unable to participate in it as a result of limited resources or direct prohibition by institutional monopolies.[7] Conversely, if the range of commercial behaviors was broad, it would suggest that households were more actively involved in commerce. Diversity in domestic economic activities, of course, can also be the product of non-commercial forms of exchange and gift giving, but it provides a starting place to begin discussion. This is a not a significant problem when the available information comes from market settings where goods by definition are moving primarily through commercial transactions.

The information discussed here comes primarily from historic descriptions of market activity in Central Mexico. The categories described are household producer-sellers who provide insight into the range of sales-oriented commercial activities that households could engage in. All households had the same options through the operation of the marketplace. They could sell a portion of their normal surplus that they did not consume, or they could produce goods targeted specifically for sale in the marketplace. Whether these goods were staple foods, fiber products, or craft goods depended on available economic opportunities and associated opportunity costs. While the historic record provides insight into domestic production activities they are mute with regard to consumption. Whether households used their gains to purchase staple foods, luxury goods, craft goods, or stored it away in some form of negotiable currency is a separate issue entirely.

As discussed in Chapter 3, markets were an important institution for household provisioning. They also provided a setting where households could produce commodities for sale to potential consumers. Markets can foster increases in the scale and diversification of production that other forms of distribution cannot. Obviously in areas where markets were small or held less frequently, the opportunities for household involvement would be less. Investigators simply need to be aware of these differences to evaluate the commercial opportunities that households could engage in.

The following pages examine whether the household played an active or passive role in the development of prehispanic economic networks. It begins by examining the role that households may or may not have played in the growth of premodern economic networks. This is followed by an Anthropological view of households based on decades of research on smallholder behavior in different areas around the world. This perspective, complemented by over a century of ethnographic research, demonstrates that households in all societies actively attempted to diversify their economic activities and to improve their economic well-being. The discussion then examines the specific forms of household commercial activity that represent prehispanic activities as well as new activities made possible by the expanding Spanish colonial economy. The chapter concludes with a discussion of three related questions. Who produced the food surpluses sold in the marketplace, how common was household diversification in agricultural households, and how widespread was household producer-seller participation in the marketplace outside the highly urbanized Basin of Mexico?

THE DOMESTIC ECONOMY IN ECONOMIC DEVELOPMENT

Henri Pirenne (1956:140–141) proposed that external trade in luxury rather than staple goods was the basis for the development of professional merchants and inter-regional exchange (Geertz 1963:42). He felt that commerce in staples was *not* important in the ancient world. Scholars who take this position make three assumptions about economic behavior. These are: 1) that agricultural production by peasant farmers was geared to auto-consumption rather than the market, 2) that commoner populations had a low purchasing power and could not stimulate exchange, and 3) the high costs of transporting bulk goods would have inhibited trade in staples (Finley 1985; Morley 2007; Parker 1984). If these three conditions were true in all situations then commerce in Mesoamerica should be restricted to trade in specialized luxury goods as Pirenne suggests.

The underlying belief is that commoner domestic households in the ancient world were impoverished and lived on the margins of survival.

Production was oriented to self-sufficiency and farmers were not market oriented because agriculture was risky enough without being subject to the uncertainties of the market and fluctuations in market prices (Morley 2007:92). Specialization in production did not occur because of the cost of moving goods over space. The result was an impoverished rural peasantry with limited purchasing power and little or no interest in goods beyond food (Finley 1985; Landers 2003:47; Parkins 1998:5). Low purchasing power made commoner households impervious to the trade in luxury goods and removed them from the normal circuit of other items such as specialized foods and manufactured goods.

While this may describe European peasant households during the medieval ages, it probably does not accurately portray the domestic economy in other areas of the ancient world. Ethnographic studies have shown that households in many tribal and chiefdom societies were relatively well off, engaged in specialized production and exchange, and actively sought the procurement of socially valued wealth objects. Moreover, the transformation from egalitarian to ranked society seems to have been a period of household affluence and inter-household competition based on feasting, gift giving, and specialized agricultural production (Hayden 2001). An important question for understanding the evolution of cultural complexity is how households were reduced to penury over the course of human history and removed from inter-regional exchange networks?

From the householder's perspective the key ingredients seem to be who controlled access to the productive resources and what demands were placed on the output that was produced. Marx referred to the first of these as the means of production and most studies of historic and prehistoric households indicate that when households had access to sufficient resources they produced a comfortable and secure livelihood for their members. Things can change when resources are restricted, but even then households are often able to intensify production without external support (Netting 1989, 1993; Stone 1986). Demands on output from social, political, or religious institutions can sharply reduce the economic well-being of commoner households and place them at increased risk. It is when these factors are combined, as they often are in peasant societies (Wolf 1966), that household well-being declines and economic impoverishment begins.

The production of agricultural goods and a strong orientation toward self-sufficiency does not automatically remove rural households from active participation in regional or even inter-regional commerce.[8]

De Ligt (1993) points out that rural Roman households consumed specialty and luxury goods in small amounts, providing a considerable stimulus for the movement of goods into and out of rural areas.[9] The demand for staple goods is always high in urban areas and it is here that households have the opportunity to sell their surplus or engage in specialized production to supply city residents (Fall et al. 2002; Netting 1990; Zeder 1988). Urban communities provide incentive for inter-regional exchange and in India created a whole network of large- and small-scale regional traders who bought grain in rural areas and transported it to cities (Chakravarti 2000; Habib 1999; Levi 1994; Sen 1998). When commerce fails, taxation systems can be used to mobilize staple goods (Hopkins 1980). Taxation or tribute systems can be constructed as "in-kind" systems of staple goods, or as monetary systems that require households to sell staples to obtain currency to pay their tax. In either case, rural households can be drawn into the larger urban-rural commercial system requiring them to intensify production and/or participate in the marketing of the goods they produce.

Trade in staple, bulk goods was neither a restriction on household participation in broader economic systems nor an impediment to long-distance trade in premodern societies. Casson (1989), for example, notes trade in both bulk and high-value goods between Egypt, Arabia, Africa, and India during the the first century AD. Likewise, Ratnagar (2004:109) records trade in food and bulk goods between Ur, Lagash, Dilmun, and Elam during the second century BC. While both of these cases involve maritime trade, they underscore that bulk staple goods were an important component of both regional and inter-regional economies of the ancient world. For more recent times Hybel (2002) argues that inter-regional trade in medieval Europe cannot be divided into an early period of trade in luxury goods, followed by a later phase involving trade in staples. Staple goods moved throughout the entire medieval ages[10] with improved systems of transportation playing a less important role than is normally assumed. Menard (1991:230) feels that improvements in maritime trade did not fuel a trade revolution during the late medieval ages and in some cases was more expensive than caravan trade.

The key is placing households and their domestic economy within the broader sphere of regional production and exchange. If they were not important producers or consumers of goods then they could not participate in commercial activity at any significant level. However, if they were not impoverished, auto-sufficient units, then their participation in regional commerce networks could have been substantially greater. The important question is how households operated under normal circumstances.

HOUSEHOLD ECONOMIC STRATEGIES

Commoner households are traditionally viewed as being auto-sufficient with little disposable income to trade for items that they do not produce. This view is true to the extent that households try to maximize their productivity and minimize their expenses. The error of this perspective is that it assumes, rather than examines, the extent of household involvement in commercial activity. In-so-doing it ignores the dynamic nature of household production strategies and the entrepreneurial way they can respond to new economic opportunities.

Research has demonstrated that households readily and frequently intensify production on their own initiative in response to both internal economic needs and external opportunities for exchange (Netting 1989, 1991, 1993). According to this approach agricultural small-holders can be dynamically entrepreneurial in resolving their needs (Stone 1986). Households readily intensify and diversify their production strategies not only for increased internal consumption, but to produce goods for sale or to exchange with other households. The result is a higher level of resource movement, commercial selling, and capital formation at the domestic level than the traditional model of household self-sufficiency normally acknowledges.

While the small-holder model was developed to describe economic practices in agricultural households, the same incentives existed in non-agricultural households. Archaeologists recognize the dynamic nature of households, but they are not usually seen as a source of economic innovation because of the difficulty of studying them in temporal segments short enough to identify changes in domestic economic strategies (Hirth 1993). Three economic forces regularly combine to diversify and intensify household production strategies: the need for survival, the desire for social enhancement, and maintenance of resource self-sufficiency.

The first of these is obvious. As the basic units of demographic and social reproduction households actively organize their subsistence activities to ensure their survivability (Netting et al. 1984; Wilk 1989; Wilk and Netting 1984; Wilk and Rathje 1982). Few social safety nets existed in pre-industrial societies for households that failed to meet their basic economic needs. As a result, households carefully anticipated their needs and geared production strategies accordingly. Although cases of agricultural underproduction have been recorded (Sahlins 1972), the ethnographic record suggests that households regularly compensated for shortfalls through crafting or other subsistence pursuits as part of a mixed economy (Sundström 1974). One strategy was to gear production to meet household needs during leans years (Halstead and O'Shea 1989; O'Shea 1989) resulting in a surplus during normal years (Allan 1965:38; Halstead 1989).

Households, of course, do more than meet basic subsistence needs. They invest in the social enhancement of their members within the communities where they live. They invest surplus in social networks through intra-community sharing and inter-group feasting (Hayden 2001; Strathern 2007). Production for social and ritual consumption is an important component of group dynamics. According to Spielman (2002:203) "ritual and belief define the rules, practices, and rationale for much of the production, allocation, and consumption in an individual's life ... It is to people's participation in, and manipulation of the ritual context that we must look to understand variation and changes in many economic practices." Wells and Davis-Salizar (2007) refer to these social and ritual activities as the ritual economy which can occupy a significant portion of the household work budget. Since these demands originate outside the household, this dimension of the institutional economy can sharply restructure the economic activities of individual households.

Self-sufficiency was a goal of every household (Gudeman 2001:43) but it was neither an attainable or desirable reality. Archaeological research has demonstrated that ancient households were never completely self-sufficient but regularly interacted with their neighbors for resources that they did not produce (Flannery 1976b). Households established and maintained inter-household exchange networks through which food and other resources could move during times of resource shortfall (Cashdan 1990; Wiessner 1982). They provided a safety net for households in an environment where there were few other means of support during times of stress (O'Shea 1989). These networks were reinforced during periods of normal abundance by the movement of redundant commodities, an artificial division of goods produced, and/or the production of speciality products for purposes of exchange (Gregory 1981; Malinowski 1922).

Together these forces provided the impetus behind household economic strategies, the most fundamental being the need to insure their economic survival. Sahlins (1972) has noted that some households knowingly fall short of meeting their needs and compensate by relying on kinsmen.[11] The development of diversified production strategies allowed households to buffer themselves against cyclical and seasonal resource shortfalls (Davies 1996; Messer 1989), as well as to produce craft goods as a means to generate additional income, and participate in inter-household exchange (Hayden 2001). Together diversification and intensification provide complementary economic strategies that households used to ensure their long-term economic well-being (Cashdan 1990; Winterhalder et al. 1999).

DOMESTIC COMMERCE IN MESOAMERICA: THE PRODUCER-SELLER

As a rule households never willingly give up control over the resources necessary for their survival unless they are forced to do so. Even when resources are constrained households find ways to innovate and improve their domestic well-being.[12] The question, of course, is how did households operate in Mesoamerica? Were they active participants in a trans-society commercial economy, or did they rarely reach beyond their local communities for the resources that they consumed? The model used here is that household involvement in commercial activity was directly proportional to the development of regional marketplaces across Mesoamerica. The marketplace provided households with commercial opportunities where they could sell processed food or to invest their labor in the production of goods specifically geared for sale.

The archaeological data suggest that the level of commercial activity increased during the two to three centuries before the Spanish conquest (Brumfiel 1986; M. Smith 2010). Historic data provide a qualitative view of the early post-conquest marketplace, the types of goods sold, and how households articulated with one another through commercial transactions. In the discussion that follows, four different classes of producer-sellers are examined that provide a picture of what market activity would have been like in AD 1519. These areas of commercial activity are: the production and sale of food, craft goods, natural products foraged from the landscape, and personal labor available for hire. These, of course, are categories of analytical convenience and it is impossible to estimate at this time the diversity and frequency with which households produced goods specifically for commercial sale.

PRODUCER-SELLERS OF FOOD AND FIBER PRODUCTS

Even the casual visitor to an open air market in Mexico or Guatemala today is struck by the quantity of fruits, vegetables, and processed food sold there. The basic role of the marketplace in the past was food provisioning just as it is today. This is evident in the accounts of Hernando Cortés and Bernal Díaz del Castillo who emphasized the variety of both cooked and uncooked food available for sale in the various marketplaces of Tenochtitlan. This is also seen in the Tlaxcala market of 1545 where 21 of the 23 items listed in the market records were food items. Food was important in urban markets where some individuals either lacked or had limited access to agricultural lands to produce their own staples.

Small domestic producers supplied an array of food and staple goods. Sahagún provides an overview of the diversity of goods sold in the Tlatelolco marketplace and the types of individuals who sold them.[13] Similar information is also available from the tax documents from the early colonial market at Coyoacan (Anderson et al. 1976). What is apparent in both of these documents is the different categories of sellers within the marketplace. As mentioned in Chapter 4, the *Nahuatl* terminology used in describing market participants distinguishes between three types of venders: producer-sellers characterized by the term *-chiuhqui*, meaning doer or maker,[14] generic sellers identified by the suffix *-namacac*,[15] and retailers who are distinguished by the term of *-necuilo*.[16] The *techiuhqui* are individuals who produced the goods that they sold which included the broad array of food produced by commoner households. Households also sold their produce to larger-scale venders, but evidence for this comes largely from the prohibitions against buying goods from commoners "on the road" traveling to the marketplace. I leave the discussion of specific commercial practices to Chapter 8 and focus here on identifying the individuals who operated as producer-sellers within the marketplace.

Table 5.1 provides a list of food and fiber goods sold by producer-sellers in prehispanic and colonial Central Mexico. Thirty-two categories of food sellers can be identified: sixteen sold unprocessed food or fiber staples and sixteen others sold processed food. The individuals selling unprocessed food and fiber products were the same persons involved in their cultivation. The individuals selling processed food may, or may not, have been cultivators. They were, however, individuals who produced the item that they sold, either by cooking or processing it into another form. Twenty-nine of these thirty-two food categories were prehispanic in origin while three were related to the new Spanish colonial economy

Few of the terms listed in Table 5.1 carry the *Nahuatl* suffix *chiuhqui* that would clearly designate these food venders as producer-sellers. Instead, they are simply listed as generic sellers with the suffix designation

TABLE 5.1: *Producer-sellers of food products*
Unprocessed food venders

Category	Nahuatl term	Notes
Cacao seller	cacauanamacac	"a cacao owner, an owner of cacao fields, an owner of cacao trees (Sahagún 1961:65)"
Chia seller	chiennamacac	"one who owns *Chia* (Sahagún 1961:67)"
Wrinkled *chia* seller	chientzotzolnamacac	"an owner of *chia*, of *chia* fields … [he is] who cleans it (Sahagún 1961:75)"
Chili seller	chilnamacac	"either … a worker of the fields, or a retailer (Sahagún 1961:67)"
Bean seller	henamacac	"The bean seller is a bean owner. Separately … [he] selects the good beans, the new crop (Sahagún 1961:66)"
Cotton seller	ichcanamacac	"is a field owner, a cotton field owner, a cotton owner; [he is] a worker of the soil, a planter of cotton (Sahagún 1961:75)"
Meat seller, butcher	nacanamacac	"a possessor of meat–a meat owner, an animal owner. He hunts … Or he is a meat dealer. He keeps [animals]–raises them (Sahagún 1961:80)"
Maguey syrup seller	necunamacac	"[is] an owner of maguey plants, a planter of maguey plants, a scraper … He extracts the syrup; he cooks it (Sahagún 1961:74)"
Herb seller	quilnamacac	"a producer of herds, a field worker, a plucker of herbs. She plucks greens (Sahagún 1961:92)"
Fruit seller	suchiqualpan tlacatl	"a fruit owner. He carries fruit upon his back–transports it … he picks, harvests, produces fruit (Sahagún 1961:79)"
Maize seller	tlaolnamacac	"The seller of maize grains [is] a worker of the fields, a worker of the land (Sahagún 1961:66)"
Tomato vender	tomanamacac	Sold multiple varieties (Sahagún 1961:68)
Egg vender	totoltenamacac	"an owner of turkeys, a breeder of fowl, a raiser [of fowl] (Sahagún 1961:85)"
Turkey vender	totolnamacac	"an owner of turkeys–a raiser, a breeder [of turkeys, a livestock owner (Sahagún 1961:85)"
Amaranth seller	vauhnamacac	"[is] an amaranth seed owner or a retailer. He sells the new crop (Sahagún 1961:67)"

Processed food venders

Category	Nahuatl Term	Notes
Squash seed seller	aioachnamacac	"sells toasted gourd seeds, those treated with maize flour, salted ones. Sells cakes of gourd seeds, seeds with honey (Sahagún 1961:68)"
Atole seller	atolnamacac	"sells hot atole . . . bean atole, toasted maize atole, fruit atole, boiled chili atole, atole with honey. She sells cold atole. It has . . . chili on, honey on top (Sahagún 1961:93)"
Chia oil maker	chiamachiuhqui	from Molina (1977)
Cooked meat seller	nacanamacac	"he sells . . . jerked meat, oven-cooked, baked, dried meat; roasted . . . cooked in an olla (Sahagún 1961:80)"
Pulque brewer	ocnamacac	Identified by Molina (1944) and Cortés (1962:88)
Pinolli seller	pinolnamacac	Prepared by mixing ground maize and *chia* flour together (Durand-Forest 1971:124)
Processed fruit seller	suchiqualpan tlacatl	"he sells . . . cactus fruit tamales . . . cooked gourds . . . sweet potatoes, manioc (Sahagún 1961:79)"
Tamale seller	tamalnamacac	Over 25 types of tamales described by Sahagún (1961:69)
Cooks and food venders	tlaqualchiuhqui, tlaqualnamacac	"sells foods, sauces, hot sauces; fried [food], olla-cooked food . . . barbequed meat . . . hot, very hot (Sahagún 1961:70)"
Fine chocolate seller	tlaquetzalnamacac	"provides people with drink, repasts . . . she adds water . . . aerates it, filters it . . . finely ground . . . with vanilla . . . with wild bee honey . . . with powered aromatic flowers (Sahagún 1961:93)"
Specialized tortilla maker	tlaxcalchiuhqui	"an owner of tortillas . . . sells tortillas which [are] thick (Sahagún 1961:69)" (Siméon 1991)
Tortilla and tamale seller	tlaxcalnamacac,	"He sells meat tamales, turkey pasties, plain tamales . . . tasty–tasty, very tasty . . . made with . . . chili, salt, tomatoes, gourd seeds (Sahagún 1961:69)"
Cooked egg vender	totoltenamacac	"He sells turkey eggs . . . [made into] tortillas, boiled in an olla, made into a broth (Sahagún 1961:85)"
Fish and lake food	xoquiiacanamacac	"He sells . . . fish wrapped in maize husks and cooked in an olla . . . dried fish . . . worm tamales . . . water fly tamales (Sahagún 1961:80)"

(continued)

TABLE 5.1: (*continued*)

Food venders of Spanish products

Category	Nahuatl term	Notes
Wheat seller	trigonamacac,	"a field owner, a landowner, a field worker (Sahagún 1961:71)"
Wheat bread baker	Castilian, tlaxcalnamacac	"He sifts . . . he kneads dough; he makes loaves; he puts them into the oven; he bakes them (Sahagún 1961:70)"
Miller, wheat flour seller	castillan texnamacac	"The seller of castillian flour . . . a miller, a flour grinder (Sahagún 1961:71)"

Note: Total number of processed and unprocessed food producer-sellers is n = 32.

namacac. This is an artifact of Sahagún's descriptive classification and the nature of the market that he is trying to describe. The marketplace at Tlatelolco included a range of venders that included producer-sellers as well as retailers who bought goods from farmers for resale. Sahagún appears to have used the term *namacac* when both producer-sellers and retailers were selling the same type of item, distinguishing between them by their activities. His brief discussion of the maize seller (*tlaolnamacac*) makes this clear when he says,

The seller of maize grains [is] a worker of the fields, a worker of the land, or a retailer . . . Each [sort] he sells separately, he sells prudently; separately the white, the black, the vari-colored; separately the soft, the yellow, the red. Each one separately he sells, that of Chalco, of the Matlatzinca, of Acolhuacan, of the people of the north desert lands; that produced in the tropics–that of the Tlahuica, of Tlaxcala, of Michoacan

(Sahagún 1961:65–66).

The producer-seller is the individual who farms his land, who owns his crop and sells his maize (Figure 5.1). The retail dealer (Figure 5.2) in contrast is described by the multiple types of maize sold. That maize grains are sold reflects the practice of removing maize from the cob and allowing it to dry for purposes of storage and preservation. The maize of Chalco and Acolhua was grown in the Basin of Mexico immediately south and east of Tenochtitlan. The other types of maize would have been imported into the Basin of Mexico through long-distance trade which was outside the scope of activities for the small-scale producer-seller.[17]

FIGURE 5.1 The farmer producing and harvesting maize

FIGURE 5.2 The maize seller

Venders are described for all major food groups including beans, *chia*, amaranth, and a range of fruits and vegetables. All are characterized in one way or another as owners of the product, workers of the fields, or owners of the fields or trees from which the products come. Fruit sellers (*suchiqualpan tlacatl*) are described as individuals who owned fruit trees, harvested, and transported fruit to the market (Sahagún 1961:79). The maguey syrup seller processed the maguey sap by boiling it to produce a thick, sugar rich syrup that was high in calories and preserved well. Even the herb seller (*quilnamacac*) is described as "a producer of herbs, a field worker, a plucker of herbs (Sahagún 1961:92)" Although some of the herbs described by Sahagún were wild varieties and could be included with foraging activities discussed later, others apparently were planted in small gardens probably by the same women who sold them.

Three venders are mentioned who sold animal products: the egg seller, the turkey seller and the meat seller. All three of these venders were also producers. The egg and turkey sellers bred turkeys to produce the eggs and the fowl that they sold. Likewise, the meat seller owned and raised the meat sold. A variety of both wild and domesticated animals are listed for the meat seller[18] that indicate both the breath of products sold in the market-place and that Sahagún is grouping a range of both producer-sellers and retailers under this category. Included in this list are the newly introduced Spanish domesticates of chickens, sheep, goats, cattle, and pigs indicating a broadening of traditional array of items sold (Sahagún 1961:80). That this group of sellers included Spanish mestizos is implied by Sahagún's illustration of the meat vender who is dressed in European apparel (Sahagún 1961:figure 134). Dog also was sold by this dealer because it was a major meat source before the arrival of the Spanish and is specifically mentioned as being sold in the Tlatelolco marketplace[19] (Díaz del Castillo 1956:216). That dog continued to be sold during the colonial period is implied by Sahagún's (1961:80) ethnocentric comment that the bad meat seller was someone who "claims dog meat to be edible."

The bulk of Sahagún's market descriptions probably date to some-where between AD 1550 and 1558 (Anderson 1994) and it is interesting to see how quickly native producers and consumers incorporated new Spanish products into their diets and commercial activities. The preco-lumbian diet was not necessarily protein poor as much as it lacked large animal food domesticates. The result was an eclectic food system that made bugs, algae, and insect larvae important consumables along with turkey, dog, fish, and hunted animals. Chickens, cattle, sheep, and goat meat were now for sale in the marketplace indicating a rapid transform-ation had occurred that incorporated new tastes and new species into the indigenous food systems (Lockhart 1992:188). Animal domesticates like chickens were welcome additions to the native diet and native producer-sellers quickly adapted their small-scale production systems to raise them. Wheat was a Spanish introduction and the presence of the wheat vender is a clear instance of the new colonial economy. That the wheat vender is described as both a land owner and a field worker suggests that it was added as a cash crop to the production cycle of some indigenous households.[20] Maize remained the dietary staple throughout Mesoamerica with wheat only raised as a speciality crop to meet Spanish demand.

The rapid economic adaptation of indigenous households to new economic oportunities is evident in testamentary wills from the late sixteenth and early seventeenth century. A good example is Bárbara Agustina, a commoner from the town of Coyoacan who raised turkeys and pigs to sell in the marketplace. According to her will of 1608 she also owned a mule used to transport her animals and other merchandise to market. The same is true for Juan Fabián, a fruit grower in Coyoacan. According to his testament of 1617, Juan owned several mules that he used to transport *zapote* (*tzapotl*) fruit from his orchards to the market-place[21] (Horn 1998:75).

Fiber products were important to prehispanic households to manufacture textiles, footgear, cordage, nets and bindings (Berdan 1987). The two principal fibers used in Central Mexico were maguey and cotton. Only the cotton seller is mentioned as a producer-seller in the Tlatelolco market where he is described as field owner, a planter of cotton, and a worker of the soil (Sahagún 1961:75). This is an interesting characterization since cotton could not be grown in the Basin of Mexico and had to be imported. The implications for this will be examined in greater detail in the Chapter 6 where itinerant and intermediate range merchants are discussed.

The Spanish also observed a large number of venders selling processed food in the marketplace (Cortés 1962:87–88; Díaz 1956:216) and Table 5.1 summarizes those listed for the Tlatelolco marketplace. Available descriptions imply that all of these venders were women (Sahagún 1961). They are identified here as producer-sellers because the tremendous variety of food dishes sold such as moles and tamales (Figure 5.3) were their own creations which took advantage of individual recipes and cooking styles. The cooked food venders included those who operated out of restaurant shops (Cortés 1962:87) as well as a myriad of street venders both in and outside of the marketplace.

The list of venders selling food includes individuals who prepared specialty beverages such as atole, cacao, and pulque. Atole was sold as both a hot and cold drink and was made from a variety of ingredients including maize, beans, fruit, chile, and honey. Chocolate was served as a cold beverage and depending on the recipe, was a mixture of various ingredients including chili, vanilla, honey, and aromatic flowers (Figure 5.4). It is likely

FIGURE 5.3 The tamale seller

that both the atole (*atolnamacac*) and cacao sellers (*tlaquetzalnamacac*) bought their varied ingredients as needed and prepared their final products in the marketplace. Pulque was also sold in and outside of the marketplace both as a fermented or unfermented beverage by the individuals who collected it.

Other items sold by women included tortillas as well as salted and roasted squash seeds made into small sweet cakes using honey. Finally, there was the bread baker who ground and baked wheat flour into cakes. That this was a colonial adaptation is evident in the vender name which uses the Spanish word for wheat (*trigo*) as the root for baker (*trigonamacac*) and is shown in Sahagún's (1961:figure 128) accompanying illustrations as a male in Spanish apparel. While tortilla manufacture was traditionally a female activity, men appear to have entered this profession by the end of the sixteenth century perhaps as organizers for larger-scale production. This is evident from the testamentary will of Don Juan de Guzmán in 1622 which stipulates that a 15 pesos debt be collected from Juan Tlaxcalchiuhqui of Coyoacan whose name in *Nahuatl* translates literally as tortilla maker. Horn (1998:74–75) suggests that Juan Tlaxcalchiuhqui may have been a Spanish-style bread baker although this is not clear.

Both processed flour and oil were sold in the marketplace. The miller is described as a vender of Castillian wheat flour. The *Nahuatl* word for this profession is *texnamacac* which simply means "one who sells ground things." During prehispanic times this would have included other types of flour such as maize and *pinolli* which was a mixture of ground maize and *chia* flour (Durand-Forest 1971:124). *Pinolli* was a flour of prehispanic origin which was prepared as a high-energy traveling food for

FIGURE 5.4 The chocolate-drink seller

both merchants and the military which Tlatelolco venders were charged to produce as a specific tribute levy. *Pinolli* was probably a fourth speciality beverage sold in the marketplace since Molina (1977) and Simeón (1991) list *pinolatl* as a drink made of ground maize, *chia*, and cacao. It is possible, therefore, that while Sahagún specifically associates this producer-seller with preparing wheat flour, this was an addition to an already established vender of other precolumbian flours. Oil made from *chia* seeds was also sold by the individuals who processed it (*chiamachiu-que*) according to Molina (1977).

Venders who primarily sold unprocessed food also sold it in cooked and processed form which is interesting for two reasons. First, it provided producer-sellers and retailers with the opportunity to increase their profit margins by "adding value" to the uncooked food they normally sold. Second, nothing spoils more quickly in the tropics than raw fish and meat.

It is not surprising, therefore, that meat venders would also sell dried, jerked, oven-cooked, baked, and stewed meat (Sahagún 1961:80), while fish venders sold dried fish and stewed fish wrapped in maize husks (Sahagún 1961:80). Egg and lake product venders were more creative, using their products as ingredients in tamales and tortillas as well as using them to prepare a broth (Sahagún 1961:80, 85). Selling their products as prepared foods allowed venders to protect themselves against spoilage by cooking foods before they went bad. Food processing was part and parcel of the shopkeeper's trade across the American frontier during the seventeenth to nineteenth centuries just to keep food from spoiling. That this also was the case for market merchants in Mesoamerica is implied by Sahagún's description of the bad vender as someone who sold spoiled, moldy, evil-smelling, rotten meat and eggs (Sahagún 1961:80, 85). This was a particularly useful strategy for retail venders (see Chapter 6).

PRODUCER-SELLERS OF FORAGED PRODUCTS AND NATURAL RESOURCES

A parallel strategy to selling food products was to collect, process, and sell naturally occurring resources available in the public domain. How open the public domain was to foraging is an interesting question, although most of the evidence suggests that the commons was an open resource zone that could be used by all community members. An attitude of open resource use is evident in the record of complaints filed in the Cabildo of Tlaxcala in 1549 and 1560 against people coming from the neighboring town of Cholula to cut firewood used to make lime. That they trespassed and used community resources was only a part of the complaint; the larger issue was that they used the firewood to make lime that was then sold back to the Tlaxcalans after getting wood for free (Lockhart et al. 1986:60). That Cholutecans would dare to cross over community boundaries to cut down trees indicates an attitude of open access to the public commons.

Documenting use of the commons is important because it reveals the existence of a viable subsistence strategy that poor households could use to support themselves. The exploitation of natural resources was seasonal work that families could use to supplement their income. Community resources were used by households in many indigenous communities well into the twentieth century for a range of activities including charcoal making, wood collecting, and resin collecting (Lewis 1951; Tax 1953).

One of the best known instances of exploiting natural resources for domestic subsistence occurred with Aztec colonization of their island home of Tenochtitlan. According to native sources, the Aztecs took refuge on the marshy island after a confrontation with the king of Culhuacan in AD 1325 (Berdan 1982:7; Durán 1994; M. Smith 1996:45). Without agricultural land to support themselves, the Aztecs faced a predicament. They could receive agricultural land by becoming subjects of Texcoco or Azcapotzalco, or remain independent and support themselves by foraging the lake's diverse lacustrine resources. Diego Durán (1994:45–46) summarizes the form of subsistence that they chose to follow:

> on market days ... their wives should go sell fish and frogs and other creatures found in the lake, together with the waterfowl they hunted. They would go without humility or submission, nor in a flattering way; they would go, not as subjects of any town, but as lords of that place which their god had given them. They fished and collected frogs and shrimp and all kinds of edible things. They collected even the worms that thrive in the water and the mosquitos that breed on the lake surface. And knowing which were market days in each town, they went to these market places as hunters and fishermen and bartered the fowl and fish and water creatures for beams and boards, for small wood, for lime and stone
> (Durán 1994:45–46).

The Aztecs became forager-sellers for everything from the fish and frogs mentioned here, to red worms and algae that they made into small loaves.[22] While the stated goal was to buy construction material, households certainly also traded these products to buy maize, beans, and other food staples. The importance of this subsistence activity is evident in the persistence that Aztec women showed in going to trade in marketplaces even when they were confronted by assaults and rape (Durán 1994:86). Trade in lake products by Aztec producer-sellers continued throughout the ascendancy of the Aztec empire (Durán 1994:105) and into the early colonial period. Documents from colonial Coyoacan indicate that Mexica boat people, as well as people referred to as the fish and lake scum sellers, were regular participants in its regional marketplace well into the middle sixteenth century (Anderson et al. 1976).

Table 5.2 lists the twenty categories of foraged products collected, processed, and sold by producer-sellers in prehispanic Central Mexico. This is a minimal list and probably doesn't cover all the foraged and collected resources sold in the Basin of Mexico much less across Mesoamerica. What it does do is document the importance of this practice in the commercial life of domestic groups. The diversified lake product venders and fishermen discussed earlier are referred to as *xoquiiacanamacac*

TABLE 5.2: *Producer-sellers: foragers, hunters, collectors*

Category	Nahuatl term	Notes
Hunter, meat seller	nacanamacac, -anqui	"He hunts; he pursues game . . . hare, . . . meat of wild beasts, of opossum (Sahagún 1961:80)"
Pine torch splitter	ocotlapanqui, ocotlapaque	Listed as a producer-vender for the market in Coyoacan (Anderson, Berdan, and Lockart 1976), ocote cutter in Huexotzinco
Pine resin seller, woodsman	ocutzonamacac, ocotzotlazqui	"a woodsman, a collector of pine resin. He collects pine resin . . . He sells uncooked pine resin; cooked pine resin (Sahagún 1961:88)"
Rubber seller	olnamacac	"a possessor of rubber, a possessor of rubber trees, a collector of rubber, collects rubber, sells rubber–balls of rubber (Sahagún 1961:87)"
Apothecary, medicine collector	pachichiuhqui	from Molina (1977)
Firewood cutter	quaquauini	"sells oak, pine alder . . . logs, toppings, kindling wood; bark . . . dart shafts, dried maguey leaves, dried maize stalks, sun flower [stalks] (Sahagún 1961:81)"
Wood seller	quauhnamacac	"a woodsman . . . He cuts with an axe; he fells trees–cuts them, tops them, strips them, stacks them (Sahagún 1961:80–81)"
Honey gatherer	quaunequanqui	A specialized craft listed at Huexotzinco (Prem 1974)
Blue dye seller	siuhquilnamacac	"a gatherer of clay . . . She mixes it with *uixachin* [leaves] with *quauhtepoztli* [bark] (Sahagún 1961:91–92)"
Liquidambar seller	suchiocutzonamacac	"a possessor of pine resin–a possessor of pine resin trees (Sahagún 1961:88)"
Lake scum seller	tecuitlachiuhqui, tecuitlanamacac	Listed as a producer-vender for the market in Coyoacan (Anderson, Berdan, and Lockart 1976)
Lime producer	tenexnamacac, tenextlati	"a shatterer of rocks, a burner of limestone, a slaker of lime (Sahagún 1961:78)"

Category	Nahuatl term	Notes
Saltpeter seller	tequixquinamacac	"a guide to places where there is saltpeter, one who heaps up saltpeter (Sahagún 1961:93)"
Chalk seller	tiçanamacac	"one who masses [chalk] with his hand … he cooks it (Sahagún 1961:94)"
Stone cutter, stone breaker	tetzotzonqui, tetlapanqui	"works with a wedge … He quarries, breaks [the rocks] … pounds, hammers them; splits them with a wedge (Sahagun 1961:27)"
Glue seller	tzacunamacac	"the digger of glue plant [roots] … beats them with a stone, pulverizes them. He sells glue plant [roots] uncooked–pulverized, ground (Sahagún 1961:87)"
Feather grass crafter (Esparto)	xomalpetlachiuhqui	from Molina (1977)
Fisherman	xoquiiacanamacac, michanqui, tlatlama	"He fishes; he catches with nets, with snares; he fishes with a fishhook; he uses a weir, a spear … He sells (Sahagún 1961:80)"
Lake products seller	xoquiiacanamacac	"a man of the water … He sells … axolotl … fish eggs … water fly eggs … water flies … water worms, worm excrement, 'worm flowers' (Sahagún 1961:80)"
Fowl or quail hunter	çolanqui, çolmani	A specialized craft listed at Huexotzinco. "He hunts; he pursues game … duck, crane, goose, mallard … quail meat, eagle meat (Sahagún 1961:80)"

Note: Total number of foragers, hunters, and collectors is n=20.

(Sahagún 1961:80) and they are described as both fishermen and insect collectors indicating that these individuals operated across the resource spectrum depending on the natural life cycle of the biota exploited.

The consumption of lake resources is a reflection of diet diversity and the demand for protein. Turkey and dog were the only two animal domestics in Mesoamerica and as a result hunting remained an important subsistence activity and profession for households right up to the conquest. Hunters were recognized personae in Central Mexican society and were the only individuals other than royal guards allowed to carry weapons in Tenochtitlan (Alba 1949:17). Hunters (*nacanamacac*) sought deer, rabbit, opossum, and any other small game such as quail (*zolanqui*) that they could find. On the lake, hunters specialized in capturing water fowl that included duck, crane, goose, and coot. Because the Basin of Mexico lakes are located along the Central American flyway, migratory fowl was a major protein source during different times of the year. Insects (*jumiles*, maguey worms, grasshoppers, etc.) were another protein supplement to the precolumbian diet.[23]

Forest products also were exploited and sold in the marketplace. Wood for construction, firewood, and pine torches were collected for market sale. Who these forager-sellers were, depended, of course, on where wood products were available for localized exploitation.[24] Tree resin was collected and sold for a variety of uses. Natural latex from rubber trees was collected and used for water proofing, chewing gum, ritual offerings, and as rubber balls used in the Mesoamerican ballgame. Since natural latex was a tropical forest import, the status of the dealers (*olnamacac*) as producer-sellers or retailers remains unclear. Sahagún also records two other types of resin sellers, the *suchiocutzonamacac* who sold liquidambar used as incense and a general resin seller called the *ocutzonamacac* (Sahagún 1961:88). The *ocutzonamacac* is described as processing his pine resin by boiling it in a pot where it was mixed with lampblack (charcoal). The *ocutzonamacac* probably is best thought of as a glue and sealer seller; not only can this recipe be used as a hot mastic, but he is located in the marketplace immediately alongside the specialized glue seller (*tzacunamacac*) who made glue from pulverized roots of forest plants (Berdan et al. 2009; Sahagún 1961:87). Finally, even a product as simple as wild grass could be cut and fashioned into usable images and amulets (*xomalpetlachiuhqui*).

There are five categories of forager-sellers who processed and sold naturally occurring earth products. The most important of these was the lime producer (*tenexnamacac*) who mined limestone and cooked it to produce lime (Figure 5.5). Lime was used in every household both to soak maize prior to cooking and in construction for stucco floors and walls. Following him in importance was the stone cutter (*tetzotzonqui, tetlapanqui*) who extracted and shaped stone at the quarry or in special constructions. Two other natural resource venders were the chalk seller (*tiçanamacac*) and the saltpeter seller (*tequixquinamacac*) who mined and sold these natural materials with minimal processing beyond simple

FIGURE 5.5 The lime seller

heating (Sahagún 1961:93–94). The fifth natural resource user was the blue dye seller (*siuhquilnamacac*) who mined blue clay and mixed it with tree leaves and bark to create this dye (Sahagún 1961:91–92).

Undoubtedly a great many other products were collected and sold in the marketplace for which there is no record. This would have included natural products used for medicinal purposes such as herbs, wood, stones, sap, roots, and leaves (Hernández 1959; Molina 1977; Sahagún 1961:28, 85). Physicians and apothecaries probably relied on experienced suppliers to provide them with medicines like *axin* that they used or sold to patients (Sahagún 1961:89). Some apothecaries (*pachichiuhqui*) collected and made their own medicines (Molina 1977). Other wild products like chicle were used for pleasure, while hallucinogenic mushrooms were employed to foretell the future or used in religious rituals (Sahagún 1979b:38–39). Add to this the greater array of non-organic products with useful applications like bitumen (Sahagún 1961:88; Wendt 2009; Wendt and Cyphers 2008) and emery (Carrasco 1980:261) and the result is a lively commerce in natural products by those who collected, processed, and sold them in the marketplace. While hunting and gathering is assumed to have declined after the advent of agriculture, it remained an important economic component in the commercial lives of many prehispanic households.

INDEPENDENT CRAFTSMEN OF MANUFACTURED PRODUCTS

The quality of prehispanic craftsmanship impressed the Spanish. Most craftsmen worked in their homes, a few worked in the marketplace, and some worked in both locales. There were also those who worked in special facilities like the *totocalli* to produce high-value goods used by the state (see Chapter 2). Archaeological research has confirmed what the historic records suggest: the vast majority of craft production in Mesoamerica was carried out by independent craftsmen working within the household (Feinman 1999; Hirth 2006c, 2009c). Recent research suggests that even the most highly skilled craftsmen probably worked at their craft on a part-time, rather than a full-time basis (Feinman 1999; Hirth 2009a). The reason for this was twofold. First, much craft activity was organized as a complement to other production activities including agriculture. Second and perhaps more importantly, the demand for craft goods was highly income-elastic for the households consuming them (Plattner 1989b:187). Purchasing patterns were directly timed to agricultural harvests resulting in highly variable demand for goods; it was safer for craftsmen to diversity into multiple forms of production than to specialize in one and pursue it on a full-time basis (Hirth 2009c).

There was little to no division of labor within crafts except in processing raw materials and making them suitable for sale to other craftsmen.[25] Artisans were highly skilled, but the output for any artisan was relatively low. This was compensated for throughout society by simply increasing the number of individuals who engaged in crafting. Zorita (1994) reports that craftsmen were widely distributed across *calpultin* rather than being concentrated in a few towns or cities (Katz 1966:51). The *Matrícula de Huexotzinco* records the number of artisans located in 23 communities in northwestern Puebla in 1560 (Prem 1974). Examination of this data reveals that artisans comprised more than 25% of the commoner households and occurred in every small town and hamlet in the region. The abundance of artisans was probably encouraged by the elite since it created opportunities for in-kind tribute levies of finished goods at the local level.

The artisans who sold their wares in marketplaces were independent producer-sellers like the farmers, food venders, and natural resource venders. They included craftsmen who produced utilitarian goods consumed by all households in society as well as artisans who made high-value luxury goods for the wealthy elite. They obtained the raw materials they used within the region where they lived, through social and commercial contacts, or within the marketplace. While they certainly could produce goods on a consignment basis, the majority of the finished goods that they made were offered for sale in the marketplace to all buyers.

Table 5.3 provides a list of craftsmen and a brief description of what they sold. Sixty craft specializations are mentioned in the sources which is twice the number of traditional crafts identified by Ixtlilxóchitl (1977). All these were discrete crafts and although the number of crafts is large, it certainly does not represent the whole array of crafts practiced in Mesoamerica,[26] much less the number of product specializations within crafts.[27] Nevertheless, their status as producer-sellers is underscored by the common designation of the noun suffix -*chiuhqui*.

The largest block of related crafts has to do with the manufacture of textiles. This is not surprising given the multiple uses textiles had in prehispanic society. Plain textiles known as *quachtli* were a form of currency (Berdan 1975; León-Portilla 1962; Rojas 1995), while decorated mantles and finished garments were used both as stored wealth and for tribute payments. It has been estimated that as much as three million textiles were paid as tribute every year by Aztec tributaries (Drennan 1984b). Berdan (1987:241) feels that this estimate is flawed and argues that annual textile tribute of 278,400 pieces of cloth is a much more realistic figure.[28] Nevertheless, an annual tribute levy of 275,000–300,000 textiles across the empire represents a significant amount of invested labor. While the number of tribute textiles was large, it does not take into account the equally large quantity of textiles produced to meet personal clothing needs, family celebrations, and local tribute obligations. What is important is that all these textiles were produced with culturally important designs by women who worked in their homes without direct supervision beyond a shared understanding of the textile quality they needed to produce.

There are thirteen crafts listed in Table 5.3 related to textile manufacture. Three of these, the dyer, spinner, and the weaver provide the structure of the basic manufacturing process. While women engaged in all three of these activities in the production of a single textile, they separated these tasks into crafts to sell specific products in the marketplace. Sahagún (1961:77) only identifies a dyer of rabbit hair

TABLE 5.3: *Craftsmen producer-sellers: artisans and craftsmen*
Crafts with prehispanic origins

Category	Nahuatl term	Notes
Smoking tube seller	acaquauhchiuhqui, acaquauhnamacac	"a maker of reed smoking tubes, a cutter of reeds ... he paints them (Sahagún 1961:88)"
Maguey cape maker	aianamacac	"the dresser of maguey leaves in order to extract the fiber (Sahagún 1961:73)"
Paper maker	amanamacac, amauitecqui	"the paper maker ... he makes it, he beats it (Sahagún 1961:78)" Also sold Spanish paper
Feather craftsman	amantecatl	"in the working of feathers two methods were used ... thus began their creations (Sahagún 1959:92–93)"
Soap seller	amolchiuhqui, amolnamacac	indigenous soap dealer and producer (Molina 1977; Siméon 1991).
Clay bell makers	cacalachiuhqui	A specialized craft from Coyoacan
Sandal maker	cacçoc, cacnamacac, cactzoc	"The sandal seller is a sandal maker ... He has ... a copper awl ... He stitches the sandals, sews them (Sahagún 1961:74)"
Garment maker	chamalochiuhqui	A specialized textile craft from Coyoacan
Basket maker	chiquiuhciuhqui	"The seller of large baskets is a maker of large baskets (Sahagún 1961:83)"
Shield maker	chimalchiuhqui	from Molina (1977)
Small (copper?) bell maker	cocoiochuihque	A specialized craft from Coyoacan
Comal maker	comalchiuhqui	"one who moistens clay, kneads it, tempers it ... flattens it ... applies a slip ... He places [unfired pieces] in the oven (Sahagún 1961:83)"
Jar maker	conchiuhqui	A specialized pottery craft from Coyoacan
Feather seller, feather spinner	hihujnamacac, hihuitzaoa	"a bird owner. She raises birds; she plucks them ... She spins feather ... into an even thread (Sahagún 1961:92)"
Weaver	hiquitqui	"one who warps ... she puts the weft in place ... She weaves; she directs others in weaving (Sahagún 1961:36)"

Category	Nahuatl term	Notes
Cotton armor maker	ichcahuipilli	Berdan 1987:241
Fiber cape maker, itinerant	icçotilmanamacac	"the maker of palm leaf fiber capes [is] a traveler (Sahagún 1961:75)"
Obsidian craftsman	itznamacac	"The obsidian seller . . . forces off obsidian blades, he breaks off flakes (Sahagún 1961:85)"
Salt maker	iztachiuhqui	"The salt producer gathers [salty] earth . . . makes brine, makes ollas for salt, cooks it (Sahagún 1961:84)"
Malacate maker	malacahuihqui	A specialized pottery craft from Coyoacan
Rope maker	mecachiuani, mecachiuhqui, tlamallique	A specialized fiber craft from Coyoacan and Huexotzinco
Tumpline maker	mecapalchiuhqui	A specialized fiber craft from Coyoacan
Arrow maker	michiuhqui, tlahuitolchiuhqui	from Molina (1977)
Sash maker	nelpilonamacac	"a cutter of cloth, a cutter of narrow strips (Sahagún 1961:91)"
Cargo basket maker	otlachiquiuhchiuhqui	"a weaver of stout cane baskets . . . He . . . splits [the canes], arranges them, establishes the rims (Sahagún 1961:86)"
Travel staff or frame maker	otlachiuhqui	A specialized craft from Coyoacan
Reed mat maker	petlachiuhqui	"the reed mat maker possesses reeds . . . He weaves reed mats (Sahagún 1961:86)"
Broom vender	popochiuhqui, poponamacac	"one who reaps with a sickle. He gathers [straw] for brooms (Sahagún 1961:87)"
Cigar seller/dealer	poquiyenamacac	A dealer in the Coyoacan market (Anderson, Berdan, Lockhart 1976). Probably a producer-seller
Coppersmith	tepuzpitzqui, tepuztecac	"he beats, he casts the copper. He blows the fire (Sahagún 1961:26)"

(*continued*)

TABLE 5.3: *(continued)*

Category	Nahuatl term	Notes
Stone cutter, architect	tetzotzonqui, tetlapanqui	"a good builder ... he builds a house ... draws plans ... builds up a foundation ... forms the walls, builds the terrace (Sahagún 1961:27–28)"
Stone cutter, sculptor	tetlapanqui, tetzotzonqui	"forms curved stone ... sculptures in stone, carves it; forms works of artifice, of skill (Sahagún 1961:27–28)"
Goldsmith, silversmith	teucuitlaoa, teucuitlapitzqui	"[He is] the final processor ... he melts, he pours the gold ... he casts (Sahagún 1961:25)"
Mirror lapidary	tezacanamacac	"a lapidary, a polisher. He abrades ... he cuts; he carves; he use glue (Sahagún 1961:87)"
Weaver of designs	tlamachichiuhqui	"a maker of varicolored capes ... She weaves designs ... forms borders ... forms the neck (Sahagún 1961:52)"
Mason	tlaquilqui, calchiuhqui	"one who makes mortar ... who spreads ... smooths, polishes ... who whitewashes (Sahagún 1961:28)"
Lapidary	tlatecqui	"He cuts stones ... grinds them down ... forms designs of them (Sahagún 1961:26)"
Border weaver	tlatenchiuhqui	A specialized textile craft from Coyoacan
Seamstress	tlatzonqui	"one who uses the needle ... She sews; she makes designs ... a craftsman (Sahagún 1961:52)"
Carpenter	tlaxinqui, quauhxinqui, quauhtlachichiuhqui	"one who uses the plumb ... he sculptures in wood, carves it, smooths the surface ... saws it, lashes it, forms tenons (Sahagún 1961:27)"
Rabbit hair dyer	tochominamacac	"a dyer, a user of dyes, a dyer [of material] in many colors (Sahagún 1961:77)"
Hide seller	tominamacac cuetlaxtli, euanamacac	Listed as a vender in Tlatelolco and Coyoacan markets (Durand-Forest 1971:124; Rojas 1995:234).

Category	Nahuatl term	Notes
Spinner	tzauhqui	"one who forms a thread ... She fills the spindle ... winds the thread into a ball ... shapes it into a skein (Sahagún 1961:35)"
Pitcher/cantaro maker	tzotzocolchiuhqui	from Molina (1977)
Beam maker	ueuechiuhqui	from Molina (1977)
Copper needle caster (see also copper smith)	veitzmallonamacac, tepuzpitzqui	"He polishes, abrades, casts copper. He makes bells, needles, awls; he pours [molten] copper (Sahagún 1961:87)"
Gourd bowl maker	xicalnamacac	"[He is a worker] who removes the ... bumps, who burnishes, varnishes, paints them (Sahagún 1961:78)"
Bag maker	xiquipilnamacac	"[He is] a cutter. He sews ... [He makes bags] small and narrow (Sahagún 1961:91)"
Fresh flower worker	xochimanque, xochichiuhqui celic	A specialized craft listed from Huexotzinco
Dried flower worker	xochimanque, xochichiuhqui vanqui	A specialized craft listed from Huexotzinco
Perfume seller	xochiocotzonamacac	A specialized craft listed by Siméon (1991). Perfume sellers normally mix their own fragrances.
Maguey garment maker	ychcamixachiuhqui, (ich) chamalochiuhqui	A specialized textile craft from Coyoacan
Pottery maker	zoquichiuhqui	"a skilled man with clay ... a fabricator ... an artist (Sahagún 1961:42)"
Wooden bowl maker	listed with çoquichiuhqui	Manufacture of wooden bowls also implied (Sahagún 1961:42)
Flute maker	zozolocchiuhqui	from Molina (1977)
Shell worker	eptli -chiuhqui	Archaeological workshop examples

(*continued*)

TABLE 5.3: (*continued*)

Craftsmen of products for Spanish consumers*

Category	Nahuatl Term	Notes
Candle maker	cantellachiuhqui, xicocuitlaocochiuhqui	"a candle maker, prepares beeswax … He forms it … places a wick (Sahagún 1961:91)"
Collar maker	cauecochiuhqui	A specialized textile craft from Coyoacan; could also be prehispanic
Cobbler	zapatosnamacac	"maker of Castilian shoes, provides soles, cuts them; stitches sandals (Sahagún 1961:91)"
Tailor	tlaçonqui, tilmachiuhqui	"a fitter … a cutter, a trimmer–a practiser of tailoring … He sews (Sahagún 1961:35)"

Note: The total number of craftsmen producer-sellers is n=60.
* It is also possible that indigenous people also were consumers of these new Spanish products

(*tochominamacac*) as a craft speciality, although individuals also dyed cotton and maguey which were the two main fibers used in Mesoamerica. The spinner (*tzauhqui*) was confirmed as a craft specialty by Cortés who observed that "all kinds of cotton thread in various colors may be bought in skeins" in the Tlatelolco marketplace (1962:88). The feather spinner (*hihujnamacac*) was a speciality artisan who spun cotton thread with feathers in it. Two types of weavers are mentioned: a generic weaver (*hiquitqui*) who manufactured plain cloth including the *quachtli*, and the weaver of designs (*tlamachichiuhqui*) who produced more complex and decorated textiles (Table 5.3).

Woven goods were fashioned into different types of apparel including capes, tunics, and breechcloths. Textiles were manufactured in both cotton and maguey and there are indications that a distinction was drawn between craftsmen who worked in these different fibers. Three different terms are used to denote a craftsmen who makes apparel: the garment maker (*chamalochiuhqui*), the seamstress (*tlatzonqui*), and the tailor (*tilmachiuhqui*). The categories of seamstress and tailor imply the manufacture of fitted garments in the Spanish style and may be colonial innovations. This is clear in the description of the tailor who is described as someone who cuts and fits clothes and he is listed as craftsman of Spanish products in Table 5.3. The seamstress, on the other hand, is described as someone who works with a needle and probably engaged in embroidery in traditional style. It is likely that all of these craftsmen worked in cotton because of the way maguey textile workers are distinguished. The generic term for a maguey garment maker is *ychcamixachiuhqui* with separate terms used for individuals who manufactured outerwear maguey capes (*aianamacac, icçotilmanamacac*).

Sub-specialization is seen in the manufacture and sale of smaller textile items. Two craftsmen were milliners, one manufacturing sashes (*nelpilonamacac*), and another producing cloth bags (*xiquipilnamacac*). Plain textiles were converted into more elaborate ones by adding decorated border pieces. This resulted in the emergence of craftsmen such as the collar maker (*cauecochiuhqui*) and the decorated border weaver (*tlatenchiuhqui*).

At the other end of the spectrum from valuable textiles were the more mundane fiber products processed and woven from reeds, palms, grasses, and other woody plants. Seven fiber craft specialists are listed in Table 5.3 who worked these products alone or in combination with other materials to manufacture household furnishings. Mesoamerican households did not have beds and people slept on reed mats that were rolled up each morning after the night's sleep. Rulers depicted as sitting on reed mats were symbolic for the place of rulership in Mesoamerica. Although many different sizes and types of mats were manufactured, there is only one term (*petlachiuhqui*) for the producer-seller who sold them. The same is true for the many different types of baskets used in household and institutional settings. Sahagún (1961:83–84) describes baskets made of different materials and in different sizes used for both storage and carrying things. Although there certainly was specialization within this craft, Sahagún only gives a single generic term for the basket maker (*chiquiuhciuhqui*) to cover all the varieties produced. The only clear differentiation is for cargo baskets made by craftsmen (*otlachiquiuhchiuhqui*) who specialized in these items. Besides being strong and of special design, these baskets were mounted on a wooden carrying frame. A number of venders in the market are referred to as "people of the basket" and it is possible that they were itinerant merchants who carried and sold their merchandise out of these specialized cargo baskets (see Chapter 6).

Fiber also was used to produce rope, twine, and sandals. The maguey fiber sandal (*icpacactli*) was the most common type of foot gear in prehispanic times and is now a thing of the past[29] (Figure 5.6). The sandal maker is referred to by various terms including *caçoc, cacchiuhqui*, and *cacnamacac* with the later term used for retail dealers (see Chapter 6). Different types of sandals were manufactured from different materials in different regions. Molina (1977) lists several types of sandals in his sixteenth-century dictionary: the high backed sandals worn by rulers

FIGURE 5.6 A pair of *icpacactli* fiber sandals bought in the Cuautla in the mid-1970s. Sandals are for a child and are made of maguey fiber

and the more common sandals made from maguey (*icpacactli*) palm (*çotolcactli*), wood (*quauhcactli, vapalcactli*), and uncured leather (*euacactli*). This reflects a level of sub-specialization in sandal making that escapes detection in the historic sources.

The rope maker (*mecachiuani, mecachiuhqui*) was an important fixture in the economy because so many items were tied or fastened with straps and bindings. Rope making was an indigenous craft that continued into the twentieth century (Parsons and Parsons 1990). A specialized rope maker manufactured tumplines (*mecapalchiuhqui*) used for hauling cargo. Tumplines were woven head bands and had to be strong, light weight, and soft enough not to abrade the forehead of the porters who used them. Finally there was the broom maker (*popochiuhqui, poponamacac*) who made several varieties of brooms.

Leather was another important resource sold in the marketplace. The hide or leather seller (*tominamacac*) is listed for both the Tlatelolco and Coyoacan markets. Although there is little information on what this vender sold, it is likely that by the colonial period it was hides of both domesticated and hunted animals. Hides were a secondary product of butchered animals and they were not sold by the same individuals who sold the meat. This implies that hides were sold fresh to individuals who processed and sold them in cured form.

Sahagún also lists producer-sellers who sold a range of items used in everyday domestic life. Prominent among these were the individuals who sold the containers used to cook, store, and serve food. Potters (*çoquichiuhqui*) manufactured cookware as well as figurines, censerware, and ceramic stoves. Ceramicists rarely produce the complete range of possible goods. Instead, they specialize in a subset of goods because of the increased production efficiency or because certain ceramic uses require specific technological properties. Examples of sub-specializations include the comal (*comalchiuhqui*), pitcher (*tzotzocolchiuhqui*), and jar maker (*conchiuhqui*) specialists. The comal maker manufactured ceramic griddles that had to resist thermal shock during use. Similarly the jar maker produced storage vessels that had to keep contents dry or permit trans-evaporation for cooling stored liquids. To these can be added the spindle whorl specialists (*malacahuihqui*) and the clay bell makers (*cacalachiuhqui*).

Other utilitarian goods sold by craftsmen included flaked stone tools, salt, ground stone tools, and military equipment. Particularly prominent among these are the specialized craftsmen (*itznamacac*) who manufactured razor sharp obsidian blades and other cutting tools from volcanic glass. These craftsmen are described as manufacturing finished goods within the marketplace (Motolinia 1973:44–45; Torquemada 1975:2:488–489). Salt was another specialized craft good. The individuals who engaged in this trade (*iztachiuhqui*) processed salt from saline marshes, springs, and marine deposits. They used a variety of solar and cooking techniques and often made the ceramic vessels used to process it (De León 2009; Parsons 2001). Grinding stones used to process food (manos, metates, molcajetes, and mortars) were an indispensable part of every household kitchen and they were sold in the marketplace by the *molcaxnamacac*.[30] Two specialized craftsmen of weaponry are mentioned by Molina (1977) who manufactured arrows (*tlahuitolchiuhqui*) and shields (*chimalchiuhqui*). Cotton armor was also manufactured by craft specialists (Berdan 1987:248), but it is unclear whether it was produced for sale in the marketplace.

Even though flowers might not be considered a utilitarian item today, they were an essential item of prehispanic life. Flowers were used to decorate buildings and special arrays were used in social events at all levels of society (weddings, receptions, funerals, etc.). The individual who manufactured these arrays was a *xochimanque* or *xochichiuhqui* and these artisans were distinguished by whether they worked in fresh or dry flowers. A related specialty item was the manufacture of perfumes. Because perfumers the world over mix their own fragrancies it is reasonable that the same was true for perfume sellers (*xochiocotzonamacac*) in Mesoamerica. Soap was another important item that was sold and manufactured by the individuals who made it (*amolchiuhqui*) (Molina 1977).

The construction trades included craftsmen who worked stone and wood. These individuals fabricated the items they used in building or manufactured them on a sub-contractual basis for others. Five specialists are listed in Table 5.3. They include the stone cutter (*tetzotzonqui, tetlapanqui*) and the sculptor (*tetlapanqui, tetzotzonqui*) who cut and shaped stone. The stone cutter is also described as an architect; someone who designed and constructed an entire structure. Related craftsman include the mason (*tlaquilqui*) who finished stucco floors and walls and the carpenter (*tlaxinqui, quauhxinqui*) (Figure 5.7). This category, included a variety of sub-specialities ranging from beam makers (*ueuechiuhqui*), and builders, to sculptors and box makers. An interesting sub-speciality listed for the market of Coyoacan was the maker of traveling staffs (*otlachiuhqui*). Whether this was a special wood product or made in a

FIGURE 5.7 The carpenter

way particular for use by porters, travelers, or merchants is unclear, but it is listed here as an example of the sub-specializations found in the fabrication of wood products.

Craftsmen who sold luxury goods in the marketplace was the hallmark of an imperial city and rulers sought to attract these artisans. Ten craft specialties producing luxury items can be identified in the textual and archaeological sources (Table 5.3). The most prominent and unusual of these crafts was the feather craftsmen (*amanteca*). Delicate feather work was used to embellish capes, skirts, head gear, warriors' costumes, dance paraphernalia, as well as items of personal adornment and small decorative furnishings. Sahagún (1959:91–97) describes three classes of feather workers based on where and who they worked for. The most skilled feather craftsmen (*tecpan amanteca*) were employed in palace workshops and made the highly adorned capes and apparel used by the rulers. Another highly skilled group were the *calpiscan amanteca* who worked in a special palace workshop (e.g. *totocalli*) to make the dance arrays of *Huitzilopochtli* and other paraphernalia used in special festivals. The third group of feather workers were the *calla amanteca* who produced goods for sale in the marketplace. This probably was the largest group of feather craftsmen who made and/or embellished a wide array of different items. Like all artisans they may also have made repairs to damaged goods that needed them although there is no direct evidence that this was the case.

Lapidaries also were highly esteemed craftsmen who produced some of the most prized wealth items in precolumbian society. Jade was particularly important and its manufacture into pendants, necklaces, ear spools, and other jewelry marked an individual's elevated social rank. Jade was considered a prerogative of the gods and was among the first gifts offered to Cortés by Aztec rulers and political emissaries.

Three types of lapidary specialists existed in precolumbian times. The term *tlatecqui* is used as a general term for a lapidary who cuts and works precious stone. These individuals worked jade as well as a number of precious and semiprecious stones including turquoise, malachite, and rock crystal. In addition to making jewelry they designed and fashioned cut stone mosaics using a variety of different precious stones.[31] One specialized lapidary is the mirror maker (*tezacanamacac*) who manufactured mirrors from obsidian and metallic ores such as illmenite by shaping, grinding, and polishing them into a smooth reflective surface. A third type of craftsman related to the lapidarian worked marine shell and although this craft is not specifically mentioned in the highland

sources, it is documented from archaeological contexts where shell artifacts were made (Balkansky and Croissier 2009; Velázquez Castro 2011).
Its omission from Sahagún (1961) may be the result of shell being worked
by the same lapidaries that worked semiprecious stones.[32]

   Metalsmiths also produced luxury goods and four specialists are listed
in Table 5.3. The first is the goldsmith (*teucuitlaoa, teucuitlapitzqui*) whose
work was highly praised by those Spanish who could look past the gold to
see their workmanship (Figure 5.8). These craftsmen worked both independently and on commission from elite patrons. Goldsmiths were closely
affiliated with the long-distance *pochteca* merchants for whom they produced an array of commodities used in trade (see Chapter 7). Copper and
bronze artifacts were also luxury goods that were manufactured by coppersmiths (*tepuzpitzqui, tepuztecac*). Copper-bronze items were symbols

FIGURE 5.8 The goldsmith

of elite status among the Tarascans of Michoacan where their production appears to have been controlled by the state (Maldonado 2009; Pollard 1987). Thin copper axes also served as a form of currency (Cardos de Mendez 1959:46; Katz 1966:59; Rojas 1995:245) which elevated the status of those craftsmen who worked in it. Specialization also is evident within the coppersmiths. In addition to smelters located close to mines, Sahagún identified specialized fabricators who made both small bells (*cocoiochuihque*) and needles (*veitzmallonamacac, tepuzpitzqui*). While some copper-bronze artifacts were utilitarian tools (e.g. needles, awls, wedges, etc.), most of the production remained focused on jewelry and small bells.

Four other semi-luxury products were manufactured and sold by the craft specialists who made them. These are smoking tube makers (*acaquauhchiuhqui*), cigar makers (*poquiyenamacac*), flute makers (*zozolocchiuhqui*), and paper makers (*amauitecqui*). Tobacco was an important product in prehispanic times that was used in healing and had ritual functions. While tobacco was not restricted to elite use, it was consumed in large quantities at important celebrations. A good deal of tobacco was smoked in tubes manufactured from reeds and filled with different mixtures of tobacco and other substances. Tobacco was also smoked as cigars in precolumbian world[33] and the cigar seller is identified as a separate vender in the market documents from Coyoacan (Anderson et al. 1976). The third speciality product was paper used by scribes for keeping records as well as by priests and ritual specialists in healing, divination, for spiritual protection, and other ritual activities.[34] As such paper like tobacco was used in a variety of important activities by both elites and non-elites. Music was also important in ritual events and musical instruments like flutes and drums were used on those occasions (e.g. *zozolocchiuhqui*).

The indigenous economy responded quickly to supply the new items demanded by their Spanish overlords after the conquest. New craft specializations appeared and indigenous merchants added Spanish products to the native goods that they sold. Two wholly new instances of crafting are evident in the sources (Table 5.3). The candle maker (*cantellachiuhqui, xicocuitlaocochiuhqui*) is an obvious colonial craft because candles were not known before the conquest. Sahagún illustrates the candle maker as a Spaniard wearing a hat in the process of making the candles underscoring the production function of this vender. The other example is the shoe maker (*zapatosnamacac*) who Sahagún specifies as making Castilian style shoes. The root prefix of the Nahualized words for both of these crafts is a Spanish word. For the candle maker (*cantellachiuhqui*) the root word is *candela*, while for the shoe maker the root word is *zapato*. In another instance of adaptability, indigenous bag makers (*xiquipilnamacac*) saw the opportunity for selling small coin bags and added them to the items that they manufactured for sale (Sahagún 1961:91).

INDIGENOUS SERVICE PROVIDERS

The question of whether wage labor was present in ancient societies is always of interest because it is a characteristic of modern societies. Marx (1964) contended that the main difference between preindustrial and industrial societies was that in the former, labor was not a commodity that could be purchased with daily wages. Marx was certainly correct in that the industrial revolution stimulated the emergence of wage labor. However the idea that individuals could sell their labor, time, and talents to others for monetary compensation is a very old principle. The key ingredient is how societies visualized labor and what precisely was sold.

In modern society wage labor is typically calculated per unit of time (e.g. hourly, daily, annually, etc.) because the labor of individuals is seen as largely interchangeable. Other societies use alternative equations such as remuneration by job or per item of piecework.[35] The key issue is that human labor can be obtained for a negotiable price. Most ancient societies had some notion of paid labor. What made it different from modern industrial settings is that the price of labor was usually linked to a specific job or set of skills. This certainly was the case in Mesoamerica where individuals could sell their labor by providing specific services to the individuals who contracted them.

Table 5.4 lists twelve service providers who offered their services for pay. Barber shops were located in the marketplace where a price was charged for a haircut and shampoo (Berdan 1975:205; Cortés 1962:87). The shoe repair specialist (*caczolchichiuhqui*) was an individual who repaired sandals, although after the conquest this probably also included Spanish style shoes. Female prostitutes (*monamacac*) and procuresses/pimps (*tetzinnamacac*) also plied their trade in the marketplace (Figure 5.9). Men and women physicians (*ticitl*) practiced on patients of the same gender who Sahagún (1961:30, 53) indicates were paid for their services. Physicians could have worked out of their homes but it is likely some of them were located in the marketplace since this is where a whole street was dedicated to medicinal plants. In the words of Cortés (1962:87), "(t)here are houses as it were of

TABLE 5.4: *Indigenous service providers*

Category	*Nahuatl* term	Notes
Canoe man	acallamocuitlaui, acallaneoani, acalpatiotl, acallaxtlauiloni	Simeon (1991) reports terms for various functions for canoe owners including freight, taxi services, and canoe rental.
Shoe repair	caczolchichiuhqui	from Molina (1977)
Singer	cuicani	"The singer . . . composes, who sets to music, originates Sahagún [songs]" (Sahagún 1961:28–29)
Prostitute, procuress	monamacac, tetzinnamacac	"She . . . seduces . . . a harlot . . . adorns herself at the market place" (Sahagún 1961:94).
Sorcerer	naoalli	"a counselor, a person of trust . . . he casts spells" (Sahagún 1961:31)
Attorney	tepantlato	"an agent . . . He collects tribute; . . . he consumes a tenth of it–he draws recompense (Sahagún 1961:32)
Physician	ticitl	"The physician [is] a curer of people . . . He provides health" (Sahagún 1961:32). "She cures people" (Sahagún 1961:53).
Solicitor, agent	tlaciuitiani, tlaciuiti	The solicitor [is] one . . . who arranges . . . He sells one's goods" (Sahagún 1961:32–33)
Porter	tlameme	"when they had assembled . . . all the loads, they . . . set one each on the hired burden-carriers" (Sahagún 1959:14).
Soothsayer	tlapouhqui, tonalpouhqui	"The soothsayer is a wise man, an owner of books [and] of writings" (Sahagún 1961:31).
Scribe, painter	tlaquilo, tlapalacuiloque, tlapalacuil	"writings, ink [are] his special skills . . . a painter who dissolves colors, grinds pigments" (Sahagún 1961:28)
Barber	tzontepeuani, tzontepeuhqui	"There are barbers' shops where you may have your hair washed and cut" (Cortés 1962:87).

Note: Total number of service providers is n=12.

FIGURE 5.9 The prostitute

apothecaries where they sell medicines made from these herbs, both for drinking and for use as ointments and salves."

At the other end of the spectrum were the scribes and singers who performed for patrons who needed their services. The scribe (*tlaquilo*) was required for record keeping in the *tecpan*. Scribes made maps, registered land allocations, kept tribute records, and recorded ritual information in screen-fold books known as codices. They were supported through the *calmecac* which was society's main educational institution. The singer (*cuicani*) was another specialized profession who sang for his or her living. Singing was considered a fine art and talented individuals were contracted for both public and private performances. This is seen in the banquets held by *pochteca* merchants in their private homes where singers were hired as part of ceremonies (Sahagún 1959:37).

Soothsayers and sorcerers were important in people's ritual lives. Soothsayers (*tlapouhqui, tonalpouhqui*) were consulted at the birth of a child to identify an auspicious day for naming the infant. Individuals were given a day-name in the *tonalpohualli* ritual calendar which carried important implications for an individual's future success in life. Soothsayers also identified favorable days for initiating important events such as the departure and return of merchants on trade ventures (Sahagún 1981:9, 27). Sorcerers (*naoalli*) would have been contracted to cast spells to influence the actions of individuals. In societies around the world, specialists of this sort are always remunerated in some form and the same was undoubtedly true in the Aztec world.

The high costs of transportation resulted in the payment of fees and wages to individuals involved in procuring and moving goods over space. Four activities are mentioned in the sources: agents and attorneys that arranged the purchase of items before they were moved, and two groups of porters who specialized in transportation for pay.

The attorney (*tepantlato*) was involved primarily in resource negotiation. Sahagún (1961:32) indicates that the attorney solicits, appeals, accuses, and offers rebuttals. Negotiation involved collection of outstanding payments as well as collecting tribute (debt) for which he received a ten percent commission. It is unlikely that Sahagún was referring to imperial tribute because that individual had the formal title of *calpixqui*. Sahagún specifies that "he collects tribute for one" which may refer to prebendal allocations of products intended to support individuals holding government offices. The solicitor (*tlaciuitiani, tlaciuiti*) was a commercial agent who was an intermediator between buyers and sellers (Figure 5.10). He apparently went into the countryside contracting the purchase and sale of commodities for himself and/or for others. He probably made his living by charging a commission; bad solicitors accepted bribes and sold other people's goods without their knowledge. This profession created a small future's market for agricultural products by contracting purchases from rural producers on behalf of retail dealers in urban areas.

Porters represent the last two service providers mentioned in the historic sources. The *tlameme* was a porter who moved cargo on his back using a tumpline (Figure 1.9). Porters were also called *momamaitoa* or *momamamanamacani*, quite literally he who sells his hands to carry. They were a recognized profession and could regularly be found in the marketplace for hire to move purchased goods to their destinations.[36] They were a hereditary profession that sometimes was imposed on groups as a tribute obligation (Hassig 1985:30). Porters were paid for their services, often in cacao beans (Hassig 1985:213) and accompanied *pochteca* merchants on long-distance trade ventures.[37]

FIGURE 5.10 The good solicitor

The *acallamocuitlaui* or canoe man also was a transportation specialist who moved goods on the Basin of Mexico lake system. Canoes transported bulk items with relatively low cost which explains why Tlatelolco developed into a large and thriving market in the center of the lake. Canoe porters were compensated for their service in three ways: canoes could be rented in their entirety, used for taxi services, or paid on the basis of freight transported (Table 5.4).

THE PRODUCTION OF AGRICULTURAL SURPLUS FOR THE MARKETPLACE

Producer-sellers were an important component of the prehispanic commercial economy bringing a variety of goods including food to sell in the marketplace. One important question for reconstructing the prehispanic food chain is whether the commoner households who sold food in the marketplace did so as specialized rural producers, or did they just sell a portion of their normal harvest to periodically meet household needs?

Both were probably true. The regular decline of grain prices at harvest time (Borah and Cook 1958:4) suggests that farmers regularly sold a portion of their crop shortly after the normal agricultural harvest. Nevertheless, commoners would have retained the majority of their maize for their own consumption. Their decision to sell a portion of their crop surplus depended upon a household's overall economic strategy and the factors of production that affected its ability to generate a salable agricultural surplus.[38]

The ability of households to produce for the marketplace depended on having sufficient land and labor for investment in agricultural production. It is here that commoner and elite households differed sharply from one another. Commoner households had limited access to land. Data from the Tepetlaoztoc area in the Basin of Mexico (Harvey 1991; Williams and Harvey 1997) and from the Tepeaca in the eastern valley of Puebla (Martínez 1984:81–85) indicate that average household land holdings ranged from 0.8 to 1.5 ha in size.[39] These were small holdings intended to meet household subsistence needs, but not providing a large surplus to sell in the marketplace. More important than the size of the land holding was its overall productivity and whether it could be cultivated continuously throughout the year. The bulk of agricultural land in Mesoamerica depended on seasonal rainfall and produced only one crop each year. Maize yields from rainfall agriculture normally produced yields from 500 to 900 kg of maize per ha (López Corral 2011) with 1,000 kg/ha being the average upper range of production for good agricultural soils. According to Sanders (1976; Sanders et al. 1979:372–373, table 1), one metric ton (1,000 kg) of maize was sufficient to meet the caloric needs of a household of 4–5 individuals. While households would have eaten and substituted other food for maize, even a 50% maize diet would not have left much of a surplus for sale in the marketplace. While some commoner households might have a small amount of surplus food to sell, the bulk of the population practicing rainfall agriculture probably did not.

Given this situation it is likely that a majority of the agricultural products sold in the marketplace came from households working improved lands or from elite estates. Only a small percentage of agricultural lands throughout Mesoamerica were improved through irrigation or the management of wetland environments.[40] Hydraulic agriculture was important because it is more stable, efficient, and supplied higher yields because a second crop could be cultivated during the dry season doubling annual agricultural yields (Armillas 1971; Mabry and Cleveland 1996:232–233; Parsons 1991; Sanders 1957, 1965; Siemens 1983).

Households with access to hydraulically improved lands had an economic advantage over those that did not. The question of course, is who had access to these lands and the potential surpluses that they could produce?

The land tenure system in the Mexican highlands placed most improved agricultural land in the hands of the elite and the commoner households that supported them. Commoner households who worked elite land holdings typically received a portion of the same land to cultivate for their own support. When these were hydraulic lands it provided households with an opportunity to double-crop and produce a larger surplus than they would under conditions of rainfall cultivation.

In the Basin of Mexico the most productive hydraulic lands were the *chinampa* fields located within and along the margins of the ancient lake system.[41] These fields could be farmed continuously by commoner households as part of both *calpulli* holdings and elite estates (Parsons 1991). *Chinampa* fields could yield 2–3 harvests each year (Palerm 1955; Parsons 1976, 1991), and it is this surplus that probably represents the greatest percentage of food staples sold in market centers throughout the basin. Under this system commoner households could produce some regular surplus for sale in the marketplace. How these surpluses were marketed must have varied. While some households would have taken agricultural products to the market themselves, others probably sold surpluses to contract agents (*tlaciuitiani, tlaciuiti*) and retail grain merchants within the marketplace.

The more important source of agricultural surplus was the private and prebendal estates under the control of elite households. These lands produced large quantities of maize, beans, and other staple foods using corvee labor from commoner households. The production from these lands was intended to support elite families and the cost of the office they held for the state (see Chapter 2). Because elite food needs were small in relation to the quantity of staples produced on their lands, a high percentage of this food would have been converted into other products in the marketplace. These estates had the capacity to supply large quantities of maize and other food staples for sale in the marketplace. While elite households could operate as producer-sellers, there is no evidence that they did so. They more likely operated as commercial suppliers selling their surpluses at discounted prices to retailers rather than marketing them themselves. These estates were an important source of food production but they did not operate, nor were they organized as commercial farms strictly for profit as elite estates did in ancient Rome (Cato et al. 1935; Tacitus 2006). Commercial farms organized for profit in ancient times needed to be organized as contiguous holdings rather than the fragmented and spatially dispersed set of small holdings found in highland Mexico.

DOMESTIC DIVERSIFICATION: THE PRODUCTION OF CRAFT GOODS AND OTHER SERVICES

The fact that most commoner households could not produce a large marketable agricultural surplus was not a deterrent to their participation in the marketplace. It may actually have been an incentive. Households are extremely flexible economic units and can quickly adjust their economic activities to the demands and opportunities available to them. Agricultural households unable to produce a salable agricultural surplus could expand domestic subsistence in other ways by selling craft goods and services. It was the pursuit of these alternative economic activities that produced the diversity of producer-seller households summarized in Tables 5.1–5.5.

It is common for households in agriculture societies to diversity their production regimes and engage in alternative activities to increase their economic well-being. Among the Hausa of Africa, most men identify farming as their profession. Nevertheless, a study of seven rural Hausa communities revealed that 90% of agricultural households engaged in some other income generating activity to improve household economic well-being (M. G. Smith 1955). Farming among the Hausa is based on seasonal rainfall and households regularly used the non-agricultural months to engage in craft production or alternative wage-earning activities.

The same would have been true in prehispanic Mesoamerica where the majority of households practiced rainfall agriculture and had the non-agricultural dry season to pursue alternative income generating activities. While commoner agricultural plots may have supplied sufficient food during normal years, unpredictable fluctuations in rainfall could reduce yields to below subsistence needs.[42] Under these conditions alternative forms of dry season production such as crafting could provide an important supplement during years when crop yields did not meet household needs. The marketplace provided the setting that enabled households to diversify their domestic subsistence activities by offering a range of products and services for sale.

Most of the producer-sellers listed in Table 5.5 may also have been involved in agricultural activities at some level. The majority of the

TABLE 5.5: *Types of producer-sellers found in Central Mexican marketplaces*

Types of producer-sellers	Number	Percent(%)
Food producers	15	12.1
Processed food venders	14	11.3
Foragers and collectors	20	16.1
Craftsmen	56	45.2
Service providers	12	9.7
Colonial specializations	7	5.6
Total number of producer-sellers	124	100

venders selling prepared foods were women who may have done so as a compliment to other subsistence activities carried out by their spouses. The same was probably also true for many of the foragers and resource collectors. Service providers such as porters, prostitutes, barbers, and solicitors may have worked more continually since they seem to be an integral part of the operation of the marketplace.

Craft production was one of the most compatible activities for producer-sellers to engage in as an auxiliary economic pursuit to agriculture. It could be carried out as a full-time speciality during the dry season, and as a part-time activity during other times of the year. Furthermore, production tasks in many crafts (e.g. weaving, basket making, stone tool production, etc.) can be broken up into small tasks that can be carried out sequentially over the course of a day or longer when time permits (e.g. Hagstrum 2001). This makes crafting compatible with many different forms of work since it can take place when bad weather or other conditions restrict other activities. Its importance as a household strategy is reflected by nearly one-half of the producer-sellers in the marketplace (n=60), being involved in some form of traditional or new colonial craft production.

CONCLUSIONS

Most discussions of ancient commerce emphasize the importance of professional merchants and long-distance trade without considering the commercial role of commoner households in the economy. The information presented here suggests that commoner households played a dynamic role in the market economies of ancient Mesoamerica. Households produced most of the food and craft goods consumed in the Aztec world. While their individual output was low, their *collective* or *aggregate* level of commercial production was high given the large number of households involved in the marketplace.

The producer-seller took many forms and this chapter has summarized the diversity of commercial activities that prehispanic households engaged in. Evidence for 124 types of producer-sellers can be identified in the early colonial sources that ranged from food production and cooked food venders to foragers, collectors, craftsmen, and service personnel (Table 5.5). While this number is large it probably represents only a fraction of the activities and services that households performed in pursuit of their livelihoods.

The diversity of producer-sellers illustrates three important features of the prehispanic economy. First, it reflects the plasticity of the domestic economy and how households could adapt to both the needs and the opportunities of economic improvement. Households have the capacity to intensify their internal production strategies and can do so without external supervision (Netting 1989, 1993). Second, production of goods for sale in the marketplace was often an important component of the domestic economy. This was especially the case for households with limited access to resources. Aztec households lacking agricultural land turned to intensive exploitation of lake resources (bugs, larvae, algae, etc.) which were processed and sold by women in markets throughout the Basin of Mexico (Durán 1994). The result was that market involvement became an important component of Aztec domestic subsistence strategies. Third and finally, the craft products produced within the domestic economy were often mobilized to meet both utilitarian and wealth good needs within sectors of the institutional economy. Elite households, for example, consumed many of the same types of utilitarian goods as non-elite households. Commoners supplied goods and services to elite households through a variety of means either as purchased items or as part of their *tequitl* and *coatequitl* obligations.

The legacy of this practice can be seen in how artisans were grouped together in tribute cadres or had their craft specialities identified in tribute censuses during the sixteenth century (Prem 1974; Rojas Rabiela 1987). Domestic producer-sellers while independent were indirectly linked to the overall operation of the institutional economy.

The foregoing discussion almost certainly oversimplifies the complexities of the prehispanic commercial world. For example, despite the diversity of household subsistence activities, there was no one-to-one correspondence in the types of activities that they engaged in. Archaeological evidence suggests that while households *might* have pursued a single supplemental economic activity, they more commonly pursued *multiple* commercial and subsistence activities to insure that household needs were met. Instead of practicing a single craft activity, domestic craftsmen often engaged in multi-crafting where two or more craft activities were carried out alongside one another within the same household (Hirth 2009c; Shimada 2007). Multi-crafting households frequently used related or complementary technologies to produce different arrays of goods. The emerging pattern for Mesoamerica is one of multi-crafting households that engaged in a mix of part-time subsistence activities to supplement agriculture. What these activities consisted of depended on the opportunities and resources available to individual households.

The Aztec world revolved around the marketplace where household producer-sellers interacted with both full-time professional merchants and household consumers. The question that remains to be answered is whether the commercial relationships observed in the Basin of Mexico existed elsewhere in Central Mexico at the time of the Spanish conquest. While difficult to answer, the information from Huexotzinco, Puebla suggests that they did. A survey of twenty-three communities in the Huexotzinco *altepetl* reveals that over 25% of tribute-paying households were engaged in some form of craft production or service activity in addition to farming. Chapter 6 examines the world of retail merchandisers who engaged in commerce at the regional and inter-regional level across western Mesoamerica.

6

The professional retail merchants

Professional retail merchants also existed in prehispanic society. Two features distinguish retail merchants from the producer-sellers discussed previously. First, these merchants engaged in commerce on a full-time basis as the primary means of earning their livelihood. While some producer-sellers may have practiced their trade on a full-time basis, most did not.[1] Second, many of these merchants were retailers in the modern sense; they bought or procured goods from others for resale at a profit. Although it may seem cumbersome to apply this modern terminology to prehispanic merchants, it is useful to do so because it identifies their role within the production-distribution network in terms that are compatible with their modern and premodern counterparts elsewhere in the world. Did merchants act as intermediary resellers at multiple levels in the distribution chain or did they obtain goods directly from producers for resale to consumers? Answering this question will clarify the structure of prehispanic economic relationships across the Aztec economic world.

Retail venders appear to have been a regular feature of both permanent and periodic prehispanic marketplaces. They had assigned locations in the large daily markets of Tlatelolco, Tenochtitlan, and Tlaxcala. While they were not shopkeepers in the sense that this institution developed in the early colonial period, they were regular outlets for the goods they sold to consumers. Identifying who these retailers were is a difficult task. Nevertheless, there are indications for thirty-nine classes of retailers in the sources as well as individuals at the fuzzy margins of retailing that include producer-sellers who engaged in small-scale retailing as an auxiliary activity.

The presence of retail activity raises the problematical issue of how merchants obtained the goods they resold. Retail selling is dependent upon two conditions: the presence of differential pricing structure and the development of a supply chain or procurement network through which goods were mobilized. The development of a commodity supply chain was a critical step in the evolution of a commercial system from one centered on producer-sellers who sold small quantities of specialized goods, to one involving more diversified retailing. To address this issue, three forms of commodity acquisition are examined and evaluated: contact acquisition, mobile procurement, and brokerage acquisition.

THE IMPORTANCE OF INDIGENOUS RETAILING

Retail sales establishments are so common in our society that what they represent for the development of commercial systems is often overlooked. The appearance of retailing indicates that the economic system has sufficient levels of demand to support merchants dedicated to procurement and resale distribution. Permanent retail outlets appear when the demand for goods becomes both large and continuous (Plattner 1989b:185). Vance (1970:16) has argued that advent of retail trade marked the end of family self-sufficiency. While this perspective is incorrect from a historical perspective,[2] it underscores the role that retail marketing had in supplying the needs of local populations. Merchant retailers service local demand by undertaking the costs of assembling commodities available for sale. The appearance of retail merchants can lead to subsequent economic developments including the extension of consumer credit, differential pricing, and the secondary marketing of local goods.

It is significant that the level of retail trade found in the Basin of Mexico at Spanish contact was comparable in scale, but not in structure, to that found in Europe at the same time. Retail trading in London, England, for example, did not begin to grow significantly until the middle of the sixteenth century coincident with the city's rapid urban growth.[3] The primary reason given for the development of London's retail trade establishments was the increase of an urban population with the disposable income to purchase luxury goods (Davis 1966:55). Important for this discussion is that the large and diverse system of retail trading found in the Basin of Mexico appears to predate the growth of retailing in London by several hundred years.[4]

It is not surprising that the complexity of prehispanic retail trading has been overlooked. In the prehispanic world most retail transactions occurred within a set of permanent and rotating marketplaces. Professional retailers were mobile and moved regularly between them. Largely missing from prehispanic societies were the isolated shop-based enterprises common in European cities.[5] Europe had a guild-based production system where craftsmen sold the goods they produced from the same shops where they worked. Craft guilds did not exist in Mesoamerica and scholars who apply this term to the Aztec economic world (Berdan 1989:89; Katz 1966:49; León-Portilla 1962:30,43) do so incorrectly without understanding the organizational differences. High costs of transportation made selling out of dispersed shop-based establishments inefficient and unfeasible. Instead retailers concentrated economic transactions in the marketplace and absorbed the transportation costs of moving goods to the consumers assembled there.

While Spanish accounts discuss the marketplace, they do not describe its internal structure or how venders actually plied their trade. The Spanish were more concerned with the type and quantity goods sold (Cortés 1962:87–88; Díaz del Castillo 1956:215–217; López de Gómara 1966:159–160) than they were with commercial structure. They were unconcerned with how the indigenous population supplied themselves as long as their economic strategies did not compete with Spanish interests. The information on retailing presented below is based primarily on a careful examination of Sahagún and the Coyoacan market sources for indications of retail activity.

IDENTIFYING INDIGENOUS RETAILERS: THE *TLANAMACAC* AND *TLANECUILO*

Information on the indigenous retail trade can be gleaned from several sources: the terminology used to describe indigenous venders, descriptions of the types of local and imported products offered for sale, the diversity of goods sold, and references to the way that retail venders conducted their affairs. By combining these criteria it is possible to compile a composite picture of indigenous and early colonial retail activity.

Terminology is an excellent place to start because of the specificity that *Nahuatl* provides for distinguishing between the types of commercial venders operating in society. As discussed in Chapter 4, separate terms are used for producer (*tlachiuhqui*), merchandiser (*tlanamacac*), retailer (*tlanecuilo*) or importer (*oztomecatl)* of goods. The two words used most often to describe retail merchants are *tlanecuilo* and *tlanamacac*. The first of these, *tlanecuilo*, was used specifically to designate retail and possibly even wholesale trade (Carrasco 1980:258; Rojas 1995). That the *tlanecuilo* was closely associated with commercial activity also is indicated by its use to refer to a usurer, that is, someone who loaned money at interest (Siméon 1991). The term *tlanecuiloqui* designated an individual who was a reseller and businessman (Siméon 1991). Sahagún (1961:42) identifies retail selling as a merchant activity when he says the "merchant is a seller (*tlanamacani*), a merchandiser (*tlanamaca*), a retailer (*tlanecuilo*) ... one who profits, who gains." Although the terms *tlanecuilo* and *tlanamacac* seem to be used interchangeably for retail selling, the former is sometimes associated with larger or more continuous commercial activity.

The term *tlanamacac* also was used as a generic reference to a merchant vender. Like other *Nahuatl* words, venders were identified by the products they sold. Thus individuals who sold chile peppers were called *chilnamacac* created by combining the word for chile (*chilli*) with the word ending for vender (*-namacac*). While *tlanecuilo* always refers to a retail merchant, the economic status and activities of the *tlanamacac* are not always apparent. Instead, the term may be used interchangeably for both a producer selling his goods or a retailer. Close examination of the sources suggests that this is not a result of imprecise or vague usage, but rather reflected the complex world of prehispanic commercial tradesmen. In a number of instances the *tlanamacaque* (plural of *tlanamacac*) appear to fulfil both production and retail functions. I believe this reflects an economic environment in which tradesmen moved fluidly between producing goods for sale in the market-place as producer-sellers, and purchasing goods from others that they offered for sale alongside their own. While many of these reselling activities may have been small in scale, they reflect a situation where individuals actively identified and capitalized on the opportunity to resell goods for profit within the marketplace. It is this commercial aptitude that created the diversity of economic behavior found in the prehispanic world.

To identify the economic activities that *tlanamacac* tradesmen engaged in requires scrutinizing the activities they were involved in. A characteristic of retailer venders was their propensity to diversify the variety of goods they sold to meet the needs of different customers. This feature is valuable for distinguishing retailers from producer-sellers, who produced a narrow range of items for sale. For example, a farmer producing chili peppers to sell in the marketplace might raise one or two different varieties depending on local growing conditions. Retailers not involved in raising the crop had more flexibility and could buy more types of chili peppers to offer their customers. Diversity of items sold, therefore, is a useful correlate of retail activity. It is this retail function that is captured for the chili retailer (*chilnamacac*) who offered twelve different types of chiles for sale.[6] As Sahagún describes,

He sells mild red chilis, broad chilis, hot green chilis, yellow chilis, *cuitlachilli, tenpilchilli, chichioachilli*. He sells water chilis, *conchilli*; he sells smoked chilis, small chilis, tree chilis ... He sells hot chilis, the early variety ... He sells green chilis, sharp-pointed red chilis, a late variety

(Sahagún 1961:67)

Diversity in the types of products offered for sale is a key feature in all of Sahagún's descriptions of market retailers. For the chili pepper retailer, diversity is expressed in the different sizes, colors, types of chilis (e.g. tree chilis, water chilis, smoked, etc.) some features of which (*cuitlachilli, tenpilchilli, chichioachilli*) remain unknown because these terms cannot be deciphered. Diversity of offerings is the same feature seen in retail venders in contemporary markets. This description could be read as a composite description of multiple producer-sellers selling the chiles that they raised except for the fact that retailers also sell imported products.

The sale of imported goods is an important feature for distinguishing retail venders. Imported goods carried higher prices because of the cost of transportation. Nevertheless, imported goods are referred to with some regularity and reveal how retail venders sought to diversify what they offered for sale. Again take the case of Sahagún's description of the retail chili pepper vender:

He sells ... [chilis] from Atzitziuacan, Tochmilco, Huaxtepec, Michoacan, Ana-uac, the Huaxteca, the Chichimeca

(Sahagún 1961:67)

In contrast to the producer-seller who grew chili peppers native to the region where he lived, the retail vender had the flexibility to sell varieties from as many different regions as he could buy them from. The chili retailer described here bought and sold chili from the Basin of Mexico (Anauac), and distant regions including the Chichimeca in the far north, the gulf coast (Huaxteca) to the east, the valley of Atlixco in Puebla (Toch[i]milco), the valley of Morelos to the south (Huaxtepec), and the area of Michoacan to the west[7] (Macazaga Ordoño 1978; Peñafiel 1885). The distances involved for importing chilis into the Basin of Mexico range from 65 to 100 km for Morelos and Atlixco, to over 200 km to reach the Huaxteca and Michoacan.[8] Transporting goods from these distances is incompatible with production strategies of producer-sellers but accords well with long-distance wholesale and retail trading practices.

Finally, there also are indications that permanent retailers existed in the larger marketplaces. Cortés (1962:87) refers to shops in the Tlatelolco marketplace where apothecaries, barbers, and food venders sold goods or practiced their trade. These locales, like stalls in contemporary market-places, provided locations where retail merchants could store goods, a unique feature of large daily markets of major cities. Retailers were also present in periodic markets held on five, eight, or thirteen day schedules. Good information is available from the mid-sixteenth-century market-place at Coyoacan which was under the supervision of the native lord, Juan de Guzmán. Coyoacan had an important market at the time of the conquest (Blanton 1996), which met weekly throughout the sixteenth century.[9] Despite its periodicity, the market was well populated with venders selling local products as well as itinerant retailers who resided outside of Coyoacan and moved between marketplaces across the Basin of Mexico.

Tables 6.1 and 6.2 summarize the retail dealers found in the Basin of Mexico during the early colonial period and provide a snapshot of what the commercial system looked like at Spanish contact. While some venders had begun to sell Spanish imports, the essence of categories remain prehispanic. Three things are striking about these categories. The first is the number of retail dealers and the diversity of goods that they dealt in. Thirty-nine types of retail dealers can be identified that bought and sold everything from food to high-value textiles and jewelry (Table 6.1). Second, there was a clear penetration of Spanish goods into the indigenous marketplace. In some cases this was a result of Spanish tradesmen entering the market, but in others it was the addition of Spanish goods to the range of items sold by indigenous merchants. Third and finally, there appears to be a degree of overlap in the sale of food and staple commodities between retail dealers and individual producer-sellers. This may reflect the shift of some producer-sellers into small-scale retailing to expand their business dealings (Table 6.2).

RETAIL DEALERS IN THE PREHISPANIC MARKETPLACE

To simplify the discussion of retail vending, dealers are grouped into seven broad categories based on the type of merchandise sold (Table 6.1). No pretense is made that this list is complete. It almost certainly is not, but it does provide a useful perspective on the complexity of economic relations reflected in resale commerce. The six categories of retail venders that carried over from prehispanic times consist of food venders, dealers of staple goods, textile and apparel suppliers, high-value merchandisers, speciality venders, and commercial specialists. The seventh category is a composite of new retailers that emerged during the early colonial period

TABLE 6.1: *Retail dealers and venders*

Category	Nahuatl term	Notes
Food dealers		
Cacao dealer	cacauanamacac, *tlanecuilo*, anoço *oztomecatl*	"an importer, a traveler with merchandise … or retailer who sells in single lots (Sahagún 1961:65)." Sells multiple imported varieties.
The *chia* and/or wrinkled *chia* dealer	chientzotzolnamacac chienecuilloque	"he sells the Chontal variety … from Oztoman, the Tlahuica variety, the Itziocan variety (Sahagún 1961:75)" Sells multiple imported varieties. (Anderson et al. 1976:144)
Chili pepper dealer	chilnamacac, *tlanecuilo*	"a retailer. He sells … those from Aizitziuacan, Tochmilco, Huaxtepec, Michoacan, Anauac, the Huaxteca (Sahagún 1961:67)" Sells multiple imported varieties.
Bean dealer	henamacac	[He sells] yellow beans, red beans, brown beans, white beans … pinto beans … wild beans (Sahagún 1961:66)" Sells multiple varieties
Fish dealer	michnamacac michnecuylo	A dealer and retailer (Rojas 1995:233). Sold a large variety of species
Fruit retailer	suchiqualnamacac	"a retailer … He sells … green maize … cactus fruit … sweet potatoes … sapotes … plums … cheeries … tomatoes (Sahagún 1961:79)." Sells multiple products
Maize dealer	tlaolnamacac, *tlanecuilo*	"He sells, that of Chalco, of Matlatzinca, of Acolhuacan … of the Tlalhuica, of Tlaxcalla, of Michoacan (Sahagún 1961:66)." Sells multiple non-local varieties.
Tomato dealer	tomanamacac	"sells large tomatoes … serpent tomatoes, nipple-shaped tomatoes … coyote tomatoes, sand tomatoes (Sahagún 1961:68)." Sells multiple varieties
Amaranth dealer	uauhnamacac, *tlanecuilo*	"an … owner or a retailer … He sells … white amaranth … bird

(continued)

TABLE 6.1: *(continued)*

Category	Nahuatl term	Notes
		amaranth ... black amaranth ... colored amaranth (Sahagún 1961:67)." Multiple varieties sold.
Dealers of staple goods		
Tobacco dealer	picienamacac	"sells fine tobacco ... small tobacco ... chews it. And some prefer wormwood (Sahagún 1961:94)"
Salt dealer	iztanamacac, iztanecuilo	"The salt retailer displays salt ... sells salt balls, salt bars, salt ollas ... thin bars ... grains of salt (Sahagún 1961:84)" Sells multiple non-local varieties.
Medicine dealer, Apothecary	panamacac	"He sells all things, medicines, herbs, wood, stones, milk, alum ... on a reed mat (Sahagún 1961:85–86)." Also a physician.
Wood dealers, split oak dealers	quauhnecuilo, auatlatzaianamaca	required having stocks in the marketplace (Durand-Forest 1971:124), Identified in Coyoacan
Gourd bowl retailer	xicalnamacac, *tlanecuilo*	"a retailer ... He sells Guatemalan gourd vessels ... bowls from Mexico ... from Tlaxcala ... from the Totonaca, Huaxteca, Tlahuica ... Michoacan (Sahagún 1961:77–78)." Imported varieties sold.
Small basket dealer	tananamacac	"sells ... palm leaf baskets; small reed, leather, wooden baskets; woven reed coffers (Sahagún 1961:84)." Sells multiple products
Textile and apparel suppliers		
Sandal dealer	cacnamacac, *tlanecuilo*	"the retailer (*tlanecuilo*) asks excessively high price for them (Sahagún 1961:74)." Sells multiple varieties.
Women's skirt cloth seller	cueitli, huipilli	Sold a variety of goods in the marketplace (Feldman 1978a:222; Durand-Forest 1971).
Fiber cape retailer	icçotilmanamacac, *tlanecuilo*	"a traveler [or] a retailer (Sahagún 1961:75)" Sells multiple varieties, an itinerant

Category	Nahuatl term	Notes
Cotton retailer and importer	ichcanamacac, ichcanecuilo, anoço *oztomecatl*	"an importer, or a retailer . . . which come from the hot countries (Sahagún 1961:75)" Sells multiple non-local varieties.
Large cotton cape dealer	quachnamacac, *tlaquixtiani*, motlaquixtiliani	"one who sells them in single lots . . . an importer, a distributor (Sahagún 1961:63)."
Decorated cape dealer	tlâmâchtilmanamacac, *tlanecuilo*, ueicapan tlacatl	"a retailer, a seller of worked capes . . . he seeks out that which he sells (Sahagún 1961:63)." Multiple designs varieties sold
Dye dealer	tlapalnamacac, chiquippantlacatl	"He sells . . . cochineal . . . chalk, lampblack . . . chicle, red ochre . . . opossum tail . . . bitumen, resin, copal (Sahagún 1961:77)"
Thread dealer	yaualli ycpatl	Sold round balls of thread (Durand-Forest 1971:123).

High-value merchandisers

Category	Nahuatl term	Notes
Greenstone dealer	chalchiuhnamacac	"He sells the different stones . . . turquoise, green stones, blue obsidian . . . jet, in pearls, in opals (Sahagún 1961:60)"
Necklace seller	coznamacac, cozcatetecpanqui	He sells necklaces of . . . obsidian, or rock crystal, of amethyst, of amber . . . of cast gold . . . necklaces of Castile (Sahagún 1961:86–87)" Sells multiple non-local varieties
Shell seller	coyolli	Sold a variety of types of shells (Feldman 1978:222)
Feather dealer, with basket	ihuinamacac, puchtecatl	"a merchant–the man with a basket . . . He sells . . . trogonorus, the troupial, the blue cotinga (Sahagún 1961:61)" Sells multiple non-local varieties.
Slave dealer	teocoani	"a leading merchant. He excels [all others]; his wealth is [as] possessor of slaves (Sahagún 10:59)" Dealers in the Azcapotzalco marketplace (Sahagún 1959:45).
Gold jewelry dealer	tlapitzalnamacac	"He sells shield-shaped necklaces . . . golden bracelets (Sahagún 1961:61)."

(continued)

TABLE 6.1: *(continued)*

Category	Nahuatl term	Notes
Bird skin dealers	tomitl	listed as a dealer in Tlatelolco (Durand-Forest 1971:124). Included tribute imports
Specialty venders		
Paper dealer, importer	amanamacac, amaoztomecatl	"the paper importer–sells coarse paper, bark paper, maguey fiber paper. He sells Castilian paper (Sahagún 1961:78)" Sells multiple varieties
Rubber seller	olnamacac	"sells rubber–balls of rubber, wide masses . . . thin masses (Sahagún 1961:87)." Sells an imported product.
Commercial specialists		
Peddlers	*tlacôcoalnamacac*	"a retailer of diverse objects . . . procures them in wholesale lots, who peddles them. He sells metal, paper, scissors, knives, needles cloth (Sahagún 1961:91)."
Banker, exchange dealer	tlapatlac, teucuitlapatlac	"The exchange dealer is a merchant . . . When silver coins are exchange . . . he gives very even weight . . . he gives good measure (Sahagún 1961:61–62)."
Retailers of Spanish goods		
Musical instrument dealer	mecahuehuetl	Dealer in indigenous and imported stringed instruments (Durand-Forest 1971:124).
Hat dealer	nequaceualhuiloni	A dealer in Spanish style sombreros (Durand-Forest 1971:124).
Silk cloth seller	seda (Spanish)	Sold imported silk from China as finished goods (Durand-Forest 1971:123).
Wool cloth dealer	tomitilmatli	listed as a dealer in Tlatelolco (Durand-Forest 1971:123)
Wheat dealer	trigonamacac, *tlanecuilo*	"a field owner . . . or a retailer. He sells white wheat (Sahagún 1961:71)."

Note: Total number of retailers listed is 39

with the new Spanish economy. This is followed by a discussion of producer-sellers who also appear to have had some small retail functions (Table 6.2).

Retail food venders

There always was a market for food in pre-industrial societies even where high levels of self-sufficiency were the norm. It is not surprising, therefore, to find retail dealers who trafficked in food products. Food shortages resulted from periodic droughts which were a regular part of the prehispanic landscape (Durán 1994:238; Stahle et al. 2011). Similarly food surpluses were needed for large-scale festivals and the consumption of food by laborers in public works projects (Durán 1971). As a result retail food venders operated in all the main food groups: basic grains and legumes, fish suppliers, fruit and vegetable providers, and as purveyors of speciality foods such as cacao.

Ten food retailers are mentioned in Sahagún (1961) as *tlanecuiloque* who trafficked in imported goods. Six of these dealt in basic grains and legumes stored in large public and private granaries (Batalla Rosado 2012; Hernández Xolocotzi 1949; Rojas 2012; Smith 2012a, 2012b). Maize and beans were the two fundamental food staples in Mesoamerica and retail venders dealt in both of them. The maize dealer (*tlaolnamacac*) sold a variety of both local and non-local maize (Figure 5.2) and is identified as a retailer (*tlanecuilo*) and importer who sold maize imported from regions as far away as Michoacan (Table 6.1). The bean dealer (*henamacac*) likewise sold a wide variety of beans grown in different areas both in and surrounding the Basin of Mexico (Figure 6.1).

Retail dealers also sold *chia* and amaranth. The *chia* dealer is identified as a retailer in the Coyoacan tax documents (*chienecuilo*) while the wrinkled *chia* dealer (*chientçotzolnamacac*) sold both local and imported grain coming from as far away as Oztoman, Guerrero located 160 km to the south (Sahagún 1961:75). The amaranth dealer (*uauhnamacac*) is identified as a retailer (*tlanecuilo*) who sold different varieties of grain. This retailer is specifically identified as an individual who bought grain, stored it, and sold it over time. According to Sahagún (1961:67) the amaranth dealer "sells the new crop, [or] he sells that which is two years old, three years old, etc." This probably reflects normal seasonal arbitrage practiced around the world where dealers bought grain in bulk at harvest when prices were low and then sold it when prices were high later in the year. The fact that amaranth was stored for three years or more suggests

FIGURE 6.1 The bean dealer

these dealers owned large granaries like those described for tribute grains (Rojas 2012). The final grain retailer (*tlanecuilo*) mentioned is the wheat dealer (*trigonamacac*), who sold wheat introduced after the conquest alongside other indigenous products.

Three fruit and vegetable retailers also are identified in the sources. The fruit dealer (*suchiqualnamacac*) is identified as selling over twenty-five different varieties of fruits (Sahagún 1961:79) which characterize the range of products from different regions imported and sold by fruit retailers. Fruit was regularly imported from Morelos during the early colonial period by merchants from the Basin of Mexico following prehispanic patterns (Gibson 1964:359). Another important vegetable retailer was the tomato dealer (*tomanamacac*). Tomatoes do not travel well and must have been grown locally. Nevertheless, the tomato dealer was again represented as selling from 7 to 12 different varieties and colors indicating the use of multiple sources of supply. As discussed earlier, chili dealers (*chilnamacac, tlanecuilo*) also were retailers who sold chilis imported from seven different areas up to 150 km or more from the Basin of Mexico (Sahagún 1961:67).

Only one food retailer sold meat products and that was the fish seller (*michnamacac*). These venders are listed as both *tlanamacac* and *tlanecuilo* in the Coyoacan tax records indicating that at least some fish sellers operated on the retail level (Anderson et al. 1976:138–149; Rojas 1995:233).

The final food retailer sold cacao used to prepared different types of specialty drinks[10] (Coe and Coe 1996). All the cacao consumed in the Basin of Mexico was imported from regions at lower elevations. In this regard, Sahagún specifically identified the cacao vender as both an importer (*oztomecatl*) and retailer (*tlanecuilo*) who sold cacao from Guatemala, Tochtepec on the Gulf Coast, and Zacatollan in the modern state of Colima. Xoconochco on the coast of Chiapas was a major producer of cacao during both prehispanic and early colonial times (Gasco and Voorhies 1989). The Guatemala cacao almost certainly came from the coastal plain located 900–1000 km southeast of the Basin of Mexico. Cacao was a valuable product that retailers continued to buy from indigenous merchants well into the colonial period (Coe and Coe 1996; Gibson 1964:348).

Dealers of staple goods

Six retail venders sold nonperishable items that were regularly consumed and in continuous demand by all households. The majority of these venders were identified as *tlanecuiloque* or retailers of imported goods. The first of these was the salt dealer (*iztanamacac, iztanecuilo*) who sold salt which was an important supplement in the prehispanic diet. The salt dealer (Figure 6.2) sold salt in different forms including bars, balls, and

FIGURE 6.2 The salt dealer

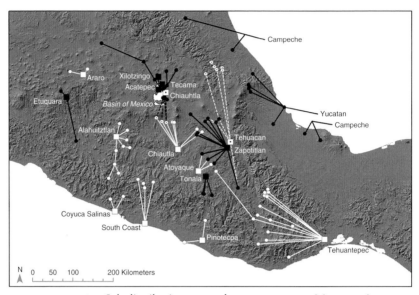

FIGURE 6.3 Salt distribution networks across western Mesoamerica

individual grains. The salt produced in the Basin of Mexico was made by leaching earth along the margins of Lake Texcoco (De León 2009; Parsons 2001) and was a briny variety that was sold in ceramic vessels. Salt dealers also sold "grains of salt–good, very white (Sahagún 1961:84)." White fine grained salt was sea salt from the coast, probably the northeastern Yucatán peninsula which exported salt all the way to the Basin of Mexico (Kepecs 2003). The salt dealer is described as a person who, "sets out on the road, travels with it, goes from market to market, makes use of markets (Sahagún 1961:84)." They represent traveling retailers and/or wholesalers who sold salt in major markets across the highlands. Figure 6.3 illustrates the range over which these merchants traveled selling salt as reported in the *Relaciones Geográficas* (Acuña 1984a–1987).

Medicine was another retail product. The apothecary (*panamacac*) sold a wide variety of herbal and natural remedies. These included fourteen kinds of different herbs together with types of wood, stones, milk, and alum. While he may have collected some of these, it is more likely that he relied on a selection of forager-collectors to provision him with a number of natural remedies. Some of the concoctions sold were undoubtedly prepared by the apothecary himself since Sahagún (1961:86) indicates that he sold things cooked in pots like skunk excretion. In this regard the medicine seller was probably part retailer and part producer-seller.

FIGURE 6.4 The tobacco dealer

Another probable retailer was the fine tobacco vender (*picienamacac*) (Figure 6.4). This individual is listed as a tradesman both by Sahagún (1961) and in the Coyoacan market documents (Anderson et al. 1976). In fact all three merchants involved in the tobacco trade (smoking tube maker, cigar seller, and the fine tobacco vender) form a continuum from producer-seller to the retail tobacconist. Tobacco had important ritual, social, and medicinal value and the fine tobacco seller prepared tobacco for chewing as well as smoking. What is important is that good tobacco was not grown within the Basin of Mexico, but was raised in lower and warmer elevations such as the Mexican Gulf Coast. It is likely, therefore, that all three tradesmen obtained their tobacco from importers who brought it from production areas to sell in leaf form. The individual recipes or blends, of course, were their own preparations. But whether tobacco was resold in unprocessed form or processed into cigars or smoking tubes, it was bought for resale by these tobacco tradesmen.

Serving vessels were an important part of household material inventories. While most were manufactured and sold by local craftsmen, some vessels were imports that were sold by retailers. The gourd bowl seller (*xicalnamacac*) was one such retailer. Gourd bowls were a beautifully carved, painted, and decorated service ware that was light enough to be imported from great distances. Sahagún (1961:77) identifies the gourd bowl seller as a retailer (*tlanecuilo*) who imported bowls from areas including Morelos, Puebla, Tlaxcala, as well as distant regions such as Michoacan, the Gulf Coast, and Guatemala. The diversity of products from distant regions again underscores the retail function of this vessel vender.

The small basket seller (*tananamacac*) was a retail vender who also sold containers. This individual is identifiable as a retailer based on the diversity of items sold. He is listed as selling eight different classes of baskets made out of four different types of materials that include reeds, palm leaf, wood, and leather (Table 6.1). The sale of baskets made of four different materials suggests that they were bought for resale from the craftsmen who worked in these different types of materials.

Another trade that was consistently referred to as a retail activity was the wood vender. The retail trade in wood products probably was related to the need to keep stock on hand to meet construction needs while at the same time taking orders for the delivery of future goods. Although Sahagún (1961:81) identifies the wood seller (*quauhnamacac*) as a feller of trees, the Coyoacan market documents consistently identify wood dealers as retailers (*quauhnecuilo*) instead of producer-sellers and they are placed in this category for that reason.[11] Some firewood and charcoal venders may also have been retailers because of the distances needed to transport these commodities. Testimony from five indigenous tribute payers[12] given in the 1553 visit of Oidor Gómez de Santillán state that it took a full day to collect and transport a single load of firewood to supply their lord (Carrasco and Monjarás-Ruiz 1976:29–49). Under these conditions, quantities of firewood or charcoal would have to be stockpiled to meet the continuous demand for cooking fuel. Retail venders could easily develop under these circumstances.

Textile and apparel retailers

Textiles were a major component of the indigenous economy since they were used as a form of currency and stored wealth as well as garments. The result was that a good deal of retail activity was associated with selling both the raw materials to produce textiles as well as finished goods. Eleven retailers can be identified; several are identified as *tlanecuiloque* while others sold imports or goods procured for resale. Cotton and maguey garments were the main items sold in the market. Because cotton was the more valuable of the two, much retail activity was directly or indirectly related to cotton textiles. By the early colonial period both wool and silk were also sold in the marketplace following traditional selling practices. Since both of these fibers were quickly incorporated into New World production systems it is difficult to determine how much of the wool and silk sold by these dealers were imported products and how much were produced locally.

The most important fiber was cotton which was sold by the cotton seller (*ichcanamacac*) who is clearly identified by Sahagún as a retailer (*ichcanecuilo*). Cotton was imported into the Basin of Mexico from lower, hotter areas such as the Valley of Morelos, the Gulf Coast, or the Pacific coast (Berdan 1987:252). Raw cotton was widely traded across Mesoamerica where it was spun into thread and manufactured into textiles. The extent of these distribution networks is illustrated in Figure 2.6. The inter-regional movement of the raw cotton allowed some areas such as Teotitlan del Camino, the Texcocan town of Tequisistlan, and towns in the Valley of Oaxaca to specialize in cotton textile production even though they did not grow cotton locally (Berdan 1987:258). Fray Alonso de Zorita underscored this inter-regional relationship when he observed that some towns in New Spain "did not grow cotton but worked it into a very good cloth. This excellent cloth was made by the people of the tierra fria (Zorita 1994:187)." It was through the importers and retailers that raw cotton was sold in the marketplaces so that this cloth could be produced in highland towns.

All prehispanic textiles were woven by women working in their homes where they dyed the fiber, spun the thread, and wove it into cloth on narrow backstrap looms (Figure 2.5). Factory style textile workshops did not exist during prehispanic times and while much of this work was carried out within the household, women occasionally purchased auxiliary materials used in textile manufacture from retailers. One such dealer was the dye seller (*tlapalnamacac*) who sold an array of dyes to color fiber prior to spinning. Twenty-six different organic and mineral substances were sold by this class of venders who, based on the quantity of items sold, probably purchased them for resale from different forager-sellers.[13] According to Durand-Forest (1971:123) balls of spun thread were sold in the marketplace by the thread dealer (*yaualli ycpatl*). Since women did all the spinning, this thread must have been purchased from the women spinners (*tzauhqui*) and specialized feather thread spinners (*hihujnamacac*) identified as producer-sellers in Chapter 5 (Table 5.3). Women could also buy products from the rabbit hair dyer (*tochominamacac*) for spinning into yarn (Table 5.3). The reselling of spun thread is a strong indication of retail activity.

Finished apparel was also sold in the marketplace. Many finished garments were manufactured in domestic settings and the presence of a vender with a stock of garments for sale in the marketplace implies a retail tradesman. Several types of garments are mentioned. The fiber cape vender (*içotilmanamacac*) was identified both as a retailer (*tlanecuilo*) and an itinerant vender who sold different types of capes. The cotton cape dealer (*quachnamacac*) was both an importer and distributor. His retail activities are identified by the statement that he sold capes "in single lots, who offers them separately (Sahagún 1961:63)" as would occur when selling to individuals in the marketplace.

Two of the most prominent apparel tradesmen were the dealers who sold decorated capes (*tlâmâchtilmanamacac*) and the textiles sold by principal merchants (*ueicapan tlacatl*). These individuals were retailers who the ethnohistoric sources indicate imported goods from long-distance trade missions. Fourteen different designs are itemized by Sahagún (1961:63–64) as sold by these retailers underscoring their role in inter-regional trade. Another retail tradesman was the vender who sold women's skirt cloth and other types of garments (*cueitli, huipilli*) in the marketplace (Durand-Forest 1971).

Footgear was sold both by the craftsmen who made them and specialized retailers (*cacnamacac*). Footgear venders are identified as retailers both by their classification as *tlanecuiloque* and the diversity of sandals sold in different types, styles, and colors. The retailers were identified with scorn by Sahagún (1961:74) as individuals who asked "an excessively high price for them. He praises them, brags of them, sells them by talking."

Three retailers can be identified who sold goods of Spanish origin. The first of these was the silk cloth vender (Durand-Forest 1971:123). These venders may have been reselling either Chinese imports procured through trade with the Philippines (Schurz 1918), or locally produced cloth. Silk raising was established in indigenous communities in Central Mexico and in Oaxaca in the early to mid-1530s (Borah 1943:9–11) so these references could refer to a combination of retail and producer-sellers of locally manufactured silk cloth.[14] Another vender mentioned is the hat seller (*nequaceualhuiloni*) who sold imported Spanish style sombreros (Durand-Forest 1971:124). The third interesting retail vender was the wool cloth vender (*tomitilmatli*) who sold cloth woven in traditional fashion from the wool of Spanish sheep (Durand-Forest 1971:123). We know that people in some highland villages raised their own sheep to free themselves from a dependence on imported cotton (Borah and Cook 1958:26). Whether these goods were woven in traditional means in domestic settings or in factory-like *obrajes* organized by Spanish weavers is unclear. Unfortunately the early colonial document that identifies all three of these retail venders (Durand-Forest 1971) is not precisely dated[15] so it is difficult to assess how the rise of *obrajes* after 1550 affected the types of both wool and silk goods sold in the marketplace.

High-value merchandisers

Wealth goods not only were visual symbols of social rank, but also were storable wealth that could be readily converted into other goods. Wealth goods entered the Basin of Mexico through the state tribute system and inter-regional trade. For example, it is estimated that as many as 278,400 textiles entered Tenochtitlan each year as annual tribute[16] (Berdan 1987:241) many of which were distributed to state functionaries as gifts or as payments for services. Once distributed, these textiles could be sold or exchanged in the marketplace for other goods. This movement of textiles provided the textile retailers (*quachnamacaque, tlâmâchtilmana-macaque*) with a ready source of both supply and demand for plain and decorated textiles depending on the system of circulation and the need for goods by individuals receiving payment from the state.

Seven types of wealth goods were sold in the marketplace that based on Sahagún's discussion imply a degree of retail trade. In some cases these venders sold exotic imported raw material that craftsmen used in wealth good production. In other instances venders sold a diversity of imported finished goods that were bought for resale.

Finely carved green stone objects called *chalchihuites* were one of the most valued substances across prehispanic Mesoamerica.[17] It is not surprising, therefore, that the greenstone dealer (*chalchiuhnamacac*) had a prominent place in the marketplace. Many of the dealers who sold greenstone objects probably were producer-seller lapidaries who carved them into finished pieces. Others, however, sold green stone in unprocessed form. These individuals appear to be retailers based on the diversity of raw material that they sold which included several types of greenstone, as well as jade, turquoise, pearls, serpentine, blue obsidian, jet, and opal. A second vender dealing in imported raw material would be the shell dealer. This vender is identified in the marketplace by both Feldman (1978a:222) and Durand-Forest (1971:124). Furthermore, Hernández states that "they sell … a thousand kinds of shell that at one time were preferred as a considerable dowry and to adorn and lend dignity to attire (Varey 2000:76)."

Two retailers are identified by Sahagún as selling finished wealth goods. The first of these was the *coznamacac* or necklace dealer. This individual is specifically identified as a seller of finished necklaces rather than as a lapidary who made them (Sahagún 1961:86–87). The jewelry he sold was either bought as finished pieces from lapidaries or contracted with lapidaries for later resale. Jewelry was listed as made from a wide array of precious and semiprecious materials including cast gold, amethyst, rock crystal, obsidian, amber, and by the time Sahagún wrote his account, even imported glass beads from Spain. Another vender who sold finished products was the *tlapitzalnamacac*. This vender trafficked in finished gold necklaces and bracelets and is identified as a person who sold rather than manufactured these valued goods.

Feathers were highly valued, especially the green, blue, and red feathers of tropical parrots and macaws. The green feathers of the quetzal bird were reserved for use by kings and their highest retainers. Feathers like textiles were items of commerce and the feather craftsmen who worked as independent artisans (*calla amanteca*) sold the goods that they manufactured in the marketplace (Sahagún 1959:91–92). These craftsmen would have obtained the feathers that they worked either directly from the merchants who imported them or through marketplace purchase. It is not surprising, therefore, that the feather dealer (*ihuinamacac*) was a prominent vender in the marketplace. Some of these venders sold feathers from local birds that they raised themselves (Table 5.3); others were retail merchants who sold more exotic feathers to the spinners, apparel makers, and craftsmen who used them. Bird skins and jaguar hides also were sold by a separate class of retail venders whose place in the Tenochtitlan market is represented on the Goupil-Aubin map by the drawing of a bird skin (*tomitl*) (Durand-Forest 1971:124). How these venders obtained these imported skins is unclear although they probably purchased them for resale from the long-distance vanguard merchants (see Chapter 7).

The final retailer dealing in wealth goods was the slave dealer (*teocoani*). Slave dealers were both retailers and long-distance merchants. They set out on long-distance trade expeditions specifically to obtain slaves for resale. Although some slave dealers were located in the Tlatelolco market (Feldman 1978a:222), most were found in the specialized slave markets of Azcapotzalco and Itzocan (Berdan 1975:197–198;

Durán 1994; O'Mack 1985:134). Male and female slaves could be bought for house service, weaving, transportation, or even field work. Manual service, however, was not the primary object of slavery. The greatest profit was made from slaves used for ritual sacrifice.

Specialty venders

There were three retail dealers in the marketplace who sold speciality items. Two of these were identified as retailers because they sold imported goods while the third sold a wider diversity of goods than he could have produced himself. The first was the paper vender (*amanamacac, amaoztomecatl*) which was used both in rituals and by scribes who recorded information in codex-style (screen-fold) books. Indigenous paper was produced in a variety of areas from both the *amate* (*amatl*) tree and from maguey (genus *Agave*) (Sandstrom and Sandstrom 1986:27). Morelos is well known for its prehispanic manufacture of *amate* paper (Hernández 1959:1:83–84) although it was manufactured in other areas of Mesoamerica as well. In the Basin of Mexico paper was an import sold by both retailers and importers (*amaoztomecatl*). Their operation as retailers is evident in that they also sold Castilian paper which was purchased for resale.

A second retailer was the rubber seller (*olnamacac*). Rubber like paper was an import, probably from the Gulf Coast. Although Sahagún (1961:87) identified this individual as an owner of rubber trees, it is likely that retail tradesman also sold imported rubber purchased from itinerant venders. The final speciality vender was the musical instrument dealer (*mecahuehuetl*) which the Goupil-Aubin map places in the marketplace where these items were sold (Durand-Forest 1971:124). The vender is represented by a guitar which reflects the new Spanish demand for string instruments in addition to indigenous instruments such as drums, rasps, different types of bells, rattles and a variety of wood, clay, shell, gourd flutes, and trumpets that also would have been sold. Since the manufacture of all these instruments requires specialized skill, the diversity of items sold suggests that this vender bought them from other craftsmen for resale.

COMMERCIAL SPECIALISTS: BANKERS AND PEDDLERS

Two other commercial specialists need special comment because they do not fit neatly into the other economic categories discussed thus far. They were the bankers and peddlers of the prehispanic world. Neither made anything for sale and like other retailers lived exclusively off the profits of their exchanges. Nevertheless, they are unique in the roles they played within and outside of the marketplace.

The exchange dealer (*tlapatlac*) was both a banker and a dealer in gold (*teucuitlapatlac*) (Sahagún 1961:61–62). Exchange dealer is the term used here because he also functioned as a money changer which is expressed by Sahagún as giving good weight, presumably in silver coins in the form of reales.[18] This individual was a rich man: specifically a merchant with possessions, goods, and gold. Part of his role was as a retailer who sold gold dust in semi-transparent quills (Feldman 1978a:222).

Several different types of goods served as money before the conquest. Cacao beans were used the most often, but plain cotton mantles, copper axe monies, and gold in transparent bird quills also had this function. The primary function of exchange dealers was to facilitate the conversion of these different currencies into one another. Although cacao beans are not mentioned specifically by Sahagún, exchange dealers may have regularly reduced currencies of high value (e.g. mantles, axe monies, gold dust quills, etc.) into smaller, fractional currencies such as cacao that could be used in the marketplace. This would have facilitated and amplified the frequency of exchange between venders and consumers. It supplied an important service within the marketplace as well as providing an opportunity to make a profit by discounting the value of goods received in exchange. Cotton mantles, for example, were grouped by size into three categories valued at 60, 80, or 100 cacao beans, which allowed plenty of opportunity to negotiate the relative value of pieces based on individual quality.

The conversion of goods may not have been restricted to the four forms of commodity money described earlier. It may have extended to an array of different products depending on the breadth of their economic interests. If exchange dealers restricted their conversion activities to wealth objects only, then their field of accumulation would be relatively narrow. If, however, they also converted basic commodities such as maize into cacao, then the commodities they accumulated would be much more diverse. Whether they traded in basic commodities is unknown but it would have been an important conduit for resource accumulation if they did.

The peddler (*tlacôcoalnamacac*) was a separate and unique category of vender who differed in two important ways from other prehispanic retailers (Figure 6.5). The first was that peddlers were mobile retailers (Geertz 1963; Plattner 1975, 1989b). Rather than the marketplace as

FIGURE 6.5 The merchant peddler

their place of sale, peddlers ranged widely across the landscape primarily selling outside the marketplace. This is somewhat paradoxical given the existence of a law that all sales had to take place within the marketplace. While it is possible that peddlers moved from marketplace to marketplace this would not have been the main market for their goods since they always were at a disadvantage vis-a-vis stationary venders who sold a greater diversity of wares. Instead, the *tlacôcoalnamacac* probably was a peddler in the traditional way that we see them ethnographically. They were small-scale mobile retailers who sold house-to-house across regions where marketplaces did not exist or were difficult to reach, most notably in rural areas of low population density. That Sahagún (1961:91) mentions the peddler in the context of the marketplace implies that they may also have frequented them although this probably was not the main focus of their operation.

The second notable feature of peddlers is that they sold a wide array of household goods. These included everything from metal, paper, and knives to scissors, needles, cloth, and bracelets. They offered a one-stop product line for the things that households could use including a few goods imported from Spain. Sahagún (1961:91) makes the point of stating that the peddler was, "a retailer of diverse objects: one who procures things in wholesale lots." Cross-cultural ethnographic studies show that the success of a peddler depends on having a diversity of useful items to sell since it was difficult to anticipate the needs of widely dispersed households (Plattner 1975). The prehispanic peddler probably solved the problem in the same way that modern peddlers do, by taking as wide an array of merchandise with them as possible. Sahagún (1961:91) underscored this strategy when he said, "he stores–as many as he can." The peddler's place of storage on the road was his *otlachiquiuitl* or stout cane cargo basket.

Sahagún's identification of peddlers (*tlacôcoalnamacac*) is the only reference that we have for them. It could be argued that peddlers were a post-conquest economic development since Sahagún (1961:91) lists them as selling metal and scissors, imported Spanish items that Hassig (1985:239) says were only sold by Spaniards. While possible, two lines of reasoning suggest that these mobile merchants followed an older pre-hispanic tradition. First, peddlers serve a very important provisioning function for low density rural populations around the world (Davis 1966:237; Geertz 1963:12; Mintz 1964:275; Plattner 1975; 1989b; Rush 1990:58; Vance 1970:73). Households in mountainous areas or scattered across the tropical lowlands would have welcomed peddlers to supply them just as they have in recent times (Kicza 1983; Redfield 1939:48). Second, Spanish peddlers would not have been readily welcomed or accepted in small, isolated native communities. It is likely, therefore, that peddlers were part of the prehispanic landscape, servicing low density areas across Mesoamerica.

The itinerancy of prehispanic peddlers was an adaptation to commercial demand and they traveled to where they could find consumers. Itinerancy was a general feature of all retailers who moved from one rotating market-place to another. It is within the context of itinerant selling that another type of itinerant tradesman needs to be mentioned, the itinerant craftsman. This was a craftsman in the role of producer-seller who traveled with the tools of his trade to produce goods for consumers who wanted them, usually in the marketplace. All producer-sellers had the ability to travel from market to market, but few did so with the specific intent of producing goods on-demand. Most traveled with finished goods because of the cost of transporting both goods and the raw materials to make them. One exception to this pattern was the itinerant obsidian craftsman who traveled with preformed obsidian cores that were used to produce the parallel sided obsidian blade which was the cutting tool of choice throughout Mesoamerica.

Sahagún (1961:85) identified the obsidian seller (*itznamacac*) as a regular producer-seller in the marketplace without specifying him as an itinerant craftsman (see Chapter 5). Archaeological research at the site of Xochicalco, Morelos has established the presence of itinerant obsidian craftsmen operating across Central Mexico as early as AD 650.[19] These artisans traveled across the highlands producing obsidian blades on-demand for consumers in the marketplace (Hirth 2006c, 2008b, 2013b). There were several reasons why this particular craft was well suited for itinerancy. First, although obsidian blades have high utility, the annual demand for them was low, around 10–15 blades for any one household depending on their length (Hirth 2006c:table 9.12). Second, the production of obsidian blades required special skill and could only be produced by a specialized artisan. Third and finally, obsidian blades dull quickly and are thus best produced at the point-of-purchase. The unusual features of this craft made itinerant obsidian crafting a viable form of mobile selling with craftsmen moving from marketplace to marketplace to sell blades on demand.

CRAFTSMEN AND PRODUCERS WITH RETAIL FUNCTIONS

One of the earliest retailers to appear in London, England during the sixteenth century was the master guild craftsman who, instead of producing all of the products he sold, bought goods from importers or other journeyman producers operating on a freelance basis (Davis 1966:63). This transformation was brought about by the pressure to sell goods at lower prices. In the process, guild craftsmen were transformed into craftsman-retailers. This transformation took place in London as a result of three conditions: urban population growth, a rise in disposable incomes, and an increase in the variety of goods offered for sale (Davis 1966:55). While craft guilds did not exist in the Basin of Mexico, the same three conditions existed there with the growth of the Aztec state.[20] It is not surprising, therefore, to see parallel economic developments in the New and Old Worlds in the way goods were sold.

As discussed in the Chapter 5, most craft goods were sold by producer-sellers who differed from retailers in that they manufactured the products sold. The scale of production was not an important variable in defining the producer-seller since they all worked within their households. Most producer-sellers across Central Mexico combined the production of craft goods or other auxiliary economic activities with agriculture to produce food for household consumption (Martínez 1984; Prem 1974).

What the economic sources suggest is that retail activity was not restricted only to individuals identified as *tlanecuilo* retailers. Some craftsmen also appear to have engaged in small-scale retail trade, that is, buying items with the purpose of reselling them. This created an interesting, if fuzzy group of individuals who were both producer-sellers and retailers. The line between the two categories was a thin one, and there is every reason to suspect that some degree of overlap would be found in any complex market economy that involved both purchase and barter. In some cases the identifications are explicit. Producers and their production activities are described and then they are identified as individuals that also bought and sold things. The things they sold can be the same or different from what they manufactured. When explicit statements are absent, retail activities can be inferred from the diversity of local and/or imported goods sold just as they were for other retailers. This is a very subjective approach, but it provides the only opportunity to probe retail patterns in the historic sources.

The resale of goods by craftsmen alongside the ones that they manufactured parallels the fluid commercial environment like that mentioned for London in the early sixteenth century. It indicates that individuals were free to explore new economic opportunities where they existed. Table 6.2 identifies six producer-sellers that also appear to have engaged in some retail selling. While I believe that light auxiliary retailing was a widespread practice within the marketplace, these were the craftsmen and

TABLE 6.2: *Producer-sellers with retail functions*

Category	Nahuatl term	Notes
Basket dealer	chiquiuhnamacac	Sells a variety of baskets in many shapes and for varied uses (Sahagún 1961:83)
Carrying basket seller	otlachiquiuhnamacac	"a possessor of stout cane baskets, buyer and seller of stout cane carrying baskets (Sahagún 1961:86)."
Reed mat dealer	petlanamacac	"He sells ... reed mats, painted reed mats ... palm leaf mats ... deep baskets ... seats with backs ... sleeping mats ... pillows (Sahagún 1961:86)." Sells multiple products
Turkey dealer	totolnamacac	"a livestock owner, a buyer and seller ... he sells Mexican turkeys, birds of Castille (Sahagún 1961:85)." Both dealers and producer-sellers
Glue seller	tzacunamacac	Probably both dealers and producer-sellers (Sahagún 1961:87).
Container dealer	zoquinanauhqui	"a dealer in clay objects, sells ollas ... pitchers ... candle holders; bowls– wooden bowls ... ladles; combs ... frying bowls (Sahagún 1961:83)." Multiple varieties sold.

food venders who engaged in it regularly enough to be noticeable in the economic descriptions. Auxiliary retail selling could have been a side-effect of barter and this possibility is discussed here.

Three of the six tradesmen listed in Table 6.2 made and sold containers used for storage in prehispanic households. Container manufacturing was a big business and it was as diverse as the individual needs of the people who consumed them. It is not surprising therefore, that it is in the area of container merchandising that producers also took on some retail functions. The pottery seller (*çoquinanauhqui*) was ubiquitous in the market-place for two reasons: pottery vessels were needed to prepare and store food and pottery vessels frequently break. While the pottery seller is often described as a producer-seller (*çoquichiuhqui*), his expanded role as a container retailer is evident in the list of goods sold. He is also described as selling non-ceramic goods that he did not produce including wooden bowls, hair combs, and merchant's bowls which were light weight gourd containers. The diversity of items sold also exceeds the range of goods that would normally be produced by a ceramic specialist. Over a dozen items are listed as sold by this vender including water jars, cooking pots, service bowls, brasiers, frying bowls, pitchers, plates, and ladles, all in different colors, polishes, and finishes. Adaptation to the changing colonial world is also evident in the sale of non-traditional goods that included ceramic candle holders and glazed ceramics (Sahagún 1961:83).

Basketry was another important craft that provided containers for domestic and non-domestic use. Two types of basket makers are identified in the sources. The *chiquiuhnamacac* was the large basket seller and from the descriptions clearly was a producer-seller (Sahagún 1961:83). Although his speciality was the manufacture of palm leaf baskets he also is listed as selling baskets made of reeds and spiny plants as well as nine different classes of baskets with different usages including holding hot foods and tortillas.

Another basket craftsman who had additional retail functions was the cargo basket seller (*otlachiquiuhnamacac, otlachiquiuhchiuhqui*). This craftsman manufactured baskets used specifically by merchants and porters for transporting goods. These ranged from simple baskets with tumplines for light weight cargo, to baskets mounted on frames for long-distance trade or heavy transport. While clearly identified as a maker of baskets, he is also identified as a person who was a possessor, buyer, and seller of stout cane carrying baskets[21] (Sahagún 1961:86). This vender was a merchant's merchant; he made and modified carrying baskets to the specifications of the carrier while also buying other baskets to have on hand for sale or to fit to carrying frames of his own manufacture. Having stocks of cargo baskets on hand was important for supplying long-distant merchants like the Aztec *pochteca* who left on trade expeditions in large groups[22] (Sahagún 1959).

The reed mat dealer (*petlanamacac*) also dealt in cane products. The reed mat was another indispensable product that was spread out on the floor to sit on during the day and sleep on at night. Many of the venders who sold reed mats also produced them. Others, however, appear to have been retailers based on the diversity of goods sold. These included plain and painted mats, mats of different size, thickness, and shapes as well as pillows, seats, stools, seats with backs, all of these goods in different colors. Besides mats they also sold a range of baskets as another category of cane product.

The glue seller was an unusual case. He was a specialist who Sahagún (1961) reports as a digger of plant roots, but who very likely also was a small-scale retailer. We know, for instance, that there were more types of mastic than just glues made from plant roots. These included resin glues made from pine and copal, bitumen mastic, and glues made from orchids and the bat excrement tree (Berdan 2006). It is unlikely that this vender procured all of these raw materials since they had to be collected from different environmental zones.[23] Instead, he likely relied on other forager-sellers to supply ingredients (see Table 5.2) to prepare glue recipes for different usages.

The final producer-vender with indications of having engaged in periodic retail activity was the turkey seller (*totolnamacac*). This individual is identified as both a livestock owner and a "buyer and seller, a breeder of turkeys (Sahagún 1961:85)." The retail function is clear whether these individuals bought chicks to raise to mature birds, or only dealt in mature birds.

THE QUESTION OF SUPPLY AND RETAIL PROVISIONING

A simple but important question is what was the mechanism used by retailers to obtain the goods that they sold? Retailers by definition are individuals who resell goods that they buy from others. They cannot exist without a source for discount buying or direct procurement. How they mobilized the resources that they sold, therefore, is a fundamental question for understanding how the economic system was structured and interconnected with the broader social and political system. Sources of supply certainly varied with the merchandise sold and where it came from. It is useful, therefore, to think of supply in terms of accumulating local or imported goods. Several alternative mechanisms may have been used to obtain both local and imported goods.

One way retailers may have accumulated stocks of local goods for sale was by *direct contact* with the individuals who produced them. Small-scale retailers can build their networks of supply through normal market interactions by offering credit or extending other forms of preferential treatment to establish bonds of economic dependency (Mintz 1964; Platt-ner 1989a). All thread, for example, was spun by women in their homes so the retailers who sold balls of thread (Durand-Forest 1971:123) would have purchased them directly from individual spinners. This type of supply network may have been the way that apothecaries (*panamacaque*) and dye dealers (*tlapalnamacaque*) obtained key ingredients from individual suppliers to make dyes and medicines. In these instances the relationship would link retail dealers and the producer-foragers who supplied them.

While individual contracting might supply individual dealers with some goods it probably would not be sufficient for retail dealers who trafficked in large quantities of food staples like maize, *chia*, amaranth, beans, and chili peppers. These foods were consumed in every household and would have moved through the marketplace in relatively high volume. Establishing contact with many small households would have been an inefficient way to mobilize resources. Not only did commoner households consume the majority of the maize and beans that they produced, but they would be reticent to sell off any anticipated surplus at a discount rate below normal selling price. While agricultural households did sell some of their normal surplus at harvest time, this would have fluctuated from year to year depending on the growing season and the size of individual harvests. A network of small-scale agricultural providers and the potential fluctuations in supply associated with them was not conducive to developing a predictable supply network for a high volume retail trade in basic grains.

A better source of supply for large stocks of food was by *direct contact* with elite estates.[24] These estates produced large quantities of maize, beans, and other staple food, but not cacao, tobacco, and other items that elite wanted to consume. The solution was to sell surplus food from their estates in the marketplace for the goods that they needed (Carrasco 1978). It is here that the retail dealers for maize (*tlaolnamacac*), beans (*henamacac*), and other staples could count on buying large stocks of food for later sale. Elite estates certainly varied in size depending on the social histories and rank of the elite families that controlled them. From a subsistence perspective these estates had more land and produced significantly more consumable food per household member than commoner households. The result was that elite estates could produce large surpluses during good years, and even small surpluses during bad years. Patterns of elite consumption and the desire for sumptuary goods probably resulted in elite households selling agricultural surpluses to *tlanecuilo* food retailers.

Food retailers, therefore, probably actively sought to buy surpluses produced on prebendal lands because they provided access to larger and more predictable sources of supply than could be mobilized from small holders. The implication, of course, is that grain retailers would have needed to maintain their own storage facilities either in their houses or somewhere in the cities where they lived. One such storage locale in Tenochtitlan was the area of Petlacalco located along the western causeway leading into the city. According to Sahagún the Petlacalco was where,

> there was stored all the food. Dried maize grains thus were kept in wooden grain bins: more than two thousand [measures of] grains of dried maize–a store of twenty years for the city. And in wooden storage bins were dried beans, chía, amaranth seeds, wrinkled chía, salt jars, coarse salt, baskets of chilis, baskets of squash seeds, and large squash seeds
>
> (Sahagún 1979b:44).

Kobayashi (1993:39) feels that the Petlacalco was the central storage district in the Basin of Mexico and may have held as many as 2,000 *cuezcomates* or granaries for storing maize, beans, amaranth, and *chia*. Even if the Petlacalco held only one-tenth of Kobayashi's (1993) estimate, excess storage capacity would have been available for use by private grain dealers if they could have rented or constructed their own granaries since only twenty-four tribute granaries were needed to store *all* of the annual tribute from the four tribute provinces in the Basin of Mexico[25] (Barlow 1949; Berdan and Anawalt 1992:2:34, 37, 47, 95).

Retailers also may have accumulated stocks through *mobile procurement* strategies. While peddlers are characterized as individuals who sell things, that is only part of the story. They also take local products in exchange for the items they sell, accumulating stocks of specific commodities that can be sold at higher prices elsewhere (Pearson 1991; Plattner 1975). Peddlers around the premodern world have been used to mobilize goods from rural areas that might not otherwise enter the marketplace. The same may also have been true of *tlanecuilo* retailers who moved from marketplace to

TABLE 6.3: *Categories of venders in the Coyoacan marketplace in the mid-sixteenth century*

	Producer-sellers (*tlachiuhqui*)		Retailers (*tlanamacac*)		Retailers (*tlanecuilo*)		Status unclear		Total venders	
	No.	%	No.	%	No.	%	No.	%	No.	%
Document 1	19	43.2	14	31.8	10	22.7	1	2.3	44	100
Document 2	17	44.7	12	31.6	8	21.1	1	2.6	38	100
Document 3	16	38.1	19	45.2	6	14.3	1	2.4	42	100
Document 4	24	58.5	9	22.0	8	19.5	0	0.0	41	100
Total	76	46.1	54	32.7	32	19.4	3	1.8	165	100

Note: The category retailers (*tlanecuilo*) includes individuals identified as formal merchants (*oztomeca*)

marketplace following the rotation of regional marketplaces. Tax records from the Coyoacan marketplace indicate that retail venders were a regular segment of its resource providers (Table 6.3). *Tlanecuilo* retailers or merchant importers (*oztomeca*) made up almost 20% of the market population and could have been over 50% of all sellers if *tlanamacac* venders also engaged in commercial retailing.[26] The movement of retailers from marketplace to marketplace would have allowed them to buy goods for resale in the same way that peddlers accumulated goods in small quantities that could be exchanged with retailers to supply themselves with goods.

A third way that retailers may have accumulated goods was through *brokerage or exchange acquisitions* that functioned in the same way that exchange dealers (*tlapatlac*) could have taken stocks of grain in exchange for cacao. Modern ethnographic studies indicate that many farmers are "target marketers" who sell food surpluses to make specific purchases for things (Plattner 1989a). In prehispanic Mesoamerica individuals entering the marketplace had three options for procuring goods: 1) barter the goods they had for the commodities they wished to purchase, 2) sell their goods in the marketplace and then use the cacao beans received in payment to purchase the goods they wanted, or 3) convert their goods directly to cacao beans with an exchange dealer and make their purchases with the money received. While the first two options would have maximized returns, they were slower and depended on finding buyers for the goods they sold in sufficient quantities to meet their needs. The third option, even if practiced for only a small percentage of the time, would have enabled specialized dealers to accumulate stocks of goods on a periodic basis as opportunities arose. Implicit in this model is that food retailers would have been able to buy food at some type of discount rate to make this process profitable.[27]

All three of these acquisition mechanisms relate to acquiring local goods. But what about non-local goods? How did retailers procure those? The answer is relatively simple: either they bought goods directly from merchant importers or from the state if goods were available from tribute stocks. While long-distance exchange is discussed in Chapter 7 it is useful to consider the general relationship that retailers had with merchants who trafficked in imported goods.

It is interesting that many of the imported items sold in the Tlatelolco marketplace also appear on the imperial tribute lists. One possibility, therefore, is that some of the high-value items obtained through state tribute were sold to retailers who marketed them to the broader society. While it is a possibility, there is no indication that this was a regular feature of state-merchant relationships. Instead there is good information that goods moved regularly between regions through trade.[28]

Four retail dealers are specifically mentioned by Sahagún as being importers. These were cacao dealers, cotton venders, cotton cape sellers, and paper dealers (Table 6.1). They are discussed as importers who sold their goods directly in the retail venue of the marketplace. They are not identified as intermediary wholesalers and if they were, it was in addition to their role as direct procurement retailers. This implies a preference for maintaining short commercial networks with importing serving retail objectives rather than wholesaler functions. This is also implied for the decorated cape seller (*tlamachtilmanamacac*) who, while not specifically described as an importer, is an individual retailer (*tlanecuilo*) who "seeks out that which he sells (Sahagún 1961:63)," implying that he travels to areas to buy and import the goods sold.

Nevertheless there is evidence to suggest that some importers operated as wholesalers, buying goods in distant areas, transporting them over space, and then reselling them to retailers in destination areas for distribution to local populations. An alternative strategy for importers would be to sell imported goods directly to consumers in local market-places that they traveled to. While possible, this would not work well for merchants who take local products (e.g. cotton, cacao, salt, etc.) to sell in distant areas since it would require arranging local housing and longer stays in the distant areas where they market their goods. More efficient would be sell their goods to established retailers in destination areas utilizing the advantages of differential pricing inherent in long-distance trade.

According to Feldman (1978a:220) the *Nahuatl* word for wholesaler was *tlaquixtiani* and appears restricted to merchants dealing in large cotton capes and high-value goods. Several researchers have speculated that wholesalers existed across Mesoamerica from western Mesoamerica to the Guatemala highlands (Ball and Brockington 1978; Feldman 1978b; Rathje et al. 1978); unfortunately there is little direct evidence to support these assertions. Importers who may have operated as wholesalers include those merchants who moved raw cotton and salt from areas where they were produced to areas where they were consumed. Until more information is available on the structure of retail merchandising the role of the wholesaler in the prehispanic economy will remain an interesting but nebulous commercial possibility.

PROFILING THE RETAILER

The marketplace is often described as a place where anonymous buyers and sellers came together for commercial transactions. While this view correctly captures the idea of economic equality within the marketplace, it misses the rich internal social dynamic that helped to structure economic interaction. Social relationships reinforced economic relationships as individuals in the marketplace fulfilled multiple roles depending on their economic objectives. Buyers and sellers, for example, often forge enduring economic relationships to guarantee continuous access to supplies of goods (Mintz 1964). It is the diversity of overlapping social and economic relationships that defines the richness and complexity of an economic system.

Larry Feldman (1978a:221) characterized the Central Mexican market economy as dominated by producer-sellers with only three types of retailers selling goods they did not produce: amaranth, *chia*, and worked capes. While Feldman was correct in his assessment of producer-sellers, he underestimated the role of retailers in prehispanic marketplaces. Professional retailers (*tlanecuiloque*) were an important fixture in the marketplace providing consistent access to a diverse array of goods (Carrasco 1980; Rojas 1995:231). They bought and sold merchandise with the goal of making a profit and operating with an economic philosophy not unlike that found in modern societies.

The retailer in Aztec society can be identified by three features: the terminology used to describe them, the diversity of goods sold, and the distances over which goods moved. Using these three criteria together helps avoid over-reading the meager sources and is better than relying on a single line of evidence to infer retail activity.[29] The diversity of goods offered for sale is an especially good indicator of retail activity for two reasons. First, producer-sellers usually did not produce the array of foods or craft goods that are listed for retailers. They were constrained by the varieties of food and natural resources available within the regions where they lived. Second, producer-sellers usually did not travel far beyond the limits of their local market region to sell goods unless strong factors compelled them to do so. I am not implying that craftsmen and other producer-sellers only manufactured a narrow array of goods because this was not the case. Archaeological evidence indicates that crafting households often engaged in several forms of production under a rubric referred to as multi-crafting (Hirth 2009a, 2009d; Shimada 2007). Nevertheless, most domestic production was small-scale and aimed at providing supplemental support for the household rather than producing to meet the demands of the market.

The analysis presented here suggests that retail vending was a common feature of highland commercial activity. Thirty-seven venders were identified as retailers in the sources, thirty-nine if the peddlers and exchange merchants/bankers are included in the equation (Table 6.1). This stands in sharp contrast with Feldman's identification of only three prehispanic retail venders. Out of the 37 retail dealers, 28 (76%) were concentrated in three economic areas: food provisioning (n=10), textiles (n=11), and wealth goods (n=7) (Table 6.1). The presence of retail venders in the food trade makes sense because of the need to maintain stocks of food in highly urbanized areas like the Basin of Mexico. Textiles along with other wealth items including feathers, jade, and cacao[30] were the basis of wealth in prehispanic society and their high value-to-weight ratio enabled them to be transported long distances across Mesoamerica. The eight other retail venders found in the sources were for high demand (e.g. salt, firewood, etc.) or light weight products that were easily transported over space (e.g. paper, tobacco, rubber, gourd bowls, etc.) (Table 6.1).

Six producer-sellers were identified that also may have some retail functions (Table 6.2). These venders are problematic. They were all described as *tlanamacaque* who appear to have sold a greater diversity of wares than they could have produced. There are three reasons for believing that some producer-sellers also had retail functions. The first is that producer-sellers, like all of the individuals selling in the marketplace, were commercial opportunists. Producer-sellers could easily slide into retail behaviors if they came across the opportunity to buy goods at a price that they could resell at a profit. This may have led to a diversification in the goods individual venders had for sale.

Second, some of the goods sold by producer-sellers went beyond the technologies they would normally employ in their individual production specialities. For example, the container dealer in addition to selling traditional pottery vessels also sold combs, wooden bowls, candle holders, and glazed ceramic wares. Combs and wooden bowls were made from different materials and glazed ceramics introduced during the colonial period represent a different technological system that required higher firing temperatures and a different form of kiln to produce them.

Third and finally, the structure of marketplace interaction would have fostered the emergence of small-scale retail behavior as a natural byproduct of the indigenous exchange economy. Many household consumers were target marketers who brought staple goods like maize, fruit, or craft goods to sell or barter for the goods that they needed. Even with the use of cacao as a form of money, direct barter would have been a quicker and more expedient way to make purchases *if* venders took goods in exchange for the wares that they sold. In many cases they probably did. Direct barter of goods was a regular feature of highland markets in the state of Michoacan throughout the twentieth century were it can still be found (Foster 1948:158; Eduardo Williams, personal communication 2013). It was a dimension of market transactions in Oaxaca (Beals 1975:137) and the state of Puebla up through the 1950s (Angel Garcia Cook, personal communication 2008).

There is every reason to believe that it was also a regular practice in prehispanic markets. Bartolomé de Las Casas (1967:I:368) observed that cacao was used to even out barter exchanges among native populations. Diego Durán (1971) is explicit in the use of barter as a widespread practice used by merchants to accumulate wealth where he states,

The third and least glorious manner of [rising in the world] was that of becoming a merchant or trader, that of buying and selling, going forth to all the markets of the land, bartering cloth for jewels, jewels for feathers, feathers for stones, and stones for slaves, always dealing in things of importance, or renown, and of high value
(Durán 1971:138).

As a widespread practice among commoner populations, Durán (1994) recounts how the practice of barter was fundamental to the survival of the Aztec population immediately after the founding of Tenochtitlan,

They fished and collected frogs and shrimp and all kinds of edible things. They collected even the worms that thrive in the water and the mosquitos that breed on the lake surface. And knowing which were market days in each town, they went to these market places as hunters and fishermen and bartered the fowl and fish and water creatures for beams and boards, for small wood, for lime and stone

(Durán 1994:45–46).

In both of these accounts barter is cited as occurring between buyers and venders within the marketplace. With barter as a widespread practice, market venders would naturally accumulate small lots of goods in the course of daily transactions that they could use or sell secondarily as retail goods depending on commercial opportunities. In this way regularly consumed staple foods like grains, chili, fruits, and vegetables can gain currency as bartered goods in market transactions. The important point here is that barter could foster secondary retail activity among producer-sellers in the normal course of selling their wares.[31]

Multiple ethnohistoric (Carrasco 1970; Durán 1994) and ethnographic studies (Beals 1975) indicate that women were always important traders in the marketplace. The same was true in prehispanic times. While Sahagún's descriptions of market venders frequently have been interpreted as male this may not be true since many of the illustrations accompanying his text indicate that women were prominent in multiple levels of commercial activity.[32] Males and females are represented about equally in the illustrations portraying different types of venders. Dealers selling high-value goods like feathers, jade, metal items, and cacao are represented as male as are those who sold Spanish related products. Females were closely associated with retail activities such as the sale of food; they are also shown as the retail venders for maize, beans, chía, amaranth, gourd seeds, fruit, and prepared foods including atole and chocolate (Figures 5.2, 5.3, 5.4, 6.1). Women are shown selling cotton capes, maguey capes, and tobacco (Figure 6.4). The maize seller in Figure 5.2 is a women sitting in front of a large sack of grain. What Sahagún's illustrations portray is the internal division of labor within households, with one member of the family involved in production while another sold finished products (Carrasco 1970, 1978:575–578). How this labor was divided along gender lines varied with the type of production and availability of labor within the household.

This study has used variability in the types of goods sold and where they originated as two criteria to identify retail activity. An alternative interpretation of Sahagún's discussion of *tlanamacac* venders would be that they are an aggregate descriptions of many different producer-venders selling in the marketplace rather than diversified retailers. I do not believe that they were, but even so, it would not diminish the level or complexity of commercial behavior found in the Aztec economic world. We know retailers existed from the specific *Nahuatl* terminology used to describe them. Reading Sahagún's *tlanamacac* venders as summary descriptions of producer-sellers would only imply a more active and vivid role of small-scale household producers in moving goods within and between regions than is argued in Chapter 5.

The fabric of prehispanic economic life was a rich and intricate weave of small-scale farmers, craftsmen, retailers, importers, and long-distance merchants. The *tlanecuiloque* were a regular part of that commercial landscape. They were retail venders of both genders who bought and sold goods for profit often on a full-time basis. The retail sale of staple goods was the basis of their domestic economy and livelihood. That they sold staple goods is logical since these goods were consumed on a continual and regular basis within society. As such they were a vital component of the marketplace offering a dependable supply of consumables to households that needed them. Chapter 7 examines the prominent and highest ranking merchants in Aztec society: the *pochteca* and *oztomeca* merchants who moved wealth goods over long distances. These were the merchants that served the state while they served themselves. They were the prominent *nouveau riche* of the Aztec economic world who supplied many of the wealth goods that enriched the state and dazzled the Spanish upon their arrival in the New World.

7

Merchant communities and pochteca vanguard merchants

Oztomecatl: The vanguard merchant is a merchant, a traveler, a transporter of wares, a wayfarer, a man who travels with his wares. The good vanguard merchant [is] observing, discerning. He knows the road, he recognizes the road; he seeks out the various places for resting, he searches for the places for sleeping, the places for eating, the places for breaking one's fast. He looks to, prepares, finds his travel rations
(Sahagún 1961:60).

Merchants who engaged in long-distance trade to obtain high-value luxury goods occupied a special place in prehispanic society. Sahagún in the preceding epigraph identifies the specialized long-distance merchant as an *oztomecatl* or vanguard merchant. Contemporary scholars have generally referred to long-distance merchants as *pochteca* because it is the most frequently used term found in the literature.[1] Determining which term to use for long-distance merchants appears to have been situational. Based on Sahagún's Tlatelolco informants, *pochteca* was a general term that referred to *all* types of professional merchants while *oztomeca* referred specifically to specialized, long-distance merchants.[2] Durán (1994) and other sources regularly used the term *pochteca* when the context was clear that they were referring to merchants in distant lands. Care needs to be exercised when reading the sources since modern scholars often uncritically associate all discussions of the *pochteca* with specialized long-distance traders instead of recognizing that the term embraced an array of retail tradesmen and merchandisers operating at many different geographical scales.

Three features mark the unique activities of all *pochteca* vanguard merchants. First, like retailers discussed in Chapter 6, they were commercial specialists who engaged in commerce on a full-time basis. While some individuals may also have had lands to support their families, the bulk of their income came from their individual entrepreneurial endeavors. Second, the risks of long-distance travel required cooperation between collaborating merchants. The result was that most vanguard merchants resided in internally stratified corporate communities that provided mutual assistance to its members. Third and finally, merchants who engaged in long-distance trade focused on the procurement of wealth goods such as jade, feathers, and richly adorned textiles. These items were important insignias of rank and status within society and a tremendous source of wealth for the merchants who trafficked in them.

This chapter explores the structure of *pochteca* groups that engaged in long-distance trade. It discusses three themes. It begins by examining the internal organization of merchant communities and the towns that contained them. Several communities with known *pochteca* groups are examined which appear to be heterogenous settlements containing merchants involved in both local and long-distance commerce. This is followed by a discussion of the social status of vanguard merchants and the functions that they provided for the society and the state. The discussion concludes with an examination of the ritual lives of vanguard merchants. Two facets of their ceremonial life are examined: the rituals associated with long-distance trading ventures and the role of ritual feasting in status acquisition within the merchant community.

THE ORGANIZATION OF PROFESSIONAL MERCHANTS

Most of the information on professional merchants comes from a few, very specific sources and the logical interpretations derived from them (Durán 1994; Garibay 1961; Sahagún 1959, 1961, 1981b; Zorita 1994). Much of this information, however, deals with the political and religious activities of *pochteca* rather than the economic details of their commercial trade. Even Sahagún's (1959) valuable narrative presented by merchant informants from Tlatelolco is a self-serving account of their service to the Aztec state. Information on their actual economic organization is limited which is unfortunate given the scale of their operations and the challenges they overcame while conducting trade.

The primary goal of vanguard merchants was trade in luxury goods (Figure 7.1). They engaged in this trade both for themselves and as agents of the state. The result was that they accumulated substantial private wealth. Despite their wealth merchants in Aztec society did not have the

FIGURE 7.1 *Pochteca* merchants and their goods

same high social position that merchants had in other Mesoamerican societies like the Yucatecan and Chontol Maya (Scholes and Roy 1968). Vanguard merchants resided in thirteen merchant communities in the Basin of Mexico (Figure 7.2) and were all members of the *macehualli* class regardless of their level of individual wealth (Berdan 1982; Carrasco 1971; M. Smith 2012c; Zorita 1994). Wealth like familiarity can breed contempt and there was considerable envy and animosity of Aztec nobles toward wealthy *pochteca*. As a result merchants hid their wealth and assumed diminutive behavior in public settings lest they be accused of challenging the social authority of the nobles (Berdan 1982:31; Wolf 1959:141).

Nevertheless, the wealth that long-distance merchants procured was vital for the growth of the economy and the operation of the state. The result was that their social status was on the rise at the time of the Spanish conquest. The principal merchants of Tlatelolco were regularly installed to leadership positions in their communities by the *tlatoani* of Tlatelolco indicating the importance of commerce for this city and their close relationship to its ruling elite (Sahagún 1959:1–2). Despite the importance of

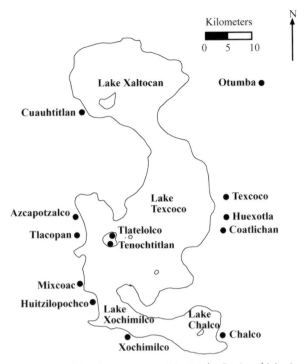

FIGURE 7.2 Merchant communities in the Basin of Mexico

imperial tribute, Tezozomoc attributed the great wealth of Tenochtitlan to the activities of the merchants and artisans who lived there (Acosta Saignes 1945:15).

Merchants had higher status in a number of societies outside the Basin of Mexico. In fact commerce in wealth goods was often in the hands of nobles rather than commoners. Merchants in Cholula were highly esteemed and the most wealthy of these had considerable political influence including the possibility of becoming its *tlatoani* (Carrasco 1966:134–135, 1970; Gaxiola González 2010:186). In the Mixteca being a merchant was an occupation and did not carry with it any class distinction. Wealthy elite of Mixtec society engaged in long-distance trade as did members of the commoner class (Spores 1984:82). The rulers of the Gulf Coast kingdom of Acalan in the state of Tabasco were all prosperous merchants. Francisco López de Gómara, secretary of Hernan Cortés observed that,

[in] the land of Acalán ... the people have the custom of choosing as their lord the most prosperous merchant, which is why Apoxpalón had been chosen, for he enjoyed a large land trade in cotton, cacao, slaves, salt, and gold ... in colored

shells, with which they adorn themselves and their idols; in resin and other incense for the temples; in pitch pine for lighting; in pigments and dyes ... and in many other articles of merchandise, luxuries or necessities

(López de Gómara 1966:354).

Maya merchants who dealt in high-value goods were known as *ah ppolom yoc* and were elite members of society (Chapman 1957a:132; McAnany 2010:256). In the Maya area like the Mixteca, commerce was an economic activity carried out by elite and non-elite alike (Roys 1943:51–52). That Maya elite engaged in commerce is clear from Landa's account of the overthrow of Mayapan where a son of the ruling Cocom dynasty escaped being killed because he was away on a trading venture in the Ulua Valley (Thompson 1970:136; Tozzer 1941:39). Finally, commerce as an acceptable activity is reflected by God L, the Maya deity of trade who takes on regal trappings after AD 900 (McAnany 2013).

The internal organization of merchant groups, like status, varied across Central Mexico depending on the society and their unique history of development. Some Mesoamerican scholars have argued that merchant groups were organized as commercial guilds like those found in medieval Europe (Acosta Saignes et al. 1975:73; Berdan 1975:147, 1982:32, 1986; Carrasco 1980:258; Cunow 1926:275–278; Durand-Forest 1971:114; Kohler 1924; León-Portilla 1962:25; van Zantwijk 1970). This characterization is a result of mistaking form with function. Merchant guilds in the Old World originally were voluntary associations with membership based on mutual commercial interest (Epstein 1991:62). Their functions were similar to those of merchants everywhere: to facilitate trade, set prices, mediate risk, regulate merchant behavior, and facilitate the conditions to accumulate wealth (Chakravarti 2005; Epstein 1991:130–135; Grief 2000:262; Jain 2005; Mauro 1993). According to Weber (2003:230), merchant guilds in Europe were often associations of foreign merchants who joined together to facilitate trade. Whatever their origin, the common denominator between merchant and craft guilds was that they were corporate commercial institutions organized around the economic needs and goals of their members. In Europe, merchant guilds were, *sui generis,* of their own making with commerce their primary reason for existence.

Merchant groups in Mesoamerica had many of the same objectives as their guild counterparts in medieval Europe. Where they differ, however, was that in Mesoamerica farmers, merchants, and artisans were all organized into groups for tributary service. As discussed in Chapter 2, every member of society had to fulfil their *tequitl* obligation to their gods and their lords (van Zantwijk 1985). Farmers fulfilled their service obligation with corvee labor while artisans and merchants fulfilled theirs by paying tribute in the goods that they produced or traded.[3] Mesoamerican merchants were organized for trade within the communities where they resided, but the internal structure of *pochteca* residential groups remains unclear. In some areas in Central Mexico merchants lived together in corporate *calpulli* and *tlaxilacalli* units, while in others they are reported in tribute cadres of twenty individuals like farmers and artisans. This contrasts with the information provided by Zorita (1994:183) who reports that merchants were dispersed across *calpulli* living alongside artisans and farmers. This contradiction may reflect regional variation in how merchants were organized or differences between merchants involved in local and long-distance trade.

In the Basin of Mexico merchants lived within *calpulli* or *tlaxilacalli* wards within the cities where they resided (Sahagún 1959:91). *Calpultin* were corporate groups with their own temple and representative leadership (Carrasco 1971). *Pochteca* participated in corporate religious ceremonies to reinforce their common identity at both the household and community level (Berdan 1975:148; Leon-Portilla 1962:30). This reinforced the idea of a common ethnic ancestry which some merchant and artisan groups traced to other distant areas of Mesoamerica.

Rudolf van Zantwijk (1985:138–142), in a careful analysis of available sources has summarized the residential location of *pochteca* groups and their hierarchical structure within Tenochtitlan. *Pochteca* resided in six different wards within Tenochtitlan[4] each of which had their own small religious sub-center. This pattern conforms to Zorita's observation that merchants resided in *tlaxilacalli* within larger urban wards. These six *pochteca* groups were linked hierarchically to a major temple within the Tzonmolco ward which presumably was the location of another *pochteca* group. *Yacatecuhtli* was known as the Lord of the Vanguard and the primary god of long-distance merchants. While the primary temple of *Yacatecuhtli* was located in the urban ward of Pochtlan, he was also worshiped at the temple of Tzonmolco. What is significant about van Zantwijk's analysis is that he identified multiple levels of organization within and between *pochteca* groups which allowed them to be incorporated into a single *calpulli* even though they resided in different residential wards.[5] This cross-cutting hierarchical structure suggests considerable flexibility in how merchant groups were organized to facilitate professional cooperation.

Calpulli membership was hereditary and not open to outsiders without the special consent of the group (Hassig 1985:118; López Austin

1973:65) and its lord (Zorita 1994:181). This was the product of both *calpulli* endogamy (Berdan 1975:149) and specific service obligations stipulated by their elite lords. Any farmer or artisan could engage in commerce as long as they fulfilled their stipulated service and tribute obligations. However, to fulfil service obligations in trade goods (*pochteca tequitl*) rather than labor, individuals had to be a member of a merchant or artisan group whose service obligations were defined in terms of cacao or craft goods.

Outside the Basin of Mexico merchants were often organized by tribute cadre that may have lacked the internal cohesion of *calpultin* (Martínez 1984; Prem 1974). In the Tarascan region all specialities from farmers to artisans, and merchants to fishermen, were organized into tribute cadres based on the service they could provide the state (Craine and Reindrop 1970:plates 2–4; de Alcalá 2013). The same is true in the Puebla-Tlaxcala region. At Huexotzinco merchants were organized in tribute cadres of twenty individuals that may represent barrio *tlaxilacalli* (Prem 1974). In a somewhat different organizational format, merchants in the Tepeaca-Acatzingo region of eastern Puebla were combined with artisans and farmers in mixed cadre of tribute payers. Here merchants and some artisans paid all or a part of their service obligation in cacao (Martínez 1984:Caudros 18–19).

Wherever they were found, merchants probably preferred to live together because they collaborated with one another in long-distance trade ventures. Merchant groups were found in many major communities across the Mexican highlands. The thirteen merchant communities in the Basin of Mexico (Figure 7.2) that were involved in long-distance trade resided in the cities of Tenochititlan, Tlatelolco, Tlacopan, Texcoco, Huexotla, Coatlichan, Chalco, Xochimilco, Huitzilopochco-Churubusco, Mixcoac, Azcapotzalco, Cuauhtitlan, and Otumba (Nichols 2013:figure 4.4; Sahagún 1959:48). Merchants from these communities regularly participated in expeditions as far away as Tochtepec, Oaxaca. Scholars have traditionally interpreted these communities as homogenous groups of specialized long-distance merchants (Acosta Saignes 1945). Recent research, however, suggests that merchant groups were more heterogenous in the types of commercial activities that their members engaged in.

THE MERCHANT COMMUNITY OF OTUMBA

The town of Otumba is a known *pochteca* community located in the Teotihuacan valley on the northeastern edge of the Basin of Mexico

(Figure 7.2). The prehispanic community covered 220 ha, had a resident population of 3,600–5,500 people, and dates to the Late Postclassic period (AD 1350–1521) (Charlton et al. 2000a; Nichols 2013:59; Sanders and Evans 2001:997). The town began as a group of *Otomí* refugees from Huexotla who settled there in the middle of the fourteenth century (Nichols 2013:58). Otumba grew into a large administrative center under the hegemony of Texcoco after its incorporation into the Aztec empire. While documentary sources state that there was a group of *pochteca* at Otumba, no information is available on the scale or structure of its merchant activities. Archaeological explorations, however, supply a picture of craft activities at Otumba that provide insight about merchant behavior (Charlton et al. 1991, 2000a, 2000b; Nichols 1994).

Surface survey at Otumba identified evidence for seven different craft industries at the site (Hirth and Nichols n.d.). Twenty different products were manufactured by craftsmen who worked in seven distinct types of raw materials[6] (Figure 7.3). Because Otumba was a known *pochteca* community, it is likely that most of this crafting was related to commercial exchange. The goods produced included obsidian blades and bifaces manufactured from locally available raw material[7]. Lapidary goods were produced that included obsidian earspools, lip plugs of both obsidian and rock crystal, and beads of both obsidian and chert. Groundstone tools were produced that included manos, metates, mortars, and scrapers (Nichols 2013:61–62; Otis Charlton 1993, 1994). Nearly every town in Central Mexico produced textiles and evidence was found for spinning, dying, and weaving of both maguey and cotton textiles (Nichols 2013:63–64).

Ceramic manufacture was the most diversified craft activity. Red pottery bowls known as Otumba Polished Tan was produced in considerable quantities (Charlton et al. 2008; Otis Charlton 1994; Otis Charlton et al 1993:163–165). Other ceramic products manufactured include figurines, pipes, flutes, bells, whistles, ball-shaped rattles, serpent-handled censers, cotton and maguey spindle whorls, and stamps for decorating textiles and other types of goods (Otis Charlton 2007). All the production was carried out in domestic contexts in a manner consistent with the producer-seller model described in Chapter 5. Otumba was also a farming community, growing food to support its merchant-craftsmen and possibly also producing dyes such as cochineal for use in its textile industry (Nichols 2013:64).

Craft goods and food products circulated through a well developed regional market system during the Late Postclassic period. Most of the

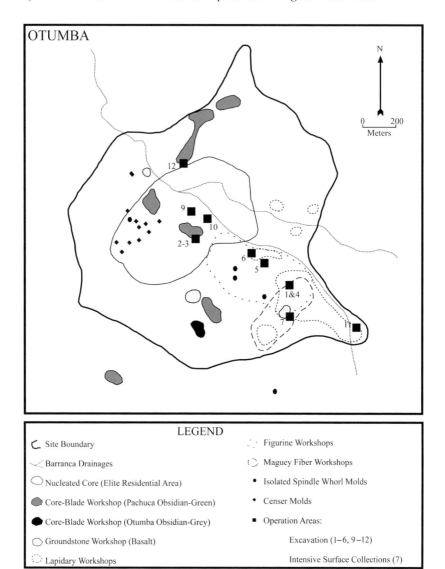

FIGURE 7.3 The archaeological site of Otumba illustrating specialized craft production areas

lapidary goods produced at Otumba appear intended for exchange out-side the community (Otis Charlton 1993, 1994). Chemical characteriza-tion studies have established that most of the Polished Tan bowls produced at Otumba were distributed to villages surrounding the city (Nichols 2013). Figurines manufactured at Otumba were distributed throughout the Teotihuacan Valley with some reaching the site of Cerro Portezuelo on the southeastern shore of Lake Texcoco (Nichols et al. 2002). Otumba participated in a lively regional distribution network and a range of goods including decorated pottery, tortilla griddles, and a range of cooking, storage, and serving wares entered the site from other manufacturing centers in the Basin of Mexico (Nichols 2013:72).

The archaeological research at Otumba provides an important economic profile of a community with a resident *pochteca* enclave. That there was a strong relationship with craft production is not surprising since artisans and merchants are often reported as residing together in the same barrio (Katz 1966:50–51; Sahagún 1959:91). While artisans often sold their own products, others manufactured goods for merchants or sold to retailers for distribution in the marketplace (see Chapter 6). Most of the goods produced at Otumba, except for some textiles and lapidary products, were utilitarian items intended for distribution and consumption within the surrounding region. This suggests that the community of Otumba was not composed *solely* of long-distance vanguard merchants. Instead, as Nichols (2013:72) has concluded, the "market areas for Aztec goods manufactured at Otumba ranged from local to international." Many Otumba merchants may have been involved in local and regional trade. It is even possible that merchants engaged in local and long-distance trade at different stages of their lives. *Pochteca* communities should be viewed as heterogenous communities of both vanguard and local retail merchants who engaged in commerce at different geographic scales and with a range of high and low-value goods.

THE MERCHANT COMMUNITY OF SANTA MARIA ACXOTLA

The *Matrícula de Huexotzinco* was compiled in 1560 and is a census of twenty-three communities within the Huexotzinco *altepetl*. Besides providing a census of community population this document identifies the profession of each household along with a measure of their socio-economic status expressed as renting or not renting property from their lords.[8] The community of Santa Maria Acxotla is located within the Huexotzinco *altepetl* and is important for the discussion here because it was composed primarily of merchants. This community was located approximately 3 km northeast of Huexotzinco and was divided into eleven barrios or *tlaxilacaltin* tribute cadres.[9] In Huexotzinco, as elsewhere in Central Mexico, these tribute cadres were organized as groups of twenty households. Carrasco (1974:6) believes that the merchants in this

TABLE 7.1: *Heads of households listed as living in the eleven barrios of Santa Maria Acxotla and the barrio of San Salvador*

Barrio name	Common households	Elite households	Total households
Teocaltitla (622r)	20	11	31
Mizquipolco (622v)	20	3	23
Couatlan (623r)	20	6	26
Tecuilhuacan (623v)	20	7	27
Chalchiuhtepac (624r)	20	3	23
Cocuixco (624v)	20	3	23
Xaltepetlapa (625r)	20	2	22
Oxihuacan (625v)	20	3	23
Tlalpican (626r)	20	1	21
Itzcoloco (626v)	20	1	21
Quetzalhuacan (627r, 627v)	40	1	41
Farmers/craftsmen, all barrios	40	0	40
Old married couples, all barrios	57	0	57
Total Acxotla households	337	41	378
Tribute paying households	280	0	280
San Salvador (Xalpatol)	67	5	72

Note: Tribute paying households are designated using the prehispanic norm that only men under fifty years of age paid tribute. Old married couples are thereby excluded even if they paid tribute to the Spanish crown.

town originated from Chalco in the Basin of Mexico where a similarly named group was found. The *Matrícula* records information on 453 individuals residing in Santa Maria Acxotla, as well as information on those who had died or run away since the last census.[10] Three hundred and seventy eight of these individuals were heads of households. Of these, 280 were commoner heads of households under fifty years of age and eligible for normal tribute service given prehispanic norms (Table 7.1). Table 7.2 records the occupations of the 280 young commoner households. Merchants and merchant craftsmen represent 240 of the 280 individuals (85.7%). The remaining 40 individuals were farmers (7.1%), non-merchant craftsmen (5.7%) and service professions (1.5%). The estimated resident population for Santa Maria Acxotla is between 1,200 and 1,525 persons.[11]

Several things are noteworthy about the distribution of occupations found at Santa Maria Acxotla. First and foremost, the data reveal that

TABLE 7.2: *Occupations of heads of households in the* Matrícula de Huexotzinco *for the community of Santa Maria Acxotla*

Occupations	Total number	Percent	No of renters	Percent of category
Farmers	20	7.1	8	40.0
Craftsmen	16	5.7	3	18.8
Merchants	238	85.0	26	10.9
Obsidian merchant-craftsmen	2	0.7	0	0.0
Professions	4	1.5	0	0.0
Total occupations	280	100	37	13.2

this was a community of commercial specialists. Fully 92% of the individuals listed as young heads of households were merchants, craftsmen, or practiced a service profession. While only one-third the size of Otumba, it appears to have had fewer farmers and higher proportions of merchant and craftsmen. Second, the low number of farmers in Acxotla (n=20, 7.1%) raises the question of whether this community was self-sufficient for all of the food that it consumed. Either food was imported to feed merchant and craftsmen households, or they also had land to grow food to support themselves (see later).

Third, the number and types of the craftsmen identified in the *Matrícula* suggests that they were linked to the economic activities of their merchant neighbors (Table 7.3). This definitely was the case for the two obsidian blade makers (Pedro Yautl and Juan Temicatl) who resided within the Quetzalhuacan barrio (Figures 7.4, 7.5h) (Prem 1974:627r). The scribal notation for this tribute cadre states that all twenty members were merchants suggesting that the two obsidian blade makers listed here were itinerant craftsmen (Figure 7.4). As discussed in Chapter 6, itinerant obsidian craftsmen circulated from marketplace to marketplace producing blades on demand. This pattern of itinerant crafting also is found in the Coyoacan marketplace tax records of 1571 where obsidian blade makers from a community outside the region supplied blades for sale presumably by direct production within the marketplace (Anderson et al. 1976:141–149; Carrasco 1978:188–195). The practice of itinerant obsidian working was present in Central Mexico by AD 650 (Hirth 1998, 2006c, 2008b, 2009b). Using experimental data, Sanders and Santley (1983:252) estimated that a single obsidian blade maker could have produced 37,500 obsidian blades in a year working on a full-time basis. Based on average consumption estimates, a single full-time obsidian craftsmen could have supplied

TABLE 7.3: *Occupations of craftsmen and professionals in the* Matrícula de Huexotzinco *for the community of Santa Maria Acxotla*

Occupations	Number
Craftsmen	
Paper maker	1
Pottery maker	10
Obsidian blade maker	2
Resin collector	1
Stone worker	3
Tobacco tube maker	1
Professions	
Doctor	3
Fiscal	1
Total	22

Note: The Obsidian blade maker is classified as a merchant in the Matricula and probably represents an itinerant blade maker. These categories represent craftsmen, merchant-craftsmen, and professions in Table 7.2.

3,125–3,750 households with all the obsidian blades needed for an entire year.[12] The capacity of the two Quetzalhuacan blade makers far exceeded the needs of Acoxtla's resident population and suggests that they produced blades as itinerant craftsmen for consumers outside the community.

The same was also true for the ten pottery makers at Acoxtla (Figure 7.5e) (Prem 1974:628v). Sanders and Santley (1983:table 11.4) estimate that a single specialized potter could manufacture 1,171 bowls or 759 jars per year. A potter manufacturing jars, bowls and basins could be expected to produce less, an average of 923 vessels per year.[13] If each household consumed 10–20 vessels per year, then a single potter could supply all the needs for 62–92 households each year.[14] At these production levels, the ten potters in Acxotla could have met *all* the needs of ceramic consumption within the village and still had goods available for export. Of course, households in ceramic making villages also would have received vessels from outside the community, through gifts, exchange, or just because households desired some additional diversity in the vessels that they used. Since the pottery makers at Acxotla resided in a community of merchants it is possible that they relied on their merchant kinsmen to market the wares that they produced much like what may have occurred at Otumba.

Six additional craft specialities were identified in Acxotla that made a variety of goods. These included: one resin collector, one tobacco tube

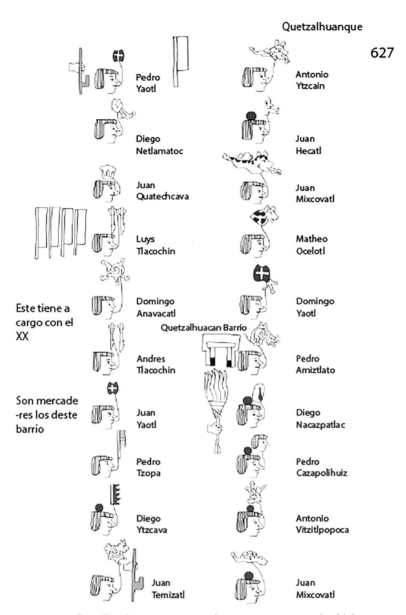

Quetzalhuanque

627

Pedro
Yaotl

Antonio
Ytzcain

Diego
Netlamatoc

Juan
Hecatl

Juan
Quatechcava

Juan
Mixcovatl

Luys
Tlacochin

Matheo
Ocelotl

Este tiene a
cargo con el
XX

Domingo
Anavacatl

Domingo
Yaotl

Quetzalhuacan Barrio

Andres
Tlacochin

Pedro
Amiztlato

Son mercade
-res los deste
barrio

Juan
Yaotl

Diego
Nacazpatlac

Pedro
Tzopa

Pedro
Cazapolihuiz

Diego
Ytzcava

Antonio
Vitzitlpopoca

Juan
Temizatl

Juan
Mixcovatl

Este dixo tiene entre estos seis terrasguerros como los [de]
mas que tienen las cabezas coloradas

FIGURE 7.4 Merchants in the Quetzalhuacan tribute cadre of Santa Maria Acxotla. The two obsidian merchant craftsmen are located at the top left and bottom of the left column and are identified by the *ixcalotli* instrument held in the hand alongside the headglyph of the craftsman

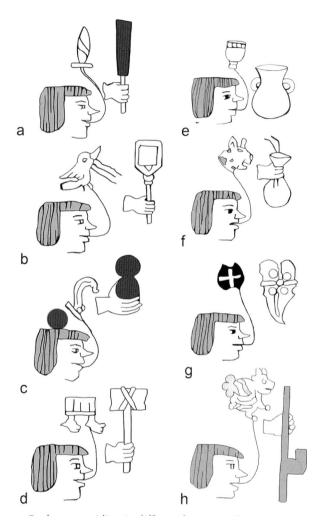

FIGURE 7.5 Craftsmen residing in different barrios at Santa Maria Axcotla.
a) tobacco tube maker, b) paper maker, c) resin collector, d) stone worker,
e) ceramicist, f) doctor, g) fiscal, h) obsidian blade maker

maker, three stone workers, one paper maker, one gold worker, and one
possible feather worker. The first three of these craftsmen made utilitarian
goods who may have sold their wares as producer-sellers in the marketplace
or consigned goods for sale with their merchant neighbors. The resin collector (Figure 7.5c), for example, would have gathered this material for trees
on the nearby mountain slopes of the Iztaccihuatl volcano and used it for
making glue and/or incense. This probably was an intermittent craft activity
since plant resins can only be gathered during specific times of the year.[15]

Tobacco was used and smoked in tubes as part of important celebrations throughout the year (Sahagún 1959; von Hagen 1999). It is likely, therefore, that the tobacco tube maker (Figure 7.5a) both manufactured smoking tubes, (*acayechiuhqui*) and served as a tobacconist (*tlapepech, tlapecho*) within the community. Whether he was a producer-seller or retailer is unclear.[16] The three stone workers (Figure 7.5d) could have shaped stone block for construction or made other goods for sale. Stone masons in Acxotla had access to basalt flows that outcrop along the eastern flank of the Iztaccihuatl volcano. Stone masons in the modern town of San Nicholas de los Ranchos exploited similar basalt flows on the northeastern flank of the Popocatepetl volcano to produce domestic milling stones for grinding corn. It is possible that stone workers in the Acxotla merchant community were involved in both of these activities.

The three remaining craft specialists were involved in making higher-value goods. The first of these was the paper maker (Figure 7.5b) who produced paper that was used by scribes for recording purposes, by midwives and health practitioners in healing and purification ceremonies, and in rituals as part of divination offerings and/or to adorn the participants or appease the gods (Sandstrom and Sandstrom 1986; von Hagen 1999). As a result paper probably was in relatively high demand, carried a moderately high price, and could have been consigned to merchants for sale as part of their commercial dealings. The gold and possible feather craftsmen are listed in the elite household registry of Santa Maria Acxotla. Both resided in the Xaltepetlapa barrio and their craft activities are inferred from their name glyphs rather than from a separate craft glyph as the craftsmen are in Acxotla. The name of the goldsmith is Juan Teocuitlachiuiqui (Figure 7.6b) whose surname directly translates in *Nahuatl* as maker of gold (Molina 1977). The glyphic expression of his name is the hieroglyph for gold like that found on the cheeks of the *Coyolxauqui*, the sister of *Huitzilopochtli* (Séjourne 1976:figure 63). Less certain is a possible feather worker named Caspal Acxoteca located with Juan Teocuitlachiuiqui in the same barrio (Figure 7.6a). His identification as a feather worker is based on his associated feather glyph and the fact that the sons of elite were urged by their fathers to take up crafting wealth goods (Carrasco 1971:373). Having resident artisans able to produce craft goods in both gold and featherwork would have been useful since they were important goods for long-distance trade as well as for personal display among elite household members.

As noted earlier, the two obsidian blade makers in the Quetzalhuacan barrio were identified as merchants by the native scribe (Prem

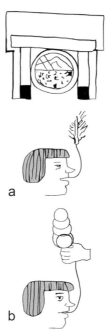

FIGURE 7.6 Two possible wealth goods craftsmen in the Xaltepetlapa barrio of Santa Maria Acxotla

1974:627r). Scribal notation within the *Matrícula* indicates that craftsmen lived side by side with their merchant neighbors and were grouped together in the same cadre for the purpose of tribute accountability. The same is true of the twenty farming households residing in Santa Maria Acxotla. This is important because it supports the view that merchant communities were heterogenous groups of merchants and producer-sellers trafficking in goods of widely differing value. One additional possibility is that craftsmen collaborated or traveled with retail merchants over short distances to sell their goods. This arrangement would have provided both safety in numbers and assistance in transporting heavy goods by those moving lighter weight items.

Evidence for merchants traveling together as composite groups comes from several sources. Durán (1994) identified that women from Tenochtitlan traveled together to sell lake products. The reason was that group travel was a safer option for women moving from town to town than traveling alone. Male merchants did the same. Tax documents from Coyoacan identified groups of venders from fourteen different towns or barrios who may have traveled together to reach its marketplace (Anderson et al.

TABLE 7.4: *Number of land renters by category in Santa Maria Acxotla*

Occupational categories	Number	No of renters	Percentage renters
Farmers*	20	8	40.0
Craftsmen*	16	3	18.8
Merchants and merchant-craftsmen*	220	26	11.8
Professions*	4	0	0.0
Old married couples*	56	19	33.9
Old widowers	20	1	5.0
Widows	55	0	0.0
Total	391	57	14.6

* These categories are heads of households of at least two individuals. Merchant-craftsmen include two obsidian craftsmen who are also identified as being merchants.

1976:146–149). Out of the 14 towns, 8 towns list anywhere from 2 to 6 different types of merchants or producer-sellers involved in selling goods. Merchants from the town of Aticpac sold five different types of goods. These included producer-sellers who sold weaving frames, cane goods, and metal products as well as retailers who sold wood products and a group of *oztomeca* merchants who sold high-value products, possibly textiles.[17] The same pattern is found for the town of Mixcoac where two classes of venders are listed: producer-sellers of ceramic tortilla griddles and *oztomeca* merchants selling high-value items. Finally, three different classes of resellers are listed from Atoyac: two selling clay dye and bark-clay concoctions and a third group selling imported cacao (Anderson et al. 1976).

A final question is whether Santa Maria Acxotla produced enough food to support its 1,200–1,525 residents. This is important because *pochteca* merchants are often perceived as full-time commercial specialists. As noted in Table 7.2 only twenty households within the community practiced farming as their primary occupation and they could not have grown enough food for everyone if merchants and craftsmen were full-time professionals. Although merchants and craftsmen did not cultivate land as part of their tribute obligation (Zorita 1994:181), they apparently did have land to cultivate for their own domestic needs (Martínez 1984).

The *Matrícula de Huexotzinco* identifies each individual that rented land for cultivation. Table 7.4 summarizes the number of individuals identified as renters in Acxotla and San Salvador. The highest percentage of renters occurred among farmers (40%) and old married couples (35.1%). Important for this discussion is that 11.8% of merchants and

18.8% of craftsmen in Acxotla also rented and cultivated land to support their families. This is logical given the statement by Oviedo y Valdés (1855:3:535) that merchants like nobles owned property that they could work and sell as they pleased.[18] Similarly, Carrasco indicates that merchants in both Xochimilco and Tepeaca had land that they farmed during the early colonial period for their domestic maintenance (Carrasco 1963, 1969, 1978:61; Scholes and Adams 1958). The merchant *calpulli* of Acxotla probably held land in common just like other *calpultin* did throughout central Mexico. The implication is that merchant and craftsmen households in Acoxtla had the capacity to be relatively self-sufficient, cultivating land that they accessed through their community or rented from their lords.

MERCHANTS IN OTHER HUEXOTZINCO COMMUNITIES

Santa Maria Acxotla was the largest, but not the only merchant community in Huexotzinco. The *Matrícula de Huexotzinco* also identifies sixty-nine merchants and five elite families living together in the new community of San Salvador located 18 km northwest of Huexotzinco. The history of this group is unclear since San Salvador was a new community formed before 1560. Two possibilities exist. Either it was a merchant community in an outlying settlement that was relocated to San Salvador during the early colonial period, or it was a subdivision of the Acxotla merchant community. The latter is favored here since the San Salvador merchants are listed along with the Acxotla merchants within the *Matrícula* (Prem 1974:629r–630r) and the five elite associated with these merchants are given the barrio name of Xapatol in the elite registry (Prem 1974:730r). Nevertheless, it is also possible that they were a separate group and are linked to Santa Maria Acxotla as a matter of convenience for purposes of collecting tribute.[19] Whatever the case, these merchants are referred to as the barrio of San Salvador within the Acxotla census document which would seem to suggest some previous linkage with this merchant community.

While most merchants were part of larger communities, they also occur as lone individuals in the communities where they resided. There are five instances of isolated merchants listed for towns in the *Matrícula de Huexotzinco* where no other merchants are registered. The first of these is an individual named Thoribio *Oztomecatl* who resided in the Yntlatlan barrio of San Juan Huexotzinco. His written surname indicates his profession as a long-distance vanguard merchant as does his glyphic name which

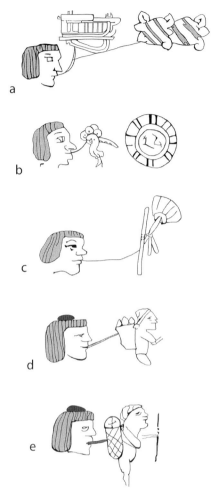

FIGURE 7.7 Individual merchants residing in the Huexotzinco *altepetl*

is a picture of a *cacaxtli* carrying frame used by merchants (Figure 7.7a). As indicated earlier, professions in the *Matrícula* are indicated by a separate glyph or word in *Nahuatl* that identifies their trade. In this case the glyph for long-distance merchant is a representation of two cargas of striped textiles. Striped textiles are the most diversified form of textile registered as tribute in the Codex Mendoza from distant regions (Anawalt 1992) and reinforces Thoribio's status as a long-distance merchant.

The second solitary merchant was Francisco Miscobatl who resided in the community of San Antonio Tlatenco. Francisco lived in a barrio named Analco Cuihitla along with some farmers and seven other craftsmen. He is identified as a merchant by the market symbol used to identify his profession (the marketplace circle with footprints in the center) located alongside his name glyph (Figure 7.7b). Unlike Thoribio *Oztomecatl*, Francisco appears to have been a simple merchant, perhaps a retailer who sold some of the products òf his neighbors. The third merchant was an individual by the name of Juan Otozmecatl who lived in the barrio of Tezoquipan in the community of Santa Maria Atenco. His profession is indicated by his name glyph which consists of the merchant's staff and fan (Figure 7.7c).

The last two merchants resided in different barrios within the community of Santa Maria Acapetlahuacan. The first of these is a merchant by the name of Augustin *Oztomecatl* who resided in the barrio of Analco. His profession as a merchant is illustrated in his name glyph as a man carrying a basket full of goods with a tumpline and a short staff (Figure 7.7d). The fifth merchant is also named Toribio *Oztomecatl* who lived in the barrio of Tepenacaçtla. Like Augustin he is represented by his name glyph of a man with a merchant's staff carrying a basket on a tumpline full of goods (Figure 7.7e). What is important about all of these merchants is that they operated on their own, unconnected to a larger merchant community. While the *Matrícula de Huexotzinco* records commercial relationships thirty-nine years after the conquest, it is very likely that these men learned their professions from their fathers and are carrying out an older tradition that extends back into prehispanic times.

RANK, STATUS, AND MERCHANT PRIVILEGE

The rank of merchants was somewhat fluid in Aztec society. While their status as *macehualtin* was hereditary, their rank within society as well as their own community could rise in proportion to their service to the state. Merchants acquired special skills as they sought out trade routes and commercial opportunities. They developed a detailed understanding of economic practices, political economy, and Mesoamerican cultural geography. This knowledge and expertise was valued and used by the Aztec state in both the expansion and management of the empire. Because of their value, successful merchants were granted special privileges and status not enjoyed by other commoners. In modern parlance merchants had limited upward social mobility. Status within their communities was based on the acquisition of wealth and the knowledge accumulated through participation in long-distance trade as vanguard merchants.

The most prominent and experienced individuals were called upon by the state to supervise economic operations within the marketplace or gathering intelligence for military operations.

Status within merchant communities was more fluid than it was within the society as a whole; it was achieved status. It was based on the same rationale used across *Nahua* society and was achieved by service to the gods and service to the state. The named positions of authority have been interpreted by some (León-Portilla 1962:39) as the formal hierarchical offices of a merchant guild which they were not. Instead, they were positions of respect acquired through years of work. Higher status among merchants was based on their commercial success and ritual performance.

The most important individuals in merchant society were the principal merchants known as the *pochtecatlatoque*. These men achieved their stature in long-distance trade as vanguard merchants. According to Acosta Saignes (1945:23) they were the old, experienced merchants who no longer traveled, but who provided advice, governed merchandising, and placed merchandise on consignment with those who did. The *pochtecatlatoque* were the ruling merchants whose high status was based on good performance and the ability to expand fair trade (Sahagún 1961:59). As Sahagún (1961:59–60) states the principal merchant is "the mother, the father of merchantry ... he is respected, venerated ... He consigns, he entrusts wares to others." The overall image is a successful merchant who nurtured and helped to develop trade benefiting the entire community. This was a position of respect and experience rather than a titled office of leadership within the *pochteca* community. According to Acosta Saignes (1945:23) this title could also be held by older women who were engaged in trade through other vanguard merchants. There were probably as many *pochtecatlatoque* within merchant communities as there were men and women capable of attaining this venerated status. In some cases Sahagún provides the names of principal merchants who were acknowledged as leaders in the merchant community by the Aztec state. When he does name them the number ranges from two (Sahagún 1959:1–2) to five (Sahagún 1959:24).

Vanguard merchants specialized in dangerous long-distance trade to obtain high-value goods. It is from this group that principal merchants were most often selected. Sahagún (1961:60) describes the *oztomeca* as a merchant who is a discerning traveler, who knows the road. Trading expeditions were organized hierarchically and operated under the direction of experienced merchants who were recommended by the principal merchants. The principal merchants also appointed a commander known as the *quappoyaualtzin* who led the vanguard merchants when they were forced into battle to protect their interests:

The vanguard merchants went in the lead, appointed by the principal merchants ... They issued orders to those who would lead the disguised merchants wherever war was to break out. Indeed in strict command over the disguised merchants ... was the one called *quappoyaualtzin*

(Sahagún 1959:24).

This would have been an individual respected for his military expertise. What is noteworthy about this position is that the *quappoyaualtzin* commanded collaborating vanguard merchants irrespective of their home of origin or ethnic affiliation. Sahagún (1959:24) indicates that the *quappoyaualtzin* commanded the joint merchant forces from all the cities in the Basin of Mexico and would determine if and where they would go to fight.[20]

Within the vanguard merchants there was another special group known as the *naualoztomeca*. These were the disguised merchants and they held a distinguished position within *pochteca* communities because they traded in dangerous areas where they were forbidden to enter by local groups. In so doing they risked their lives and if discovered they were executed as spies (Sahagún 1959:22). The risks they took were for the expressed purpose of procuring wealth and information. In return they were revered for the service that they provided.

Sahagún (1959:21–24) records that the disguised merchants received the name of *naualoztomeca* through their exploits in the highland area of Zinacantan, Chiapas (Figure 7.8) where they were forbidden to trade by the local population.[21] Zinacantan was an important trade center where highland merchants obtained goods from the Maya area (Cardos de Mendez 1959:59). The inhabitants of Zinacantan were all said to be merchants who did not engage in cultivation or craft production. This was probably more boast than truth, but it underscored the fact that Zinacantan was a regional trade center where a wide range of goods including salt, feathers, animal skins, and amber could be obtained. According to Ximenéz (1920:360): "There are those from this town (Zinacatan) throughout this land who are leaders of each town and only being from Zinacatan gives the right to say that they are merchants.[22]"

The merchants of Zinacatan apparently maintained tight control over commerce in their region and for this reason wanted to forbid outsiders from entering its markets. Maya traders came to Zinacantan from the Verapaz region to sell goods including quetzal feathers and liquidambar (Cardos de Mendez 1959:75, 1975). The principal merchants of

FIGURE 7.8 Two *naualoztomeca* disguised merchants entering the province of Zinacantan

Zinacantan probably wanted to control this trade and exclude foreigners who might procure goods directly from Maya traders.

Sahagún (1959:21) indicates that the disguised merchants were most active during the reigns of the Aztec kings of Axayacatl and Tizoc before Zinacantan was conquered by the Aztecs in AD 1486 by Moctezuma Xocoyotzin (Durán 1994). Their goal was to obtain amber, animal skins, and quetzal, blue cotinga, and honeycreeper feathers. Zinacantan was an area of Tzotzil Maya so the *naualoztomeca* disguised themselves as Otomí, Chontal, or even Tzotzil by learning these languages, cutting their hair to the style of each, and coloring their body with red ochre. They entered the region around Zinacantan in this way to trade obsidian blades, needles, shells, cochineal, alum, red ochre, and strands of rabbit fur. That merchants took utilitarian goods with them suggests that they interacted directly with common people in the marketplace.

This was dangerous work that had a very high economic return. Sahagún (1959:21–22) tells us that the *naualoztomeca* were the first to procure both the feathers and the amber used to make the regalia and lip plugs used by rulers and great warriors. If identified as interlopers the disguised merchants had to fight their way to safety. Because of the danger, successful trading ventures were treated as military conquests and merchants dressed in regalia that distinguished their accomplishments upon their return to Tenochtitlan. While profit was their motive, their account to Ahuitzotl the Aztec *tlatoani* has a different twist. To him they emphasized that their goal was to conquer this land for the Aztec god *Huitzilopochtli*. While they did not conquer Zinacantan they presented Ahuitzotl with the tabulation of the number of merchants who had died and a summary of the strategic information that they collected during their trading venture.

A group with similar functions as the disguised merchants were the *teiaoaloanime* or spying merchants. Frances Berdan (1975:160) suggests that they may have been disguised merchants of lesser status and possibly a separate arm of the state. While the latter is a possibility, I believe they represent the *naualoztomeca* serving in their more restrictive role of collecting strategic information for the state. As merchants traveled they heard and saw things of use to Aztec rulers. For example, the first sighting of Spanish reported to the Aztec court came from a merchant who spotted the Juan de Grijalva's expedition off the coast of the Yucatán in AD 1518[23] (Dibble 1981:45).

As a rule the best place to collect military intelligence was in the marketplace where merchants could estimate population size and the types of goods available for tribute (Berdan 1975:290; Orozco y Berra 1940:107). It was also the place to judge the political climate of subjugated provinces within the Aztec empire and to determine whether revolt was in the wind. After all, the marketplace was where people met and voiced their opinions about a great many topics. Even undisguised, an Aztec merchant could collect a considerable amount of information in the course of normal business dealings simply by observing, listening to conversations, and talking to local people who frequented the marketplace. It is for this reason that Aztec rulers always met with vanguard merchants after their return from long expeditions. This is indicated in the account of the return of the *naualoztomeca* from Zinacantan:

And when they came to reach their homes, thereupon the disguised merchants sought out the principal merchants; they discussed with them the nature of the places they had gone to see. Accurately did they set forth their account of all that had happened there. And when the principal merchants had heard the exact account, thereupon they led them before the ruler Auitzotzin; before him they set forth all which hath been told which had happened there at Tzinacantlan

(Sahagún 1959:22–23).

The slave dealers known as the *tecoanmime* were another important category of merchants who engaged in long-distance trade.[24] These merchants were distinct because the slaves they trafficked in often were used in ritual human sacrifice. The distinctiveness of the *tecoanmime* can be seen in their ritual practices. Most *pochteca* worshiped the god *Yacate-cuhtli* (Sahagún 1959:27) who was embodied by the merchant's walking staff and linked to safe travel. Unlike other *pochteca*, the *tecoanmime* worshiped *Tezcatlipoca* as their patron deity (O'Mack 1985:114,125). Slave dealers worked both inside and outside of the empire and Sahagún (1959:18) notes that they participated in long-distance trade expeditions to obtain male and female slaves for sale. Slave dealers were closely associated with the *tealtiliztli* or Bathing of Slaves ceremony (see later) and this profession may have been restricted to individuals who had achieved this distinction (Berdan 1975:160; Town-send 1992:187). Whether this actually was the case is unclear.

Aztec society was enough of a meritocracy to recognize that the individuals selected for positions of responsibility needed to possess the qualifications, experience, and abilities to carry out the tasks that they were assigned. Success in commercial activities was an avenue for social advancement and made merchants eminently qualified for certain tasks. Foremost among these were the merchants who were appointed as marketplace supervisors and judges (*tianquizpan tlayacaque)* (Berdan 1975; Durand-Forest 1971, 1994:175). These individuals kept order, set price ceilings, and identified fraud where it occurred (Kurtz 1974:698; van Zantwijk 1970:7). Assigning this task to experienced merchants was logical since they understood proper and improper economic dealings. According to the informants for Tlatelolco,

And thus was it that the work of the principal merchants became precisely that they cared for the market place. They sponsored the common folk, so that none might suffer, might be deceived, tricked, mistreated. These same pronounced judgment upon him who deceived others in the market place, who cheated them in buying and selling. Or they punished the thief. And they regulated well everything: all in the market place which was sold; what the price would be Sahagún
(1959:24).

Merchants advocated and practiced a high standard of ethical behavior and had their own courts to deal with the commercial and non-commercial misconduct of their members (Hassig 1985:118; León-Portilla 1962). This is made clear by Sahagún where he states,

And thus did the principal merchants, the disguised merchants, conduct themselves: quite apart did they pronounce their judgments; independently were sentences meted out. A merchant, a vanguard merchant, who did wrong, they did not take to some else; the principal merchants, the disguised merchants, themselves alone pronounced judgment, exacted the punishment, executed the death penalty … He who had done wrong they killed, they slew, there at the *quauhcalli*, or anywhere; perhaps indeed in his home they killed–slew–him

(Sahagún 1959:23).

The experience of vanguard merchants in long-distance travel and international affairs often made them the best choice for a range of state related duties. For example the *oztomeca* regularly served as guides for the army during military campaigns (van Zantwijk 1970:7). They knew the routes to distant places as well as where cities and fortifications were located. Most of the knowledge of areas targeted for conquest would have been collected by the *naualoztomeca* and *tecoanmime* in the course of their normal economic pursuits so it was natural that these individuals were called upon to provide logistic information during military campaigns.

The cross-cultural experience that merchants acquired also made them qualified for filling positions as ambassadors (Katz 1966:71; León-Portilla 1962:30). This was an extension of their role as economic representatives and commercial agents for the king. According to Alba (1949:2), for a merchant to serve as an ambassador he had to have high social standing in the community, be educated in the *calmecac*, be honorable, and be a good orator.

LONG-DISTANCE TRADE AND THE AZTEC STATE

Vanguard merchants engaged in long-distance trade because it was an avenue to accumulating enormous wealth. The Aztec elite also were interested in wealth which was mobilized through a range of institutional channels (see Chapter 2). But the elite also recognized that merchants enriched Aztec society (Durán 1994:64)[25] and for this reason they were given considerable leeway as independent commercial entrepreneurs within the kingdom. Their economic acumen was valuable and in Texcoco principal merchants served on an economic council within the palace of Nezahuacoyotl (Katz 1966:79).[26]

A number of scholars have argued that despite their non-elite status merchant trade operated as an official arm of the state's administered economy (Carrasco 1978; Chapman 1957a). This belief comes from the influential work of Karl Polanyi (1957; Polanyi et al. 1957) and Ann Chapman (1957a, 1957b) which shaped the views of several generations of Mesoamerican scholars. Chapman believed that long-distance trade could not be carried out through normal commercial activity. Instead, she argued that fractious political groups, rough geography, and poor transportation technology meant that trade was organized as a separate institution and carried out as state-directed administered activity (Chapman 1957a:114–115). Pivotal for inter-regional trade was the existence of ports-of-trade in politically neutral areas where merchants could interact as representatives of their respective polities. From Chapman's perspective political relationships defined the *modus operandi* of Aztec merchants. Vanguard merchants were viewed as operating exclusively beyond the limits of the empire (Chapman 1957a:122; Townsend 1992:189) with their sphere of operations expanding ever outward as the empire expanded.

This argument was based on a selective reading of ethnohistoric sources which were interpreted through the lenses of Polanyi's model of administered economy. Little evidence exists for the port-of-trade model that Chapman proposed (Berdan 1978; Gasco and Berdan 2003; Voorhies 1989). Instead, a great deal of variation can be found in the degree of neutrality that important trade centers maintained. Politically neutral trade centers like Acalan were not frequented by Aztec merchants (Berdan 1975:184), and the important trade center of Xoconochco was conquered and directly incorporated into the Aztec empire as a regular tribute province (Berdan and Anawalt 1992; Voorhies 1989).

While vanguard merchants were important economic auxiliaries, the Aztec state did not structure state economic policy to benefit the activities of the *pochteca*. State economic policy was structured to benefit the state and its elite. That was the sole purpose of Aztec economic policy. Where those interests paralleled one another, merchants engaged in private commerce alongside, or at the same time that they served the state. Merchants were commercial opportunists who visited trade centers within and outside the empire, both with and without politically negotiated treaties of interaction. The principal merchants (*pochtecatlatoque*) are described as the companions of the governors and rulers (Sahagún 1959:3). I believe this refers, in part, to the role they played as king Ahuitzotl's commercial agents in long-distance trade. The best example of operating with the authority of the state is Ahuitzotl's use of vanguard merchants to trade with independent groups on the Mexican Gulf Coast. Examples of initiating trade without state support occurred when merchants penetrated enemy lands as disguised merchants. Let us take a closer look at the way merchants acted as the king's personal commercial agent in long-distance trade.

The Ahuitzotl account is related to the expansion of trade into the province or country of Anahuac Xicalanco located on the Gulf Coast. The province of Anahuac Xicalanco was made up of a number of independent

FIGURE 7.9 Ahuitzotl turning capes over to the merchants of Tenochtitlan and Tlatelolco

towns located between the Coatzacoalcos river and the Laguna de Terminos (Scholes and Roys 1968:31). According to Sahagún (1959), Ahuitzotl called the principal and disguised merchants to the palace where he gave them 1,600 large cotton capes (*quachtli*) to trade on his behalf in Anahuac.[27] These capes were divided equally between the merchants of Tenochtitlan and Tlatelolco (Figure 7.9) who then took them to the marketplace where they were exchanged for high-value capes with royal symbols, fancy breech cloths, and embroidered skirts.[28] Sahagún clearly specifies that these items were the exclusive property of Ahuitzotl which the merchants carried for him as agents to Anahuac Xicalanco. Sahagún provides a long list of the personal goods that merchants took to trade on their own behalf during this trip. The list of the merchant's personal goods included items made of gold and rock crystal for the Anahuac elite as well as a range of goods used by commoners.[29] It is interesting that while the goods of Ahuitzotl carried his emblem, the merchant property did not, suggesting they traded goods with appeal to both elite and non-elite. Figure 7.10 illustrates the high-value goods returned to Ahuitzotl at the end of the trading expedition.

FIGURE 7.10 Merchants returning goods to Ahuitzotl after a trade mission

The description of the merchant's entry into the province of Anahuac indicates that at least a portion of the trade with Xicalanco was arranged through political agreement (Berdan 1986, 1987:251). *Pochteca* from multiple cities traveled together as far as Tochtepec. From there merchants from the five cities of Tlatelolco, Tenochtitlan, Atzcapotzalco, Cuauhtitlan, and Huitzilopochco proceeded armed at night to avoid attack. However, as they approached Anahuac they sent messengers to their ruler upon which,

the rulers of Anauac sent emissaries to meet them. [These] also went girt for war ... Thus they went forth to meet them in the midst of the enemy's land, so that [the merchants] could arrive there [in the province of] Anauac Xicalanco

(Sahagún 1959:18).

Clearly this was dangerous territory, but the fact that the rulers of Anahuac sent an armed escort to meet Aztec *pochteca* indicates that a treaty for safe passage had been established. It is within this context that Sahagún (1959:17) specifies that "Anauac was not the place of entry for everyone, because it was the trading area of [the merchants of] Ahuitzotzin."

Economic interaction commenced after safe arrival at Xicalanco. Sahagún only records the interaction between merchants on behalf of Ahuitzotl and the rulers of Xicalanco. Goods were not exchanged, but were presented as gifts after which the rulers of Xicalanco reciprocated with gifts of their own. As Sahagún recounts,

when the merchants reached Anauac Xicalanco [and] the rulers who governed the cities ... thereupon they gave to each of them all the items of trade–the precious capes, precious skirts, precious shifts, the property of Auitzotzin ... And then the rulers of Anauac Xicalanco, Cimatlan, [and] Coatzaqualco reciprocated with the large green stones, ... and fine bottle-green jadeite, and turquoise mosaic shields; ... and large red sea shells, ... feathers of the red spoon-bill, the toupial, and the blue honeycreeper; ... and the skins of wild animals[30]

(Sahagún 1959:18–19).

The context of interaction between elite was one of reciprocal gift exchange. It is likely that after this interaction merchants traded their personal goods with both elite and non-elite alike.

There are multiple examples of *pochteca* merchants trading in areas without state support. In fact it is their disingenuous characterization of their commercial exploits "to seek land for the master, the portent, Uitzilopochtli (Sahagún 1959:4)," that led scholars (e.g. Carrasco 1978; Chapman 1957a) to classify merchants as an official auxiliary of state expansion. Vanguard merchants went disguised and/or armed and into enemy territory to trade where they could. Their most heralded campaign was the siege of the merchant stronghold of Quauhtenanco in the province of Ayotlan in Xoconochco. Sahagún's Tlatelolco informants embroidered the account of the siege of Quauhtenanco by claiming they waged war for four years, eventually conquering the province for incorporation in the Aztec empire. This was not true. The merchants residing in Quauhtenanco very likely were attacked repeatedly by hostile parties from Ayotlan, Tehuantepec, Comitan, and Xoconochco. But Isaac (1986) doubts whether the combined armies of these enemy provinces would have marched hundreds of kilometers to attack a band of *pochteca* merchants. If they had, they would have defeated them quickly and soundly. Instead, he feels the tale of the four-year siege was a self-serving summary of all the hardships experienced by *pochteca* during their commercial operations in Chiapas.

This is confirmed by both Durán and Tezozomoc. Durán (1994:374–381) recorded that king of Tehuantepec asked Ahuitzotl for help against his enemies in Xoconochco, Xolotla, and other southern Mazatepec groups. Assistance was requested because their alliance with the Aztecs had resulted in the murder of "merchants from Tenochtitlan that had gone there to trade (Durán 1994:374)." In response Ahuitzotl raised an army and together with the army of Tehuantepec conquered Xoconochco and its allied cities. Tezozomoc (1980) concurs. His account deviates from Durán's by implying that the merchants killed were from Tehuantepec rather than Tenochtitlan (Tezozomoc 1980:550). It is possible that merchants from Quauhtenanco participated in the campaign and actually received some of the honors that Sahagún's Tlatelolco informants claimed Ahuitzotl gave them[31] (Sahagún 1959:6). But it is unlikely that merchants regularly participated in military campaigns as it would have made them targets of retaliation during their travels. Although the province of Tochtepec was the main base of operations for vanguard merchants they were not involved in its conquest and addition to the empire. While Tochtepec is listed in the Codex Mendoza, it appears to have been conquered by Nezahualcoyotl in an joint Aztec-Texcoco military operation who installed a tribute collector (*calpixqui*) there to oversee its administration (Carrasco 1999:342).

While the precise role of merchants in the conquest of Xoconochco is unclear, vanguard merchants were organized for military action to protect themselves while they were on the road. As a result they were able to take advantage of their military preparedness and training when it was in their economic advantage to do so. A recently discovered document dating to 1543 is an account of military aid provided by *Nahuatl* merchants to the Tarascan lord of Tzitzispandaquare (Monzón et al. 2009). According to the account written in P'urhépecha, twenty *Nahuatl* merchants assisted Tzitzispandaquare, the son of Tangaxoan and the previous ruler of Tzintzuntzan, to reconquer and take control of the city. The military role of these twenty merchants was apparently indispensable in Tzitzispandaquare's consolidation of power. As a result of their support they were consolidated into an elite lineage within Tzintzuntzan's ruling society. After conquest these *Nahuatl* merchants were given land and the labor to work it, solidifying their position in Tarascan society that can be traced well into the sixteenth century.

What is important about this historical text is that it underscores the active and opportunistic role that merchants played in the political and economic landscape in which they operated. This event probably took place sometime in the early fifteenth century perhaps between AD 1430 and 1440. While we do not know precisely where these merchants originated from, the Basin of Mexico is the most likely locale. That they were willing to provide Tzitzispandaquare with assistance suggests that they were already trading in the area around Tzintzuntzan at the time of conflict. Their military training provided them with the opportunity to serve a foreign lord and in the process gain access to lands, titles, and noble status that they could not achieve as wealthy commoners within their own society. This instance of military intervention suggests that vanguard merchants did indeed serve as a paramilitary presence in areas outside the empire which they could use in strategic operations that benefitted the merchant communities to which they belonged.

FIGURE 7.11 The slaying of traveling vanguard merchants

Killing and harassing merchants was a common reason for going to war (Figure 7.11) (Hassig 1985:120). The murder of Aztec merchants was the reason for declaring war against Tepeaca, Tehuantepec, Ahuilizapan (Orizaba), Tizauhcoac, Coixtlahuaca, and the cities of the Huasteca (Berdan 1975:Carrasco 1980:257, 1999:410; Durán 1994:160, 176, 182; Katz 1966:68). Tezozomoc (1980:550) indicates that indigenous groups viewed commerce with the Aztecs as a form of cowardly submission and killing its merchants was an act of defiance. Within the empire this was the equivalent of killing tax collectors or ambassadors and was a signal of revolt that required a military response. But there also were the economic reasons why killing and harassing merchants could not be tolerated.

Commerce had to proceed because both merchants and artisans brought wealth to their cities. The Aztec *tlatoani* made this clear to the people of Tepeaca when he said,

be especially careful to protect the merchants ... since these are the ones who enrich and ennoble the earth. They feed the poor, they maintain the villages, and should anyone mistreat them, harm them, you will notify this court as soon as possible, for their offense is punishable by death

(Durán 1994:158).

Merchants supplied artisans with raw materials to practice their trade (Katz 1966; Rojas 1995). Since artisans often fulfilled their *tequitl* service by paying a tax-in-kind (*tlacalaquilli*), attacks on merchants directly reduced the creation of artisan wealth. Merchants also operated as commercial agents, trading goods consigned to them by wealthy elite. In these instances killing merchants was a direct assault on the wealthy elite of the Aztec state and could not be tolerated.

Frances Berdan (1975, 1982) has argued that conquered provinces often depended on *pochteca* merchants to supply them with the goods they needed to pay their tribute but could not produce. The Oaxacan town of Pochutla, for example, was required to pay tribute in copper which had to be purchased from merchants (Acuña 1984a:196). Likewise, the people of Iztepexi in Oaxaca had to pay tribute in gold and feathers which they obtained from merchants as payment for serving as *tlameme* porters in trade expeditions to Tehuantepec and Xoconochco (Acuña 1984a:255; Berdan 1975:117). In the complex tribute system of the Aztec empire there were plenty of opportunities for merchants to procure and sell goods needed to meet provincial tribute demands.

A recent analysis of Aztec tribute by Gutiérrez (2013) indicates that the flow of tribute was more dynamic and flexible than previously thought. As discussed in Chapter 2, a comparison of the local tribute record of the goods paid by Tlapa, Guerrero does not match the list of goods arriving in Tenochtitlan.[32] The analysis reveals two important elements of the tribute system. First, the value of the goods paid in Tlapa exceeded the value of the goods demanded by 13–14%. Gutiérrez suggests this over payment represents the cost of supporting the local *calpixqui* and the collection of tribute. Similar differences can be noted for the community of Pochutla that supplied gold dust, jewels, copper, feathers, and clothing to Tochtepec as tribute of which only jewels, feathers, and clothing reached Tenochtitlan; the gold and copper may have been used locally or employed to purchase some of the tribute items required. Second, tribute flows were not rigidly fixed. The goods collected locally were different from those demanded as tribute by the Aztec capital. Gold and mantas were the primary items paid as tribute in Tlapa. But the tribute reaching the Aztec capital included both shields and warriors' costumes, gold dust and tablets, rubber cakes and figures, finished garments, and gourd vessels (Gutiérrez 2013:table 6.2).[33]

The detailed annual Tlapa tribute record spanning thirty-six years from AD 1486 to 1522 (Gutiérrez 2013) illustrates that the level of imperial tribute was always changing with the needs of the state. Moreover, the tribute items paid at the local level were not the same as those depicted in Aztec tribute documents. What was important was that the goods were of equivalent value. This created a problem for the regional tribute collector who was responsible for meeting imperial tribute demands. The problem may have been solved by an intricate process of resource conversion using merchants as agents to procure non-local goods for regional tribute collectors (Gutiérrez 2013:142). The relationship between merchant and tribute collector is found in the *Codex of Tepeucila* where the *tequitlato* and local lords borrowed forty-five gold pesos from *pochteca* merchants to meet the tribute demands of their Spanish overlords (Herrera Meza and Ruíz Medrano 1997:33).

The picture that emerges from Gutiérrez's analysis is that meeting tribute obligations was not a static, on-demand mobilization system. Instead, it made dynamic use of commodity valuation, tribute negotiation, and conversion of goods through commercial agents. During the colonial period the goods used to meet tribute demands were often "produced" through *granjería,* a system of managed collaboration at the community or regional level. Raw cotton paid as tribute in one village (*tlacalaquilli*), would be transported to other communities and woven into finished goods using service labor (*coatequitl*) to meet tribute needs. This system of "working the tribute" (Miranda 1952:35) almost certainly extended back into the prehispanic past (Gutiérrez 2013:157). The concept of *granjear,* meaning to trade, traffic or earn a profit in something, is expressed by the *Nahuatl* verb *ixnetia* which means to make something appear or to produce.[34] Merchants would have played a dynamic role in this system by supplying raw material for production activities or finished goods as required. If the role of the *calpixqui* was as much to create the tribute as it was to collect it, then merchants would be well qualified for appointment to this administrative post (Townsend 1992:188).

Several scholars have suggested that the Aztec state intentionally founded marketplaces across the empire to help merchants move goods between regions (Carrasco 1980; Chapman 1957a). The most cited case is the founding of the large market of Tepeaca after the province was conquered by Moctezuma Ilhuicamina. An Aztec *calpixqui* named Coacuech was placed in Tepeaca to collect the mandated tribute and to oversee the marketplace. Moctezuma Ilhuicamina commanded that the marketplace contain "rich cloth of all kinds, precious stones and jewels, featherwork of different colors, gold, silver, and other metals, the skins of animals such as jaguars, ocelots and pumas, cacao, fine breechcloths, and sandals (Durán 1994:159; Carrasco 1980:257)." The richness of this marketplace would, of course, generate revenue from its market tax. But more importantly, it would have provided access to an array of exotic goods required as tribute by groups in the eastern provinces who did not have access to them. In this way the Tepeaca marketplace would have been a small source of revenue for the local *calpixqui* while also providing access to wealth goods to meet tribute demands in neighboring provinces. This market also would have attracted merchants moving into the highlands from both the south and east. The expansion of the Tepeaca marketplace could also have been part of a broader Aztec economic strategy designed to draw merchants away from the large Tlaxcalan marketplace in Ocotelulco (see Chapter 3 for information on this marketplace).

Vanguard merchants provided important information and services for the Aztec state, but they were not a formal arm of an administered economy as some scholars have argued (e.g. Carrasco 1978; Chapman 1957a). The state utilized merchants to help manage economic aspects of the empire, collect military intelligence, and to serve as agents-of-commerce for the elite who entrusted them with goods to trade. Attolini Lecón (2010:70) has suggested that the Aztecs were not interested in direct control over long-distance trade, but shaped it in subtle ways with regulations about markets and the transportation of goods. This may be true, but the subtlety with which this was done may have been largely unintentional. Merchants took advantage of the uneven distribution of natural resources and were actively involved in moving goods required to meet tribute payments from one region to another. It is possible that their greatest service to the institutional economy was that they evened out variation in supply and demand inherent in the ever changing tribute system. This economic activity, of course, was a for-profit enterprise.

THE RITUAL LIFE OF MERCHANTS

A great deal can be learned about the practical morality of merchant behavior from the secular and religious rituals that they practiced. Ritual as it is used here refers to action wrapped in symbolic meaning (Keltzer 1988:9). It is the symbolism attached to specific behaviors that makes them meaningful within the contexts where they are practiced. Ritual fulfils a variety of functions for its practitioners. It imparts meaning to the world, provides cohesion to organizations, and is used to invest and divest power. Here the concern is with what merchant ritual can tell us about how they perceived economic pursuits in relation to the social and perceived spiritual forces in which they operated.

As discussed earlier, merchants living in *calpultin* had a strong sense of corporate identity. Rituals within merchant communities had several functions. First, they provided the mechanism through which the risks, rewards, and psychological uncertainty of their economic ventures were expressed and resolved. Second, rituals publically marked and recognized the achievements of individuals within the community of merchants. Finally, rituals such as the *tealtiliztli* ceremony served to interface the merchant community with the broader society (see later). All merchant rituals simultaneously invoked elements of both the social and spiritual landscapes in which their members operated. As in all facets of *Nahua* society, the gods were an ever present force in people's daily lives, determining their destiny based both on godly service and the predestined elements of their individual birth. Sahagún's interest in understanding "pagan" religious practices led him to collect a significant amount of information on domestic ritual from his Tlatelolco informants that directly reflect the beliefs and practices of prehispanic merchants (Sahagún 1959).

Preparation rituals for merchant ventures

Nahua society characterized life as precarious and full of danger. Travel was especially risky because it took the individual away from the safety of their local village and into strange and unknown country. The way to avoid life's pitfalls was to be alert, prudent, humble, and disciplined. The road of life was characterized by Sahagún as a journey,

on earth we travel, we live along a mountain peak. Over here there is an abyss, over there is an abyss. Wherever thou art to deviate, wherever thou art to go astray, there wilt though fall, there wilt though plunge into the deep. That is to say it is necessary that thou always act with discretion in that which is done, which is said, which is seen, which is heard, which is thought

(Sahagún 1969:125).

Long-distance trade involved risk at several different levels. The first was the physical risk of travel and the dangers of being attacked, robbed, and killed on the road. This was a result of being a foreigner in a strange land and was an ever present aspect of a vanguard merchant's life. The next dimension of risk involved the spiritual dangers of moving into unknown areas. The *Nahua* pantheon was replete with deities who were capricious in the way they treated mankind and whimsical in their bestowal of favor or disfavor (Nicholson 1971; van Zantwijk 1985). What made merchant activity especially risky was that they sought to accumulate the wealth of the gods. This made trade risky since acquiring wealth for oneself meant expropriating it from the gods. The capricious nature of the gods and the need to be humble in the accumulation of their riches is clarified by Sahagún where he says,

Travel with care in the plain, in the desert, lest our lord the protector of all, the master of the heavens [and] of the earth, will somewhere destroy thee ... and ... if thereby the protector of all should entrust thee something of his riches, his wealth, do not let thyself be arrogant

(Sahagún 1959:13).

Ritual, therefore, was a constant aspect of merchant life. They were practiced before a merchant venture, during the expedition, and after its successful completion. Merchants prepared sacrifices and offerings on all these occasions to negotiate their worthiness for a successful trip. These offerings were reciprocal debt payments. Not only were humans in debt to the gods for sacrificing their lives at the world's creation, but the acquisition of wealth on earth depended on procuring their favor (Carrasco and Sessions 1998:149). Merchant ritual was intent on purifying the individual, currying spiritual support, and recognizing the omens that could foretell good outcomes or avoid disaster.

Trading ventures were preceded by a series of departure rituals to prepare merchants for the ordeal ahead. Departure of a merchant expedition had to begin on a propitious day of the *tonalpoalli*, the Aztec's 260 day sacred calendar.[35] Once the day was set, goods and expedition members were assembled and prepared. The day before departure merchants purified themselves by washing their heads with soap and cutting their hair. After departure they did not cut their hair or wash above the neck in an effort not to disturb their *tonalli* soul which the Aztecs believed resided in their head (López Austin 1988:321).[36] They cut papers in commemoration of the fire god (*Xiuhtecuhtli*), the earth deity (*Tlaltecuhtli*), and *Yacatecuhtli* the patron god of the merchants.[37] Merchants decorated the end of the staves with these papers and with liquid rubber which they worshiped as the manifestation of their god (see Figure 7.8). Since the merchant always carried his walking staff, his god went with him and before him down the road he traveled.

Once this was completed, merchants prepared a debt sacrifice to the gods. Ceremonial papers were cut and sacrifices were made both in the courtyard and before the hearth of their houses. Quails were sacrificed and merchants pierced their ears and tongues with obsidian blades to draw blood that was cast into the fire of the hearth and offered in the courtyard to the four directions. This blood offering was intended to appease the gods for offenses that they had committed and to purify themselves for departure. In a final act of autosacrifice, bloodied papers were burned together with white copal in their hearth fire and the smoke was read to divine the success of the venture. If all was done correctly and the paper and incense offerings burned well, the merchant would be psychologically prepared for the journey and would conclude that, "He hath been good to me, the master, our lord. I shall indeed reach the place where I am to go (Sahagún 1959:11)."

While it is risky to speculate on the meaning and imagery of this ceremony, there are a number of continuities with ethnographically known purification ceremonies in *Nahuatl*, *Otomí*, and Tepehua communities. For example, paper effigies are cut of both the fire and earth deities to which blood sacrifices of birds are offered as part of fertility, pilgrimage, health, and protection rituals (Sandstrom 2015; Sandstrom and Sandstrom 1986). The fire deity in these ceremonies resides in the hearth stones and is the manifestation of the home providing protection to members of the kin group. According to the *Otomí* the fire god carries a walking stick and accompanies the Sun on its daily travels across the sky. The earth god is a representation of fertility and also travels. Among contemporary *Nahuatl* the earth god has control over the life and death of merchants as they moved across the earth's surface (Sandstrom and Sandstrom 1986:49, 78). In all ethnographically documented ceremonies blood is poured on all the paper images of good and evil spiritual entities to appease them or attract them in prescribed fashion. For prehispanic vanguard merchants setting off on an expedition, protecting their kinsmen at home and themselves on the road were critical ingredients for success. Paper and cutting paper imagery were likely critical elements in the ritual offerings to these protective deities.

At dawn of the day of the expedition's departure Aztec vanguard merchants invited ranking members of their merchant community to their houses for a feast. The goods to be traded were exhibited and the elder, ranking merchants who stayed behind would extol expedition members to travel with care, to make their journey with courage, and to be humble and diligent in their venture lest the gods destroy them (Sahagún 1959:12–13). This was a solemn occasion because of the dangers that merchants would face on the road (Sahagún 1979a:61–68).

From this point on preparations shifted to departure. Each individual transferred goods, equipment, and provisions to the house of the expedition leader where they were displayed for community validation and loaded onto *cacaxtli* cargo frames. They waited for nightfall to load everything onto the boats that they used to transport themselves across the lakes surrounding Tenochtitlan. After solemn farewells each departing merchant took a lump of copal from a green gourd and cast it into the courtyard fire. Thus they set out together on the evening of the propitious day of departure. None of the merchants looked back since it was considered a bad omen to do so (Sahagún 1959:16).

Little is known about the rituals that merchants practiced while they were away from home except that they were cognizant of the physical and spiritual dangers that they faced. Merchants regularly paid homage to the cross-road *cihuapipiltin*. These were the dangerous spirits of women who died in childbirth and to whom shrines were erected at major cross-roads. Merchants made offerings at these shrines throughout their travels (van Zantwijk 1985:156) as well as in each temple or town through which they traveled. If they did not stay in a town they made offerings in the fields where they slept (van Zantwijk 1985:159).

All precolumbian people believed that certain animals were harbingers of omens. Merchants feared the high pitch cry of the white hooded hawk (Carrasco and Sessions 1998:149) which they believed indicated future sickness, robbery, attack by wild animals or even death. The words of the expedition leader upon hearing the cry of a hawk reflect the fatalistic approach with which merchants approached their circumstances:

Be of good cheer, O my sons ... Of what profit is it that we are afflicted? Let no one be sad or heavy of heart. In truth for this we came: we came to die ... (therefore) ... Let no one feel womanish in heart. Yield completely to death; pray to our lord

(Sahagún 1979a:154).

Unknown places always caused unrest and nervousness because of the possibility that unseen spirits could cause them harm. In these circumstances merchants offered sacrifice and appealed to *Yacatecuhtli* for protection. Sahagún communicates the angst that merchants felt on the road when they found themselves in an unknown place:

And if somewhere night fell, they gathered, joined, crowded, and assembled themselves somewhere at the foot of a tree or the opening of a gorge, and bound and tied, fastened together ... all their staves, which represented their god *Yacatecuhtli*. Here, before him, they did penance, bled themselves, cut their ears,

and drew straws through them; ... (and) ... If nothing befell them, their hearts
were therefore again a little lifted

(Sahagún 1979a:154–155).

The return from an expedition was also carefully planned. Again a
propitious day was selected for the merchants' arrival (e.g. 1 house,
7 house, etc.). To insure this occurred, merchants would stop at an
intermediary town outside the Basin of Mexico like Itzocan, Puebla
and remain there between 10 and 20 days so that they would arrive
home on a good day (Sahagún 1959:31; van Zantwijk 1985:159). Upon
their return merchants only entered their home city after dark, going to
the house of a merchant leader where they presented themselves before
returning home.[38]

The ritual to purify merchants after their return was called the
necxipaquiliztli, or the washing of feet. At midnight merchants would
quickly perform autosacrifice offering blood to both *Yacatecutli* and
Xiuhtecuhtli, the old fire god. This blood offering was to repay the gods
for a safe return (Sahagún 1959:27). The merchants' traveling staves
representing the god *Yacatecutli* were taken to the *calpulli* temple where
the sacred staves were placed. A feast was then organized to celebrate
their return and to recognize the bounty that the gods had bestowed on
them. It was here that returning merchants were both praised and admonished by their elders so they would remain humble in the face of their
newly acquired wealth.

Ritual feasting and social rank

Ritual is used to communicate information about social position and to
invest or divest power in both individuals and institutions. The rituals
that do this may be commonplace or formalized depending on how
societies are structured (Drucker and Heizer 1967). Although merchants
were not members of the elite, they had several special privileges including the ability to own land, sacrifice slaves, and wear symbols of distinction at certain festivals (Berdan 1975:144). Status within merchant
communities was achieved rather than ascribed. Nevertheless, the social
roles that merchants fulfilled in society were approved by ruling elite.
Sahagún (1959:1–3) states clearly that the principal merchants
(*pochtecatlatoque*) of *Tlatelolco* were installed by its rulers.[39] These were
the merchants called the companions of the ruler (Sahagún 1959:3).
Moreover, merchants acted with the authority of the rulers to

recommend and/or appoint experienced merchants to important social positions across society.

Upward social mobility within the merchant community was based upon an individual's ability to sponsor a set of costly feasts that advanced their prestige and status.[40] Ritual feasting marked changes in status and reinforced values and relationships within the merchant community. Young boys moved from inexperienced youths participating in their first long-distance trade venture (*pochtecatelpopochtin)*, to apprentices (*tlazcaltiltin*), and full adult merchants who could trade on their own or as agents for others (see Chapter 8). These changes in status were affirmed by the merchant community in the feasting cycle. Feasting was the primary way a merchant demonstrated his success and prestige was accumulated by sponsoring thanksgiving feasts that mobilized wealth in visible ways.

Sahagún (1959) provides information on several of the ritual feasts that merchants sponsored. His descriptions suggest that feasts served two different functions. Their stated purpose was to thank the gods for the wealth accumulated and to pledge their continued reverential service. The unstated purpose of ritual feasting was to build prestige both inside and outside of the merchant community through the invitation of the honored guests to the event. All feasts began and ended by recognizing the gods. Small feasts began with a commemorative prayer proclaiming the mercy of god and reiterating that the merchant has remembered to support the poor, old, and destitute members of his family and community (Sahagún 1959:33). More elaborated feasts involved presentation of offerings at the main temple of *Huitzilopochtli*, at the ward temples of merchant *calpultin*, and in the house of the sponsoring merchant (Sahagún 1959:37–38). These offerings included quail sacrifices, flower arrays, and offerings of tobacco, paper, rubber, and copal. While some feasts were given by individuals, the elaborate ones were jointly sponsored by groups of principal merchants.[41]

The social networks built during these feasts are evident in the list of attendees. Guests of honor included military knights, army generals, masters of youth, and noblemen. Experienced warriors were invited to be the attendants at these feasts to distribute food. The inclusion of warriors in these festivities may be symbolic or it may reflect the practice of taking a few warriors along for protection on merchant ventures. In any event the symbolism is strongly militaristic in nature. The warrior attendants offered tobacco smoking tubes to guests which are described as spears or spear throwers. Likewise attendants carried bowls to receive the used tobacco tubes from guests which were likened to military shields. In the same way guests were offered shield flowers and stick flowers to recognize the service that warriors provided in going to war to nourish the gods. Feast attendees could be served hallucinogenic mushrooms which induced visions about the future lives of members of the merchant community.

The key to a successful feast was that it was concluded with excess. Wealth was not intentionally wasted like it was in the Northwest Coast potlatch (Codere 1966; Drucker 1967), but there was suppose to be an abundance of resources left over. Wastefulness was not in accordance with the prudent behavior required of merchants, nor would it have shown proper respect to the gods for the wealth they had bestowed on the sponsor. Instead, the presence of large quantities of left-over food and other supplies was a good omen for the sponsor of the feast and was a portent for continued future prosperity. Sahagún's Tlatelolco informants make this clear when they specify,

If nothing remained of the flowers, tubes of tobacco, food, [or] chocolate at the time of the distribution of the leftovers ... the old men considered of him who fed the people ... that ... nothing more would be to his merit; nothing more would be his reward. Always it resulted that the master, our lord, became irritated
(Sahagún 1959:42).

It is reasonable to suppose that left-over food was distributed to poor members of the community since this was a regular admonishment of elders to younger merchants as they strove to achieve commercial success.

The biggest and most important ritual festival that wealthy merchants could participate in was the *tealtiliztli* also called the Bathing of Slaves ceremony. The culmination of this ceremony involved the public sacrifice of slaves during the *Panquetzaliztli* (raise the banners) festival given in honor of *Huitzilopochtli* as the fifteenth public feast of the solar year (Durán 1971). This festival commemorated the birth of *Huitzilopochtli* and was celebrated close to the winter solstice when the sun was low on the southern horizon and about to begin its journey back toward its zenith at the center of the universe.[42] The *Panquetzaliztli* ceremony was dedicated to war and the human sacrifices offered during the celebration were seen as renewing the world order. The songs and dances exalted the bravery of the warriors who supported the god's rebirth after the winter solstice. It was during this festival that merchants could offer "bathed slaves" as sacrificial offerings to *Huitzilopochtli* (Aguilera 1989:132). Their inclusion in this ceremony was symbolically very important to merchant identity because it placed them on a near equal plane with warriors in providing the blood of sacrificial victims to nourish the gods.

The origin of an Aztec merchant's ability to offer humans for sacrifice can be traced back to the story of merchants being besieged in Quauhtenanco. Sahagún (1959:3) tells us that merchants fought and took captives in the four year campaign, "some took twenty, some took fifteen," and it is from this event that the participating merchants could wear the netted capes of warriors on special occasions. Whatever captives were taken in the Quauhtenanco campaign were undoubtedly returned to Tenochtitlan for sacrifice during the *Panquetzaliztli* festival.

The bathing of slaves ceremony represented the culmination of merchant's lifetime achievement.[43] It was the most expensive, most involved, and most public of merchant activities. It was not a single event, but a series of feasts and activities that spanned a year or more. The merchant who became a Bather of Slaves was recognized as a wealthy individual who the gods had blessed, and an individual who had dedicated his life to serving the gods by providing them with blood sacrifices. In this way he achieved respect that approximated that given to warrior knights who obtained sacrificial victims in battle. Bathers of slaves (*tealtianime*) were prestigious individuals within the merchant community and completing this ceremony may have been a component of becoming a principal merchant (*pochtecatlatoque*).

The *tealtiliztli* was practiced to varying degrees in other *Nahua* communities across the Mexican highlands. Merchants also sacrificed slaves in Cholula. Acosta Saignes (1945:36) argues that this was because *Yacatecuhtli* was a version of the god Quetzalcoatl who was worshiped in Cholula. The occurrence of this practice outside of the Basin of Mexico suggests a widespread desire by merchants to participate in the blood sacrifice owed to the gods they worshiped. The merchants who bathed slaves dramatically increased their individual prestige while at the same time providing god-service for the group as a whole. Bathing slaves also was a special prerogative of some wealthy craft groups who could financially undertake the corresponding costs. In addition to merchants, goldsmiths also purchased, prepared and sacrificed slaves during the *tlacacaxipehualiztli* (skinning of victims) festival which was the second of the eighteen feasts of the solar year (van Zantwijk 1985:160–161). It is likely that the honor to do so was accompanied with some of the same type of ritual events practiced by wealthy *pochteca*.

The decision to become a *tealtianime* was an aspiration that required many years or even decades to attain. It was a very expensive undertaking whose exact cost could not be precisely fixed because of the way that events surrounding the dedication events could unfold. Sahagún (1959:47) estimated that the event required anywhere between 800 and 1200 large decorated capes and 400 decorated loincloths just for the gifts given to distinguished invitees during the celebration (van Zantwijk 1985). Individuals that received gifts within the merchant community included the principal merchants, other *tealtianime*, all the disguised merchants, and the slave dealers. Many gifts were also given to important, high ranking elite outside the merchant community. These included military generals, distinguished warriors, judges, administrators, and all the princes of the reigning elite families. Giving gifts during these festivities validated the role of merchants in serving the gods and engendered elite support in a world where the envy of their wealth could cost them their very survival (Sahagún 1959:47; van Zantwijk 1985:148).

The aspiring *tealtianime* would begin by purchasing between one and four slaves in the slave market at Atzcapotzalco (see Figure 3.3). These were not ordinary slaves: they were men and women of good appearance and with special singing and dancing skills that slave dealers set aside for this honor. Slaves were dressed as warriors in fine apparel and displayed their singing and dancing talents in the marketplace before they were bought. The price of these slaves varied from 30 to 40 large capes depending on their countenance and abilities. After purchase they were taken to the house of the sponsor where a small house with a flat roof was erected on which the slaves destined for sacrifice would dance. Their predestined role as sacrificial victims was recognized by the community and they were watched carefully so they would not escape.

The material goods needed for the festival including food, cacao, salt, dishes, baskets, and charcoal which were bought, or contracted to be bought, so they would be ready on the appointed day when slaves would be sacrificed. When preparations were complete the sponsoring merchant would set out for the merchant enclave in Tochtepec. This trip, like all long-distance trips, involved the solemn preparatory ritual described earlier. Nevertheless, this was not a commercial venture *per se*, although it is likely that trading occurred along the way. Instead the merchant took items with him that were used to sponsor a feast for merchants in residence there. The purpose for this trip was largely ritualistic because Tochtepec was the furthest permanent outpost of Basin of Mexico merchants.[44] This was the first in a series of feasts and was designed to incorporate merchants on active trade missions into this important event.

Upon reaching Tochtepec the *tealtianime* candidate went to the communal house of his *pochteca* group and then to the temple of *Yacatecutli*. Here he displayed the symbolic traveling staff prepared for each of the individuals to be sacrificed. On those staves he laid out the elaborate vestments they would wear at the time of their sacrifice. These vestments remained in the temple throughout the length of his stay. He then prepared a feast where he invited all of the prominent merchants, slave dealers, and other *tealtianime* present in Tochtepec. It was at this feast that he announced his intention to stand before *Huitzilopochtli* and make his sacrificial offering. Within this context the merchant's rationale for the *tealtiliztli* ceremony is evident: merchants like the eagle and jaguar warriors made personal sacrifices to serve the gods and thereby received their wealth. According to Sahagún (1959:51) it was in the display made in Tochtepec that a merchant spread his fame among his colleagues and incited others to follow his example. This was perhaps the most important feast for acquiring prestige within the merchant communities since it was at Tochtepec that all the most active *pochteca* and *naualoztomeca* were found.

After returning from Tochtepec the candidate called together the merchant leaders of his *calpulli* to review the preparations for the four feasts to be performed in Tenochtitlan during the *Panquetzaliztli* festival. This evaluation insured that there were enough resources to conduct the feasts successfully, since failure to do so brought shame on the entire community. A favorable day sign (1 house, 2 flower, 2 monkey) was then selected to announce the feast. The merchant leaders then reminded the candidate to give gifts to the earthly representatives of *Huitzilopochtli*, namely the rulers and their civil servants. By doing so they would be given life on earth (Sahagún 1959:56–57). It is hard not to see this as a double entendre. On one hand it recognizes that the elite were their lords and the representatives of their gods on earth. On the other hand, it also hints at the need to curry the favor of the elite who were always jealous of merchant wealth.

After the arrangements were reviewed, a feast was held to announce that the candidate intended to bathe slaves. This celebration was called the *teyolmelahualiztli* and was the first of four feasts that he had to sponsor. Its goal was to "direct the minds of men" that all would do their duties for god. There was no turning back once this announcement was made. The second celebration was called the *tlaxnextiliztli* feast. Here the slaves intended for sacrifice were displayed in their finest garments and they danced and sang for the invited guests. This was an important but risky event for the merchant sponsor. If the slaves danced poorly, it reflected badly on the candidate. If the slaves danced extremely well, or had other praiseworthy talents, the wealthy nobles invited to the feast as guests could request to buy them.[45] This saved the slaves from sacrifice, but it was a significant setback to the sponsoring merchant because it meant that he had to wait until the next *Panquetzaliztli* festival to sacrifice the number of intended slaves. According to van Zantwijk (1985:167) this provided a check on ambitious merchants who wanted to advance too quickly up the social hierarchy.

The remaining two celebrations were held during the *Panquetzaliztli* festival. The third banquet was the *tealtiztli* feast held on the eleventh day of the festival. It was the day upon which the slaves were bathed and ritually purified. Their final purification was carried out in the *calpulli* temple where the sacrificial victims were joined by the priests in charge of the sacrifice. It was during this ceremony that the sponsor received the title *tealtiani* (he who bathes slaves) (van Zantwijk 1985:149). Between the fifteenth and nineteenth days of the festival the sponsor and other aged merchants fasted in preparation for the sacrifices performed on the twentieth and last day of the *Panquetzaliztli*. On the evening of the nineteenth day, feasting was carried out in the home of the sponsor and the slaves were taken to the Temple of *Huitzilopochtli* and given intoxicants in preparation for their sacrifice the next day. From there they went back to the *calpulli* temple where a vigil was held throughout the night (Sahagún 1959:63).

On the morning of sacrifice, a procession referred to as the serpent dance was begun in which all the individuals intended for sacrifice moved quickly throughout the city. During the procession they were taken to the *calpulli* of Coatlan where they engaged in ritualistic combat. Bathed slaves were given shields and obsidian-bladed swords and fought with armed warrior knights. If an intended sacrificial victim was "captured" in the combat, the sponsor was given the opportunity to ransom him back so that the slaves could continue on to their sacrifice. If the sponsor was unable to do so the slave was sacrificed on the spot and the merchant lost his opportunity to present him to *Huitzilopochtli*. It was yet another opportunity for the secular elite, especially the warrior knights, to benefit economically by ransoming captive slaves at the expense of the merchants.[46]

From here all victims were taken to the temple of *Huitzilopochtli* where they were arranged in rows. The temple courtyard was filled with spectators including the Aztec *tlatoani* who watched the sacrifices unfold.

War captives were sacrificed first, led to the temple summit by their accompanying captor. Then the bathed slaves of the merchants were sacrificed. This was greatest moment of honor in a merchant's life. He and his wife would accompany the slaves to the temple summit in front of the assembled multitude. The slaves would be sacrificed and their bodies rolled down the temple steps. The merchant sponsor would then descend and his household attendants would carry the bodies to his home where the flesh was cooked and served to the members of his family in the final celebration meal. Trophies of the victim's cut hair and sacrificial clothes were kept by the merchant until his death.

Only a few merchants could accumulate the wealth to ceremonially bathe and sacrifice slaves. Nevertheless it was an important event for the entire community. It underscored the participation of merchants in the celestial task of serving and feeding the gods. In economic terms the distribution of gifts was an expensive, but practical way to curry the favor of the elite and the experienced warriors who supported them. The capture of four sacrificial victims was the way that valiant warriors entered the ranks of the knight societies. It is not surprising, therefore, that merchants also aspired to bathe and sacrifice four slaves. It was their way to emulate service to the gods as valiant warriors. It is for this reason that much of the symbolism used in the ceremony invoked the symbols of military combat.

CONCLUSIONS

Vanguard merchants occupied a special place in the Aztec economic world. They sought out exotic goods and moved them over long distances. Traveling long distances involved both physical and spiritual risk. *Pochteca* who undertook long-distance trade did so primarily as a full-time economic specialization. They lived in well integrated corporate communities, membership to which was largely closed except through marriage. These groups were not guilds as we know them from medieval Europe. Instead, merchants were organized as *calpultin*, clan-like or community based organizations that shared a common ancestry, profession, and worshiped the same patron god. Even in areas of highland Mexico where *calpultin* were replaced by tribute cadre, the merchant *calpultin* appeared to have remained largely intact. The reason for this was twofold. First, the risk of long-distance trade required sustained collaboration between merchants who knew and could rely on one another. I believe that merchants carried each other's goods and when attacked had to fight to protect themselves. In these circumstances knowing who you could depend on was the key to survival. Second, long-distance trade was a lucrative venture and for this reason entry into the profession and the knowledge needed to practice it was closely guarded. Merchants retained their own internal forms of organization as long as they provided elite with wealth goods as their *tlacalaquilli*.

Merchants occupied a special, but unusual position in highland societies. They were members of the commoner (*macehualli*) class but could amass enormous wealth through commercial activity. Their wealth made them the object of envy by the elite who could put merchants to death for being "haughty" (Katz 1966:75). Merchants mediated this precarious position by maintaining a humble demeanor and providing valuable services for the state. They provided raw materials for craftsmen and served as spies and guides for the army. Their economic acumen was valued and they supervised the marketplace as well as advising rulers on economic matters. Finally, rulers consigned their personal wealth to the care of merchants who acted as commercial agents to build wealth on their behalf.

The oral narratives from Sahagún's informants indicate that merchants wanted to see themselves not as servants to the state, but as servants of the gods. They saw their role in long-distance commerce as a sacred activity in the same way that warriors served the gods. Warriors went into battle and risked their lives to procure sacrificial victims to nourish the gods. Merchants went armed into foreign lands and risked their lives to procure the hidden wealth to glorify the gods. The *tealtiliztli* ceremony provided merchants with the same opportunity to nourish the gods as the warriors who risked their lives in battle. Chapter 8 returns to more practical economic concerns by examining the tactical procedures and operating principles that merchants used to conduct both local and long-distance commercial exchange.

8

The tools of the trade and the mechanics of commerce

Every economic system has a set of beliefs and operating principles that guide economic interaction. Without them economic interaction would not be possible. Notions about gifting, reciprocity, value, and maximization all impact how individuals interact with one another. Maxims such as "do onto others as you would have others do onto you" and "let the buyer beware" establish very different criteria for how individuals operate in economic relationships.

The larger and more internally specialized an economic system becomes, the more tools and economic instruments are created to facilitate interaction or to overcome the obstacles that impede it. These instruments include formal and informal currencies, credit and credit cards, loans and interest, and a range of formal contracts and the contract law that attend them. The type and volume of goods circulating in commercial settings are a function of these operating principles and economic instruments. As economic systems grow in size, new forms of economic organization appear and operate alongside preexisting forms without replacing them. Economic systems are by nature plastic and polymorphic, and become increasingly so as they grow in size.

This chapter examines the basic economic instruments and principles of operation found in highland *Nahua* economies. In common parlance these are the tools of the trade and the rules of the road. The best information on these subjects comes from Sahagún's Tlatelolco merchant informants which is fortunate because they were the individuals who evaluated what constituted acceptable economic behavior both in and outside the marketplace. The discussion begins with the general principles operating at all levels of *Nahua* society and then examines the evidence for specific economic features such as the use of agents, consignment selling, brokers, factors, and interest bearing loans. While the Aztec world lacked many of the tools of modern capitalism, the entrepreneurial spirit was clearly present and supplied the engine behind commercial interaction.

THE NAHUA MORAL ECONOMY

The moral economy refers to the fundamental beliefs on which economic interaction is based. It consists of the shared interests and norms of behavior which underlie all economic interactions (Gudeman 2001). They are based on the moral values taught to children during their upbringing and reinforced through social interaction within the community where they reside. The economic behaviors that these beliefs and values engender, of course, are a balance between the desires and self-interests of the individual and the altruistic obligations that individuals have to their family and community. However expressed, the moral economy is the foundation on which honest or dishonest economic exchanges reside.

The household was the center of early childhood education. It was where social mores were learned and responsibility to family and community was indoctrinated. Sons and daughters were taught from an early age to be well-behaved and moderate in all things. Exemplary behavior was a blend of obedience, humility, diligence, thankfulness, honesty, modesty, and respectfulness (Sahagún 1969:2–3, 12–13). Where encouragement failed, punishment for bad behavior followed. Children of both genders were required to contribute to the maintenance of the household from an early age. Young boys were taught the trades of their fathers and young girls were taught to spin and weave. As they grew, all children attended the *cuicacalli*, the house of song. Song and dance were aspects of many religious rituals and their lyrics contained important information that reinforced many of the same prudent behaviors learned at home. Young boys later went to the *calmecac* or the *telpochcalli* where they learned the importance of public and religious service (Berdan 1982, 2014).

The value of hard work and honesty echo in the admonitions of *pochteca* elders to both young and journeyman merchants during a feast celebrating a successful trade venture,

even if thou hast here given us food [and] drink, hast thou perchance thus stopped our mouths? Are we therefore afraid of thee? Can our occasion for rearing [and] training perhaps no longer be? Where didst thou get that which thou gavest us to eat [and] drink? Perchance thou didst go somewhere to remove it from one's pot ... Perhaps thou playest *tlachtli* or *patolli*, or thou hast filched some woman's belongings: her goods. Thou hast robbed someone ... This we do not know; but [if so] ... no longer wilt thou have merit nor be deserving[1]

(Sahagún 1959:29).

While merchants in many societies were viewed as devious and dishonest (McCormick 2001:12; Simmel 1906; Vance 1970:62), unflagging honesty was actually the *sine qua non* of successful commerce in pre-industrial settings (Das Gupta 2001b:105; Grief 1989:868, 2000:265). The warning against playing *tlachtli* (the ball game) or *patolli* (a board game of chance) were not bad in and of themselves. They are looked down upon here because of the gambling and betting often associated with them (Aguilar-Moreno 2007:361–363). It is this dimension of fairness, honesty, and the need to work hard, rather than take risks that is the foundation for the moral economy in ancient Mesoamerica.

THE COST OF MOVEMENT: A TUMPLINE ECONOMY

Moving goods in Mesoamerica was costly. It lacked beasts of burden that could pull carts or carry loads and it had few navigable rivers outside of the coastal plain. As a result, the bulk of goods in the highlands moved by human porters (*tlameme*) much like they did across Central Africa. Porters carried goods in baskets or on *cacaxtli* cargo frames with the aid of a tumpline. The tumpline was a strap that transferred the weight of the load to the forehead of the porter instead of onto the shoulders as is the case with the modern back-pack. This passed the load weight directly down the spinal column to the pelvis without straining the arms or shoulders. It allowed loads to be carried by balancing the load against his back and leaning forward (Figure 1.9).

Transportation limits were set by how much weight a porter could carry. Since human porters are energetically inefficient in comparison to other forms of ancient transportation, it is assumed that bulk goods did not move very far except through tribute demands (Drennan 1984b; Slyuter 1993). One of the problems in modeling Mesoamerican transportation systems is the use of unrealistically low estimates of what *tlameme* porters normally carried. The Spanish conquistador Bernal Díaz del Castillo observed that two *arrobas* (23 kg) was the standard cargo weight for porters.[2] Most scholars have used the 23 kg load because it was the normal cargo associated with public service during the colonial period[3]

(Borah and Cook 1958; Hassig 1985, 1986). This is unfortunate because 23 kg does not reflect the size of loads *tlameme* could and probably did carry when they engaged in trade or moved goods for themselves.[4] Light loads of only 23–30 kg were probably used for moving goods in rapid relays.

The ethnohistoric and ethnographic evidence from Mesoamerica indicates that *tlameme* porters regularly carried loads heavier than 23 kg. Geronimo de Mendieta (1945), another reliable sixteenth-century Spanish source, records that highland natives regularly carried loads of 3–4 *arrobas* (34.5–46 kg) in one *jornada*. The *jornada* was one day's normal travel which ranged from 5 to 6 Spanish leagues (26–33 km) depending on terrain and conditions (Borah and Cook 1958:42; Hassig 1986).[5] Information from the *Minas de Cobre* written in 1533 provides good information on the transportation of copper ingots in the old Tarascan domain (Warren 1968). Here *tlameme* porters regularly carried loads of between 32 and 72 kg over distances of between 21 and 43 km depending on terrain (Pollard 1987:748–750). Likewise, Thomas Gage, an English visitor to Mexico in 1648, says that 50–60 kg was a common load for native porters. Ethnographic information from the nineteenth and twentieth centuries indicates that tumpline merchants carrying commercial loads for themselves regularly moved cargos weighing in the 40–70 kg range, with maximum loads reaching as high as 85–90 kg (Table 8.1). Finally, illustrations from the sixteenth century often depict porters carrying individuals instead of loads of goods (Figure 8.1). This role of the porter as a prehispanic taxi cab illustrates their ability to carry loads of at least 55–70 kg.

Cross-cultural evidence suggests that porters regularly carried loads heavier than 23 kg. Table 8.1 summarizes available information on load sizes carried by human porters for nine different areas of the world. For the most part 40–60 kg (88–132 lbs) seems to be the range of loads carried by farmers in China, India, and Japan. In Pakistan head loads range from 20 to 40 kg while the use of shoulder baskets enable porters to carry cargos of 75–100 kg. Commercial porters in Nepal regularly carried loads between 58 and 88 kg during the late twentieth century. In the early twentieth century commercial porters carrying tea hauled loads of 76–120 kg (167–264 lbs) over the Himalayas with the highest recorded load being 164 kg (360 lbs). What is clear is that human porters around the world often carried 1.5–2.5 times their normal weight when there was a desire or need to do so. It is incomprehensible to think that Mesoamerican merchants would not have carried equally heavy loads. A great deal

TABLE 8.1: *A cross-cultural comparison of porter cargos within Mesoamerica*

Region	Century	Load	Load weight (kg)	Source
		Mesoamerican porter loads		
Central Mexico	Sixteenth	Normal	23 kg	Díaz del Castillo 1956
Central Mexico	Sixteenth	Normal	34.5–46 kg	Mendieta 1945: 1:122
Michoacan	Sixteenth	Normal	32–72 kg	Pollard 1987:748; Warren 1968
Guatemala	Early seventeenth	Normal	50–60 kg	Gage 1929:234
Michoacan	Late nineteenth	Normal	63 kg	Lumholtz 1902
Michoacan	Late nineteenth	Maximum	86 kg	Lumholtz 1902
Guatemala	Mid-twentieth	Normal	68 kg	Bunzel 1959:30
Guatemala	Mid-twentieth	Normal	45 kg	Hammond 1978
Guatemala	Mid-twentieth	Maximum	91 kg	Tax and Hinshaw 1969:83
		Global porter loads		
China	Early twentieth	Normal	47–59 kg	Clark and Haswell 1967:189
China	Early twentieth	Village average	59 kg	Fei and Chang 1949; Clark and Haswell 1967:183
India	Early twentieth	Head load, jute	40 kg	Clark and Haswell 1967:189
Japan	Early mid-twentieth	Normal	45 kg	Clark and Haswell 1967:183
Nepal	Late twentieth	Commercial porters	58–88 kg	Malville 1999
Old Assyrian trade	3000 BC	Estimated	30 kg	Dercksen 1996
Pakistan	Early twentieth	Head loads	20–40 kg	Clark and Haswell 1967:183
Pakistan	Early twentieth	Shoulder baskets	75–100 kg	Clark and Haswell 1967:183
Tibet	Early twentieth	Commercial porters, normal load	76–120 kg	Malville et al. 2001:45
Tibet-China	Early twentieth	Commercial porters, heaviest load	164 kg	Malville et al. 2001:53

FIGURE 8.1 A *tlameme* porter carrying an individual

of long-distance merchant trade consisted of high-value and light weight goods which absorbed the high costs of transportation (Blanton and Feinman 1984; Drennan 1984a; Katz 1966:66). Nevertheless, future research needs to incorporate these higher load values into models of prehispanic long-distance trade.

The need for porters was high and as a result they formed a recognized occupational group across the highlands (Clavijero 1974:238). Boys began using the tumpline at the age of five (Berdan and Anawalt 1992) and became acclimated to carrying heavy loads over the course of their lives. The occupation of *tlameme* was a necessary, but low status profession which anyone could perform because there always were loads to be carried (Hassig 1986:135). Work as a *tlameme* was associated with poverty and used as a metaphor for bad fortune (Sahagún 1979a:152).

Tlamemes were needed by merchants and they traveled with them on long-distance trade ventures (Sahagún 1959:14). As mentioned in Chapter 7 the town of Iztepexi, Oaxaca obtained the gold and feathers they had to pay as tribute by working as porters for *pochteca* merchants (Acuña 1984a:255; Berdan 1975:117). The need for a consistent supply of porters was so high that the Aztecs required that the town of Tepeaca provide *tlamemes* as part of their tribute obligations (Durán 1994:155).

Although the Spanish introduced mules in the colonial period, *tlamemes* continued to move goods throughout the sixteenth century. The Spanish system supplemented rather than replaced the indigenous system of native porters (Hassig 1986:134; Rees 1975). The advantage that mules had over porters was not in the weight that they carried (115 kg) since a *tlameme* could carry about the same load weight[6] (see Table 8.1). Their advantage was that a single driver (*arriero*) could easily manage 4–5 mules. Nevertheless, *tlamemes* continued to be used throughout the sixteenth century for five reasons: 1) mules and carts were not always available, 2) the cost of investment in mules and carts was high, 3) terrain and the absence of roads made some areas accessible only by porters, 4) *tlamemes* took care of themselves and were less work than mules, and 5) despite legal restrictions, *tlamemes* were a cheaper commercial option than mules (Hassig 1986:137). Between 1530 and 1541 licenses were given allowing merchants to use gangs as large as 1,000–3,000 *tlamemes* to move cacao and grain over space. The number of complaints about *tlameme* abuses indicates that they were a regular part of the landscape up through the end of the sixteenth century. Even legislation against using *tlamemes* did not ease the abuses since the laws applied primarily to their use by Spanish merchants; native merchants could use them without restriction. What brought the use of *tlameme* transport to an end in the early seventeenth century was the dual effect of continued population reduction and the gradual improvement of roads.

DEAL MAKING: THE MECHANISMS OF SUPPLY AND EXCHANGE

The fundamental purpose of economic exchange is to procure items to meet demand. How exchange takes place can vary from society to society and from individual to individual. As discussed in Chapter 4, the concept of "profit" certainly existed in the prehispanic world. The *Nahuatl* word for profit (*tlaixtlapana*) literally means to split or divide something in face-to-face dealings (Table 8.2). The implication is that negotiated exchange was intended to produce "an increase." While making a profit

TABLE 8.2: *A vocabulary of* Nahuatl *economic terms*

Nahuatl words	Morphology and literal definition	Colonial economic context
Nahuatl **verbs**		
cemana	*cem*, entirely, as a whole; *ana*, to take. "to take whole amounts"	To wholesale
chihua	*chihua*. "to do, make, perform, engender"	To manufacture, make
cohua	*cohua*. "to buy something" (co- has implications of "turning" or "returning" in many *Nahuatl* words indicating that word possibly had an archaic reciprocal meaning "to trade")	To buy
huiquilia	*huica*, to take, accompany, be responsible for; -*lia*. "to take, carry something for someone"	To owe (money)
ixnextia, ixnextilia	*ix* is from the noun *ixtli* which means face, eye or surface; *neci* which means "to appear, to produce money or tribute"	To haggle, make a profit face to face
namaca	*na*-, archaic form of the indefinite reflexive *ne*- and was originally a reciprocal; *maca*, to give. "to sell something" although archaically it possibly meant "to give in return for something"	To sell
necuiloa	*necuiloa*, "to bow, bend, twist something, to engage in commerce"	To deal
patilia	*patilia*, "to sell, exchange or barter"	To exchange something with someone
pialia	*pia*, to keep, have custody of; -*lia*. "to keep something for someone"	To owe (money)
-*tech necuiloa*	-*tech*; *necuiloa*. "to make an investment with someone"	To loan with interest, to invest

Nahuatl words	Morphology and literal definition	Colonial economic context
-tech tlaixtlapana	*-tech*; *tla-*; *ix-* (from the noun *ixtli* which means face, eye or surface); *tlapana*, to split or divide something with someone.	To loan with interest, to invest, to profit
tiamiqui	origin of the *tianquiztli*, market.	To engage in commerce
tianquiztoca	*tianquiztli*; *toca* to follow. "to follow the market"	To trade in the market
timotlapatilia	*ti-*, subject you or we; *mo-* reflexive; *tlapatilia* (from *patla)*, "to barter, exchange, or do buisness"	To barter something with someone
tlacohua	*tla-*; *cohua* "to purchase"	To purchase
tlaixtlapana	*tla-*; *ix-* (from the noun *ixtli* which means face, eye or surface); *tlapana*.	To profit
tlanehuia	Originally seems to have meant to borrow and return the same thing	To rent from someone for money (land), to borrow
tlaneuhtia	*tlanehuia*;-*tia*. "to cause something to be borrowed"	To lease something to someone for money, to lend
tlapatilia	given as reflexive (*nino-*); *tla-*; *patla*, to exchange something;-*lia*. "I exchange things for myself"	To exchange, operate in the market
tlaquehualtia	*tlaquehua*, -*ltia*. "to hire someone"	To hire someone
tlatennonotza	*tentli* for "lips" and *nonotza* for "converse"	Molina (1977) – to make or negotiate an agreement or contract
tlatolcaquilia	*tlatolli*, words; *caquilia*, to accept a request, their words.	Molina (1977) – to give credit
tlaxtlahua	*tla-*; *ixtlahua*, "to pay for something"	To pay for something
tzatzilia	*tzatzi*, to cry out, shout or howl; with *tia* and if preceded by *nitla* or *titla* it can mean to declare the price of something	To state or ask the price of something for sale

(*continued*)

TABLE 8.2: *(continued)*

Nahuatl words	Morphology and literal definition	Colonial economic context
***Nahuatl* nouns**		
oztomecacalli	*oztomecatl*, disguised merchant; *calli*, house	Merchant hostel
patiuhtli	*patla.* usually appears possessed (*i-pati-uh*) meaning "its price" and refers to what something could be exchanged for	Price, worth
tiamicoyan	*tiamiqui*; passive -o; locative – yan. "place where trade or business takes place"	Market, places where trading occurs
tiamictli	from *tiamiqui*	Merchandise
tiamiquiztli	*tiamiqui*; *-liztli.* "the act of selling and buying or doing business"	The act of selling and buying
tianquiztli	from *tiamiqui*	Marketplace
tianquizcayotl	*tianquiztli*; *-ca-*; nominal suffix -yo. "the essence of the market, something characteristic of the market"	Market merchandise
tlacocohualoni	*tla-*; *co-*, distributive of *cohua* implying many repetitions; *cohua*; nonactive agentive – *loni.* "instrument for buying things"	Currency
tlacohuani	*tla-*; *cohua* "the act of buying things"	Somebody who buys something
tlacohualli	from *cohua.* "something bought"	A purchase
tlacemanani	*tla-*; *cem; ana.* "one who takes whole amounts"	Wholesaler
tlachiuhqui	*tla-*; *chihua*; *-qui.* "maker of things"	Producer, vendor, craftsman
tlaciuitiani	*tla-*; *cui* "the act of taking things?"	Solicitor (Sahagún 1961:32–33)
tlacocoaliztli	*tla-*; *co-*, distributive of *cohua* implying many repetitions; *-cohua*; *-liztli.* "the act of buying things"	A purchase, the act of buying
tlacohuani	*tla-*; *cohua*; *-ni.* "he who buys things"	Buyer

Nahuatl words	Morphology and literal definition	Colonial economic context
tlaixtlapanaliztli	*tla-*; *ix-* (from the noun *ixtli* which means face, eye or surface); *tlapana*, to profit; *-liztli*. "the act of profiting by multiplying ones possessions by loaning" with usury.	Usury (Molina 1977)
tlaixtlapanqui	*tla-*; *ix-* (not identified); *tlapana*; *-qui*.	Investor, profiteer
tlamama, tlameme	from *mama* and *meme*, to carry something	Porter
tlamieccanquixtiani	*tla-*; *mieccan*, many times, places or points, *quixtia*, to leave or withdraw; *-ni*. "someone who divides something into many parts, charges usury with interest."	Usurer (Siméon 1991)
tlamieccanquixtiliztli	*tla-*; *mieccan*, many times, places or points, *quixtia*, to leave or withdraw; *-liztli*. "the act of dividing into pieces or loaning with usury.	Usury (Siméon 1991)
tlanamacac	*tla-*; *namaca*; *-c*. "seller of things"	Seller, vendor, merchandiser
tlanamacaliztli	*tla-*; *namaca*; *-liztli*. "the act of selling things"	Sale, act of selling something
tlanecuilo	*tla-*; *necuiloa*. "he who bends, twists things, engages in commerce"	Dealer, also swindler, sharp dealer
tlaquixtiani	*tla-*; *quixtia*; *-ni*. "one who removes things"	Importer, wholesaler
tlaquehualli	from *tlaquehua*	A person hired to do something
tlaxtlahuilli	from *ixtlahuia*	Payment to someone (salary)

was clearly a skill, it was also seen as a function of one's good fate and being born on a propitious day for a life of commerce. Being born on the day 4 dog, for example, was seen as a favorable augury for success in commerce, especially raising and selling dogs. As Sahagún relates,

His dogs would grow; none would die of sickness. As he trafficked in them, so they became [numerous as] the sands ... Thus the breeding of dogs resulted well with him. He sold them all. And all which were born, all came to be capes [for him]. Also owners and breeders of dogs became rich, and the price of dogs was so high, because they were eaten and needed by the people in days of old

(Sahagún 1979a:19–20).

Economic Anthropologists have long recognized that accumulation and gaining advantage through exchange is possible in all societies, even in those that lacked general purpose currencies (Barnett 1968; Harding 1967; Herskovits 1965; Pospisil 1968; Radford 1968). In Mesoamerica goods could be acquired using both indigenous money and through barter. In both cases, value was established actively through haggling.

Barter was the basis for all early economic exchanges and certainly was practiced across prehispanic Mesoamerica. By barter I mean the direct exchange of one commodity for another irrespective of place or setting.[7] It is a means for transferring goods between individuals through negotiation. Barter can take place in a wide range of settings, from the patio of a household to a busy marketplace. Berdan (1975:217) believes that although several forms of money were used in highland marketplaces, barter remained an active component of market interaction. This enabled commoners operating as target marketers to exchange small quantities of the goods (i.e. maize, chile, and fruit) for specific commodities without having to first sell them. This meant that market venders could have taken in a variety of staple products like maize in exchange for goods. While this is not mentioned in colonial period sources, it is a fundamental way that exchanges occurred in many traditional markets around the world (Bohannan and Dalton 1965; Stanish 2010; Stanish and Coben 2013).

Francisco Hernández specifically identified barter as a widely practiced economic activity across Central Mexico.

They had no system of weights and measures. They did not have metal money, instead bartering or using cacao seeds

(Varey 2000:77).

And again,

They lived by means of the barter system ... with people providing one another with freshly picked fruit, until the day that coins ... began to be minted

(Varey 2000:107).

The concept of barter as a form of exchange is expressed in *Nahuatl* in several ways. The word *patilia* literally means to exchange something with somebody (Table 8.2). Likewise the word *timotlapatilia* means to barter something with someone.[8] We see this word used in Motolinia's sixteenth-century confessional guide (Christensen 2011; Dibble 1988; Motolinia 1950, 1973) where the priest asks about improper and deceitful behavior in the marketplace. He inquires, "And when you sell something, or buy something, or exchange something at the market place, do you deceive others and cheat people?" The meaning of *timotlapatilia* as barter in this context is made clear by its juxtaposition with the alternatives of buying and selling. A number of scholars have cited the fundamental importance of barter in economic exchanges throughout Mesoamerica (Alba 1949:47; Muñoz Carmargo 1972:265) and Chapman (1957a:128) felt that all foreign trade was based on barter. Barter as discussed in Chapter 6 is still practiced on a small-scale in Michoacan and other areas of Mexico.

Establishing value through barter usually follows one of two paths. One approach is the use of fixed rates of exchange (e.g. two apples for one orange) with negotiation over the quality and size of the items (Mayer 2002). The other is through haggling and lively negotiation (Malinowski 1922). The word *ixnextia* is the *Nahuatl* word meaning to haggle (Table 8.2). It literally means to make a profit face-to-face.[9] Likewise, the word to negotiate is *tlatennonotza*, the entomology of which is constructed from the word *tentli* for lips or mouth and *nonotza* meaning to converse, discuss, or come to an agreement (Table 8.2). Finally, the word for asking the price of something is *tzatzalia* (Table 8.2). Rojas (1995:260) sees negotiation over price as active haggling since the root for *tzatzalia* comes from the verb *tzatzi* which means to shout, sing, or cry (Siméon 1991). Anyone who has been in Mexico can appreciate the lyric nature of market interaction as stall and street venders call out prices of goods for sale. It is also evident in the speech scrolls placed in front of the mouths of the market venders illustrated in the Florentine Codex such as the maize seller (Figure 5.2) and the bean seller (Figure 6.1. The two-way dimension of negotiation is illustrated in Sahagún's depiction of interaction with the tobacco dealer (Figure 6.4). This dimension of negotiation is reiterated by Sahagún (1961:63) who states that a good merchant as an individual who is just, fair, and "who adjusts the price."

CURRENCY AS MEDIUM OF EXCHANGE

The use of money in ancient Mexico has been thoroughly discussed by modern scholars (Berdan 1975; Durand-Forest 1971; León-Portilla 1962;

Rojas 1995). Several forms of money facilitated buying and selling in the marketplace although the prehispanic view of money was different from ours. Modern money is a general purpose currency that simultaneously serves as a medium of exchange, a unit of account, a standard for payment, and a means of storage (Dalton 1965; Plattner 1989b; Weatherford 1997). Money in the Aztec world was a special purpose commodity with agreed upon values that served as mediums of exchange (LeClair and Schneider 1968:467).

The *Nahuatl* word for money is *tlacocohualoni* which came in several forms.[10] The most common types of money were cacao (chocolate) beans, standardized textiles (*quachtli*), T-shaped copper axes, and gold dust in transparent feather plumes (Clavijero 1974:236, 257; Katz 1966:59; Rojas 1995:244–245). Copper axes and gold dust had recognized value but did not circulate widely as a form of money. Moreover all these forms of money probably varied in value and importance over space and between cultures.[11] Rojas (1995:245) indicates that copper axes were used in exchange for things of low value while the value of plumes depended upon the amount of gold dust that they contained. Both of these items moved as tribute within the Aztec empire.[12]

The two most important forms of money were *quachtli* textiles and cacao beans which functioned together in a system of interchangeable denominations. *Quachtli* were plain white cotton textiles that according to Sahagún (1959:48) circulated in three different size-value denominations calculated in cacao: small *quachtli* were worth 65 cacao beans, medium sized *quachtli* were worth 80 cacao beans, and large *quachtli* were worth 100 cacao beans. Besides size, quality and tightness of weave would also have affected value. Rojas (1995:244) feels that *quachtli* were produced specifically for exchange rather than as a separate use item that had value. While a possibility it is more likely that their value derived from the combined effect of their standardized sizes and the fact that they could be made into clothing. Berdan (1975:227) notes that *quachtli* were more important and had a higher degree of negotiability in the pre-conquest documents than in colonial ones. Textiles of different types were a standard item in the Aztec tribute system and *quachtli* were regularly used to pay fines (Garibay 1973:89). They had fungible value as Sahagún notes when he describes their ability to be exchanged for food in the marketplace:

Behold, here the husband provideth … [his wife] … with merchandise, five large cotton capes with which thou wilt negotiate at the market place, with which thou

wilt procure the sustenance, the chili, the salt, the torches, and some firewood, that
thou mayest prepare food

(Sahagún 1969:132).

Quachtli fell out of use quickly during the colonial period when they
were replaced by Spanish coin (Rojas 1995:255). The last clear reference
to the regular use of *quachtli* as currency dates to 1530. This is when
tribute paid to Spanish encomenderos switched from *quachtli* to staple
goods (Garibay 1961:176–177). The indigenous currency that continued
and expanded in use during the colonial period was cacao.

Cacao had a special place in Mesoamerican prehistory. According to
Hernández: "The seed of the cacao tree served instead of money, and this
is what they used to buy things (Varey 2000:108)." Four types of cacao
were grown in Mesoamerica, three large bean varieties which were regularly used for money, and a small bean variety regularly consumed in
beverages[13] (Berdan 1975:fn 61). Cacao was consumed as a beverage
during all important social and ritual events[14] (Durand-Forest 1967).
Cacao was grown in areas below 1,000 m in elevation and as a result
was the object of long-distance exchange into the highlands. The high
demand for cacao made it a commodity that always was accepted in trade
and transformed it into a fractional currency in Mesoamerica. The
sixteenth-century writer Bartolomé de las Casas (1967:I:368) says that
cacao beans were used to even out barter exchanges when exact equivalents could not be found (Berdan 1975:223). Its widespread use as a
currency is recorded by Cortés who states that cacao was:

a fruit resembling our almonds which they sell crushed, and of which they have
such stores that they are used as money throughout the land to buy all necessities
in the public markets and elsewhere

(Cortés 1962:79).

The Spanish quickly recognized that cacao functioned as money and
secretly looted the royal storage area of cacao during their stay in Moctezuma Xocoyotzin's palace where Torquemada (1975:I:472) reported that
40,000 cargas of cacao were stored.[15] Cortés paid his troops in cacao
during the first years of the conquest (Durand-Forest 1971:fn116) which
was the most expedient way for them to provision themselves with basic
necessities. Torquemada (1975:III:228) reports that the Spanish gave
cacao beans to beggars and the poor according to their faith and charity.
The Spanish referred to cacao as *moneda menuda* or small money because
it could be used for any number of small or large purchases both in and
outside the marketplace (Torquemada 1975:III:228).

We know that cacao was an effective currency for two reasons. First, the Spanish continued to use it well into the colonial period until the production of silver coinage covered the demand for fractional currency. Second, cacao was counterfeited during prehispanic times which underscores its importance as a currency if people took the time to counterfeit individual beans. Demand for cacao increased after the conquest as more individuals consumed it as a drink (Christiansen 2011). The region of Xoconochco remained a primary production area for cacao until the market collapsed in the seventeenth century[16] (Lewis 1976:131). Although the Spanish got involved in its production after the conquest (Ortiz Díaz 2010:252), the transportation and exchange of cacao remained largely in the hands of indigenous merchants throughout the sixteenth century. Indian merchants trekked to Xoconochco from Mexico City, Tlaxcala, Cholula, and Oaxaca to buy cacao transporting it to central Mexico using *tlameme* porters (Berdan 1986:293; MacLeod 1980; Ortiz Díaz 2010:251; Szewczyk 1976:140). While indigenous merchants commonly used groups of 15–35 porters, one Indian merchant was given a license to use 1000 *tlameme* porters to bring cacao to Mexico City in 1542 (Hassig 1986:141).

Table 8.3 provides a summary of known prices for commodities during the first twenty-five years after the conquest. The "small change" dimension of cacao is evident in the number of different food items that could be purchased for a few cacao beans. The price of a year's labor was calculated in terms of the subsistence value of 20 large *quachtli* valued at 100 cacao beans each; this was the normal price paid when someone sold themselves into slavery (Durand-Forest 1967:179). *Quachtli*, therefore, can be thought of as larger denominations of cacao and when they were used together they functioned as an integrated and divisible system of all-purpose commodity money.

RULES OF THE ROAD: STRATEGIES FOR INTER-REGIONAL EXCHANGE

All travel outside the local community was risky and even moving between neighboring communities could be problematical when local animosities developed over fractious personal relationships, land disputes, or political tensions. These types of problems are illustrated by a disagreement that arose in the Basin of Mexico between the communities of Tenochtitlan and Coyoacan separated by only 13 km.[17] According to Durán,

TABLE 8.3: *The cost of goods in cacao*

Item	Cost in cacao beans	Date	Source
1 large tomato, 1 tamale, 2 cactus fruits, 4 ripe chiles, 20 small tomatoes, chopped firewood	1	1545	Anderson et al. 1976
1 avocado: fully ripe to newly picked	1–3	1545	Anderson et al. 1976
1 fish wrapped in maize husks	3	1545	Anderson et al. 1976
1 turkey egg	3	1545	Anderson et al. 1976
1 salamander	2–4	1545	Anderson et al. 1976
1 strip pine bark kindling	5	1545	Anderson et al. 1976
1 day's labor	20	1521–1526	Borah and Cook 1958:45
1 small rabbit	30	1545	Anderson et al. 1976
1 small *quachtli* cloth	65	Contact	Sahagún 1959; Durand-Forest 1971
1 medium *quachtli* cloth (*tecuachtli*)	80	Contact	Sahagún 1959; Durand-Forest 1971
1 large *quachtli* cloth (*totolcuachtli*)	100	Contact	Sahagún 1959; Durand-Forest 1971
1 forest hare	100	1545	Anderson et al. 1976
1 turkey hen	100	1545	Anderson et al. 1976
1 canoe of potable water	100; 1 *totolcuachtli* worth 100 cacao	Contact	Sahagún 1959; Durand-Forest 1971
1 turkey cock	200	1545	Anderson et al. 1976
Subsistence for 1 year, the price for selling yourself into slavery	2,000; 20 *totolcuachtli* worth 100 cacao/cloth	Contact	Durand-Forest 1967

(*continued*)

TABLE 8.3: (*continued*)

Item	Cost in cacao beans	Date	Source
1 slave for sacrifice	3,000–4,000; 30–40 *totolcuachtli* worth 100 cacao/cloth	Contact	Sahagún 1959; Garibay 1961:177

Note: Prices changed throughout the colonial period as a result of inflation with the value of cacao ranging from 100 to 200 cacao beans to 1 Spanish tomín or silver real. According to Rojas (1995:255) the value of the real was regulated at 140 cacao beans in 1555 and then 120/real in 1590. The value of cacao in the 1545 Tlaxcalan document published by Anderson et al. 1976, equates 1 tomín to 200 "full" cacao beans or 230 "shrunken" beans (Berdan 2014:126).

One fine day some Aztec women were on their way to the market at Coyoacan with their merchandise, to buy and sell as usual ... When they reached the place of the guards, the latter came out and, as these men were declared to be enemies of the Aztecs, they robbed the women of everything they carried, then raped them and made them flee. The women, tearful and full of anguish, returned to the Aztec city and told their husbands what had occurred. Everyone was overwhelmed by this disagreeable incident and the king of Tenochtitlan gave orders forbidding the people to go to the market at Coyoacan. But some persisted, believing that only common thieves had robbed and despoiled the Aztec women. And so, stubbornly going to this market, they continued to be robbed and assaulted

(Durán 1994:86).

Safety was a persistent concern and several strategies were employed to mediate the risks of travel and assault. Durán's account underscores one fundamental rule of the road: travel in groups. The women on the way to Coyoacan were *macehualli* producer-sellers of the goods they sold (see Chapter 5). The fact that no men accompanied the women suggests two things. First, they took small amounts of items to sell, and second, they were accustomed to make this trip together without additional protection. The goods taken from them may have consisted of prepared food or lake resources which Aztec women sold in the marketplace (Durán 1994:105).

It is likely that all producer-sellers and retail merchants regularly traveled in groups outside their communities to avoid theft along the road. This is implied by the tax documents from the Coyoacan which lists the individuals trading in the marketplace. Tax document 4 groups sellers by the communities they came from. As a result spindle makers, tobacco sellers and tobacco-tube makers, wood dealers, pine-torch splitters, sandal makers, and *oztomeca* merchants are grouped by place of origin instead of by the goods they sold (Anderson et al. 1976:147–149). While this may be a device used to organize the tax report rather than a reflection of how the marketplace was structured, it suggests that sellers from the same towns may have traveled together in small groups along the same routes. Durán (1994:106) reports that merchants trafficking in cotton traveled in groups over the 50–100 km between Morelos and the Basin of Mexico.

Vanguard merchants always traveled in caravans over the distances that they traversed. These caravans were led by the merchant who organized it and the success of the venture was often determined by his skill, preparations, and knowledge.[18] The composition of the caravan was diverse and consisted of everybody from experienced merchants and professional porters, to apprentices and young boys going on their first long-distance venture.

Sahagún (1959:14–15) indicates that loads were kept light upon departure for porters and merchants alike. Moreover, young boys carried nothing. The reason for this was to facilitate climbing hills (Sahagún 1981b:III:26). Light loads meant faster movement which was essential in hostile areas where stealth and speed were main elements of safety. This also served to condition their bodies for the long trek ahead since the first few weeks on the road were strenuous no matter how experienced a merchant was. Finally, light loads at the beginning of the trip did not imply light loads at its end. The goods taken for trade were generally lightweight, high-value commodities, but a successful venture would imply returning with heavy loads of high-value merchandise. The conversion of Ahuitzotl's 1,600 *quachtli* to high-value decorated cloaks and gold jewelry condensed both the value and the weight of the load taken to trade (Sahagún 1959:7). Better to start light and return heavy than the other way around.

Once on the road professional merchants and small groups of producer-sellers probably traveled together from home to market, or from market to market. Acosta Saignes (1945) and Chapman (1957a) incorrectly proposed that vanguard merchants only traded outside the empire. Aztec merchants regularly frequented marketplaces both inside and outside the empire where goods could be purchased from local individuals selling to outside buyers. The reason for this was simple: marketplaces were the most secure places to conduct trade. The roads leading to marketplaces were normally guarded and local elite took responsibility of supervising the marketplace to ensure fair dealings and reasonable security. Failure to do so had dramatic effects since an attack on merchants often led to declarations of war.

Vanguard merchants took provisions with them for use on the road but this was not necessary for individuals operating between regional marketplaces. The sequential timing of marketplaces made it possible for merchants to move at a normal pace trading goods from market to market as they worked their way across the landscape (see Chapter 3).

Environmental diversity across the highlands made local marketplaces the bulking points for an array of regional resources as well as the specialized craft goods manufactured from them. They were perfect spots to acquire local goods at the lowest prices. One such example was the Mixtec marketplace at Coixtlahuaca where merchants regularly obtained feathers, cacao, fine gourd bowls, clothing, and thread made of rabbit fur (Berdan 1988:642). It was here that 160 merchants from the towns in the Basin of Mexico were killed in a plot to incite the Aztecs to declare war.[19] The number of merchants trading in Coixtlahuaca was high and included those from the Puebla-Tlaxcala region, the Mixteca, and the Valley of Oaxaca. It is possible that the merchants from these other areas exceeded those from the Basin of Mexico.

The logistics of trade increased in complexity with the time spent away from home and the distance traveled. After safety, the two critical concerns of merchants on the road were food and lodging. According to Sahagún (1959:14) vanguard merchants took prepared travel food such as *pinolli* with them on their expeditions.[20] *Pinolli* was a high calorie mixture of toasted maize flour, herbs, spices, and possibly ground nuts, *chia (Salvia hispanica)*, and *huauhtli (amaranthus* sp.). While recipes varied, it was the prehispanic equivalent of the modern tail mix and high energy drinks consumed by hikers and marathon runners. *Pinolli* was mixed with water, did not require cooking, and was drunk cold; it was a perfect food for merchants on the road.

Trail food like *pinolli* probably was not the everyday staple of merchants on the road. Marketplaces then as now, were always places where prepared foods could be purchased (Sahagún 1979b:67). Vanguard merchants took utilitarian goods with them to trade in the marketplace so it is possible that they bartered these goods for provisions to feed themselves. Nevertheless, merchants around the world are notoriously frugal and probably prepared their own meals whenever possible with ingredients carried with them or purchased along the way. Peddlers (*tlacôcoalnamacac*) operating outside of marketplaces probably arranged eating and housing arrangements with the individual families that they interacted with over their normal circuits. This appears to have been the case at Xochicalco, Morelos where itinerant obsidian craftsmen who sold blades in its marketplace were also the primary suppliers of raw material for local craftsmen (Hirth 2008b). It is likely that these itinerant craftsmen were housed and fed in the households of Xochicalco craftsmen as part of their reciprocal economic relationships (e.g. Heider 1969). In desperate situations Aztec law allowed hungry travelers to take up to twenty ears of corn from the first furrow along the road (Alba 1949:22). How widely this convention was recognized throughout Mesoamerica is unclear.

Theft was often punishable by death especially when it occurred in the marketplace (Alba 1949:21). The punishment for theft depended on the conditions surrounding it, with harsher punishment for crimes against the elite. Small crimes like the theft of less than twenty ears of corn could result in simple repayment. Nevertheless, stealing the same amount from a noble's field was punished by being sold into slavery. Cases of desperation allowed for more lenience (Alba 1949:22). In all cases, however, withdrawals of maize were restricted to the first row of the field as a safeguard against having entire fields looted during times of famine and impacting the survival of the household to whom the field belonged.

Another basic problem for traveling merchants was where to find safe lodgings. They most likely stayed with trade partners or related merchants in diaspora communities whenever they could (e.g. Curtin 1984). Martinez (1984) believes that merchant groups from Chalco and Xochimilco had small barrios of distant kinsmen in Tepeaca who provided lodgings when they visited the market there. This more likely was the exception rather than the rule. Other than the special community of Tochtepec, there is no indication that diaspora communities were maintained for this purpose as they were in other parts of the ancient world. The most likely practice for most commercial travelers was to overnight in the marketplaces and at the shrines that they visited during their travels.[21] This would have been highly desirable if merchants were allowed to enter marketplaces at night since they were safe zones, supervised and policed by local authorities.

The need for safe lodgings also resulted in the appearance of merchant hostels located along key commercial routes.[22] These hostels were known as *oztomecacalli*, literally merchant houses. These were not houses pertaining to specific merchant *calpulli* as Sahagún (1959) describes for the merchant community of Tochtepec; instead these hostels provided lodgings to all travelers. Bernal Díaz del Castillo noted the presence of these hostels during the march to Tenochtitlan (Katz 1966:65). While it is unclear how common *oztomecacalli* were along major trade routes, merchant rest houses are also reported from the Yucatán peninsula (Roys 1939; Scholes and Roys 1968:60). As a rule the Yucatecan Maya were generous and hospitable to travelers and only merchants were expected to pay for their stay if they lodged with families during their travels (Cardos de Méndez 1959:61).

Of course there were times when no safe lodgings could be found and merchants had to make rough camp in a sheltered or hidden place. This was the most dangerous and least favored option. When this occurred merchants gathered together, did penance, prayed to *Yacatecuhtli*, and hoped for the best (Sahagún 1979a:155).

Vanguard merchants reduced the dangers of the road by traveling in large caravans under the direction of an experienced merchant. The preparations for these expeditions reveal a great deal about their organization and some of the strategy employed to yield success (Sahagún 1959:14–16). Merchant expeditions were voluntaristic ventures. All community members willing to submit to the authority of a lead merchant could participate. The merchant's reputation and the success (or failures) of previous expeditions were the determining factor in his ability to recruit competent participants. Expedition members included a cross-section of the merchant community, from youths on their first trip to experienced career merchants. The training of merchants began as apprentices on these expeditions.[23] Throughout their upbringing youths were admonished by their parents and elders to learn through observation, show humility, be brave, and accept correction for their errors without complaint. These were the behaviors considered essential to surviving the dangers of the road.

The success of the expedition depended on the lead merchant making wise decisions while on the road. The expedition leader made all of the logistical arrangements for the expedition. He performed the ceremonial rituals and set the date for departure (see Chapter 7). He acquired the travel rations, gourds and drinking vessels used on the trip, assembled the merchandise of all the individuals who were invested in the venture, and hired the professional porters that would accompany them on the trip. He also oversaw the packing of the *cacaxtli* cargo frames and the division of weight so everyone carried a light load. All these preparations were done in the house of the lead merchant to maintain secrecy about the scale of the expedition and the wealth it carried.

One commercial strategy revealed in the discussion of expedition preparations is that more individuals invested in the merchant venture than actually made the trip. Expedition members took loads of goods on consignment from both principal merchants and merchant women which they sold on their behalf over the course of their travels (Sahagún 1959:14). We do not know if fees or commissions were charged for acting as commercial agents but I suspect that they were (Rojas 1995:247). Likewise, no information is provided about whether goods were entrusted to specific individuals or distributed to various participants as was the case for Ahuitzotl's consignment of goods to the *pochteca* community. Whatever the arrangement, consigned goods were almost certainly partitioned and kept separate throughout the expedition from the privately owned goods of caravan participants. This would have been necessary to preclude co-mingling of assets and the temptation to under-represent the return to the owners of the goods consigned.

The result was that merchant caravans were large heterogenous groups composed of individuals at different stages in their professional careers and carrying a diversity of both utilitarian and wealth goods. The wealth goods taken on these ventures included richly decorated capes trimmed with feather work, elaborate breech cloths and embroidered skirts, as well as an array of gold ornaments that included pendants, rings, and ear flares. The utilitarian goods intended for trade included obsidian and copper ear flares, obsidian razors with leather handles, pointed obsidian blades, rabbit fur, needles for sewing, shells, alum, and dyes such as cochineal (Sahagún 1959:8, 12). The utilitarian goods, in addition to procuring food provisions on the road, could have been used to acquire small lots of valued items offered for sale by local producer-sellers. Caravans from the same community probably included merchants with different specialties such as itinerant obsidian craftsmen who could produce blades for sale in local marketplaces. This certainly was the case for caravans from Santa Maria Acoxtla in Huexotzinco where two obsidian craftsmen are listed as members of their merchant community (Figure 7.4).

Even large caravans attempted to move quickly through unfamiliar or dangerous territory (Garibay 1961:57; Sahagún 1959:15) although speed was not their only defense. *Pochteca* merchants traveled armed but preferred to avoid a fight rather than engage in one. The division of cargos between multiple porters was an effective strategy to minimize loss if one or more porters were killed in an attack and their cargos lost. Segmented cargos also would have helped reinforce group interdependence and solidarity when they were on the road.

The practice of carrying divided or segmented cargos is implied by the unusual events that Sahagún describes for merchants returning from a successful expedition. He states:

> And as to goods ... Not at one's [own] home did one arrive, [but] perhaps at the house of his uncle or his aunt ... or it was only someone else's house into which he went–one who was of good heart, who told no lies. Nor was he a thief; he was prudent. And this owner of the goods did not acknowledge them; he did not take the goods himself, he did not claim them as his own. And there ... into as many cities as he bore their goods ... He did not claim the goods, the property, as his own. He only told them: ... (those who guarded the goods) ... They are not my goods which I have carried; they are the goods of our mothers, our fathers, the merchants, the vanguard merchants
>
> (Sahagún 1959:31).

Three aspects of this statement imply that merchants carried divided cargos. First, the merchants state that the goods are not his own. Second, ownership was assigned, at least in part, to merchant women and principal merchants who consigned goods for trade at the start of the expedition (Sahagún 1959:14). Third, goods were not taken to either the merchant's private home, or to the home of the expedition's leader who organized the venture. Instead, they were taken to an honest and impartial third party where they were placed under guard until they were collected by their owner. Who was the owner? Apparently *not* the merchant who transported them. This division of merchandise insured that profits from consigned goods would reach their rightful owners and there would be no question about the honesty with which consigned goods were handled.

The care taken with the final division of goods suggests that consignments were kept separate throughout the expedition to prevent commingling with the private property of the merchants who traded them. It is even possible that consigned goods were traded by one merchant and accounted for by another. While this would not have eliminated all opportunities for dishonesty, the emphasis on corporate accountability and reputation within the moral economy of merchant communities would have greatly reduced the temptation to engage in dishonest practices.

Commercial success meant that merchants returned more heavily laden than when they left. The profit from their transactions was in the form of cacao, capes, jade, and other raw materials which would have been both bulkier and heavier than many of the high-value gold goods taken with them on their outward journey (Sahagún 1959:8). Even if the hired porters stayed with them the entire journey, heavier loads inevitably reduced the mobility and speed with which merchants traveled. One solution to this problem was to purchase slaves for use as porters on the return trip. That this was a regular practice is implied by Sahagún's description of the return journey of vanguard merchants to the Basin of Mexico. He states that merchants followed the roads with purpose until they reached the town of Itzocan, Puebla where they awaited for a favorable day sign to return home. Itzocan, was famous for its large slave market and was where the Aztecs kept a garrison of troops (Asselbergs 2004:41; M. Smith 2012c:112). If slaves were used as porters they could be sold there for a good price and then other porters hired or the loads repacked for the short trip home. This was probably a common practice since the *tecoanmime* dealt in slaves (Acosta Saignes 1945:10). Slaves were regularly used as porters in southern Mesoamerica where they were sold in foreign ports along with their cargos (Attolini Lecón 2010:66; Chapman 1957a:134).

FACILITATING EXCHANGE: AGENTS, BROKERS, AND FACTORS

One way to judge the complexity of a commercial system is by the type and number of commercial instruments that it contains. Commercial instruments refer to the economic tools and agreements regularly used to facilitate exchange. In the modern world these include business contracts, loans, rental agreements, and all forms of insurance. Commercial instruments also existed in the ancient Old World in the form of comenda agreements (Abu-Lughod 1989:217; Dyer 2005:14; Grief 1989; Rossabi 1993:354; Yoshinobu 1970:31), maritime insurance (Bayly 1983:418; Moore and Lewis 1999:210; Reed 2003:35), and annuities. Even simple things like minted currencies were important commercial instruments in the way they facilitated exchange in the era when they were invented. Commercial instruments expedite exchange even when they are against the law. For example, commercial loans were made throughout medieval Europe even though they were considered to be usury and against the law. The problem was deflected by structuring the loans as currency conversions (Parks 2005).

The commercial tools employed in ancient Mesoamerica were relatively simple. Cacao and *quachtli* facilitated exchange and most production was organized at the household level. Wage labor as we know it did not exist. The marketplace was the central economic institution in society and most business dealings between non-kinsmen were conducted there.

Transactions between business associates both within and outside the marketplace were based on the principles of reciprocity, integrity, and honesty. Severe legal sanctions existed against theft and dishonesty but the need to enforce them seems to have been more the exception than the rule. Mesoamerican commerce did not employ writing, oath taking, or other physical sureties to structure business relationships and as a result many of the subtleties and complexities of these dealings are lost. Nevertheless, there is enough indirect evidence to suggest that structured business agreements were made between individuals on a regular basis which included using agents and factors, as well as making loans and charging interest.

Brokers and factors were used as commercial agents to assist in conducting trade over long distances. Both types of agents served the economic interests of their clients and their function was the same: to facilitate the movement, purchase, or sale of goods. Brokers and factors did not operate free-of-charge, but were paid a commission for conducting business. In the cross-cultural perspective the difference between these two types of agents is in the degree of permanency in the client–agent relationship. *Brokers* are agents with short-term economic relationships with their clients that normally did not endure beyond a specific transaction.[24] *Factors* also function as agents, but differ from brokers by establishing enduring and ongoing economic relationships with their clients. Factors in a real sense were commercial associates of their clients whether their relationship was one of business partner, employee, regular customer, or perpetual creditor. They were nodes in dendritic commercial systems through which goods moved on a regular basis.[25]

The practice of consigning goods to other merchants at the beginning of a long-distance trade venture is an example of using brokers to engage in commercial exchange. Goods were assembled and entrusted to other merchants who acted as agents on the owner's behalf. The individuals identified as consigning goods in Sahagún (1959) were the principal merchants and the merchant women, probably widows of former merchants who may have lived off the returns from these investments. This practice was presumably available to anyone in the merchant community with goods to invest in trade but could not travel themselves.[26] What is important is that goods were consigned to merchants, who as far as can be determined, were not necessarily family members of the consignors.[27] The practice of consigning goods appears to have been a regular economic practice. In describing the principal merchant, Sahagún (1961:60) states that he is, "a governor of merchantry. He consigns, he entrusts wares to others. Wares are consigned, marketed, sold." This brief description does not clarify whether merchants received a commission or percentage of the goods procured instead of doing so free-of-charge. Nevertheless, since this is described as a commercial relationship, it is likely that agents received some economic return for the work invested in conducting the exchange.

That the consignor–broker relationship was a formal one is implied by the way consigned goods were handled in preparation for a trade expedition. Consigned goods were not given directly to a specific individual as part of their personal inventory of goods. Instead, they were assembled and displayed separately as consigned goods in the house of the expedition leader. This served as a public proclamation to the merchant community that a consignment was made as part of the trade venture. It also allowed individuals to view the quantity and quality of goods being consigned. This is important because the community as a whole could then judge whether the return from the consignment was "reasonable" given the success of other merchants participating in the expedition. Public opinion and an emphasis on integrity probably was a key feature of a merchant's image and a strong motivating factor for ensuring the honesty of brokers viz-a-viz the consignments entrusted to them.

The use of factors established an enduring economic network through which goods flowed on a regular and predictable basis. The factor-client relationship also provided the framework for creating and cementing economic relationships between diaspora communities (e.g. Curtin 1984). The best direct evidence for the ongoing use of factors comes from southern Mesoamerica where elite members of society regularly engaged in trade. At the time of the conquest, the province of Acalan was very important in long-distance trade. Acalan is a *Nahuatl* term meaning land of the boats. Itzamkanac was the capital and it was here that the ruler and primary merchant named Paxbolonacha resided.[28] Hernan Cortés visited Acalan in 1525 during his march to Honduras and provides valuable information about Paxbolonacha and the nature of his commercial activity (Cortés 1962; Herrera y Tordesillas 1725, 1934; López de Gómara 1966). Paxbolonacha, referred to as Apoxpalón in the Spanish sources, regularly used agents to engage in trade and conduct business in the towns outside of Acalan (Scholes and Roys 1968). According to López de Gómara,

In the land of Acalán ... Apoxpalón ... enjoyed a large land trade in cotton, cacao, slaves, salt, and gold (although this was not plentiful and was mixed with copper and other things); in colored shells ... in resin and other incense for the temples; in pitch pine for lighting; in pigments and dyes ... and in many other articles of merchandise, luxuries or necessities. For this purpose he held fairs in many towns, such as Nito, where he had agents and separate districts for his own vassals and traders

(López de Gómara 1966:354).

Two things are particularly interesting about this account from a commercial point of view. The first is the diversity of both high- and low-value commodities that Paxbolonacha trafficked in. The second is the scale of his operations. While the province of Acalan is located on the Mexican Gulf Coast, the town of Nito was located on the Gulf of Honduras, east of the Yucatán peninsula. The distance from Acalan to Nito was 1,500 km by canoe around the Yucatán peninsula or 415 km overland across the Peten. Since canoes were the main way to travel in Acalan, it is likely that Nito was reached by following the maritime route. The reference to Paxbolonacha's trade in salt reinforces the likelihood that he used a maritime route since salt was not produced in either Acalan or Nito, but was obtained primarily from the north coast of Yucatán (Andrews 1983; Cardos de Méndez 1975; Kepecs 2003). Cacao produced in both Acalan and Nito was probably used along with other goods to procure Yucatecan salt.

What Paxbolonacha and the merchants of Acalan developed was a network of factors that obtained goods in one locale and resold them in another. This network was based on the placement of factors as permanent commercial agents in foreign towns to engage in trade on the merchant's behalf. This was the case in Nito where merchants of Acalan occupied a whole ward of the town. They apparently were permanent residents in Nito since they were ruled by Paxbolonacha's brother (Scholes and Roys 1968:58). While little is known about them, these Acalan residents appear to have formed a diaspora community in the Nito area for the purpose of trade.[29]

The use of factors produced a network through which ongoing trade took place. They required special facilities to conduct operations that included dormitories to house merchants, production facilities, and warehouses to store goods. The use of factors was relatively common across southern and eastern Mesoamerica. According to Scholes and Roys (1968:3), wealthy merchants from Xicalango, Tabasco; Potonchan, Campeche; the interior of Yucatán, and Chetumal along the east coast of Yucatán all had factors, factories, and permanent warehouses on the Ulua River in Honduras. This trade was important enough that when the Spanish set out to conquer Honduras, the ruler of Chetumal sent a force of fifty war canoes to defend his commercial interests on the Ulua river (Scholes and Roys 1968:317).

The question of course is did Aztec *pochteca* do the same thing? Did they also use factors where appropriate to establish enduring commercial contacts in the areas where they traded? The answer is probably yes. The community of Tochtepec very likely contained factors who operated in consort with vanguard merchants. Tochtepec was a base of operations used by all *pochteca* groups from the Basin of Mexico. It had *calpulli* houses, *calpulli* temples, and storage facilities for merchants engaged in trade with adjacent regions. Given the concentration of merchants at this locale it is likely that other groups came to Tochtepec to trade with *pochteca*. While the information about Tochtepec is limited, we know that *pochteca* had warehouses and used factors in the Chontalpa of eastern Veracruz in the towns of Mecoacan, Chilateupa, and Teutitlan Copilco (Scholes and Roys 1968:31). It is the reference to these merchant factors and facilities that led Ann Chapman (1957a, 1957b) to propose that these communities functioned as ports-of-trade for Aztec *pochteca*. A combination of ethnohistoric and archaeological evidence also suggests that the town of Naco on the Ulua river may also have had a colony of *Nahua* traders (Roys 1943:117; Scholes and Roys 1968:321; Thompson 1970:78; Wonderley 1986; Ximénez 1920).

The role of factors in the ancient world has always been the same: to sell the goods they have to offer and to buy goods as part of extended procurement chains for sale elsewhere. The use of factors and resident commercial agents is an effective way to penetrate foreign economies to acquire resources. Where market systems exist, the marketplace is the natural focal point for procuring resources through trade. In non-market economies, or where marketplaces are held infrequently, large surpluses may be difficult to mobilize even with elite involvement. Under these circumstances the use of factors provides a way to assemble resources in small lots over prolonged periods of time. This may explain the presence of factors in southern Mesoamerica where populations were more dispersed and marketplaces were held as periodic religious fairs. They are not apparent in central Mexico where the marketplace was the primary vehicle for mobilizing and purchasing key resources. In areas where markets were active the use of factors was less common.

MAKING LOANS AND CHARGING INTEREST

The level of commercial activity in both ancient and modern societies is based on the amount of disposable wealth or income available to purchase goods. Access to fungible wealth is a necessary prerequisite for merchants to buy goods for resale. They can either provide the capital themselves, obtain it through a cost-sharing arrangement (e.g. comenda), or procure it through an interest bearing loan. Documenting the presence of formal loans, therefore, is important because it indicates the development of an economic rationale beyond simple credit or delayed return.

There was no formal system of banking among the Aztecs. The individuals who came closest to fulfilling this role were the exchange dealers (*tlapatlac*) discussed in Chapter 6. The function of these individuals was the conversion of high-value commodities and other goods into smaller, fractional currencies such as cacao beans that could be used in the marketplace (Sahagún 1961:61–62). They also would have converted bulk goods into condensed wealth that could be transported over space. These individuals were rich merchants who made their living by converting goods at a discount rate which they could resell at full or higher value. In this way they were like the early bankers of Europe who began as merchants involved in discounting the value of different currencies used to purchase and sell goods moving between countries (Parks 2005).

Loans become a dynamic element in commercial transactions when they carry interest due upon repayment. The information on interest bearing loans is extremely limited because they were suppressed by the Spanish church. The idea of charging interest was a Christian heresy and a damnable sin. It was seen as an unnatural act in the same way the Catholic church viewed rape, homosexuality, and incest. Putting money to work in agriculture or a business venture was the "natural way" to make a profitable living. But loans were necessary for economic growth during the colonial period, so a series of ways emerged to circumvent the problem. One approach used by the Spanish was to structure the loan as an annuity with an annual payment and full face value redemption at the end of its term. These were referred to as *censos al quitar* (Burns 1999) and were used by convents and monasteries throughout New Spain to make income off endowments given to the church.[30] Direct interest bearing loans were forbidden so it is interesting to find reference to them as a *Nahua* practice in the colonial literature.

Two lines of evidence suggest the possibility that loans were made in the prehispanic world. The first is the linguistic evidence for words in *Nahuatl* that translate into the concept of charging interest. Since this practice was a Spanish heresy, the presence of these words in *Nahuatl* suggests it was a pre-conquest practice. The second line of support comes from references to loans and interest found in the accounts themselves.

The Spanish work-around for granting a loan without using a word for "interest" was captured by the phrase *dar a logro* (Molina 1977). *Logro* means to obtain, so the phase glosses the idea of receiving interest with the idea "to give to obtain." Although charging interest was forbidden, Molina (1977) did not hesitate in translating "dar a logro" into *Nahuatl* as *tetech nitlanecuiloa* and *tetech nitlaixtlapana*. *Necuiloa* means to bend or twist something (like an arm in our thinking) and in economic contexts to engage in commerce. *Tetech* means "with somebody," so the idea of interest is "I engage in commerce with someone." The phrase *tetech nitlaixtlapana* likewise means to make a profit with someone, in this context as a loan with interest. Siméon (1991) translates usury directly as *tlamieccanquixtiliztli*.

References to charging interest also are found in early colonial sources. The first comes from Sahagún's discussion of a bad merchant. He is identified as "... a practiser of trickery, an illicit trafficker. He tricks others, practices usury, demands excessive interest (Sahagún 1961:59)." Two things are of interest here. The first is that it is a merchant who is making a loan which confirms that loans were part of the commercial world they operated in. The second is that the interest charged was viewed as excessive. What this implies is that charging reasonable interest was acceptable.

A second reference to making loans with interest comes from the *Codex of Tepeucila*. A loan is mentioned as background in litigation against Andrés de Tapia by the indigenous leaders of the Cuicateca community of Tepeucila, Oaxaca. According to the source the *caciques* and *tequitlato* of the town were forced to borrow forty-five gold pesos from merchants in Tenochtitlan and Texcoco to pay tribute to their encomendero in 1535. The conditions of the loan imposed an interest rate of 200% which returned three pesos for every one borrowed (Herrera Meza and Ruíz Medrano 1997:33). This rate of interest by any scale was usury, but the merchants apparently were well within their rights to ask for it. Furthermore, their method of collecting the loan was brutal with as many as hundred *pochteca* descending on Tepeucila to collect the debt. When they arrived they chased the *cacique* and other leading citizens out of town (Gutiérrez 2013:158; Herrera Meza and Ruíz Medrano 1997:36)! It should be noted that high rates of interest have traditionally been associated with loans based on repayment in kind. In Morelos during the late twentieth century rural farmers who borrowed seed corn from merchants were required to repay it at the 100% interest rate at harvest, a mere six months after the initial loan was made.

The Tepeucila account contradicts the statement by Zorita (1994:135) that loans were made without charging interest of any kind. What Zorita is probably describing is a loan in-kind where the same type of good that is loaned is returned after a period of time to the lender. These loans required repayment in-kind in a greater amount than was initially lent, creating the appearance of no interest being charged when it actually was (León-Portilla 1962:50). Loans appear to have required a bond or quantity of material goods be placed on deposit until the loan was repaid. This involved pawning or giving a material surety to the lender during life of the loan. This could result in pledging the service of a son as a slave to the lender until the debt was paid (Alba 1949:46–47). Individuals seeking loans without the means to place goods on deposit could pledge themselves as the bond. Failure to repay resulted in their becoming a slave of the lender. These obligations were transferable to the decedents of the debtor, with the wife or son becoming a slave if the debtor died before repayment[31] (Torquemada 1975:II:566). Slavery was also the punishment if an agreement was broken or if a piece of land used to guarantee a loan was sold before repayment (Alba 1949:22; Calnek 1978:111).

CLOSING THE TOOLBOX

This chapter has examined the principles of operation of highland *Nahua* economies and some of the commercial tools that merchants used to carry them out. This information is not easy to obtain. The precolumbian world did not employ forms of writing or other physical recording devices to identify ownership, or to establish, validate, or reinforce business agreements. Mesoamerican economy was an oral economy, reinforced by good reputation, public witness, and honesty before God. This practice did not change a great deal for native peoples during the colonial period. Indigenous merchants continued to conduct their business transactions using tradition and established social networks of mutual dependence.[32] The result is little documentary evidence regarding the scale of commerce and how transactions were struck. This together with the fact that professional merchants guarded the information about where to obtain resources has produced a scarcity of information on their modes of operation.

The moral economy emphasized service, honest dealing, and hard work which allowed households to take advantage of economic opportunities when they presented themselves. Differences in elevation over relatively short distances created a landscape that juxtaposed different resource zones and stimulated a great deal of household level exchange. The major impediment to large-scale resource movement was the lack of beasts of burden and the absence of navigable rivers. The result was that most goods moved through exchange networks on the backs of human porters. The purpose of exchange ranged from fulfilling household subsistence needs to accumulating wealth for its own sake. Barter and fungible wealth in several forms of commodity money were used to facilitate commercial exchange.

Trade and travel were a risky business the further individuals got from home. Vanguard merchants traveled the furthest distances and attempted to mediate the risk of their trips by carefully following prescribed rituals, traveling in groups, frequenting supervised marketplaces, and finding safe lodgings in merchant hostels (*oztomecacaltin*). The success of long-distance trading ventures depended on finding profitable merchandise and avoiding trouble. Here the experience and knowledge of the merchant leader was critical for success.

Vanguard merchants did not venture blind into distant lands. They used established contacts from previous trips and searched for new opportunities where they could find them. Individuals placed goods on consignment with merchants who conducted business on their behalf for a commission or on a shares basis. In areas where markets were held less frequently they probably established commercial relationships with local merchants to conduct trade on their behalf. The practice of settling factors in distant regions may have helped create some of the *Nahua* diaspora communities found throughout Mesoamerica at the moment of conquest. Merchants were commercial creatures and they made and obtained loans to conduct business well into the colonial period despite the disdain of the Spanish church against all forms of interest as usury. It is likely that loans were an instrument of last resort rather than an active tool of commerce because of the high rates of interest charged.[33]

Highland *Nahua* society lacked a number of the economic tools of modern capitalism. What it did not lack, however, was the entrepreneurial spirit or the broad based involvement of individuals in commercial practices. Chapter 9 examines some of the general features of the highland *Nahua* commercial society and places them in a comparative framework with other ancient and premodern societies around the world.

9

Conclusions

More than a century ago Emile Durkheim observed that societies with higher levels of economic interdependence were more tightly integrated socially than those that were not. Durkheim referred to this economic interdependence as organic solidarity and felt that the social structures that emerged from the division of labor produced and supported larger and more durable societies. Commerce and exchange is the manifestation of economic interdependence and is a good point of departure for examining the scope of economic interaction in ancient and premodern societies around the world. It serves as a means of assessing not only internal integration as Durkheim suggested, but also the level of interaction between societies and across political boundaries.

The fundamental objective of this volume has been to explore the scale, complexity, and integration of the Aztec economic world so that it could be incorporated into a broader comparative discussion of ancient economy. What can be observed at the moment of the Spanish conquest was the end product of several thousand years of economic interaction between people located in ecologically diverse environmental zones in close proximity to one another. The organic development of marketplaces within different resource zones helped to stimulate commerce even under conditions where all goods moved on the backs of human porters. This system of regional commercial symbiosis was the foundation of the highland *Nahua* economy.

What the Aztecs added to this economic landscape was military conquest that extracted a huge quantity of wealth from a tribute empire covering between 160,000 and 165,000 sq km across Mesoamerica.[1] This wealth was funneled into the Basin of Mexico and the three primary cities of the Aztec military alliance: Tenochtitlan, Texcoco, and Tlacopan. It stimulated a wave of economic development as it trickled down into society through state sponsored festivals, elevated elite consumption, and rewards to warrior knights and military personnel. The tribute extracted from the Aztec empire also had a twofold effect on the conquered provinces. It forced an increase in regional production to meet Aztec tribute demands and stimulated inter-regional commerce within the empire to obtain the goods that provinces could not produce. The combination of these economic and political forces created the economic affluence and level of commercial activity that the Spanish encountered in AD 1519.

The discussion that follows will attempt to place the economic development of western Mesoamerica into a framework suitable for comparison with other societies in the ancient and premodern world. What developed in western Mesoamerica was a multi-tiered commercial system that included everything from simple producer-sellers to professional retailers and merchant importers with some wholesale and banking functions. The underlying catalyst for this system was the development of early marketplaces that provided the opportunity for both part-time and full-time professional merchants to buy, sell, trade, and barter goods in an open and direct way. What is particularly significant is that the level of market activity found in western Mesoamerica during the early sixteenth century is equal to, if not slightly higher than, what is found in Europe at the same point in time. While goods moved over greater distances in the Old World because of better systems of transportation, the level of commerce and the integration of rural households into the regional economy may have been greater than some areas of Europe because of the structure of regional market systems in western Mesoamerica.

COMMERCE AND THE ANCIENT ECONOMY

Determining the level of commercial activity in ancient society provides important information about seven important aspects of its past economy. First, the more commercial activity found in ancient or premodern societies, the more we can be assured that economic decisions were made by individuals without state directed involvement. Archaeological research has shown that commoner households were actively involved in commerce across the Mexican highlands at both the local and regional level (e.g. Brasswell 2003; Hirth 2013a, 2013b; Minc 2009; Pollard 1982, 2003; M. Smith 2003a, 2003b, 2010). The research presented here identified 124 producer-sellers who sold a range of different products in marketplaces within the Basin of Mexico alongside 39 different types of retail merchants. This certainly is not an inclusive list of all the commercial specialists found across the Aztec world, but it does reflect the type of economic diversity that existed at the time of the conquest.

Second, high levels of independent commercial involvement means greater variation in the types of goods produced and sold. Over 700 unique products (SKUs) were identified in historic sources which were only a fraction of the goods produced and offered for sale in highland marketplaces. Diversity in the type of goods sold is a measure of the level of consumer demand as well as the level of entrepreneurial activity involved in meeting it. Consumer demand was high and cross-cut all levels of *Nahua* society. Nevertheless, commercial activity reached its highest levels in the Basin of Mexico where the wealth entering through the tribute empire fueled a level of trickle down consumerism not found in other areas of Mesoamerica at the same time.

Third, commerce is the most effective way to move products rapidly from producers to consumers. In highland Mesoamerica large quantities of goods were mobilized through the marketplace, centralizing resource procurement, and making it both highly efficient and predictable. Markets were supervised by political leaders who provided the oversight to resolve disputes, maintain security, and insure fair practices. Beyond that, however, they operated largely on their own with minimal administrative interference. Fourth, the more centralized commercial activities became, the less costly it was to move goods within society. This is important in an area like Mesoamerica with some of the greatest transportation constraints in the ancient world. The level of commercial activity found here, however, suggests that some of our assumptions about transportation efficiency limiting exchange are either incorrect, or do not capture the way that prehispanic households operated with regard to resource provisioning. Modern scholars model resource movement in terms of relative transportation efficiency; it appears that ancient Mesoamerican people used a different logic.

Fifth, a great deal of commercial activity in the Aztec economic world was in the hands of commoner households. Small-scale craft production provided important resource gains that contributed to annual household subsistence. The size of that contribution is difficult to determine although it probably varied inversely with the amount of land that households had available for agriculture. One important aspect of Mesoamerican craft production that has been identified archaeologically was the tendency for full-time artisans to engage in multiple craft activities (multi-crafting) rather than specializing in a single craft at the household level (Hirth 2009a). The use of complementary technologies in multiple craft activities enabled households to broaden their response to market opportunities where they existed. Sixth, as mentioned earlier, commercial activity promotes higher levels of organic solidarity and economic interdependence between households in society (Durkheim 1984:200–225). While this is an obvious result of commerce, rates and levels of consumption are rarely examined as a measure of economic integration even though they provide a useful analytical framework for comparative economic analysis.

Finally, commercial activity provides insight into the riskiness of the economic environment. Travelers in the ancient world, especially those carrying valuable goods were always at risk of assault. Political unrest had a strong negative effect on commercial activity often changing the routes along which it moved. The higher the level of risk, the more economic activities were embedded in social or political relationships (Martin 1986:109–110). Conversely, the less risky the economic environment, the more goods moved over space and the higher the level of participation by individuals in the marketplace. This was the situation found across the Aztec world in the early sixteenth century. Whether out of fear of political retaliation, or because of a general toleration for traveling merchants, commerce was a regular feature of the Aztec economic world.

The prehispanic economy was complex and entrepreneurial. Despite the sophistication of precolumbian market systems and the level of commerce that they supported, prehispanic societies were a long way from the nascent capitalistic economies found at the beginning of the industrial revolution. The reason was not simply the lack of appropriate technology since this is not a precondition of capitalism or even the development of complex economic organization (Carneiro 1974). Instead, the structure of highland prehispanic economy was the product of several intersecting economic conditions: an ecologically diverse highland environment, a limited market in land, the absence of a free market in labor, and a transportation system limited to human porters. The indigenous response to these conditions was the development of a richly textured system of inter-locking marketplaces.

THE MATERIAL CONDITIONS OF COMMERCIAL ACTIVITY

The environmental conditions of the Aztec commercial world were discussed in the introduction to this volume. Its most important feature was the close juxtaposition of different environmental zones containing an array of distinct natural and agricultural resources. Environmental diversity within highland Mesoamerica occurs as pockets of different resources within a mountainous hill-country. Changes in elevation and variable rainfall patterns create variation within the highlands placing different lowland tropical and highland sub-tropical resources within a day or two walk of most areas (Figure 1.8).

Environmental diversity was an important incentive for small-scale economic interaction to develop across the highlands. The proximity of different resource zones made it possible for households in one ecological zone to procure resources from another, either through direct procurement or through trade with households residing there. The GIS spatial analysis of environmental diversity summarized in Figure 1.8 illustrates that over 85% of all households lived within 30 km, or one day's journey or less, from a different major ecological resource zone at least 1 sq. km in size. The symbiosis that emerged provided the foundation for the later levels of inter-regional commerce found at all levels across the Aztec economic world. Households were involved early in the procurement of resources from these different zones as a dimension of normal household provisioning. Small-scale inter-regional exchange probably developed with the appearance of the first settled villages around 1200 BC (Flannery 1976a; Hirth et al. 2013). The environment did not determine the structure of economic relationships, but it did provide the opportunity for different forms of economic synergism to develop. What emerged was a system of interconnected regional marketplaces where households could pursue a range of both independent resource procurement strategies and commercial pursuits.

The Aztec commercial world was a premodern economy in the sense that it did not develop large-scale markets for land, labor, or capital like those found in modern capitalistic economies. Some specific types of land could be bought and sold between elites but this practice appears limited in extent. Labor could be contracted for specific duties, jobs, or periods of time depending on the skills of the individuals involved. Slaves existed in the prehispanic world but they were not widely used as labor in either agriculture or craft production. Regarding the demand for capital, small loans apparently could be obtained but only with very high interest rates. Personal loans were secured by a pledge of material goods or bonded service, and where they occurred, were based on the inter-personal relationships of the individuals involved.

Land and labor were not free market commodities in the sense that they are today; access to both were embedded in the social structures that governed them. While each individual maintained control over the majority of their own labor, a portion of it was committed through *tequitl* obligations to serve the gods, society, and the governing elite. Corvee labor was mobilized from commoner households to support the production of goods for the institutional economy. There was little latitude for, or evidence of, large-scale "private" initiatives either in agriculture or craft production by individuals operating strictly in their own self-interest. Production within commoner households was organized using resident labor or labor that could be mobilized through immediate kinship or community relations. Production for elite households employed corvee labor as part of the institutional economy. Labor could be hired by an individual for specific tasks like transporting goods by porters, but this was for a specific purpose and work-for-wage was not a general principle or practice across society.

It is interesting that in the absence of wage labor, slavery did not develop as an institution to meet labor needs. Instead, slavery was considered an unfortunate condition of life arrived at by incurring debts or being captured in war. Debt slavery resulted in becoming the servant of one's creditor. Captives taken in war were not put to work: they were put to death as sacrifices to nourish the gods (Boone 1984; Townsend 1992). Thousands of war captives were sacrificed annually in Aztec ritual ceremonies (Cook 1946). While the Aztecs saw human sacrifice as a necessity, the ancient Greeks (Casson 1991:45; Finley 1959; Starr 1977), Romans (Bradley 1987; Jongman 1988:67; Rauh 1993; Scheidel 2012), Egyptian Mamluks (Abu-Lughod 1989:213–214), and other ancient societies would have seen this as a waste of productive labor and financial value (E. Williams 1994). In most cases debt slaves were used for domestic service (Rojas 1995:207). Only in a few instances were slaves used for manual labor[2] such as agriculture.[3] Slavery was more common in southern Mesoamerica among the Maya, where slaves were used to tend cacao orchards which required year-round attention (Scholes and Roys 1968:28), haul cargo, and to paddle trade canoes (Cardos de Mendez 1959:130; Kepecs 1998:111). Gerónimo de Aguilar was a Spaniard who was shipwrecked on the coast of Yucatán in 1511 and made a slave. His account indicates that slaves received rough treatment among the Maya.[4]

All Mesoamerican societies were agrarian. Land was the essential ingredient for household and community subsistence as well as supporting the elite. Most land was held as community property under elite control. Elite held hereditary estates that were used for their support although most land was not private property. A great deal of institutional

land consisted of prebendal assignments (e.g. Table 2.1). Prebendal lands
were assigned to an individual or the office they held and were intended to
provide the resources needed to cover the associated costs. Usufruct or use
rights to land were granted to individuals through the social and political
prerogatives of ruling elite. The same was true for commoners: they
accessed land through membership in their *calpulli* or through contract-
ual agreement with a ruling lord.

Among commoners land use passed from father to son but it was not
owned by the individual who used it (Harvey 1984:90). Except for some
elite holdings (*pillalli, tecpillalli*), most of the land including that worked by
commoners could not be bought, sold, or accumulated on an individual
basis independent of social oversight. Access to land depended on an
individual's position in society and commoners lacked the ability to accumulate land outside the social relations of their community that governed
its distribution. Hereditary elite ownership of land may have been increasing in frequency in the Basin of Mexico with the construction of new wet
land *chinampas* fields in the southern lakes region (Parsons 1991). The two
land categories that appear to have become hereditary holdings were the
pillalli lands of the nobles and the *huehuetlalli* ancestral lands of specific
groups. The conditions under which land could be sold remain unclear.
Offner (1981b) reports two types of both *pillalli* and *tecpillalli* in the
province of Texcoco that were distinguished from one another depending
on whether they were worked by renters or free commoners. Both types of
tecpillalli could be sold irrespective of whether they were cultivated by
renters or free commoners (*macehualtin*); this differs from the *pillalli* land
which could only be sold if it was worked by renters (Offner 1981b:46).

The reason for these different terms of sale are not clear, but may have
to do with the length of time that these lands remained under individual
elite control. The fact that private land emerged so quickly in the first
decades after the conquest suggests that both elite and commoners recognized the concept of hereditary control and its transfer to other users. By
1560 land purchases had become common enough in some areas that an
early form of purchasing agent for land (*tlalcouhqui*) was listed in the
Matrícula de Huexotzinco (Prem 1974).

The indigenous transportation system was a major constraint to commerce and the movement of goods over space. Industrial and pre-
industrial economies are often compared on the basis of their production
capacity. But it was not the manufacture of large quantities of goods at a
low cost that fueled the industrial revolution. What fueled the industrial
revolution was the ability of merchants to find markets and distribute

manufactured goods, which in turn enabled new forms of organization (factories, workhouses, and joint stock companies) to take shape and employ economies of scale in their production facilities. High production capacity meant nothing if manufactured goods could not be distributed to the consumers who wanted them. This is where merchants were indispensable for the development of industrial production. Without worldwide distribution networks early industrial enterprises would have choked on their own production capacity.

Without a reliable, low cost system of transportation production entities were doomed to remain small and could not employ economies of scale in the production of goods. It is in this regard that Mesoamerican economic systems were especially challenged. Mesoamerica had the poorest transportation system in the ancient world and by all logical accounts should not have had a commercial economy. But it did and therein lies the paradox. Transportation efficiency affected, but did not determine, the scale of commercial relationships or the structure of the economic system in which they operated. From an evolutionary perspective Mesoamerican commerce appears to have grown out of an early involvement in small-scale regional and inter-regional household exchange. The development of marketplaces concentrated those exchanges in a central place and in the process made household procurement and exchange more efficient. Marketplaces amplified the number and type of exchanges possible by facilitating interaction between people of different ethnic groups who might otherwise not have interacted. As a safe place for interaction, they also provided a venue for individuals involved in long-distance exchange.

THE MIRACLE OF THE MARKETPLACE

The marketplace developed not as a *result* of the large-scale movement of goods, but as a *solution* to reduce the cost and facilitate the movement of goods over space. This may sound like a contradiction but it is not. China and Mesoamerica stand out as two areas in the ancient world with highly developed market systems (Blanton 1996; G. Skinner 1964; M. Smith 1979). Movement of goods in both these areas depended heavily on high cost, overland transportation.[5] Marketplaces thrived in areas of high transportation costs because they reduced both the marginal cost of provisioning for buyers and the marginal cost of selling by venders.

Households across the Aztec economic world never were completely self-sufficient for all the goods that they consumed. Instead they relied on exchange for a significant number of staple goods that they did not produce.[6] The advantage of the marketplace was that it allowed households to bundle their provisioning activities into a single trip rather than engaging in them on a per-item acquisition basis. Markets reduced the total time and distance of provisioning activities and lowered marginal provisioning cost for each item procured. While this did not reduce the cost or difficulty of transporting individual items from home to marketplace, it permitted households to travel farther because of the increases in efficiency obtained by combining multiple procurement activities in a single trip.[7] Marketplaces allowed households to combine buying and selling into a single event. Any public function that brought people together was an opportunity to offer goods for sale[8] and it is possible that some markets developed as a side product of other ritual and public assemblies (e.g. Abbott 2010; Burger 2013; Malville 2001).

The marketplace also supplied merchant sellers with several advantages. Most importantly it brought buyers together into a large temporary demand pool. This had several effects. First, it reduced the marginal cost of selling goods to consumers congregated in a single locale. Second, the marketplace provided merchants with an assembly point for goods from local sellers. Third and most importantly, the seller effectively shouldered the burden of assembling and transporting goods to the marketplace. Rotating periodic marketplaces enabled merchants to move across the landscape from marketplace to marketplace making goods available to consumers even in lightly populated rural areas.

The marketplace was the engine behind a great deal of the commercial activity found across the Aztec world. When the marketplace first appeared is unclear[9] although archaeological research suggests that markets were present in the Valley of Oaxaca by at least 500–350 BC[10] (Blanton et al. 1993:29). They are believed to have provisioned the large urban centers of Teotihuacan and Monte Alban during the Classic period (AD 200–650) and were clearly present at Xochicalco by AD 650 (Blanton 1978; Hirth 1998, 2009b; Millon 1973). Markets had a long trajectory of development and were operating in the highlands for at least 2000 years before the Spanish invasion.[11]

The marketplace emerged as the central focus of provisioning households with goods that the household could not produce themselves. It was the point of intersection between the domestic and institutional economies. It was where tribute goods could be converted into staple goods and where food could be converted into storable wealth. Moreover the marketplace was the locale where petty trade could be conducted by households to obtain basic necessities. Small-scale market selling was the fulcrum on which highland craft production pivoted. Craft goods produced in the household could be sold to retailers or marketed directly to the consuming public by the artisans who made them. Independent craftsmen operated as entrepreneurs and it was the ability of individuals to buy and sell in the marketplace that created the diversified commercial economy that the Spanish encountered upon their arrival in prehispanic Mesoamerica.

COMMERCIAL COMPLEXITY IN THE AZTEC ECONOMIC WORLD

A large portion of this study has focused on documenting the economic diversity found in the Basin of Mexico and elsewhere at the time of the Spanish conquest. This diversity has been described at three different levels: the independent producer-seller, the regional merchant retailer, and the long-distance vanguard merchant. Together they document a multi-tiered commercial system that ranged from intermittent hawking of goods to full-time involvement in trade as a primary livelihood.

The independent producer-seller was the foundation of the economic system. They produced goods in their homes, gardens, and fields selling them in the marketplace to meet household subsistence needs. Most artisans were not full-time specialists. Instead, they appear to have had agricultural fields that household members worked to produce food.[12] Some crafts such as ceramic manufacture and salt making were seasonal activities that were practiced with high intensity during the dry season. The involvement in household level crafting certainly varied from region to region. There were more economic opportunities for households in towns with marketplaces and large resident populations than in lightly populated rural areas.

The range of producer-sellers was identified and discussed in Chapter 5. They were small-scale producers whose manufacturing capacity was limited to the resources and labor that could be mobilized within their households. Different types of producer-sellers – 124 types – are identified in the sources who sold goods in the marketplace. Sixty of these producer-sellers were craftsmen practicing both indigenous crafts and producing new items for Spanish consumers (Table 5.3). The diversity of the goods produced for sale suggests two things. First, it indicates that most households were not auto-sufficient for the greater array of tools, equipment, and consumables that they used in daily life. Instead, they depended on craftsmen for many of their household goods which included: equipment to process, cook, serve, and store food; household furnishings such as mats, brooms, rope, and chests; general consumables including cutting tools, dyes, spinning equipment, and soap; and items of individual attire including sandals, cloaks, bags, and belts. Second, if sixty crafts are mentioned in the sources then it is likely that there were many others that went unmentioned since the Spanish were unconcerned with the material dimensions of indigenous life.

Since the primary role of the marketplace was to provision the household, food was a major item bought and sold there. Sixteen sellers of unprocessed food were identified who produced and sold the major grains, meat, vegetables, fruit, and spices essential for the Mesoamerican diet. Cooked and processed foods also were sold in the marketplace which probably teemed with individuals selling pulque, cacao, tamales, atole, and tortillas. Indigenous marketplaces have always been a place to get a hot savory meal and the same was certainly true in the prehispanic past.

Raw materials also were sold in the marketplace. Nineteen foragers and resource collectors were identified who sold forest products (resin, pine torches, rubber, and wood products) as well as natural or processed minerals (stone, chalk, lime, dyes, and saltpeter) and wild foods (fish, insects, lake algae, and rabbit). Twelve service providers are referenced in the sources that included physicians, attorneys, prostitutes, barbers, sorcerers, and shoe repairmen. Together these 124 types of producer-sellers represent the numerous individuals who sold food, craft goods, and their personal skills to meet the needs of a commercial society. A high number of producer-sellers in society is a predictable outcome of a poor transportation system which makes alternative, centralized production and distribution cost-prohibitive (R. Smith 1978:18).

Commerce wasn't limited to producer-sellers. Retailers and possibly a few wholesalers also were active in the marketplace. Several things are important about the presence of these commercial specialists. First, retailers by definition are individuals who made all or the majority of their living through buying and selling. The fact that their livelihood depended on the gains from reselling underscores the existence of a profit motive as the basis for commercial exchange. Second, the existence of retailers shows that demand for consumer goods was continuous. Retailing is a logical extension of urban living where the demand pool for food and other goods is directly proportional to the size of its resident population.

Retailers were present in the daily markets of Tlatelolco, Tenochtitlan, and Tlaxcala. They also are reported in marketplaces in the Basin of Mexico that operated on a rotating schedule. Rotating markets required that retailers travel with their merchandise from venue to venue. It is possible that retailers may have left some goods in the care of market officials or trusted care keepers to minimize the cost of transporting large inventories from marketplace to marketplace. The Spanish priests were continually impressed with the good behavior of the indigenous people and in 1537 observed that Indians in the Gulf Coast always spoke the truth and "never took people's property, even it if lay around on the road for many days (Motolinia 1950:166)." In another statement Motolinia summarizes how merchandise was left without fear in the Zapotitlán marketplace in southern Puebla,

And it is true that at the end of this month of February, 1541, in a town called Zapotitlán that an indian left over one hundred loads of merchandise in a place in the middle of the market, and it remained there both through the night and during the day, and not a thing was missing. On market-day, which is every five days, each person stands by the merchandise that he has to sell. In the middle of the five-day period there is another small market, and for this reason the merchandise is always left in the *tianquizco* or market-place, except during the rainy season. But this simplicity has not reached Mexico or its vicinity

(Motolinia 1950:166).

That goods could not be left unattended in the marketplaces around Mexico City may be more a function of Spanish influence than a lack of honesty on the part of the highland *Nahua*.

Thirty-nine different types of retailers were identified who sold both local and imported goods. Eleven of these were food retailers who provided a day-to-day reliable source for food staples. Another eleven were involved in the trade in textiles or other types of apparel. This confirms Zorita's observation that there were many cloth merchants across New Spain who moved textiles between regions to sell (Zorita 1994:253). The remaining retailers sold items ranging from household staples to high-value goods and speciality items. Where did retailers buy the goods they sold? Either from the craftsmen who manufactured them or from other merchants who trafficked in them from outside the region. The presence of commercial agents and solicitors suggests that local goods were frequently mobilized through agreements or contracts of supply.[13]

Six additional retailers were identified as producer-sellers who also bought goods for resale. This hybrid merchant is not an anomaly unique to the Aztec commercial world. They were a common feature of the economic landscape during the eighteenth and nineteenth century in Britain well into the industrial revolution. According to Jefferys (1954) British producer/retailers developed as a response to increased demand for goods from their clientele. Craftsmen operating out of their shops (the equivalent to producer-sellers) had two options. They could either increase their level of production or add more and varied goods to what they sold by purchasing them from other craftsmen. Following the second option resulted in the emergence of hybrid producer/retailers. Like in Britain, the presence of this hybrid category reflects the adaptation of the producer-seller to an increasingly complex commercial world.

Also present were itinerant merchants who sold a heterogenous array of household goods door-to-door outside the marketplace. While this would seem to contradict the norm to buy and sell in the marketplace, it was probably tolerated and even encouraged in areas of low population density where marketplaces were widely spaced or absent altogether. Webber and Symanski (1973) argue that venders will become mobile retailers where transportation costs are high and population density and demand per unit area is low. Other specialized venders included the banker and wholesaler. Bankers were exchange merchants who converted goods into negotiable currencies and vice versa. Wholesalers are more problematic. The Nahuatl word for wholesaler is *tlaquixtiani* (Table 8.2) and Feldman (1978a:220) feels these individuals trafficked in textiles and a few other high-value goods. It is likely that the term is also appropriate for some cotton and salt merchants who may have preferred to sell to local venders instead of taking the time to sell all their goods themselves in the marketplace. The practice to sell wholesale rather than retail follows Mintz's (1964) strategies of small-scale trading where profitability is dependent on increasing the number of transactions in the course of one's commercial life, an important consideration where most of the time involved in commerce is consumed by transportation.

THE LONG-DISTANCE VANGUARD MERCHANT

At the top of the commercial food chain were the groups of vanguard merchants who dealt in wealth goods over long distances. Among the Aztecs these merchants were commoners who could accumulate great wealth. The Aztecs believed that all wealth belonged to the gods (Sahagún 1959:55) and one obtained it only if *Huitzilopochtli* revealed it to you. The secret to acquiring wealth was to be hard working, honest, humble, and reverent to the gods. But this alone was not a guarantee for its acquisition since wealth was seen as being hidden in the crags and hollows of the earth.

Long-distance travel was risky and merchants were subject to robbery and death on the road. But as rich commoners life was also risky at home.

Vanguard merchants trafficked in elaborate textiles, feathers, cacao, slaves, and all other high-value goods moving across Mesoamerica. As they became wealthy they drew the envy of the elite class. To escape persecution they hid their wealth and provided services to the Aztec state. They supplied artisans with high-value raw materials and paid tribute to their lords in cacao. They served as commercial agents for the Aztec *tlatoani* and traded on his behalf in foreign areas. In-so-doing merchants benefitted from the *tlatoani*'s protection, obtained safe passage through dangerous areas, and conducted trade for their lord as well as for themselves.[14] They were armed for their own protection and often had to protect themselves from attack in areas outside the empire. They assisted Tzitzispandaquare the Tarascan prince in his consolidation of power at Tzintzuntzan indicating that they could be a small but significant paramilitary force in their own right. The *pochteca* vanguard merchants served as spies collecting intelligence for the Aztec state and as guides in times of war. Finally, high ranking merchants could be appointed to supervise the marketplace or to act as tribute collectors in key provinces.

Vanguard merchants validated their individual accumulation of wealth through their service to *Huitzilopochtli* which they characterized as a form of warfare: going into dangerous territory and engaging in combat on the God's behalf. The wealthiest merchants extended this rationale to include providing victims for sacrifice like warriors did. They did this through the *tealtiliztli* celebration where they expended huge quantities of wealth to buy and offer slaves for sacrifice. This ceremony could extend over several years and involved sponsoring a series of feasts where distinguished elite were honored and given expensive gifts. Once completed the sponsoring merchant obtained the title of *tealtianime*, was recognized as a leader in the merchant community, and depleted his wealth as a result of providing largesse to the elite. All in all the *tealtiliztli* celebration was an effective economic leveling mechanism that kept *pochteca* wealth within acceptable limits.

The long-distance *pochteca* operated inside and outside the empire. Inside the empire they traveled from marketplace to marketplace trading their goods for items with high-value. They traded on the principle of buy cheap and sell dear whenever they could. Risks were higher outside the empire and in some cases merchants went in disguise; these individuals were referred to as the *teiaoaloanime*. *Pochteca* became an important but unofficial component of the Aztec tribute system because of the high-value goods merchants trafficked in. While many areas paid tribute in local goods or resources, tribute levies of some provinces consisted of non-local goods that had to be obtained through inter-regional exchange. Aztec merchants offered non-local tribute goods for sale in areas where they knew they were needed or obtained them as consignments through special contracted requests. Similarly local merchants may have taken to the road to obtain them in marketplaces where they could be found. That merchants supplied non-local goods required for tribute payments to local populations is evident in the Relación de Tetiquipa y Cozauhtepec where it says that the residents bought the copper bells, ingots, and axe money that were needed to meet their tribute needs in the local marketplace (Acuña 1984b:183). While some authors have assumed that Aztec *pochteca* merchants operated primarily outside the empire (Acosta-Saignes 1945; Chapman 1957a) this does not conform with the many reports of merchants operating within and traveling between important marketplaces.

MEDIATING THE MERCHANT'S DILEMMA

Hans-Dieter Evers (1994) has discussed what he identifies as the merchant's dilemma created by engaging in inter-regional trade in socially conscripted economies. The trader's dilemma in broad terms consists of the social pressures that can impede the accumulation and retention of capital necessary to engage in trade (Lloyd 1953:42). The dilemma arises in the face of the pressures brought upon a merchant to invest his wealth in the local community for the benefit of its members. In small communities wealthy individuals are regularly called upon to sponsor community functions. If the merchant acquiesces to these community pressures he runs the risk of not having enough capital to conduct his business. As a member of the community he has the advantage of buying local goods at the insider price established by the moral economy. While advantageous for selling local goods outside the community it has its down side. As a community member he is also expected to sell goods at reduced insider rates to other villagers even if they were purchased at a higher external market price. Neighbors and relatives will ask for loans and may not repay them, much less repay with any form of interest. Professional merchants, therefore, can be targeted as a resource for community development which conflicts with their personal commercial interests.

The merchant's dilemma was mediated in several ways across the ancient world. The first was for the merchant to leave the community and operate as a foreign resident in a distant community. This transformed merchants into trader-strangers as originally observed by

Simmel (1906). This could result in the creation of merchant diaspora as distinct ethnic or religious groups within local communities (Cohen 1971; Curtin 1984; Dobbin 1996; Levi 2002). Foreigners do not have the same demands and pressures placed on them to invest in local activities until they return to their home communities. Second, they could depersonalize economic relations somewhat through market interaction although this did not allow them to escape social obligations. Finally, they could accumulate cultural capital by sponsoring socially approved activities that deferred financial obligations or shelter resources in ways that left capital partially intact. Examples include making endowments to temples that could be borrowed back interest free or becoming the temple manager and receiving fiduciary advantages as a result (Rudner 1987; Stein 1960).

Vanguard merchants in the Aztec world used several of these solutions to minimize the commercial drain on their resources. The most important was that they remained organized in their own communities. While sometimes recognized as having foreign origins (Martínez 1984), many *pochteca* groups operated as internally stratified but independent local communities within *calpultin*. *Calpultin* boundaries were maintained by group endogamy and worship of patron deities. The primary deity of merchants across Central Mexico was *Yacatecuhtli* known as the Lord of the Vanguard[15] (Thompson 1966:162). This corporate organization allowed merchants to maintain their integrity as an individual tribute body as they applied their expertise in long-distance trade. Although wealthy merchants certainly were called upon in matters concerning the needs of their group this did not extend beyond the limits of their own *calpulli*.

While *pochteca* groups have names that suggest foreign origins they do not appear to have operated as strongly integrated diaspora communities as was common in other areas of the ancient world. Perhaps the closest instance to a diaspora community was the settlement of Tochtepec shared by all *pochteca* communities from the Basin of Mexico. The widespread operation of marketplaces across Mesoamerica appears to have mediated against the development of diaspora communities. The reason was that the open, depersonalized structure of the marketplace facilitated interaction between local and foreign merchants. There was little need to relocate a community to conduct trade in a region; foreign merchants just had to attend local marketplaces when they were convened.

The problems researchers face in reconstructing merchant behavior stems from three sources. First, merchants by their very nature are secretive. Their wealth is based on trade secrets: knowing where to obtain goods inexpensively and where to sell them at a significant profit. Native merchants did not use writing to formalize business dealings so very little information is available from indigenous sources. Second, the Spanish had no interest in the everyday life of commoner households much less their commercial dealings. The result is that very little information is available on indigenous commercial activity from colonial documents. Finally by the mid-1550s native merchants were transforming rapidly with the conditions of the new colonial economy. Trade in many traditional sources of merchant wealth (e.g. feathers, jade, shell, etc.) was gone or drastically shrinking. The two most productive forms of exchange that remained were trade in cacao and textiles. The tribute network had changed significantly and with it the profitable role that merchants previously provided as intermediaries to procure tribute goods not locally available. The new market was in European goods and indigenous merchants were largely precluded from dealing in imported goods from Spain. While indigenous merchants continued to trade using *tlameme* porters, they were out-competed along many routes by Spanish *arrieros* driving strings of mules. It is within this context that Sahagún's Tlatelolco informants remember the glory years of *pochteca* trade before the conquest and the important roles they played in the operation of the Aztec state (Sahagún 1959).

THE AZTEC COMMERCIAL WORLD IN CROSS-CULTURAL PERSPECTIVE

The present study is intended as a contribution to the comparative study of ancient and premodern economy. While researchers have long recognized the important role that the economy plays in the evolution of historic and modern nation states (Abu-Lughod 1989; Braudel 1986; Marx 1964; Pomeranz and Topik 2006; Wallerstein 1976), there have been relatively few comparative studies of past economic systems (e.g. Trigger 2003; Wolf 1982). The reason for this is twofold. First, the best information on ancient economic systems comes from societies with literary traditions that provide information either as written documents or as inscriptions on monuments. This has produced a good understanding of the economic institutions of Greece, Rome, and southwestern Asia. While it is now possible to talk comparatively about ancient economic structures in the Mediterranean world (e.g. Finley 1985; Postgate 2004; Scheidel 2012; Starr 1977; Veenhof 2003), the same cannot be said for Africa, parts of east Asia, and the New World. Second, the long standing interest in the development of capitalism and the industrial revolution has produced a good understanding of the historic development of the European world-system (Wallerstein 1976). One unfortunate result of this has been the characterization of ancient and premodern economic systems in the third world as undeveloped or subsidiary to those of European societies (Frank 1966, 1976).

The approach taken here is that the comparative study of ancient and premodern economies offers an excellent analytical framework for reconstructing the structure and organization of past socioeconomic systems. This study has attempted to identify the main forms of economic organization found throughout the Aztec commercial world. Understanding those forms of organization is a first step in identifying how commerce in New World societies was similar to, or different from, state level economies elsewhere in the ancient world. The Aztecs employed many non-capitalistic forms of organization to produce and distribute the resources necessary for their growth and survival. What made them unique was their highly developed market system. Identifying the complexity, scale, and operating principles that enabled them to combine non-capitalist forms of production with commercial forms of distribution through the market system is a valuable case study for the comparative study of ancient economy.

The preceding discussion has outlined multiple modes of production and distribution that operated simultaneously within Aztec society. These modes of organization were grouped into two levels of economic activity described as the domestic and institutional economy. Like other areas of the ancient world, the domestic economy was the primary unit of both production and consumption. Most households engaged in farming which could be combined with supplemental craft production, hunting, and collecting activities. What is important from a comparative perspective is that commoner household labor was not permanently attached to land either through restrictive fealty obligations to their lords or through the ownership of private property. Access to land was established through social relations either to a hereditary land holding group (e.g. the *calpulli*), or through negotiated service relationships to a lord with governing rights over a territorial domain (the *altepetl*). This made it possible for both individual households and small groups to change location for the purpose of accessing more resources if circumstances permitted.

The farmer was a valued individual in the *Nahua* world and elite sought to attract commoners to their domains. The reason for this was twofold. First, they were the primary producers of food and craft goods as well as the basis for the semi-professional militia that formed the army.[16]

Second, support for the elite and all public institutions depended upon corvee labor to produce the resources that they used. Labor, therefore, was the source of both increased economic well-being and military power. There was no concern over commoner households being deposed from their fields or denied access to common land as occurred in England in the fifteenth century with the enclosure acts (Beresford 1998; Thompson 1991). Commoner labor was the fuel that powered the prehispanic economy. Besides providing labor to farm elite fields, commoner households supplied the labor for all public works projects.

Households produced the majority of utilitarian and high-value craft goods consumed in society. Craft production employed the labor available within the household or that could be mobilized through kinship relationships. Craft production was not organized by artisan guilds as it was across Europe.[17] In the Aztec world children learned crafting from their parents and there were no restrictions on who could engage in craft activity. Craft goods were sold in the marketplace where fair prices were established by a combination of both demand and the officials who oversaw the market's operation. There were as many artisans in the society as the market was able to support. Furthermore crafting was not limited to urban centers as it was in Europe where production quality was supervised by guild officials. Instead crafting occurred anywhere that households had access to resources and a marketplace to sell finished goods.

The institutional economy consists of both the formal and informal ways that resources are produced above the level of individual households. As discussed in Chapter 2 the primary way that formal institutions were supported was by the production of goods on lands assigned to specific purposes. Labor was drawn as corvee drafts on a rotating basis from commoner households. Revenue was collected as service or as in-kind staple goods. This differed from forms of land poll taxes found in the ancient world that extracted resources directly from the household and estate units that produced them.[18] In the Aztec world most institutional resources were not extracted directly from household subsistence stocks, and as a result, was less exploitive than forms of Old World taxation. In bad years household and institutional revenue streams were impacted equally and institutional resources might not even be collected so that they could be used by households with resource shortfalls (Zorita 1994:194); this was not the practice in many parts of the Old World which collected fixed amounts when taxes were due.

All levels of the institutional economy benefitted from having more available labor. Even where land was scarce, more labor meant either more intensive forms of production or out-migration of groups to areas where agricultural land was still available. Elites benefitted from the high commoner-to-elite ratio. In prehispanic times the service demand on commoner labor was low. Zorita (1994:188) states that before the Spanish arrived, "each man gave only a little, yet the whole came to a great deal because there were so many people." In terms of the total amount of labor worked, "each man's portion of labor was small, and his turn of domestic service came one or two times a year at most (Zorita 1994:188–189)." The hardship that the native population suffered during the colonial period was a result of population decline without a change in the level of tribute.[19] This is reflected in the amount of labor needed to produce the 278,400 total tribute textiles that Berdan (1987:241) estimates as the annual Aztec tribute levy.[20] With an estimated population of between 5 and 10 million people within the empire (Sanders 2008:69; Webster and Evans 2013:636), the annual tribute level would be one textile for every 3.5–7.2 households.[21] This is not a heavy tribute level considering that the Aztec empire covered between 160,000 and 165,000 sq kms.[22]

The marketplace was the institution that enabled the economy to grow to the size and complexity described here. Marketplaces were large by European standards and probably were both more numerous and held more regularly. The Tlatelolco marketplace with its 60,000 daily attendees was the largest market that the conquistadors had ever seen. Although the comparative information on sixteenth century markets in Europe is limited, Tenochtitlan was larger than any other sixteenth century Spanish city. From another perspective the daily attendees in the Tlatelolco market was larger than the entire residential populations of all the contemporaneous Spanish cities other than Granada (Chandler 1987). The Spanish had every reason to be impressed. Only two cities in Europe, Constantinople and Paris, were larger than Tenochtitlan. London and Amsterdam which would grow into major cities by the end of the century were still smaller.[23] The reason that prehispanic markets were so large is that retail shops were rare to nonexistent in Mesoamerica.

Other than sheer size, the Tlatelolco market impressed the Spanish because of how it was organized; it was highly centralized. Markets in large urban cities in Europe often were polyfocal depending on their individual histories. Sixteenth-century markets in London were fragmented into seventeen small retail centers[24] (C. Smith 1999:table 7). Market centralization in the Aztec world allowed for more efficient supervision. Furthermore, small markets in Europe often were specialized by the products sold[25] while Aztec markets had food, utilitarian goods, and wealth goods in separate sectors within the same marketplace. The produce diversity found in the Tlatelolco market was typical of large indigenous markets across the highlands. Ralph Beals (1975:136) reports that over 500 products were sold in traditional markets in Oaxaca, which is certainly a shadow of the type of complexity the Spanish would have observed in Tlatelolco. All of the goods available in Aztec society would have been sold in the Tlatelolco marketplace except perhaps for some of the speciality items made in the *totocalli* that carried the *tlatoani*'s emblematic designs.

While marketplaces were a mainstay of the highland Mesoamerican landscape, there is no reliable estimate of how many existed across the Aztec empire (but see Figure 3.6). The only area where a reasonable estimate of the density of marketplaces can be made is in the Basin of Mexico and the adjacent area of northern Morelos. Twenty-nine major market centers are known from the Basin of Mexico (Blanton 1996; Blanton and Hodge 1996) which are spaced an average 16 km from their closest neighboring market-place (Figure 3.5). On average this would place towns distributed across the landscape within 8 km from the nearest provisioning marketplace. In terms of market use this represents a round trip distance that could easily be traversed on foot in a single day. Blanton (1996:59) suggests that 8 km was the maximum radius of a market service area with 4–8 km the more likely average (Stark and Ossa 2010:105). Fifteen markets are known from northern Morelos [26] (Maldonado Jiménez 1990). The distance between the neighboring marketplaces in this area is only 8.2 km. The households in this area of Morelos were better served than those in the Basin of Mexico being only 4–5 km from a provisioning marketplace (Figure 3.5).

The average spacing of 4–8 km between market towns and their hinterland users conforms to what William Skinner (1964) observed for traditional marketplaces in rural China. Skinner found that market towns were spaced an average of 8 km apart with an maximum walking distance of a peasant family to the nearest marketplace of only 4.5 km.[27] The similarity between market spacing in highland Central Mexico and high-land China is striking and suggests a similar adaptation to the high costs of transporting goods overland by peasant households. This is closer spacing than was found in rural France during the nineteenth century where forty-five weekly markets had an average catchment size of 7 km. Correspondingly, where the focus was on herding the service catchment of specialized animal markets in areas like western Brittany was much larger often constituting two to three days of travel time (Landers 2003:100).

The Aztec market system provided an effective provisioning network. Although the record of small and intermediate sized marketplaces is far from complete, the majority of rural households in the central highlands appear to have been within a day's round trip travel from a market town. This both facilitated household provisioning and helped reduce the cost of moving goods over space. Nevertheless, professional merchants were a common feature of Mesoamerican society, operating at both the regional and inter-regional level. Merchants in the Aztec world were *macehualli* commoners while long-distance merchants in the Gulf Coast and throughout the Maya area tended to be members of the elite. This difference in merchant status may be due to the greater degree of economic symbiosis found in the highlands which enabled commoner households to become involved in inter-regional trade from the very beginning of settled village life. Whatever the cause of these social differences, long-distance merchants trafficked in high-value items that made transporting goods by land a profitable endeavor.

While merchants in different societies share many of the same economic goals, the organization and methods of operation of Aztec merchants differed from those in the Old World in several ways. As mentioned earlier, merchants guilds did not exist, nor were diaspora communities needed to establish or maintain commercial linkages in the Aztec commercial world (e.g. Curtin 1984). Likewise, *pochteca* did not regularly engage local agents or brokers to procure or sell goods as was common in other areas of the ancient world (Goitein 1967:185–190; Hill 1966; 1988; Sundström 1974:57–60). The reason for these differences was a product of the marketplace where merchants could interact with local buyers and sellers on a one-on-one basis. Marketplaces by definition were places where both local residents and foreign strangers could enter for purposes of exchange. As a result there was no need for intermediary economic agents to establish economic interaction between people from differing cultural backgrounds.

Kurtz (1974) identifies the presence of factor markets in land, labor, and capital as a main feature of modern market economies. Factor markets did not exist in the Aztec commercial world as they did in other Old World economies (Isaac 2013). The common denominator of factor markets is the ability to access or purchase land, labor, and capital using a single unified currency which was absent in the Aztec world. In the Old World gold and silver were standards of value that facilitated exchange and could be procured through loans to purchase both land and labor. In the Aztec world cacao beans and textiles served currency functions as did copper axes and gold dust; other high-value items such as jade and featherwork items served as stored wealth. Mesoamerican commerce did not suffer despite the absence of a unified currency. It operated effectively and efficiently with multiple forms of commodity money which served as units of account to facilitate exchange and economic interaction.

The absence of formalized currency has been cited as a feature of a primitive or underdeveloped economy (Dalton 1965). While formalized currency can certainly increase the speed and ease of transacting exchanges, it also has had negative results. In colonial times the demand for gold and silver undermined indigenous wealth and service economies and led to the imposition of oppressive head taxes and forced labor in Spanish mines. In the seventeenth and eighteenth century the economic policy of mercantilism was employed to maintain control over the flow of resources and currency into and out of European countries (Wallerstein 1980). The result was the development of nation-centered economies with colonial dependencies. By comparison, prehispanic economic systems were more diversified and stable. They did not have a unified currency, but this did not impede the development of an active commercial system that moved goods within and between all levels of prehispanic society.

AT THE CLOSE OF BUSINESS

It has been argued that the Aztec world did not have a market economy in the sense that supply and demand directly influenced scale and timing of production decisions (Carrasco 1981; Isaac 2013). This generalization is basically true insofar as it lacked factor markets in land, labor, and capital like those found in Europe at the same time. But the important question is how important were these features to the development of commercial economy in the Aztec world? I believe not very. The absence of strong factor markets certainly distinguish ancient and premodern economies from those of the modern world. But the Aztec world was not commercially crippled by their absence. To the contrary, commerce in the Aztec world was alive and well, equaling if not surpassing the number of economic exchanges found in even the largest contemporary commercial centers in the Mediterranean world.

What the Aztec world had was a marketplace economy. Goods were produced and offered for sale in the marketplace because there was a demand for them. Demand for goods directly affected household production strategies because without the marketplace households would not have produced goods that they could not sell. In this sense market forces were operating but not in the way that we see them affecting the move-ment of land and labor in the modern world. Comparative analysis needs to identify the economic structures operating in ancient and premodern societies so that a reasonable approximation of their similarities and differences can be made. This study has summarized the economic struc-tures found across the Aztec world and is a first step in this direction.

In conclusion it is useful to reiterate a few caveats stated at the beginning of this volume. First, the historic sources on Mesoamerican economic activity are very limited. There is no solution to this except additional scrutiny of colonial archives matched with problem-oriented archaeo-logical research. What has been attempted here is to push the meager historical sources to their maximum limit and to extract as much economic data as possible. Theoretical discussions are often made without data, but where data exist they should be exploited to their fullest as the basis for modeling what is known about the ancient past.

Second, most of the information available on commercial activity in the Aztec world comes from the Basin of Mexico. The Basin was both an exceptional and atypical area in the early sixteenth century. It was the center of the Aztec empire and benefitted from the massive influx of tribute wealth that either trickled down to the local population or was consumed in local, state supported projects. This new wealth certainly intensified the level of commerce within the Basin of Mexico and helped to underwrite the expansion of intensive agriculture within the southern lakes region.[28] Nevertheless, all of the same economic structures found in the Basin of Mexico were also present in other parts of the Aztec economic world. While the scale of commercial activity probably was greater than other areas of Mesoamerica, it did not differ in kind. The marketplace was the central economic institution throughout western Mesoamerica and it fostered the same range of economic activity every-where where it occurred. The marketplace shaped the Aztec commercial world and its attendant economic structures and should be included in comparative studies with other ancient and premodern societies.

Finally, while the discussion has employed formal economic termin-ology it recognizes the importance of cultural context in structuring the social and economic values with which society operated. Economic behavior was shaped by, and embedded in, other social institutions. Identifying the modes of organization for production and distribution is the starting point for a meaningful cross-cultural analysis of economic structure. Social institutions were discussed in Chapters 2 and 3. The discussion emphasized the importance of households who were in business for themselves. The goal of commoner households was to live comfortably and reproduce while elite households sought to expand in size and improve their social standing and wealth. In this sense I have referred to household endeavors as entrepreneurial. While this may seem inappropriate to those who confine the use of this term to capitalistic societies, even a rudimentary examination of the ethnographic literature shows that households were not economically passive. They had fundamental subsistence goals to meet and actively worked to improve their overall economic well-being when they had the opportunity to do so.

While this analysis has focused on the commercial structures we need to remember that goods also moved through other forms of distribution outside the marketplace. Food, craft goods, and natural resources also moved from household-to-household through gift and reciprocal exchanges as they had since the advent of settled village life. Some may argue that the examples of commercial behavior presented here was the exception rather than the rule, with the bulk of Mesoamerican households mired in auto-consumption and with little involvement in the marketplace. If this was the case then the same was true of *all* of Europe at the same time. John Landers (2003:100) has estimated that throughout the eighteenth century when the industrial revolution was in full swing, less than 15% of total production in rural areas was consumed away from the point of production. How this compares to production in the Aztec world is unclear and can only be resolved by focused comparative, cross-cultural research. Hopefully this study places the Aztec world into a framework that makes future comparisons possible.

Notes

Chapter 1

1 That the Aztec of Tenochtitlan referred to themselves specifically as the Culhua-Mexica should not be a surprise. As a rule prehispanic people referred to themselves as members of a particular ethnic or community group. The island of Tenochtitlan continued to be occupied after the Spanish conquest when it was gradually transformed into modern day Mexico City.

2 The Aztec world encompassed a diverse array of important indigenous language groups including Nahuatl, Huastec, Mixtec, Otomí, Tarascan, and Zapotec speakers to name a few. These language groups did not form integrated societies.

3 The small indigenous city-states known as *altepeme* were referred to by many different names depending on the language spoken. For a discussion of how the prehispanic *altepeme* were organized see Hirth (2003, 2008a).

4 The three highest mountains in Mexico are Popocatepetl at 5,426 m msl, Pico de Orizaba at 5,636 m msl, and the Nevada de Toluca at 4,680 m msl.

5 Ross Hassig (1985) feels that a normal *jornada* representing one day's journey on foot during the colonial period ranged from 21 to 29 km depending on topography. Thirty km is used here as the normal maximum day's travel during the prehispanic period. What this means is that even at the maximum separation of 90 km all indigenous communities would have been within a three *jornada* journey to another ecological resource zone.

6 The lakes in these regions varied in size and permanence. The lake system in the Basin of Mexico is particularly well known. It was permanent and in the rainy season, lake levels were managed to prevent flooding both in Tenochtitlan and the *chinampas* agricultural fields. The lakes in both the Puebla-Tlaxcala region and the Valley of Toluca are less well known and primarily were impermanent seasonal marshlands that formed during the rainy season (López Corral 2013).

7 The power of ecological diversity is especially evident in the New World in the Andes of South America where the juxtaposition of different resources zones led to highly complex social and economic structures to access and distribute

different goods (Hirth and Pillsbury 2013; LaLone 1982; Murra 1972, 1980, 1985). While the Mexican highlands lack the sharply contrasting vertical ecological zones of the Andes, the degree of environmental diversity still brought different resource zones in close proximity to one another.

8 The town of Ecab was a very important commercial center in northeastern Yucatán because of its location near major coastal salt works (Kepecs 2003).

9 The best account of large maritime canoes comes from Christopher Columbus' fourth voyage where a large trading canoe was encountered near the Bay Islands, Honduras that contained twenty-five men. Las Casas (1877) reports that it was sailing from the Yucatan peninsula and also contained a number of women. Thompson (1949, 1970:126–134) discusses the maritime trade and trade routes in and around the Yucatan peninsula.

10 Written documents containing valuable economic information began to appear across the Near East between 3000 and 1800 BC. (Dercksen 1996; Nissen et al. 1993; Pettinato 1991; Postgate 2004; Veenhof 2003). The origin of writing in this area is closely tied to economic transactions with its precursors in the form of ceramic bullae dating back to as early as eighth and ninth millenium BC (Schmandt-Besserat 1978). Written documentation is also present in the Old World in the form of letters and accounts (Goitein 1967; 1973; Goitein and Friedman 2008), dedicatory inscriptions (Chattopadhyaya 2005; Stein 1960; Young 2001:81), and commercial manuals (Casson 1989; Khachikian 1966; Pegolotti 1936) all of which provide valuable information for commerce in different areas of the Old World. Likewise, long-distance commerce along the silk road between Europe and China has been amply documented (Abu-Lughod 1989; Allsen 1997; Hirth 1966; Hirth and Rockhill 1911) and information from shipwrecks document shifts in maritime commercial activity (Hopkins 1980; Worrall 2009).

11 The available bibliography for studying the emergence of capitalism and the industrial revolution in the western Mediterranean is immense (e.g. Baechler 1976; Chang 2008; Pellicani 1994; Perelman 2000; Weber 1992). The early origins of the important components of modern economy include: coinage (Weatherford 1997), banking and lending institutions (Andreau 1999; Hunt 1994; Postgate 2004:135; Weatherford 1997:64–79), maritime commerce (Berggren et al. 2002; Das Gupta 2001a; Reed 2003), relations of indebtedness (Graeber 2011a, 2011b), the emergence of private property (Hudson 1996; Hudson and Levine 1996), and double entry book-keeping (Bresson n.d.; Weatherford 1997:78). Moreover the emergence of capitalism has focused attention on the development of its primary institutions including forms of industrial production and the joint stock company (Braudel 1986; Landers 2003; McKendrick et al. 1982).

12 To estimate the number of commoner households involved in precolumbian commercial dealings requires archaeological investigations that systematically explore small-scale domestic crafting and production for commercial sale. I know of nowhere where this question has been asked and explored comprehensively, either in Mesoamerica or any other area of the ancient world.

Chapter 2

1 Commercial transactions are defined here as balanced and immediate reciprocal exchanges where equivalent values are established through active negotiation. This type of transaction has been referred to as market exchange whether it occurs in or outside a central marketplace (Garraty 2010; Hirth 2010; Pryor 1977).

2 The use of slaves in agriculture was limited in Central Mexico because production here was focused on subsistence production and individual land holdings were limited in size. In the absence of the ability to use labor to intensify agriculture, using slaves as farm hands simply added more mouths to feed. Slaves were more widely used in agriculture in the Gulf Coast and the Maya region where they were employed in the cultivation of cash crops such as cacao (Attolini Lecón 2010:59). In the Maya region slaves were also used in long-distance transportation to carry loads or to paddle trade canoes (Attolini Lecón 2010:66).

3 The reasons foreign merchants in other societies often marry into local communities is to facilitate and strengthen trading relationships with their host populations and to provide a base where visiting merchants from their home groups could reside on a temporary basis (Curtin 1984).

4 The fact that households are risk minimizers has led some investigators to misconstrue some of their economic behaviors as oriented to minimizing effort rather than maximizing returns (Sahlins 1972). Part of this misunderstanding stems from focusing on one dimension of household subsistence behavior (e.g. subsistence agriculture, herding, crafting, etc.) or the individual economic initiatives of household members based on age or gender rather than the full range of household subsistence production (e.g. Netting 1990).

5 Women did an enormous amount of work and contributed greatly to the economic diversification found in domestic units. Bauer (2010:184) estimates that just grinding maize and preparing tortillas for family food needs occupied anywhere from 5 to 6 hours of work/day. This represents a 35–42 hour work week, a full-time job by modern standards.

6 According to Durand-Forest (1967:116–117) 20 large *quachtli* each worth 100 cacao beans were sufficient to support a person for an entire year if goods were bought entirely in the marketplace.

7 Colonial sources from Tepeaca indicate that each household was given between four and five parcels of land for their own support and one additional parcel of land to cultivate as part of their *coatequitl* obligation for their lords (Martínez 1984). If we assume that these parcels were of equal size, then the domestic economy would have controlled 80–83% of the total land and the agricultural surplus that it produced. Closer examination of parcel size, however, suggests that plots cultivated for lords were slightly smaller than those allocated to commoners (López Corral and Hirth 2012a:85). Since these parcels were attached to individuals scattered across the landscape there would have been little difference in the productivity of household and elite plots (López Corral 2011).

8 Examples of group land ownership as a means of reducing both subsistence risk and the costs of operation include the pioneer settlements at Jamestown, Plymouth, and Salt Lake City in American pioneer history, Hutterite colonies,

the Israeli Kibbutzim, the twentieth-century Mexican Ejido, and the medieval open field season (Ellickson and Thorland 1995).

 9 Not all *calpultin* held land. In urban areas *calpultin* grouped artisans and other residents in residential wards. In these cases *calpultin* may have lost all of their land holding functions and served merely as an administrative structure to group individuals along class and professional lines.

10 In Nahuatl the word *cocoliztli* means sickness or pestilence (Molina 1977).

11 The word for beggar in Nahuatl is *motlahtlaihtlani*, one who seeks alms (Karttunen 1983).

12 In ancient Israel gleaning was the practice of collecting the unharvested grain that was intentionally left in the fields to support members of the community in need. The practice involved gleaning the *pe'ah* (meaning corner) which involved leaving uncut grain in the corners of the field for those in need. The amount of grain left uncut was at the discretion and compassion of the field owner. An analogous practice to gleaning in ancient Israel was the practice of *leket* (also meaning gleanings). This practice involved collecting the sheaves of grain that fell from the reapers hand during harvest and which they were not supposed to retrieve so it could be collected by those in need. A good illustration of both these practices can be found in the biblical narrative in the book of Ruth.

13 Sahagún (1953:23, fn 13) is cited as identifying *yacacolli* as a type or species of maize. Since wild maize is not known from Mesoamerica the most likely candidate for a related wild form is teosinte.

14 A large theft could result in death (Alba 1949:21)

15 This famine is often referred to as the famine of the year 1 Rabbit in the Aztec calendar. This refers to the year AD 1454 which was the most devastating year in the span of four years when famine predominated (Bierhorst 1992). Tree ring dating confirms the present of significant decrease in rainfall and plant growth over this time span (Therrell et al. 2004).

16 The towns from which the Totonacs bought slaves included Tenochtitlan, Texcoco, Chalco, Xochimilco, and Tlacopan (Durán 1994:24). It is notable that even the large towns of Chalco and Xochimilco were affected despite their having large numbers of *chinampas* fields within the lake bed at their disposal. It would appear that the drought was significant enough to drop lake levels below usable levels.

17 Distinguishing between different types of extraction and the way that these resources are produced is akin to the Marxian recognition that different modes of resource production exist within society (e.g. Wolf 1982).

18 Based on colonial records the most common items that households were taxed to support the elite were textiles, turkeys, and firewood. The other common instance of taxation occurred on individuals who brought goods to sell in the marketplace. What the scope of the market tax was is unclear although following the norms of Nahua resource mobilization, it probably was small and in proportion to what was needed to operate the marketplace.

19 Prebend allocations were common across western Europe during the medieval period and were the stipends furnished by a cathedral or collegiate church to support a clergyman in its chapter.

20 While the amount of food produced on private and prebendal estates was small in relation to the total percentage of food produced in society, it

probably represents a large percentage of the real, mobilized surplus available for society through the marketplace.

21 *Tecpantlalli* land would have supported the elite families of *tecpan* lords as well as the costs of related administrative activities, feasts and festivals, maintaining land registers, managing their tribute obligations, and overseeing the maintenance of their cult temple and associated *telpochcalli* or *calmecac* school (Evans 1991).

22 According to Ixtlilxóchitl (1891:2:171) this type of land could comprise up to one-third of the land in conquered areas. It indicates that lands and the labor that worked them could be reassigned after conquest to individuals in the victorious army.

23 Martínez (1984:85) calculates the braza as 3.34 m in length to make this calculation which raises field size to 0.67 hectares. Reexamination of the size of the braza suggests that it corresponds to the indigenous measurement of the *cemmatl*, the distance between outstretched hands. The best estimate for the size of the *cemmatl* is 1.67 m in length which reduces the size of the field to 1,673 sq m, or 0.167 ha. For additional discussion on indigenous measurements see López Corral and Hirth (2012a).

24 Martínez (1984:cuadro 11) uses the larger sized braza of 3.34 m to calculate the total amount of institutional fields farmed for the elite to range from 66 to 1,077 ha. Use of the *cemmatl* of 1.67 m for the size of the braza reduces the total of the size of the fields cultivated to support elite families of different size to between 16.5 and 269 ha.

25 Based on the reading of this document, Hicks (1978) felt that the braza measurement of 3.34 m is appropriate for estimating this field size.

26 The figure of 400,000 tortillas seems extraordinarily high as a daily figure but it is what is reported in the document. If each person in the palace consumed twenty tortillas per day this amount would have been sufficient to feed 20,000 people. It is possible that the sum of 400,000 is an exaggeration or a recording error.

27 The standard size of plots was 0.1673 ha in size. Households had 5–8 plots for their own use and one plot to cultivate for the elite (Martínez 1984:85). The range of land each household had to cultivate was 1.0038–1.5057 hectares. This meant that the elite field represented 16.7% of the total land cultivated when the household had 5 plots for their own use and 11.1% when the household had 8 plots for their own use.

28 Fields of two different sizes were cultivated by artisans for elite: 100 brazas long by two brazas wide, and 80 brazas long by three brazas wide (Martínez 1984:118). Using the indigenous measure of the *cemmatl* (1.67 m) for the braza produces an estimate of only 557.78 and 669.34 sq m for these two field sizes respectively. These estimates are substantially smaller than the 0.2231 and 0.2725 ha estimated for these fields by (Martínez 1984:118) based on his use of a larger braza.

29 According to Durán (1994:336) once the tribute was brought in, craftsmen in the *totocalli* including "the artisans, silversmiths and lapidaries, and feather workers were given all they needed for making the jewelry, feather ornaments, diadems, and precious objects that the kings and great lords were given."

30 That craftsmen lived in their own residence is implied in Sahagún's description
   of the *totocalli* feather workers since he prefaces it by stating that his description relates to "the manner in which the inhabitants of Amatlan, the orna-
   menters worked feathers for adornment (Sahagún 1959:91)." In other words,
   the craftsmen from the ward named Amantlan that worked in the *totocalli*.
   López Austin (1973:67) believes that feather workers in Tenochtitlan also
   lived in the barrio of Tzonmolco (see also Rojas 1995:162)

31 The conquests of the Triple Alliance took place in a piecemeal fashion and all
   groups in the Basin of Mexico were not conquered until AD 1465, fully thirty-
   seven years after Aztec independence from Tepanec overlordship.

32 Everybody paid tribute in what they produced, which was referred to as
   tlacalaquilli (Gutiérrez 2013:143). In the words of Juan Bautista de Pomar
   in 1582, "Lo q[ue] les daban de tributo era de los frutos naturales de cada
   tierra, dando cada indio la parte q[ue] le cabía, conforme a la hacienda q[ue]
   poseía, [segun] si era mercader u oficial, y, si labrador, al respecto de la tierra q
   [ue] labrada;" This included cacao, cotton spun thread, bee honey (Acuña
   1986:53).

33 It has been suggested that the Aztec state specified the collection of exotic
   tribute goods that were not available locally as a specific way to benefit
   merchants (Chapman 1957a). There was no reason for the state to do so.
   The state just had to stipulate the goods to be collected and let the local
   population solve the problem. Furthermore, the level of animosity that the
   elite felt toward rich *pochteca* merchants makes it unlikely that the state would
   intentionally strive to enrich them.

34 This information was recorded by Juan Ximénez Ortiz in the *Relación de
   Itztepexic* in 1579 where he reports, "Y [dicen] que la plumería y oro que así
   tributaban lo[s] iban a buscar a Teguantepeque, y a la provincia de Soconusco
   y [a] Guatemala, alquilándose en cargar mercadurías de mercaderes, y en
   beneficiar y cultivar tierras en la d[ic]ha provincia, donde se detenían seis y
   siete meses, y un año."

35 Berdan's (1992a) estimate of 128,000–255,360 textiles paid annually as tribute
   is conservative in contrast to scholars who have estimated tribute at anywhere
   from 2,088,000 to 3,116,560 textiles per year (Berdan 1992a:156; Drennan
   1984b:109; Rojas 1995:255). The variance in these tribute estimates is a result
   of reading the tribute documents in two different ways. The *Codex Mendoza*
   was prepared by a Nahua scribe and then glosses were added in Spanish to help
   explain the document. The Spanish glosses on the Mendoza indicate that each
   symbol represented a "carga," of twenty items. Berdan (1992a) observes that
   the word "carga" was added on with carats, perhaps as a second thought. The
   Mendoza also lists that payments were due twice a year. The *Matrícula de
   Tributos* deals with most of the same tribute provinces but can be read differently. Here the Nahua scribe listed sums of textiles but no additional specifica-
   tion of cargas was added, so the most conservative interpretation is that this is a
   list of individual textiles. However the *Matrícula* gives a different collection
   sequence indicating that textiles were paid every eighty days, or four times per
   year. The tabulation of textiles as individual items is also what is presented in
   the tribute summary provided in the *Información de 1554* (Scholes and Adams

1957). The preponderance of evidence available at this time suggests that the tribute is listed as individual textiles.

36 The three sources that contain tribute information are the *Codex Mendoza* (Berdan and Anawalt 1992), the *Matrícula de Tributos* (Reyes 1997), and the *Información de 1554* (Scholes and Adams 1957).

37 Several other provinces in the Aztec empire also paid their tribute tax in gold. These included the provinces of Coayxtlahuacan/Coixtlahuacan and Tlach-quiavco which supplied twenty gourds of gold dust annually; the provinces of Coyolapan (n=20) and Tlalcozauhtitlan (n=40) that paid tribute in gold disks; and, the three provinces of Tochtepec, Cuetlaxtlan, and Xoconochco that supplied gold ornaments or ornaments set in gold (Berdan and Anawalt 1992).

38 The total value of goods listed in the Tribute Record of Tlapa was 13,678 tribute mantas. The value of goods listed in the Codex Mendoza was 12,020 tribute mantas and 12,080 tribute mantas in the *Matrícula de Tributos*. The value of the Tlapa tribute, therefore, is 13.79% greater than that listed for the *Codex Mendoza* and 13.23% greater than that listed for the *Matrícula de Tributos*.

Chapter 3

1 Market exchange as the term is used here includes both the barter of one type of good against another and the purchase of goods using a formal currency (Dalton 1965; Plattner 1989b).

2 An alternative term for market exchange would be negotiated reciprocal exchange. Active negotiation over price and value is documented for both hunting and gathering groups (Steward 1938) and tribal societies (Harding 1967; Malinowski 1922; Strathern 2007). It occurs in decentralized contexts when interaction occurs between trading partners or with itinerant peddlers. It also occurs in centralized locales with purchases in retail shops or a central marketplace.

3 The number of people who came into Tenochtitlan to visit the market complicates accurately estimating the size of the city. Population estimates for the size of Tenochtitlan's resident population vary widely from 120,000 to 225,000 people (Calnek 2001:721; Sanders 2003; M. Smith 2012c:190). The most likely size for the city based on a careful evaluation of the ethnohistoric and geographic information is Sanders' (2003:203) estimate of 120,000–150,000 persons. This lower estimate is based on a careful consideration of variable population densities in different sectors of the city (Sanders 2003) instead of average population densities for the city as a whole (Rojas 1995:66–68; Smith 2008:152). Sanders subdivided the city into sectors of variable population density that included high, middle, and low class residential areas, the civic-ceremonial center, and chinampa fringe areas on the margins of the city.

4 The advent of keeping inventory records on SKU stock keeping units was made possible with the advent and use of modern computers. In a recent study William Beinhocker (2006:9) reports that retailers have estimated the material diversity of commercial products available for purchase in retail outlets in New York City at more than ten billion (10,000,000,000) SKUs.

5 The reason that obsidian blades were produced in the marketplace is because many of the artisans were itinerant craftsmen who circulated from marketplace to marketplace. Archaeological research at the site of Xochicalco, Morelos has shown that manufacture of obsidian blades in the marketplace was the preferred pattern for both itinerant and resident obsidian craftsmen at least as early as AD 650–900 (Hirth 2006a, 2009b, 2009d, 2013b).

6 We tend to think of baths in the European and Asian sense of soaking in water. More common in Nahua society was the use of the *temazcalli* or sweat bath that involved washing after sitting in a steam heated chamber. The *temazcalli* was used by doctors and midwives for healing as well as physical and/or spiritual cleaning and may have been near the area where apothecaries and doctors were found. The *temazcalli* was a common feature of most Aztec houses and was presided over by the goddess Temazcalteci (Aguilar-Moreno 2007:150). What appears to be a public *temazcalli* has been excavated in the central administrative precinct of Xochicalco which dates between AD 650 and 900.

7 It is clear from the rest of the account that he is comparing his reference of shops to those found in the Ocotelulco marketplace. Since this is the only daily market apparently held in Tlaxcala it is unlikely that he is referring to temporary booths in other five-day marketplaces. This intriguing passage is the only account that suggests the existence of a shop-level economy operating in Nahua society even on a small scale. If accurate it could also refer to selling out of craftsmen houses. In any event this is a topic for future archaeological testing.

8 The five-day rotating schedule was based on the indigenous Mesoamerican calendar. The five-day rotation was shifted to a seven-day rotation after the conquest to conform to the Christian calendar used by the Spanish. This shift did not occur without some costs. The longer periods between market days carried a slightly higher increased risk of food spoilage (Hassig 2001:150).

9 In the Mixteca region the term for market (*yahui*) was applied to the Spanish word for plaza (Terraciano 2001:248) suggesting that the normal location for the marketplace was in open plazas in the center of town.

10 It is likely that judges serving in the marketplace in Tlatelolco and Tenochtitlan were appointed by the *cihuacoatl*, the principal advisor and administrator under the Aztec *tlatoani* (Alba 1949:26; Clavijero 1974:550).

11 The practice of having a special building or facility to regulate commercial activities in large marketplaces was a trans-Mesoamerican practice. In highland Guatemala the public authority regulating commerce in the marketplace was the *popol pat*, which also was the largest council house of the town (Feldman 1985:15).

12 Like the Aztecs of Tenochtitlan the people of Tlatelolco probably built and cultivated small *chinampa* plots within the lake around their island. Whether they also had land on the mainland is unclear but with the growth of the city over time, land shortages for purposes of subsistence agriculture probably existed.

13 Durán (1994:247–262) describes the political events in considerable detail. Over a small insult, the Tlatelolco king Moquihuixtli and his general Teconal

decided to wage a sneak attack against Axayacatl the *tlatoani* of Tenochtitlan. The plot was discovered and the Tlatelolcans' were quickly defeated resulting in the tribute levy of 20% on market products sold by merchants.

14 Sebastian Moreno testified in 1578 that if people paid, they did so in small amounts of the goods they sold. Otherwise they might pay 2–3 cacao beans. Conversely Juan Jacobo said that when he collected the tax, people who sold things would pay one or two cacao beans if they sold something, and they would pay nothing if they didn't sell anything (Carrasco and Monjarás-Ruiz 1978:41–42). At 180–200 cacao beans per tomin/real, a 1–2 cacao levy was insignificant if goods were sold. In purchasing power this 1–2 cacao levy was the equivalent of 57–63 grams of maize in 1560.

15 In the early sixteenth century the gold peso was the primary unit of account even though gold pesos never circulated (Borah and Cook 1958:9). Each peso was divided into 8 *tomines* with each *tomín* consisting of 12 *granos* of gold representing 96 *granos* to the peso. The Coyoacan tax documents are from the middle sixteenth century. After 1538 the Spanish monetary system was reestablished at one peso of base gold (of 8 tomines) to be equal to 8 silver reales.

16 Coyoacan tax document 3 indicates that tax was paid once a year (Anderson et al. 1976:144–145). Coyoacan market tax document 4 reports that the market tax was paid every 30 days (Anderson et al. 1976:148–149). The other two documents (1 and 2) do not specify when the tax was paid (Table 3.2). Although there clearly is a discrepancy in reporting I believe Berdan (1988) is correct in using the yearly payment information because it conforms with when the normal tribute and taxes were collected during both the precolumbian and colonial periods.

17 The price of maize in 1550 was 3 reales/fanega in 1550. The price increased in 1560 to 4 reales/fanega and this is the price used in this calculation. According to Borah and Cook (1958:11) a fanega of maize was 46 kg. Maize could be bought cheaper in rural areas (Restall et al. 2005:91) but the prices used here represent the prices for maize in Mexico City.

18 The full tribute paid by Coyoacan's 3,652 tributaries during the sixteenth century as reported by Carrasco and Monjarás-Ruiz (1978:84) was 1,386 pesos and 6 tomines, 39,780 cacao, 3,834 turkeys, 1264 fanegas of corn, and 447 mantas.

19 If one assumes that Coyoacan tax document 4 is correct and that the market tax of 9 pesos, 5 tomines was collected every 30 days, then the amount of market tax yearly rises by a factor of 12. Under these conditions the average annual market tax collected from Coyoacan would be 114 pesos, 6 tomines. This monetary value equals a purchasing equivalent of 10,764 kg of maize which is enough to support ten commoner households for a year. While significant, this larger estimate is still only 8% of what is raised from the supporting populations' normal service tax/obligation to their lord.

20 The Spanish attempted to raise money from market sales in two different ways. One was charging a market tax on all goods sold. The second was to require sellers to purchase a license called the *alcabala* to sell in the marketplace. Because of protests over the first of these the Spanish enacted the *alcabala* in 1591 which was a sales tax that amount to about 2% of the value of goods sold (Terraciano 2001:249).

21 Another level of market stimulation was the silk raising industry which was encouraged as a means of expanding community income (Borah 1943). The silk industry was particularly important throughout the southern highlands and collapsed during the last quarter of the sixteenth century (Terraciano 2001:246).

22 Examples of marketplaces along trade routes include those found in Timbuktu (Bovill 1970; Miner 1953) and in the commercial cities located along the overland silk road to China.

23 Market importance did not covary exactly with its rotational cycle. Both the marketplaces at Tochpan and Tzicoac held large markets that were convened every twenty days (Frances Berdan, personal communication, 2014).

24 The English translation of Clavijero (1974:235) is by Berdan (1975:168).

25 This is logical given the geopolitical landscape. Goods entering the Valley of Puebla from the south via the Tehuacan valley and east from Veracruz along the Orizaba pass could either proceed to large market at Cholula or to the larger daily market at Tlaxcala. The Tepeaca market effectively intercepted and stalled a good amount of goods from moving on to Tlaxcala. In terms of a geopolitical strategy, the expansion of the marketplace at Tepeaca and stocking it with wealth goods may have been a more effective strategy to isolate Tlaxcala economically than the supposed political blockade and embargo enacted by the Aztecs.

26 Richard Blanton (1983; Blanton et al. 1993:22–31) has argued that the origin of marketplaces in the Valley of Oaxaca was related to the intensification of agriculture coincident with the emergence of the state at Monte Alban between 500 and 300 BC. The motivation was the need for specialized goods by households involved in intensive agriculture that they could not produce themselves. William Sanders (1956) speculated that marketplaces in Central Mexico were a product of inter-regional trade across different environmental zones. For a discussion of market origins and some of their archaeological correlates and documented occurrences see Hirth (1998, 2009b, 2013a).

Chapter 4

1 The quote, money makes the world go around comes from the lyrics of a song written by Irving Berlin from the musical play *Cabaret*. While a parody of life in Berlin during the 1930s, it is a statement that both Karl Marx and Adam Smith could agree with when viewing the economic motivations of individuals and governments alike.

2 The tumpline, referred to in *Nahuatl* as the *mecapalli*, was a strap attached to a carrying frame or basket that transferred the weight of the load carried on the back, to the forehead of a porter (Molina 1977). By leaning forward and maintaining a rigid spine, a porter could carry much more weight using a tumpline than if loads were simply balanced on the head as was the practice in Africa. Karttunen (1983) also identifies the tumpline with the *Nahuatl* word *eltapechtli*.

3 There are three primary tribute documents for the Aztec state. These are the *Codex Mendoza* (Berdan and Anawalt 1992), the *Matrícula de Tributos* (Reyes

1997) and *Sobre el modo de tributar los indios de Nueva España a su majestad, 1561–1564* (Scholes and Adams 1958). While these documents contain much useful information about the economic structure of the Aztec tribute system, they do not provide any information about the structure and operation of precolumbian commerce beyond providing a backdrop for identifying where local resources could be found within the Aztec domain.

4 Gerardo Gutierrez (2013) has observed that the document listing the tribute paid by Tlapa to Aztec Tenochtitlan resembles a modern spreadsheet in the way tribute was tabulated quarterly. This resemblance is coincidental and there is nothing to indicate that it was anything other than a list of tribute paid.

5 In Central Pennsylvania farmers involved in the direct marketing of the goods they produce also regularly buy other items for resale at local farmer's markets and their roadside stands. The goods I have documented as resale items in these markets include, but are not limited to: apples, oranges, Christmas trees, pumpkins, apple cider, jams and jellies, homemade pies, ice cream, mushrooms, caramel, honey, and maple syrup. It is relatively common for apple orchards to buy or trade for varieties of apples that they do not produce for resale to their clientele.

6 One large-scale society that operated quite well without merchants was the Inka society of Andean South America. Here the large-scale inter-regional movement of resources was coordinated by the Inka state (La Lone 1982). It was only on the northern edge of the empire where specialized merchant groups continued to operate and provision regional elites with high-value prestige goods (Salomon 1977, 1987).

7 This is especially clear where the Chinese state consciously tried to exclude or outlaw merchants from distributing goods at different points in time. During the Song period the state monopolized the production and distribution of salt as a major source of state revenue. Although merchants were specifically excluded from selling salt, the state quickly found that they could not effectively and profitably distribute salt in areas of low demand and/or poor transportation without using merchants. The costs of state directed distribution were too high; merchants were a much more cost efficient alternative (Lee-fang Chien 2004).

8 The individual decision making role of the merchant was more apparent in the past than it is today. In the world of cell phones and the internet it is hard to imagine being cut off from information on price and supply at the global level. In the past communication was slow and often inaccurate, requiring merchants to make most of their buying and selling decisions on imperfect information and their hard-won experience.

9 The problem as Gudeman (2001:98) sees it is that there is no consistent theory of what constitutes profit. He agrees with Robinson (1960:79) that neoclassical economics fails to provide a general theory of profit. Profit motivation is even more difficult to identify because it deals with the individual preferences that vary with circumstances.

10 Non-monetary resource accumulations invested in the infrastructure at the household and community level is sometimes called landesque capital because it represents the expenditure of labor mobilized through a variety of monetary and non-monetary means.

11 Favored client relationships are called *pratik* in Haiti by Mintz (1964). The economic means used to create these relationships include granting credit, reduced prices, gifts, or bulk discounts. They are usually designed "to stabilize and secure sources of supply and loci of demand" (Mintz 1964:262). Social relations used to forge commercial ties include kinship, friendship, gossip, and hosting prospective clients.

12 Rural shop keepers often sold on credit and took produce as payment. This could mean processing pigs into hams and cucumbers into pickles before they could be resold (Vance 1970:76).

13 The putting out system is also called the *verlagssystem* and is very old in France. A law from AD 1275 reports the operation of a putting out system for silk production in Paris where spinsters were forbidden to pawn mercers of silk given them by merchants for spinning into thread (Braudel 1986:316). While widely used in early textile manufacture, putting out systems were also used to manufacture durable goods such as nails and cutlery (Braudel 1986:298).

14 The statement in *Nahuatl* that Sahagún recorded is: "In puchtecatl ca tlanama-cani, tlanamacac, thanecuilo, tlaixtlapanqui, tlaixtlapanani, tlatennonotzani, tlamixitiani, tlapilhoatiani. In qualli puchtecatl, tlaotlatoctiani, tlanênemitiani, çan tlaipantiliani, tlanamictiani, tlaimacazqui teimacazqui (Sahagún 1961:42–43)."

15 The verb *tlaixtlapan(a)* may also reflect the idea that the goods received in exchange for others can be divided and separated into the cost of the original item exchanged, plus the increase in value that the exchange produced (profit). I thank Mark Christiansen for helping to deconstruct the etymology of the concept of profit.

16 Several types of indigenous money in the form of cacao beans and textiles (*quachtli*) were in use before the Spanish conquest. Cacao continued in use after the conquest with one hundred cacao beans equal to one Spanish real. The advantage of the cacao was that it was divisible into amounts suitable for the purchase of small value items. Because of the shortage of Spanish currency the cacao bean continued in use as the daily currency throughout the sixteenth century.

17 The format of confessional manuals was to ask questions of petitioners giving them the opportunity to recognize and respond with the appropriate confession of wrong doing. In Molina's confessional manual the question is asked, *cuix tetech titlayxtlapan*, did you gain a profit off someone? The same root word for profit (*tlaixtlapan*) is used here as we find in the discussion of profit by Sahagún. (Christiansen 2011).

18 I am using the term status to refer to the economic role of the participants in the market and not to refer in any general way to their social rank or level of economic well-being.

19 These three terms are especially clear in the discussion of venders in the early colonial market of Coyoacan (Anderson et al. 1976; Rojas 1995).

20 The *Nahuatl* for this passage is, in tlaolnamacac, milchiuhqui, tlalchiuhqui, anoç tlanecuilo.

Chapter 5

1 This quote from François Quesnay concerns the economic orientation of rural peasants (Braudel 1986:177). Quesnay favored subsistence consumption over luxury consumption as the fundamental engine for economic development. Although it is from the mid-eighteenth century well into the industrial revolution, it reflects the orientation that also was probably true of all rural peasant farmers throughout the pre-industrial and ancient world.

2 The premise underlying this argument is twofold. First, that commoner households did not have the purchasing power to consume goods not directly related to meeting their food and clothing needs, and second that only the high price of luxury goods had the ability to overcome the high transportation costs involved in moving them over long distances. For discussion of long-distance trade in high-value luxury goods see Abu-Lughod (1989), Bernstein (2008), Oka and Kusimba (2008), Pirenne (1956), and Schneider (1977). There are many specific examples of the importance of long-distance trade (Allsen 1997; Bovill 1970; Curtin 1984; Daaku 1970; Dale 1994; Goitein 1967; Ratnagar 2004; Tracy 1990, 1991; Weatherford 2004).

3 The literature arguing the importance of wealth goods over staple goods in ancient trade is immense. The inability of peasants to contribute significantly to emerging economy has been argued to be the result of their poverty and the lack of disposable income to purchase non-local products (Braudel 1986:135; Dyer 2005:127–135; McKendrick et al. 1982) and the assumed self-sufficient orientation of rural domestic farming (Halperin 1994:143–149; Waters 2007). The high cost of transporting bulk staple goods is a significant factor in why goods only moved far under special circumstances when technology permitted (Adams 2012; Berggren et al. 2002; Hopkins 1978:43–45; Hugill 1993; Landers 2003:73–93).

4 The demand for luxury goods by political-religious institutions and the appetite for luxuries by nobility is well documented. For instances see Allsen (1997), Liu (1988), Martin (1986) and Weatherford (2004). Likewise the demand for goods created by concentrated urban populations (Appleby 1976; Fall et al. 2002; Kron 2012; Zeder 1988) and its effect on their regional hinterlands have a long discussion (Hoselitz 1955; Jacobs 1969; Wrigley 1978). The high demand for food around urban centers can be met by specialized agricultural production (Yoshinobu 1970:85) supplied by small holders (Dandamayev 1999:363; Frayn 1979; Habib 1982), estate production (Cato et al. 1935; Percival 1976), or a combination of both.

5 Some information on production and consumption can be obtained in the historic record from wills and testaments (Horn 1998; Kellogg and Restall 1998). Unfortunately estate inventories are the residual remains of economic activity and do not provide a comprehensive picture of what domestic production and consumption consisted of on an ongoing basis.

6 Equifinality refers to the problem that similar artifact distributions can be produced by different forms of behavior. In this case similar levels of consumption of goods within households could be a result of different combinations of gift giving, inter-household reciprocal exchange, and market

exchange. The problems of equifinality increase when small samples of archaeological material are used to reconstruct economic behavior.

7 For example, if households live by the only salt source in a region they have the option of exploiting it for commercial gain because individuals far from the source may need or desire salt, but not have the means to exploit it easily. In contrast if households live by a salt source that we know was used, but don't exploit it, then it is possible that there was some form of restricted access to the resource. Ways that access can be restricted include private ownership as well as mediated control through social, political, or religious institutions. The opportunities for commercial exchange may exist or not depending on the social and natural environments in which households find themselves.

8 Luuk De Ligt (1993:107) points out that we should not confuse per capita demand of speciality goods in rural households with total aggregate demand. The idea here is that poor households may only consume imported goods under special circumstances (celebration or sickness) in small quantities. When taken together in the aggregate, however, this level of consumption can be an important stimulus to the movement and consumption of non-local goods.

9 Tony Waters (2007:40) in his cross-cultural study of subsistence agriculture observes that it is common for households to buy small imported items from local shops or itinerant peddlers supplying both a demand for trade and the need to sell local goods to obtain them.

10 Berggren, Hybel, and Landen (2002) argue that subsistence and exchange economies have always been linked. For example, they argue that technological improvements in the production of beer during the thirteenth and fourteenth centuries transformed it into an important export commodity throughout Europe. German brewers learned to preserve beer using hops. This enabled them to lower production costs by reducing its alcoholic content and transporting it over longer distances without it spoiling. During this time the level of production rose and about one-half of the 457 brewers in Bremen, Germany became beer exporters (Berggren et al. 2002:121).

11 The failure of households to produce the level of resources necessary for their survival is best perceived as falling along a continuum. At one end are the households that produce sufficient resources during normal times and only fail to meet subsistence needs during periods of unanticipated shortfalls. Halstead and O'Shea (1989) provide a discussion of these societies. At the other end of the continuum are households that intentionally do not produce enough resources to meet their known resource needs and rely on patronage relationships with kinsmen or other households to support themselves. The Iban of Borneo and the Mazulu societies of Africa are examples of this situation (Sahlins 1972:tables 2.7–2.8).

12 A good example of creative household innovation to obtain access to new resources in Europe during the medieval period is the practice of assarting and clearing new lands to relieve themselves of labor obligations on the feudal manor (Stinson 1983). Other examples would be the micro-division of work to support more people and the ever present rural to urban migration to look for more productive work opportunities (De Haan 1999).

13 While Sahagún's account refers specifically to the range of goods sold in the Tlatelolco marketplace, the same types of goods and people selling them are reported in market accounts for other areas of Mesoamerica.

14 The term *chiuhqui* comes from the verb *chihua*, to make. It is used as a suffix to describe the maker of a specific type or class of items. For example the word *conchiuhqui* would be used to identify a maker and seller of ollas (cooking pots), where the prefix *con* comes from the word for olla which is *comitl* (Durand-Forest 1971:124).

15 The word *tlanamacac* is the word used for a generic vender. The word *petlanamacac* would refer to a generic vender of reed mats, where the prefix *petla* comes from the word for reed mat which is *petlatl*, while *namacac* refers to the act of selling.

16 The word for retailer is *tlanecuilo*. In Nahuatl the suffix *necuilo* is added to prefix of the word for the item being sold such that the word *ichcanecuilo* would refer to a cotton retailer where the prefix *ichca* comes from the word *ichcatl* for cotton. This term may be used specifically to refer to larger-scale dealers, including wholesalers.

17 Maize from the Matlatzinca would have come from the Toluca valley due west of the Basin, while Michoacan lies farther to the west and northwest. Maize of the Tlahuica would have come from Morelos due south of the Basin of Mexico while maize from Tlaxcala would have come from the Puebla-Tlaxcala valley further to the east. While the reference to maize from the north desert lands is unspecific all of these areas lie outside the Basin of Mexico. These different types of maize would have been deemed desirable and imported because of their different colors and properties of taste (Sahagún 1961:66).

18 The types of wild animals listed as being sold include deer (venison), rabbit, hare, duck, crane, goose, mallard, general bird meat, quail, eagle, and opossum. Domesticated animals include the turkey and the meat of newly imported Spanish animals including chickens, cattle, pigs, sheep, and goats (Sahagún 1961:80).

19 Dog (*chichi, ytzcuintli*) is not mentioned by Sahagún (1961:80) as one of the animals sold by the "good" meat seller, only the "bad" meat seller. One possibility is that this may reflect the rapid replacement of dog in the diet by the more productive Old World domesticates of cattle, sheep, and goats. More likely, however, it reflects Sahagún's evaluation of dog meat. That the bad meat seller still offered it for sale reflects its continuation in the native diet as an acceptable food.

20 That indigenous households were involved in the production and sale of wheat is indicated by designating the seller also as a field worker, something the Spanish in the middle sixteenth century did not regularly engage in.

21 The archive testament for Bárbara Agustina is discussed in Karttunen and Lockhart (1976:90–100), while that of Juan Fabián is located in Anderson et al. (1976:58–63).

22 Red worms were made into small cakes known as *ezcahuitli* and were paid by the Aztecs as tribute to Atzcapotzalco for fifty years (Durán 1994:57). Algae, insect eggs and other insect products were also regularly collected from the lakes and used as food (Parsons 1996)

23 *Jumiles* are a small insect much like a lady bug that are often sprinkled on food and eaten live. Grasshoppers remain a popular component of the regional diet in Oaxaca whose consumption has followed migrants from that state north into the United States.

24 The hill region behind Coyoacan in the southwestern portion of the Basin of Mexico was well-known for its carpenters and wood suppliers which are frequently mentioned in the marketplace tax records during the colonial period (Anderson et al. 1976).

25 For example, an obsidian miner at the quarry would shape the stone into cores and preforms for various types of tools to make them lighter to transport over space. The craftsman that purchased obsidian cores benefited from that initial shaping. While this represents a division of labor between two craftsmen in the complete sequence of producing stone tools, it is sequential in the sense that it occurs between, rather than within, a single crafting enterprise.

26 An array of specialized items were produced that very likely also were specialized crafts for which there are no mention in the sources. Examples would be net makers, canoe makers, grinding stone manufacturers, charcoal makers, and weapon and armor makers to name a few.

27 Sahagún provides a generic word for potter (*çoquichiuhqui*), but we know from experience that potters usually specialize in certain sizes and types of items produced. This variation includes cooking vessels, cooking braziers, storage jars, service ware, chili graters, tortilla griddles, figurines, spindle whorls, spinning bowls, ceramic censors, effigy vessels, musical instruments, and mortuary vessels among others. The same would be true for many of the other crafts listed in Table 5-3.

28 Berdan's lower estimate is based on reading the tribute records as individual counts of textiles rather than cargas of twenty pieces as calculated by Drennan.

29 Maguey fiber sandals were still being made in Morelos and sold in the Cuautla market in the 1970s. At that time they were no longer in everyday use but were used primarily as foot apparel for the deceased when they are buried.

30 While manos and metates were always made from stone, the *molcajete* is a chile grater used in preparing sauces and can be a ceramic vessel with a scored grater surface on the interior of the vessel. Ceramic *molcajetes* were more common than stone ones in the Basin of Mexico at the time of the conquest although the name probably remained the same for the producer-seller who manufactured them in stone. Ceramic *molcajetes* would also have been produced and sold by potters.

31 Finely made stone mosaics were manufactured into pendants, ear spools, mirror backs, as well as covering funerary masks. Lapidary mosaics were also incorporated into finely made gold work. Examples of precolumbian mosaic art can be found in museums in Mexico, the United States and Europe (e.g. McEwan 2006; Saville 1922; Urcid 2010: plates 62–65).

32 One place where a specialized shell workshop has been identified archaeologically is in the Valley of Oaxaca where marine shell was fashioned into beads, pendants, ear spools and other miscellaneous ritual paraphernalia (Feinman and Nicholas 1993, 2000).

33 Cigars were smoked in precolumbian times especially in the Maya area where they are occasionally shown being smoked by God L as can be found at Palenque in the main bas-relief carving at the Temple of the Cross.

34 Paper was used to make sacrifices and clothing for the gods. It was also used to absorb the blood sacrifices made in autosacrifice before they were burned as offerings. Paper was a special offering made by merchants to the god Huitzilopochtli for safe passage during their travels. As a portent of these offerings, merchants often wrapped paper around their travel staffs which they worshiped as representatives of their patron god Yacatecuhtli (Sahagún 1959:9–11).

35 In US colonial history indentured servitude would be another example of remuneration for work over a negotiated or stated period of time. The period served was based on the size of the monetary outlay incurred by the individual in the form of passage, room and board, and loans to those who came to the New World from Europe. Often at the end of the time of service an additional monetary stipend could also be stipulated as part of the agreement (Moraley 1743; Souden 1978; E. Williams 1994:10–19)

36 In the colonial period these market porters were called *ganapanes* (Rojas 1995:145) and they continued to be used because of convenience and a shortage of other forms of transport. According to Molina (1977) the proper Nahuatl word for porter is *tlamama*.

37 Frances Berdan (1975:168) reports that porters from the region of Iztepexi regularly served as porters for *pochteca* merchants on trade expeditions on the way to Tehuantepec, Xoconochco, and Guatemala.

38 I am using surplus in this context to refer to the amount of a crop produced by the household and available for sale after its own auto-consumption needs are met. The level of surplus in this context is dependent on a range of factors that include general household production goals, the type and amount of land the household can cultivate, the internal consumption demands, and how fluctuations in climate affect overall crop yields.

39 Aurelio López Coral (personal communication) calculates the average size of family holdings for households in the community of Tepeaca to be 1.4–1.5 hectares per family. Families working on the land held by elite estates were given 5–8 sections of land for their own support of 0.17 ha/section as long as they cultivated at least one section of the same land for the elite household (Martínez 1984:81–85). The result was that commoner households had from 0.85 to 1.36 ha of land to cultivate during the rainy season.

40 Two forms of wetland agriculture have been identified and discussed in Mesoamerica. One is chinampas agriculture (Armillas 1971; Parsons 1976) frequently found in highland areas in permanent marsh and lake environments. The other is raised field agriculture frequently found in seasonal catchment areas in the Maya lowlands (Puleston 1978; Turner and Harrison 1981). The use and management of concentrated water resources allows cultivators to extend production into the dry season when agriculture is not normally possible.

41 Chinampa agriculture like that found in the Basin of Mexico has some of the highest agricultural yields known for ancient agriculture (Sanders 1976). The

success of the system depended on growing crops on raised beds within a marsh or lake environment so that water is constantly available for plant growth without inundating the fields. The expansion of chinampa agriculture was the focus of a large-scale hydraulic project by the Aztecs in the southern lakes region of the Basin of Mexico. This project involved constructing an intricate system of canals and diversion ponds to manage the annual fluctuations in lake levels that were the result of seasonal rainfall (Luna 2014; Parsons 1976, 1991).

42 A recent study by Aurelio López Corral (2011) shows the severe effects that fluctuations in rainfall can have on agricultural yields across Central Mexico even during years with average rainfall. In a study of agricultural production in the Valley of Puebla in 2009, López Corral (2011) recorded losses on 90% of agricultural yield due to cessation of rainfall during the canicula in what was otherwise considered to be a year with normal average annual rainfall.

Chapter 6

1 It is likely that some artisans, especially those residing in the Aztec capital of Tenochtitlan practiced their craft on a full-time basis because goods were readily salable in the marketplaces and because they lacked alternative agricultural land. Most producer-sellers throughout Central Mexico, however, combined selling their products, crafts, or services with some amount of agricultural production. Accordingly they would not be full-time professionals in the strict sense of the term since they only engaged in commercial activities on a seasonal or periodic basis. Craftsmen who produced luxury goods in state workshops like the *totocalli* would have been an exception to this pattern.

2 Vance (1970) visualizes the relationship between household self-sufficiency and retailing in absolute terms: once a retail item is purchased, a household is by Vance's definition no longer self-sufficient. Vance's premise is inherently a false one. It is incorrect because historically forms of gift and reciprocal exchange were distributing products between households and eliminating their economic isolation for thousands of years before the appearance of commercial retailing.

3 London grew from 60,000 persons in 1540 to between 300,000 and 400,000 persons in 1640 (Davis 1966:56). This represents a doubling of population every 35–40 years as a result of large rural to urban in-migration.

4 It could be argued that certain places like the urban center of Teotihuacan had just as rich and as complex system of retail trading by AD 500 as was found in Aztec Tenochtitlan in AD 1521. This was probably true for the city of Teotihuacan which certainly was supplied through several urban marketplaces. The difference, of course, is that the pattern of retail marketing was spread widely throughout the Basin of Mexico and beyond at the time of the Spanish contact, which does not seem to be the case with Teotihuacan. Large sites which could have supported regional marketplaces were rare during the Classic period because of Teotihuacan's domination of the economic system (Blanton et al. 1993; Evans and Webster 2001; Sanders et al. 1979).

5 A possible exception to the absence of a shop-based commercial system is the reference by Hernando Cortés (1962:50) to the existence of shops outside the marketplace in the city of Ocotelulco in the province of Tlaxcala. If this observation is accurate it implies a different kind of economic structure than is recorded elsewhere in Central Mexico. This would need confirmation through focused archaeological investigation.

6 While many types of chile were grown in prehispanic Mesoamerica, Siméon (1991:102) identifies twelve types of chile that were recognized as distinct varieties in the Nahuatl language.

7 The location of Atzitziuacan mentioned in the account remains unknown although it was not located within the Basin of Mexico. It too was an import into the Tlatelolco market.

8 These distances are given as direct line map measurements and would not reflect the actual travel paths of the merchants who would have followed them. Their routes would have been longer, less arduous, and designed to follow safe communication corridors that linked major settlements and population centers.

9 Many marketplaces held on 5-, 8- 13- or 20-day schedules under the indigenous system (Gibson 1964:356; Hassig 1982a) were shifted to the weekly intervals using the Christian calendar. In 1550 the Coyoacan market was changed from a 5- to a 7-day market cycle with the market held on Mondays during the normal Spanish work week (Gibson 1964:357).

10 Durand-Forest (1971:115) and Hernández (Vaery 2000) note that there were four main varieties of cacao, the smallest variety called *tlacacahuatl* was the one used for drinking.

11 The four Coyoacan market documents were written at different times by different recorders, yet they all follow the same pattern of identifying wood venders as retailers rather than producer-sellers. There are nine references to wood dealers in the four Coyoacan market documents which in all nine cases are referred to as *tlaneculio* retail dealers. These dealers paid the highest market tax in the market and did so because Coyoacan was the center of an active and thriving market in wood products because of its nearby forests. This higher tax revenue was probably based on a high volume of sales for these products.

12 The five individual tribute payers were Pedro Tlacotec of Tlacatecol, Joan Toquiasuchil de Tlacaquen, Pedro Sucamyl de Myhualco, Andres Yautle de Culnazalcinco, and Gonzalo Gualacique de Xometitlan (Carrasco and Monjarás-Ruiz 1976:29, 36, 40, 44, and 49).

13 One particularly important dye was cochineal obtained from the insect larvae of *Dactylopius coccus* raised on the leaf of the nopal cactus. Cochineal became a large-scale export industry in colonial New Spain during the middle sixteenth century (Donkin 1977; Gibson 1964).

14 Even if all of the silk sold in the market in Mexico City was produced locally in the highlands of Mexico it is still likely that the venders were retailers because it would have been imported from Huexotzinco and the Valley of Puebla rather than grown locally.

15 The document that Durand-Forest (1971) obtains this information from is the map of the Tenochtitlan marketplace referenced as manuscript 106 in the Goupil-Aubin collection of the National Library of Paris.

16 Richard Drennan places the level of annual textile tribute as high as three million pieces of cloth collected annually. This figure overestimates the textile tribute by counting the number of textiles recorded as cargas of twenty rather than as individual pieces (see Berdan 1987).

17 The value of jade was related to its color. Green stone was considered to be a living material and a sacred substance by all societies across Mesoamerica. As a revered material it was reserved for use as offerings for the gods and by elite individuals ruling in their stead.

18 Determining value by weight in this case of silver to gold was a Spanish colonial convention that used a scale. In prehispanic times value was figured in count or volumetric measure which were periodically reviewed and evaluated for accuracy.

19 The Epiclassic period dates to AD 650–900, fully 600 years before the first mention of the Aztecs in the historic literature. Obsidian blade production appeared and spread widely across Mesoamerica between 1000 and 700 BC and was an indispensable component of household consumption patterns from an early date (Clark 1987; Hirth et al. 2013). The pattern of itinerant obsidian blade production was established at least as early as AD 650 and continued down to the Spanish conquest.

20 The flow of tribute wealth into the state facilitated the growth of the city and the expansion of Tenochtitlan's urban economy. An increase in urban populations together with a rise in disposable wealth created a situation where craftsmen and other producer-sellers expanded their commercial behavior to include a range of other retail activities.

21 The *otlachiquiuhchiuhqui* is identified as "a weaver of stout cane baskets, an owner of stout cane baskets, a possessor of stout cane baskets, a buyer and seller of stout cane carrying baskets" (Sahagún 1961:86).

22 The experienced professional merchant certainly would have his own preferred carrying gear. But novices were often taken on trips under the tutelage of experienced merchants (Sahagún 1959) that could lead to the need for purchasing multiple carrying baskets on short notice to outfit expeditions. The need to maintain stocks would be amplified if there were preferred times of the year to leave on long-distance trade ventures.

23 If bitumen was a regular mastic sold by this vender it would have to have been imported from the Gulf Coast where it is collected.

24 Although some food staples were mobilized through the state tribute system most of the maize, beans, chía, and amaranth collected through tribute appear to have been earmarked for consumption within the palace and not available for sale to commercial agents.

25 The annual food tribute in maize, beans, amaranth, and chía listed for the entire Aztec empire in the Codex Mendoza is eighty-eight tribute bins or storage granaries (Berdan 1992a:154). Sixty-four of these granaries were for food tribute pledged from provinces outside the Basin of Mexico which probably were stored and used in those outlying regions.

26 Retailers predominate in the Coyoacan tax documents. Tax document 4 in Table 6.3 has a high figure of 58.5% for producer-sellers. This is partially a result of double counting vender categories since unlike the other three documents, venders are listed by upper or lower division within the Coyoacan *altepetl*.

The result is that a number of the producer-seller categories for carpenters, sandal makers, spindle whorl makers, pine torch splitters, etc. are listed twice rather than once as they are in the other three market documents.

27 There is no specific information that this occurred except that some level of differential pricing mechanism had to exist for retailers to operate as a viable commercial option. Minimally, differential pricing may have operated on a seasonal basis with more food stock taken in at harvest when prices were lower and held until times of the year when prices rose.

28 The Codex Mendoza indicates, for example, that chili peppers were tribute items paid by three Huaxteca provinces in the far northeastern corner of the empire. These three provinces were Tuchpa, Tzicoac, and Oxitipan (Berdan and Anawalt 1992:2:131, 137, 140). Although the Huaxteca was the only province that paid tribute in chili, these peppers were imported and sold in marketplaces from a much wider area including the far western region of Michoacan (Table 6.1). This at least indicates that the network for imports that retail venders regularly accessed was broader and more diverse than the state-sponsored tribute system.

29 Reliance on terminology alone to identify retail activity as Feldman (1976, 1978a) has done is somewhat unreliable because of the frequent use of the term *tlanamacac* or *tlanamacaque* to identify individuals who sell things. Reading of the sources indicates these terms simply refer to the generic category "seller" and do not distinguish whether they are producer-sellers or retailers in the sense we are interested in them here.

30 In this analysis cacao was considered as a food category. But cacao actually had two uses in prehispanic society, as a beverage and as a currency used to purchase goods. Different types and species of cacao may have been used for these two different purposes which makes it possible to classify cacao as either a food or a wealth item.

31 The extent to which barter would foster or inhibit secondary retail activity would depend to a great extent on the exchange rate at which products moved. It would be difficult to monitor exchange rates in barter transactions. If merchants could procure goods through barter at discount rates they could find themselves in a favorable position to resell them at the going market rate and make a profit.

32 A male dominated view of the marketplace is implied in the discussion of market participants by those who translated Sahagún's Nahuatl information into Spanish and English. As a rule gender is not specified and venders are just described in terms of the activities they engage in. Because Sahagún takes the care to specifically identify some producer-sellers as women when they are engaged in traditional female tasks (cooking, spinning, and weaving) it might be assumed that other venders are males. This was not his intent and just the result of the way the account was constructed and the gender neutral language in which it was presented.

Chapter 7

1 Modern scholars who refer to long-distance merchants as *pochteca* include: Acosta Saignes (1945), Berdan (1975, 1980), Bittmann Simons and Sullivan

(1978), Carrasco (1978), Chapman (1957a), Katz (1966), Rojas (1995), and Salomon (1977)

2 That *pochteca* was a general term to refer to all professional merchants is clear from the way it was used with adjectives in *Nahuatl* to refer to generic terms like merchant woman (*pochtecacihua*) and old merchants (*pochtecaueuetque*) (Berdan 1975:155).

3 The payment of tax in the goods traded by merchants was called *pochteca tequitl* illustrating that this payment was seen as a material equivalent to labor service paid by farmers (Molina 1977).

4 The six urban wards where merchants resided were: Pochtlan, Ahuachtlan, Atlauhco, Acxotlan, Tepetitlan, and Itztulco (van Zantwijk 1985:138).

5 van Zantwijk (1985) saw this hierarchical structure as a dimension of the *pochteca* being organized into merchant guilds. Although it certainly reflects higher levels of professional cooperation, caution needs to be exercised so as not to draw incorrect parallels with guilds as we know them from the Old World.

6 These twenty different products were produced in five different crafting activities at Otumba: flaked stone, ground stone, lapidary, weaving, and ceramic production. The raw materials worked include obsidian, chert, rock crystal, basalt, clary, cotton, and maguey.

7 The obsidian sources used include the local source of Otumba and the Sierra de Pachuca source. The Sierra de Pachuca source is located 49 km from the site of Otumba.

8 What makes the *Matrícula de Huexotzinco* unique is that it provides a head glyph for each individual, lists their name with an accompanying name glyph, and records their trade or profession in an additional glyph. The status of renter or *terrazguero* is indicated by placing a red dot over their head of the listed individual. The absence of a dot implies that they had their own land.

9 Gerhard (1986:145) and Prem et al. (1978) could not identify the exact location of Santa Maria Acxotla within the Huexotzinco *altepetl*. The most likely location for this community is in the open piedmont east and below the original town of Huexotzinco near the marketplace town of San Francisco Tianquiztenco. This location is the most logical given the sequence of town visitations presented in the *Matrícula* and the probability that a major community of merchants would be located near the region's central marketplace.

10 The 453 individuals listed for Santa Maria Acxotla are: 280 young heads of commoner households, 41 elite heads of households, 57 old married couples, 12 widowers, 55 widows, and 8 sick and incapacitated individuals. Also listed are 68 people who have died since the last census and 22 men who have run away. Residents for the barrio of Xalpatol are also listed in the Santa Maria Acxotla tabulation who reside in the town of San Salvador. The Xalpatol barrio contains 67 merchants and five elite households.

11 The estimate of 1,200–1,525 people is derived in the following way. The 280 heads of commoner households were assigned a population of 3–4 persons/household (840–1,120) while the 41 elite households were estimated as being slightly larger at 4–5 persons (164–205). The number of old married couples (n=57) was multiplied by two (114) to which were added single counts

for the 75 widows, widowers, and sick even though we do not know their ages or whether they had children resident with them. The resulting total for these population ranges was 1193–1514 persons.

12 The number of households a single obsidian craftsman could support depended on the size of the household, the length of the blades the craftsman produced, and the household's annual need for cutting edges. Hirth and Castanzo (2006: table 9.12) summarize the various estimates of obsidian blade consumption found in Mesoamerica. Although these estimates range widely from 4 to32 blades per year, most fall clearly within the range of 5–15 blades per year. Santley's (1984:61) estimate of 10–12 blades per year is reasonable. The production capacity of the two Acxotla obsidian craftsmen far exceeded local consumption demands even if the highest rates of 20–32 blades per year is used to estimate the community's consumption needs (Clark 1986; Hay 1978). At consumption rates of 20–32 blades/year, the two craftsmen still could have provided the obsidian blades consumed by 2,343–3,750 households.

13 An average production of 923 vessels per year is reasonable for domestic production. Arnold's (1988) study of domestic potters in the Tuxtla region reports an average of 30 vessels fired in modern kilns (Pool 1993:406). This represents just over 2.5 firings per month over the length of the year to produce the estimated output of 923 ceramic vessels. If potters worked only during the dry season their output would be significantly lower.

14 The information on ceramic consumption is difficult to accurately assess from ethnographic data given the changes in modern household assemblage composition. Nevertheless, Pool (1993:table 4) and Rice (1987:table 9.4) summarize the available data. Annual ceramic replacement rates range from low (2–5 vessels) and medium (13 vessels) to very high (33 vessels/year) (Pool 1993:403). The estimate of 10–15 vessels per year used here is seen as a medium to high level of ceramic usage.

15 In addition to resin collecting being seasonal, the part-time nature of this activity is reinforced by the fact that the resin collector is listed as a farmer who rented land from his lord.

16 Tax records from the Coyoacan marketplace show that tobacco tubes and processed tobacco were sold by separate venders. Tobacco sellers are recorded in all four of the tax inventories while cigar sellers are recorded in three; all seven of these tobacco products are listed as being sold by resellers (*tlamanacac*). Conversely tobacco tube sellers are listed in three of the four market tax documents as producer-sellers (*-chiuhqui*) and once as a reseller (Anderson et al. 1976).

17 While cane goods and warping frames would be relatively inexpensive commodities, metal goods consisting of copper-bronze items and the goods sold by *oztomeca* merchants were high-value items.

18 The statement from Oviedo y Valdés (1855:3:535) is "Solo los señores, e algunos sus parientes e algunos principales e mercaderes, tienen heredades e tierras propias, e las venden e juegan, quando les paresce." Only the rulers and some of their relatives and other principal leaders and merchants have granted estates and their own land, and they sell, work administer, and arrange them as they like (translation by Gerardo Gutierrez).

19 Merchants residing in Acxotla were assigned as tribute payers to an elite lord named Pedro Tlackin (Prem 1974:626r). Merchants in the barrio of San Salvador were assigned to a separate lord named Diego Mineuh who was one of the five elite households residing in the Xapatol barrio (Prem 1974:629r)

20 The cities that Sahagún (1959:24) identifies as being under the command of the *quappoyaualtzin* include vanguard merchants from Tenochtitlan, Texcoco, Huexotla, Coatlinchan, Chalco, Huitzilopochco, Mixcoac, Azcapotzalco, Cuauhititlan, and Otumba.

21 Sahagún (1959:21) refers to this area as Tzinacantan. The area around Zinacantan, Chiapas is well known from the ethnographic work of Frank Cancian (1965, 1972), Evon Vogt (1969), and Jane Collier (1973).

22 The original Spanish is: "Son los de este pueblo en toda esta tierra como principales de cada pueblo y solamente por ser de Zinacantan se hacen honra por decir que son mercaderes (Ximenéz 1920:360)."

23 This sighting was recorded in pictographic form in the Codex en Cruz. Elizabeth Boone (2000:230) suggests that symbols of eyes portrayed in codices represent the watchfulness of Moctezuma's spying merchants.

24 Various names are given for slave dealers which include *tecoanmime, tealtinime, teyaohualohuani*, and *yiaque* (Acosta Saignes 1945:23; Orozco y Berra 1940:107).

25 The respect for merchants and craftsmen is revealed in a statement to Ahuitzotl which Tezozomoc (1878:461, 521) accredits to the Cihuacoatl where he says, "los que adornan y resplandecen (sic) esta gran ciudad son los oficiales de obras mecánicas, como son plateros, canteros, albañiles, pescadores, petateros, loceros y lapidarios, cortadores de las piedras finas, en especial los tratantes ... y mercaderes; a estos estimó muy mucho mi buen hermano Moctezuma Ilhuicamina (Tezozomoc 1878:461, 521)."

26 In describing the functionaries of the Texcoco palace Ixtilixochitl states, "el cuarto consejo fue el consejo económico. En él se reunían todos los administradores (mayordomos) del rey y algunos de los principales comerciantes de la ciudad, para ocuparse en cuestiones económicas y con el tributo real (Katz 1966:79).

27 These were most likely *quachtli*, plain white tribute capes or clothes.

28 The goods bought with the 1,600 *quachtli* were, "ruler's capes, feathered in cup-shaped designs, and those of eagle face designs, and striped on the borders with feathers; and rulers' breech clo[uth]s with long ends; and embroidered skirts [and] shifts (Sahagún 1959:8)."

29 The goods listed as property of the merchants include: "golden mountain-shaped mitres, like royal crowns; and golden forehead rosettes; and golden necklaces of radiating pendants; and golden ear plugs; and golden covers used by women of Anauac–with these the princesses covered their bodies; and rings for the fingers, called *matzatzaztli*; and golden ear plugs, and rock crystal ear plugs. And the things used by the common people were obsidian ear plugs, [or] tin, and obsidian razors with leather handles, and pointed obsidian blades, and rabbit fur, and needles for sewing, and shells. All these were prepared as goods exclusively of the merchants (Sahagún 1959:8)." Also taken were

cochineal, alum, birthwort, and cosmos suphureus (Sahagún 1959:18). The reference to "tin" ear plugs probably refers to copper ear spools.

30 The complete list of the goods that the lords of Xicalanco gave to the merchants for Ahuitzotl were: large round green stones, cylindrical green stones, green stones cut on a bias, the finest emerald-green jade, fine bottle-green jadeite, turquoise mosaic shields, green pyrites, large red sea shells, red coral shells, flower-colored shells, yellow and ocelot-colored tortoise shell cups, red spoon-bill feathers, toupial feathers, blue honeycreeper feathers, yellow parrot feathers, and jaguar skins (Sahagún 1959:18–19).

31 Sahagún's account has Ahuitzotl going out to meet the returning victorious merchants in Acachinanco (Sahagún 1959:4). This did not likely take place since according to Durán (1994) Ahuitzotl accompanied his army in the Xoconochco campaign. It is likely that Sahagún's merchant informants took considerable liberties with the facts and drew a symbolic parallel to later events since Acachinanco is the place near Mexico City were Cortés was granted an interview with Montezuma and other Aztec nobles during the Spanish conquest (Simeón 1991:6). Participating merchants did receive special devices and apparel that they could wear in public as a result of participation in the Xoconochco campaign.

32 The inventory of goods arriving at the *petlacalco* in Tenochtitlan are recorded in the *Matrícula de Tributos* (Reyes 1997), the *Codex Mendoza* (Berdan and Anawalt 1992), and the *Información de 1554* (Scholes and Adams 1957).

33 The exact list of goods recorded on tribute documents in the Aztec capital of Tenochtitlan include warrior costumes with shields, bars of gold, tecomates of gold dust, huipiles, cloth decorated with stripes, plain cloth, gourds for consuming cacao, cakes of rubber, rubber in the shape of human figures, and turkeys (Gutiérrez 2013:151, 157).

34 The *Nahuatl* word *nextia* is the causative form of *neci* (to appear). In economic contexts or where money is involved it refers to "money, tribute and to be produced or available." The *ix* is likely from *ixtli* (face) which was commonly used to refer to "the eye or more generally that something appears." In the context of goods, tribute or money *nextia* would serve as a verb "to make something appear, or to produce it (Mark Christensen, personal communication 2013).

35 The first day of several of the thirteen day periods were considered especially propitious for setting out on a merchant venture. Four especially lucky days were: 1 *cipactli* (1 crocodile), 1 *coatl* (1 snake), 1 *ozomatli* (1 monkey), and 7 *coatl* (7 snake). Directionality was also significant and the 1 crocodile and 1 snake were associated with the east while 1 monkey and 7 snake were associated with the west (Sahagún 1959:9; van Zantwijk 1985:153).

36 The Aztecs believed they had three souls. The *tonalli* resided in the head and was the soul of will and intelligence. The *teyolia* was located in the heart which was where the soul of fondness and vitality was located. The *ihiyotl* was the soul of passion, luminous gas, and aggression and was believed to reside in the liver (Carrasco and Sessions 1998:123; Ortiz de Montellano 1989:199).

37 *Yacatecuhtli* (Lord of the Vanguard) the patron god of the merchants also was known by several other names including Yacapitzauac (Sahagún 1981a; Thompson 1966:160) and Cocochimetl (O'Mack 1985:118). This variation in naming

was most likely a product of the specific merchant group. For example, Quetzal-coatl was the primary god of the merchants in Cholula outside the Valley of Mexico.

38 This description is drawn from Sahagún's account provided by his Tlatelolco informants. Although it recounts the return of merchants to Tlatelolco it is assumed that the same practice was followed by *pochteca* merchants living in other cities within the Basin of Mexico.

39 The principal merchants who were installed or vested by different Tlatelolco rulers include: Itzcoatzin and Tziuhtecatzin installed by the ruler Quaquauh-pitzauac (AD 1379–1418); Cozmatzin and Tzompantzin who were principal merchants under Tlacateotl (AD 1418–1427); Tollamimichtzin and Mic-xochtzinyautzin who were installed by the Tlatelolco king of Quauhtlatoat-zin (AD 1428–1460); Popoyotzin and Tlacochintzin who were installed under the ruler Moquiuixtzin; and Quauhpoyaualtzin, Nentlamatitzin, Vetz-catocatzin, Canatzin, and Veiocomatzin who may have been the principal merchants under the reign of the Aztec king of Ahuitzotl (AD 1486–1502) (Sahagún 1959:1–3).

40 van Zantwijk (1985) feels that merchant feasts were part of a cycle of ritual *cargos* or tasks very much like the elaborate cargo system described ethno-graphically from a number of areas of Mesoamerica. Feasts were important, but I feel it is unlikely that they were part of a formal cargo system in the sense that we know it from modern ethnographic work (Cancian 1965; Flannery 1972; Monaghan 1995) because cargo systems were a post-colonial response to the loss of elite leaders that sponsored community celebrations.

41 This is clear when at one rather elaborate feast Sahagún (1959:38) describes the high ranking individuals who were invited to dance. Joint sponsorship of the feast is implied by his words, "But the principal merchants did not dance; they only sat; they remained watching, because it was these who gave the banquet (Sahagún 1959:38)."

42 *Huitzilopochtli* was the patron god of the Aztecs and the embodiment of the sun god (Tonatiuh). Conducting this ceremony at the winter solstice provided *Huitzilopochtli* with the blood nourishment necessary for him to return in strength during the coming year.

43 Townsend (1992:190) speculates that the Bathing of Slaves ceremony was initiated early in a merchant's career, to initiate new merchants into becoming professionals. This was tactically impossible given the cost involved, the solemnity of the event, and the significance it had for marking a merchant as a leader both in his profession and the society as a whole.

44 Tochtepec was both the outpost from which *pochteca* penetrated distant and hostile lands like warriors and the point from which they returned "victori-ous" with the wealth of the god.

45 According to the Codex Matritense (1906), "if one of 'those who were bathed' proved to be a well-educated person, who could sing well and was otherwise well trained in the art of living, and made a good impression on account of his outward appearance and inward qualities, the nobles would take such a person aside." The translation of the original *Nahuatl* is provided by van Zantwijk (1985:316–317).

46 Elsewhere Sahagún (1981a) gives a different account of combat during the *Panquetzaliztli* festival where combat is described as a fight between captured warriors intended for sacrifice and the bathed slaves with warrior knights joining in the fray. Instead of ransom, warrior knights captured by the bathed slaves were sacrificed. This narrative presented in Book 2 of Sahagún (1981a:145–146) is less complete than that presented in Book 9 which I believe is the longer and more complete account of this ritual combat.

Chapter 8

1 *Tlachtli* and *patolli* were games of chance and were considered one of the lewd vices to which an individual could fall.

2 An arroba is a Spanish measure of 11.5 kg (Hassig 1986).

3 The 23 kg load was legislated as the standard load for service portage during the colonial period. Hassig (1985:33) notes the account of Bernal Díaz del Castillo was written well after the 23 kg load limit was instituted and may not reflect a prehispanic practice.

4 Robert Drennan (1984a, 1984b) recognized that 23 kg was an unusually light load for modeling prehispanic trade. His solution was to model trade using the arbitrarily larger porter load of 30 kg.

5 Borah and Cook (1958:42) define a *jornada* as one day's travel for a *tlameme* under load. This was six Spanish leagues or six hours travel at average pace of 2.5 miles/hour to produce a maximum day's travel of 15 miles (33 km) per day.

6 Mules normally carried 20 kg which is within the range of a human porter. Good (1995) cites late twentieth century examples where porters actually carried more weight than mules. Carts with two large oxen could pull 40 *arrobas* (460 kg) with one driver (Hassig 1986:137). The problem was the scarcity of good roads except between major settlements which limited the feasibility of large scale cartage.

7 This contrasts with the use of the term barter by Blanton (1998:464) and others (Humphrey and Hugh-Jones 1992) as restricted exchanges that took place between individuals or groups in socially isolated settings. My use of the term barter does not make location an important ingredient in defining the term. It is simply the balanced and negotiated exchange of one good for another.

8 The entomology of *timotlapatilia* is: *ti-* is the subject designation for you or we while *mo-* indicates it's a reflexive action. The root *tlapatilia* comes from the word *patla* which means to exchange or trade. Together the word means to barter, exchange, or do business with someone.

9 The idea of active negotiation in *ixnextia* comes from the root word *ix* derived from the noun *ixtl* meaning face, eye or surface combined with the word *neci* which means to appear (Table 8.2). In other words to make something appear from face-to-face interaction. This idea of face-to-face dealings is represented in the words *tlaixtlapana* (to profit), *tech tlaixtlapana* (to loan), and *tlaixtla-panaliztli* (usury), and *tlaixtlapanqui* (investor) (Table 8.2).

10 Gerardo Gutierrez (personal communication, 2015) notes that in Sahagún (1959) the term *tlacocohualoni* is used to describe the act of buying. He suggests that an alternative etymology might be that *tlaco* is associated with one-half. That is where "to measure and divide in halves" is used as a metaphor to buy and sell and make profit. It is possible that in colonial parlance, Molina may be refering to a coin of a medio or one-half of a real.

11 A wider range of valued items served as money among the Maya. These included cacao beans, copper bells, shells, colored stones, copper axes, jade beads, and feathers (Cardos de Mendez 1959:46; Tozzer 1941:94–96).

12 It is possible that the Spanish took special notice of gold and copper because they were metal like their own currencies. Clavijero (1974:236, 527) mentions that pieces of silver were also used as money but it is likely that these were copper-silver alloys that moved in a variety of forms. Both Tepequaquilco and Quaiuhteopan paid tribute to the Aztecs in copper axes (Litvak King 1971; Rojas 1995:245). Tlapa was one of the provinces in the Aztec empire that paid the largest quantity of gold as tribute (Gutiérrez 2013).

13 The three cacao varieties regularly used for currency were *cacahuatl*, *mecacahuatl*, and *xochicahuatl*, while the small been variety (*tlalcacahuatl*) was more often used for drinks (Durand-Forest 1967:158; Hernández 1959: II:303).

14 There were three primary beverages consumed on festive occasions in Central Mexico at the time of the conquest. These beverages were cacao, chian made from Chenopodium seeds, and pulque (Rojas 1927:165).

15 A *carga* of cacao represented a full porter load which contained a total of 24,000 cacao beans (Borah and Cook 1958:12).

16 The production of cacao was extended to Venezuela during the sixteenth century and it became an agricultural export early in the seventeenth century to Spain via the port of Veracruz. The growth of cacao as an export in the seventeenth century was due to its increased consumption in the European market (Arcila Farías 1975).

17 Tenochtitlan is 11.6 km from Coyoacan by canoe. The account suggests that the women had traveled by land which was 13 km to Coyoacan from the west edge of Tenochtitlan along the Calzada de Chapultepec.

18 The leader of the merchant expedition was called the *tachcauhchiuhtiaz*, which directly translates as "he who would lead or become the leader (Berdan 1988:650)."

19 Durán (1994:182–183) indicates that the 160 merchants came from a number of towns in the Basin of Mexico including Texcoco, Chalco, Xochimilco, Tenochtitlan, and several of the other Tepanec towns.

20 *Pochteca* merchants took *pinolli* on their expeditions as a main travel ration (Sahagún 1959:14). It was mixed with water and drank. It was extremely nourishing and fought hunger.

21 I have observed venders in the 1970s regularly sleeping in the marketplaces both in Cuzco, Peru, Antigua, Guatemala, and the periodic fair at Mazatepec, Morelos, Mexico.

22 The equivalents of these places in the Old World were caravanserai located along important caravan routes. Although similar in function, there was no

need in ancient Mexico for large courtyards because no beasts of burden were employed in indigenous caravans.

23 It is likely that youths who were not members of *pochteca* communities learned the skills and established the necessary economic connections by accompanying their parents or other community members involved in commerce.

24 The role of the broker was to assist the merchant in the sale of merchandise without becoming involved in the sale-purchase chain. Brokers were commonly used across the pre-industrial world to solidify long-distance exchange relationships. In Africa neutral brokers were a common way to mediate exchange between different ethnic groups and to ensure a high degree of honesty and fair play (Cohen 1966). In the Muslim world the use of brokers is well documented in the inter-cultural maritime trade with India during the eleventh and twelfth centuries. Letters and documents in the Cairo Geniza record the regular use of Hindu brokers by Jewish merchants who shipped, bought, and sold merchandise along maritime routes between Egypt, Saudi Arabia, and northwestern India (Goitein 1967, 1973).

25 Factors form enduring business relationship with their clients. They engage in multiple, commercial transactions, and in the case of employees or trading partners, owe their livelihood to the success and maintenance of ongoing business relationships. When client-factor relationships are built on kinship or ethnic affiliation they can create long-distance diaspora networks (Curtin 1984). These sustained business practices create the need for permanent facilities (warehouses, domiciles, and processing areas) in the areas where factors do business. Examples for the use of factors can be found in many areas of the pre-industrial world including Rome (Finley 1985:44), Medieval Europe (Abu-Lughud 1989), Central Asia (Levi 2002), Indonesia and the Phillipines (Dobbin 1996:166; Geertz 1963; Rush 1990), and all the chartered European trade companies from the sixteenth to nineteenth centuries (Bayly 1983; Cheong 1997; Daaku 1970; Pearson 1988).

26 Support for the idea that investment through consignment was open to a wide range of individuals in the *pochteca* community comes from the statement given by Sahagún's informants that the goods brought back by a merchant from a trading expedition were not his goods but the goods of "our mothers, our fathers, the merchants, the vanguard merchants (Sahagún 1959:31)."

27 Family and kinsmen often functioned as brokers in other ancient societies. The key to defining the relationship is that there was economic return in either profit or reciprocal services provided between the consignor and the consignee.

28 Itzamkanac the capital of Acalan is probably the modern archaeological site known as El Tigre located in southwest Campeche. For a discussion of the archaeological features of El Tigre see Vargas Pacheco and Teramoto Ornelas (1996).

29 What constitutes permanent or semi-permanent residence in a diaspora community is subject to debate since a great deal of variability is found with merchant communities throughout antiquity. What is often the case is that

the community is permanent while its residents cycle between homeland and diaspora communities. This was clearly the case with Old Assyrian merchants who lived in diaspora communities such as Kanish for fifteen years or more before returning to their home city of Assur (Veenhof 2003:81).

30 According to Burns (1999) convents were particularly active in making these annuity loans. They acquired capital resources from the daughters sent with their dowries when they entered the convent. The *censos al quitar* were a way to generate an income from these capital resources by loaning it out to members in the community.

31 According to Motolinia (1971: 370), "When someone took mantas on credit, or something of equal value, from some merchant, and died without paying, the merchant had the authority to make a slave of the widow for the debt. If the deceased had left a son, the son was made a slave and not the mother (translation by Berdan 1975:62)."

32 The 1573 will of Don Juan de Guzmán, the *Nahua* ruler of Coyoacan, recorded that the Spanish peddler Alonso de Yépez be paid fifty pesos owed him for business dealings (Horn 1998). This was placed in his will as a testament in lieu of Alonso de Yépez having any written document or contract for their business dealings. This suggests that even significant business dealings were conducted by verbal agreement without written contacts even fifty years after the conquest when Spanish influence across society was strong.

33 José Luis de Rojas discusses types of contracts and loan agreements that he believes were practiced among the Aztecs. These include the "permuta, compra-venta, deposito, comision, prestamo, prenda, fianza, arrandamiento, aparceria, donacion y trabajo (Rojas 1995:246–247)."

Chapter 9

1 The limit of the Aztec empire is illustrated in Figure 1.1. Conservative estimates place the population of the empire at between 6 and 10 million people (Webster and Evans 2013:636). The area of highest population density within the empire was the Basin of Mexico which was the home to 1–1.2 million people distributed over 7,000 ha (Sanders et al. 1979:378; Webster n.d.; Whitmore et al. 1990:33). This was the Aztec homeland and its large population gave the Aztecs a tactical military advantage as it could field an army that normally was significantly larger than many of their adversaries.

2 José Luis de Rojas (1995:116) cites Motolinia saying that owners of slaves did contract them out to carry cargos in the marketplace as a means to make money.

3 Rulers sometimes gave slaves to especially talented artisans engaged in the production of high-value goods to encourage full-time production. The ruler Nezahualcoyotl gave slaves to skilled artisans living in Texcoco so they could engage in craft production on a more regular basis. The Aztec ruler Moctezuma also gave two slaves to skilled artisans to farm their plots for the same reason (Katz 1966:52).

4 Bernal Díaz del Castillo (1956:43–46) records the account of Gerónimo de Aguilar. In the words of Díaz del Castillo (1956:46), "Cortés questioned

Aguilar about the country and the towns but Aguilar replied that having been a slave, he know only about hewing wood and drawing water and digging in the fields, that he had only once travelled as far as four leagues from home when he was sent with a load, but, as it was heavier than he could carry, he fell ill."

5　China clearly was not as restricted in its transportation options as was Mesoamerica. Carts were used to move goods and where possible large quantities of goods were moved along major rivers. Despite these advantages many of China's markets depended on movement of goods over land.

6　Traditional peasant households in some areas of Oaxaca obtained as much as 50% of the maize they consumed from outside the region where they lived reflecting the high dependence on the marketplace for basic provisioning (Beals 1975:136). Prehispanic households across the highlands were likewise dependent on trade for some staple resources while producing most of their own food. Households, for example, procured the majority of their cutting edge as obsidian through inter-regional exchange.

7　These efficiencies of procurement are the foundation for the emergence of market hierarchies as predicted by Central Place Theory (Chorley and Haggett 1967; Christaller 1966; Losch 1938; C. Smith 1976). It is the demand threshold for different types of goods that creates a market hierarchy where the higher order levels of the hierarchy offer more different types of goods for sale than lower levels.

8　The advantage of timing marketplaces to coincide with public events was recognized by the Spanish who established markets on Sundays so peasants could combine economic provisioning with their travel from rural areas to attend church (Bromley and Symanski 1974:9).

9　Marketplaces probably emerged across the Central Mexican highlands coincident with the appearance of increasingly localized ceramic spheres after 500 BC. Inter-regional exchange networks continued to operate but ceramic assemblages become more and more regionalized as local economic systems grew in strength and integration around this time.

10　Blanton (1983) has argued that the origin of the marketplace in the Valley of Oaxaca was linked to the emergence of intensive forms of year-round agriculture. While plausible, there is no direct archaeological evidence to suggest that this was the case. Marketplaces appeared across Central Mexico without any connection to irrigation or other forms of intensive agriculture. A marketplace was operating at Xochicalco at least as early as the Epiclassic period (AD 650–900) where no intensive agriculture is found (Hirth 1998, 2000).

11　While markets had a long history of development in the highlands, their role in eastern Mesoamerica among the Maya is less clear. Although marketplaces are present in several areas of Maya-land in the early sixteenth century, they are not as frequent or as large as those found in the central and southern Mexican highlands. For a discussion of the possibility of markets in the Maya lowlands during the Classic period see Masson and Freidel (2013) and Shaw (2012).

12　The preponderance of evidence across Central Mexico suggests that crafting households had supplemental agricultural fields for household maintenance. What the situation was in the Aztec capital of Tenochtitlan is unclear since city residents suffered from a shortage of agricultural land from its foundation

(Durán 1994). A higher level of commercial activity and artisanship may have existed there from the beginning of the city out of economic necessity.

13 These negotiated agreements would be for goods on-hand as well as for future goods. These agreements would represent formal purchase contracts and would have conformed to the law if goods were delivered in the marketplace where buying and selling was to take place. For efficiency purposes food was probably bought from large estates rather than small farmers, while craft goods would have been contracted from individual artisans.

14 The best documented instance of a safe passage agreement is recorded for their trade into the province of Anahuac Xicalanco (Sahagún 1959).

15 The maintenance of foreign ethnic identify helped reinforce *pochteca* boundaries. This is seen in the worship of Yacatecuhtli in the community of Otatitlan along the Rio Papaloapan in coastal Veracruz. Morante López (2010) associates Yacatecuhtli with the black face Christ worshiped in Tlacotepec, Puebla and Esquipula, Guatemala as part of the religious syncretism that occurred during the sixteenth century. Yacatecuhtli is also known as Yacapitzauac.

16 By semi-professional soldiers I am referring to the knight societies that were composed of accomplished commoner warriors who demonstrated their combat abilities by taking multiple sacrificial victims that were offered as human sacrifices to the gods. For more discussion of the military system see Berdan (1982), Hassig (1988), and M. Smith (2012c).

17 In Europe and elsewhere guilds sought to control the production of certain goods, maintain profitability, control prices, prohibit competition, and manage risk. European guilds were organized at the level of individual communities and as a result its membership was integrated through a range of religion and co-fraternal activities rather than through kinship relations (Epstein 1991; Golas 1977; Wolek 1995).

18 Examples of poll or head tax used in the old world include the household tax in ancient Israel (Exodus 30:11–16), the Roman poll tax on subjects in conquered provinces, and *jizya* tax among Muslim groups. In Europe forms of poll taxes on movable property appear in England and Scotland during the thirteenth and fourteenth centuries.

19 Zorita (1994:189) makes clear that the economic pressure on native populations during the sixteenth century was due to population declines when he states that in prehispanic times, "one Indian pays more tribute today than did six Indians in that time, and one town pays more in gold pesos today than did six towns of that kind that paid tribute in gold."

20 The 278,400 pieces of cloth are estimated as 60,400 tribute cloaks paid four times per year, 14,400 loin cloths, 20,800 women's tunics, and 1,600 skirt sets (Berdan 1987:239–241).

21 This estimate calculates the average size of the domestic unit at five people per household which for a population of 5–10 million people represents 1,000,000–2,000,000 households. When the 278,400 tribute textiles are divided by the number of households, each household would be required to produce between 0.28 and 0.14 textiles per year.

22 William Sanders and colleagues estimate that the Basin of Mexico had the highest population in Mesoamerica at the time of the conquest with over

1,000,000 people located in 7,000 sq km (Sanders et al. 1979:378). That would place between 5 and 10% of the entire population in the Aztec empire within only 4% of its total area. While the Basin of Mexico was densely occupied because of the highly productive *chinampa* agriculture located there (Parsons 1991), so too were other areas of the empire including the Mixteca and the Valley of Oaxaca.

23 The growth of Amsterdam in the seventeenth century to become a major financial and trading center with 200,000 people was due in large part to the emergence of the Dutch East India company as a major commercial power and Holland's continued relationship with the Spanish monarchy. In 1500 its resident population did not exceed 15,000–20,000 persons. London grew rapidly throughout the sixteenth century but at 1519 only had a population between 50,000 and 60,000 people (Chandler 1987).

24 Paris may have been somewhat different as it was the largest city in the western Mediterranean during the sixteenth century that had a large central market in Les Halles (C. Smith 1999:172).

25 Marketplaces in London were often the result of specific licensing arrangements made by the crown. This was the case with city markets that were established by charter (C. Smith 1999:30). Over 2,000 weekly markets and annual fairs were established in rural England in the late Middle Ages in hope that towns would grow, peasants could sell goods to get money to pay their taxes, and traffic to markets would produce revenue for the lords from tolls (Dyer 2005:20). To a large extent rural fairs in England during the sixteenth century were strongly oriented to wholesale activity and purchasing stocks for sale elsewhere (Cox 2000:195).

26 The Morelos markets listed by Maldonado Jiménez (1990:mapa 26) are: Atlatlahuacan, Axochiapan, Cuauanahuac, Huaxtepec, Hueyapan, Jantetelco, Nepopoalco, Ocotepec, Ocuituco, Tepoztlán, Tetela, Tlayacapan, Totolapan, Yacapichtlan, and Yautepec.

27 Skinner's analysis was based on the examination of thirty-four market towns in and around Chengtu, China (G. W. Skinner 1964:22–26).

28 For a discussion of this intensification of agriculture and how it relates to the influx of Aztec tribute see Blanton and Feinman (1984).

Glossary of Nahuatl and early colonial Spanish terms

altepetl, pl-altepeme the local territorial political domain
arroba A Spanish measure of 11.5 kg
cacaxtli frames for carrying cargo
cacique a leader
calmecac school for elite male youths
calpixqui, pl-calpixque tribute collector
calpuleque calpulli elite
calpulli, pl-calpultin barrio or an internally strategified social group censo
    al quitar annuity with an annual payment used in lieu of charging
    interest on a loan
chia Chenopodium
chinampas wetland raised field agriculture
chiuhqui suffix for producer-seller
cihuapipiltin female spirts of the cross-roads
coatequitl work carried out with corvee labor
cochineal insect used to make red dye
cocoliztli sickness, pestilence
Coyolxauqui Moon goddess, sister of Huitzilopochtli
cuauhpipiltzin warrior knights
cuezcomate storage granary
cuicacalli the house of song, a school for youths
grana Spanish word for cochineal dye
granjear trade or traffic in something
granjería cooperative system to produce tribute
huahtli amaranth
Huitzilopochtli patron god of the Aztecs

ixnetia make or produce something
jornada 1 day's travel on foot, 26–33 km
lienzo an indigenous map
macehualli, pl-macehualtin commoners, free-holders
maitl arm, leg
mayeque, sing- mayé commoners, renters
mecapalli tumpline carrying strap
Moctezuma Ilhuicamina an Aztec tlatoani
Moctezuma Xocoyotzin Aztec tlatoani at the time of the conquest
momoztli market shrine
motlahtlaihtlani beggar
Nahua shared culture of nahuatl related groups
Nahuatl language of the Aztec and other groups in Central Mexico
namacac suffix for market vender
naualoztomeca the disguised merchants
necxipaquiliztli washing of feet ceremony for returning home
Otomí group of Oto-Manguean speakers in Central Mexico
oztomecacalli, pl-oztomecacaltin merchant hostel
oztomecatl, pl-oztomeca long distance vanguard merchant, importer
Panquetzaliztli winter solstice, raise the banners ceremony
patolli a board game of chance
petlacalcatl tribute steward of the petlacalco
petlacalco treasury storehouse in Tenochtitlan
pilli, pl-pipiltin hereditary elite
pinolli high calorie travel food
pochtecatelpopochtin young boys on their first merchant venture
pochtecatl, pl-pochteca merchant
pochtecatlatoque the principal merchants, served as market administrators
quachtli standardized lengths of tribute cloth used as money
quappoyaualtzin merchant military commander
quauhcalli jail
Quetzalcoatl Feathered serpent deity, patron god of Cholula
tachcauhchiuhtiaz leader of a merchant expedition
tealtianime bather of slaves title
tealtiliztli Bathing of Slaves ceremony
techiuhqui an individual who produced what he sold
tecoanmime slave dealers, merchants
tecpan lord's place, palace and center of administration
teiaoaloanime spying merchants
telpochcalli school for male youths

temazcalli sweat bath
Tenochtitlan capital city of the Aztecs
tepantlato litigant attorney
tequitl obligation
tequitlato overseer of tribute service
terrasguerro farmer renting land
teyolmelahualiztli First feast of four in the tealiliztli ceremony
Tezcatlipoca patron deity of slave dealers
tianquiz marketplace
tianquizpan tlayacaque market supervisor
tianquiztli marketplace
tierra caliente hot lands below 1,000 m msl
tierra fria cold lands from 2,000–2,800 m msl
tierra helada frozen lands above 2,800 m msl
tierra templada temperate lands between 1,000–2,000 m msl
tlacalaquilli tribute in goods
tlachiuhqui producer-seller
tlachcocalco armory
tlachtli the rubber ball game
tlacôcoalnamacac peddler
tlacochcalco, pl-tlacochcalco slave
tlaixtlapana profit
tlalmaitec another term for mayeque
Tlaltecuhtli the earth deity
tlameme, tameme porter
tlanamacac, pl-tlanamacaque market vender
tlanecuilo, pl-tlanecuiloque market retailer
tlapatlac, teucuitlapatlac banker, money changer
tlaquixtiani wholesaler
Tlatelolco, Tlaltelolco adjoining city to Tenochtitlan on Tenochtitlan
  island and the location of the large market
tlatoani, pl-tlatoque ruler
tlaxilacalli, pl-tlaxilacaltin a small residential unit
tlaxnextiliztli Second feast of four in the tealiliztli ceremony
tlazcaltiltin apprentices, young merchant apprentices
tonalli the soul, resided in the head
tonalpohualli 260 day ritual calendar
totocalli craft workshop in the state pleasure garden of Tenochtitlan
Xiuhtecuhtli fire deity
Yacatecuhtli patron god of merchants

Bibliography

Abbott, David 2010 The rise and demise of marketplace exchange among the prehistoric Hohokam of Arizona, in *Archaeological approaches to market exchange in pre-capitalistic societies*, C. Garraty and B. Stark eds., pp. 61–83. University Press of Colorado, Boulder.

Abu-Lughod, Janet 1989 *Before European hegemony: The world system A.D. 1250–1350*. Oxford University Press, Oxford.

Acheson, James 1994 Welcome to Nobel country: A review of institutional economics, in *Anthropology and institutional economics*, J. Acheson ed., pp. 3–42. University Press of America, Lanham

Acosta Saignes, Miguel 1945 Los pochteca: Ubicación de los mercaderes en la estructura social Tenochca. *Acta Antropológica* 1(1).

Acosta Saignes, Miguel, Miguel León-Portilla, Ann Chapman, and Amalia Cardos de Méndez 1975 *El comercio en el México prehispánico*. Instituto Mexicano de Comercio Exterior, Mexico City.

Acuna-Soto, Rodolfo, David Stahle, Malcolm Cleaveland, and Matthew Therrell 2002 Megadrought and megadeath in the 16th century Mexico. *Revista Biomedica* 13:289–292.

Acuña, René 1984a *Relaciones Geográficas del siglo XVI: Antequera tomo primero*. Serie Antropológica, 54. Instituto de Investigaciones Antropológicas, UNAM, Mexico City.

   1984b *Relaciones Geográficas del siglo XVI: Antequera tomo segundo*. Serie Antropológica, 58. Instituto de Investigaciones Antropológicas, UNAM, Mexico City.

   1985 *Relaciones Geográficas del siglo XVI: Tlaxcala tomo segundo*. Serie Antropológica, 59. Instituto de Investigaciones Antropológicas, UNAM, Mexico City.

   1986 *Relaciones Geográficas del siglo XVI: Mexico tomo tercero*. Serie Antropológica, 70. Instituto de Investigaciones Antropológicas, UNAM, Mexico City.

1987 *Relaciones Geográficas del siglo XVI: Michoacán.* Serie Antropológica, 74. Instituto de Investigaciones Antropológicas, UNAM, Mexico City.

Adams, Colin 2012 Transportation, in *The Cambridge companion to the Roman economy*, W. Scheidel ed., pp. 218–240. Cambridge University Press, Cambridge.

Aguilar-Moreno, Manuel 2007 *Handbook to life in the Aztec world.* Oxford University Press, Oxford.

Aguilera, Carmen 1989 Templo Mayor: Dual symbol of the passing of time, in *The imagination of matter: Religion and ecology in Mesoamerican traditions*, D. Carrasco ed., pp. 129–135. BAR International Series 515, Oxford.

Ahrndt, Wiebke 2001 *Edición crítica de la relación de la nueva españa y de la breve y sumaria relación escritas por Alonso de Zorita.* INAH and Bonn University, Mexico City and Bonn.

Alba, Carlos 1949 *Estudio comparativo entre el derecho Azteca y el derecho positivo Mexicano.* Ediciones especiales del Instituto Indigenista Interamericano 3, Mexico City.

Allan, William 1965 *The African husbandman.* Oliver and Boyd, Edinburgh

Allsen, Thomas 1997 *Commodity and exchange in the Mongol empire.* Cambridge University Press, Cambridge.

Anales de Cuauhtitlan 1975 Anales de Cuauhtitlan, in *Codice de Chimalpopoca: Anales de Cuauhtitlan y leyenda de los soles*, Primo Feliciano Velázquea, trans., pp. 3–68. UNAM, Mexico City.

Anawalt, Patrica 1992 A comparative analysis of the costumes and accoutrements of the Codex Mendoza, in *The Codex Mendoza*, F. Berdan and P. Anawalt eds., vol 1, pp. 103–150. University of California Press, Berkeley.

1992 Codex Mendoza tribute textile design motives, in *The Codex Mendoza*, F. Berdan and P. Anawalt eds., vol 1, pp. 247. University of California Press, Berkeley.

Anderson, Arthur 1994 Los primeros memoriales y el Códice Florentino. *Estudios de Cultura Náhuatl* 24:49–91.

Anderson, Arthur, Frances Berdan, and James Lockhart 1976 *Beyond the codices.* University of California Press, Berkeley.

Andreau, Jean 1999 *Banking and business in the Roman World.* Cambridge University Press, Cambridge.

Andrews, Anthony 1983 *Maya salt production and trade.* University of Arizona Press, Tucson.

Anonymous Conqueror 1971 Relación de algunas cosas de la Nueva España y de la gran ciudad de Temestitán, escrita por un compañero de Hernán Cortés, in *Colección de documentos para la historia de México 1*, J. García Icazbalceta ed., pp. 368–398. Editorial Purrúa, Mexico City.

Appleby, Gordon 1976 The role of urban food needs in regional development, Puno, Peru, in *Regional analysis, vol 1: Economic systems*, C. Smith ed., pp. 147–178. Academic Press, New York.

Arcila Farías, Eduardo 1975 *Comercio entre México y Venezuela en los siglos XVI y XVII.* Instituto Mexicano de Comercio Exterior, Mexico City.

Armillas, Pedro 1971 Gardens on swamps. *Science* 174:653–661.

Arnold, Philip 1988 *Ceramic production and consumption in the Sierra de los Tuxtlas, Veracruz, Mexico.* Research Paper Series No. 21. Latin American Research Institute, University of New Mexico, Albuquerque.

Asselbergs, Florine 2004 *Conquered conquistadors: The Lienzo de Quauhquechollan: A Nahua vision of the conquest of Guatemala.* University Press of Colorado, Boulder.

Attolini Lecón, Amalia 2010 Intercambio y caminos en el mundo Maya prehispánico, in *Caminos y mercados de México*, J. Long Towell and A. Attolini Lecón eds., pp. 51–77. UNAM and INAH, Mexico City.

Baechler, Jean 1976 *The origins of capitalism.* St. Martins Press, New York.

Balkansky, Andrew, and Michelle Croissier 2009 Multicrafting in prehispanic Oaxaca, in *Housework: Craft production and domestic economy in ancient Mesoamerica*, K. Hirth ed., pp. 58–74. Archaeological Publications No 19, American Anthropological Association, Washington D.C.

Ball, Hugh, and Donald Brockington 1978 Trade and travel in prehispanic Oaxaca, in *Mesoamerican communication routes and cultural contacts*, T. Lee and C. Navarette eds., pp. 107–114. Papers of the New World Archaeological Foundation, No. 40. Brigham Young University, Provo, Utah.

Barlow, Robert 1949 *The extent of the empire of the Culhua Mexica.* University of California Press, Berkeley and Los Angeles.

Barnett, Homer 1968 Making money, in *Economic Anthropology*, E. LeClair and H. Schneider eds., pp. 374–380. Holt, Rinehart and Winston, New York.

Batalla Rosado, Juan José 2012 Análisis de la representación de depósitos de almacenamiento en los códices, in *Almacenamiento prehispánico del norte de México al altiplano central*, S. Bortot, D. Michelet, and V. Darras eds., pp. 187–202. Laboratorie Archéologie des Amériques, Mexico City.

Bauer, Arnold 2010 Molineros y molenderas: Technología, economía familiar y cultural material en Mesoamérica: 300 a.C.–200 d.C., in *Mestizajes tecnológicos y cambios culturales en México*, E. Florescano and V. García Acosta eds., pp. 169–199. CIESAS, Mexico City.

Bayly, Christopher 1983 *Rulers, townsmen and bazaars: North Indian society in the age of British expansion, 1770–1870.* Cambridge University Press, Cambridge.

Beals, Ralph 1975 *The peasant marketing system of Oaxaca, Mexico.* University of California Press, Berkeley.

Beinhocker, Eric 2006 *The origin of wealth.* Harvard Business School Press, Boston.

Benet, Francisco 1957 Explosive markets: The Berber highlands, in *Trade and market in the early empires*, K Polanyi, C. Arensberg, and H. Pearson eds., pp. 188–217. The Free Press, Glencoe, Illinois.

Berdan, Frances 1975 Trade, tribute and market in the Aztec empire. PhD dissertation, Department of Anthropology, University of Texas, Austin.

   1978 Ports of trade in Mesoamerica: A reappraisal, in *Mesoamerican communication routes and cultural contacts*, T. Lee and C. Navarette eds., pp. 187–198. Papers of the New World Archaeological Foundation, No. 40. Brigham Young University, Provo, Utah.

1980 Aztec merchants and markets: Local-level economic activity in a non-industrial empire. *Mexicon* 2:37–41.

1982 *The Aztecs of Central Mexico. An imperial society.* Holt, Rhinehart and Winston, New York.

1985 Markets in the economy of Aztec Mexico, in *Markets and marketing*, S. Plattner ed., pp. 339–367. University Press of America, Lanham, Maryland.

1986 Enterprise and empire in Aztec and colonial Mexico, in *Economic aspects of prehispanic highland Mexico*, B. Isaac ed., pp. 281–302. JAI Press, Greenwhich, Connecticut.

1987 Cotton in Aztec Mexico: Production, distribution and use. *Mexican Studies/Estudios Mexicanos* 3:235–262.

1988 Principles of regional and long-distance trade in the Aztec empire, in *Smoke and mist: Mesoamerican studies in memory of Thelma D. Sullivan*, J. Josserand and K. Dakin eds., pp. 639–656. BAR International Series 402, Oxford.

1989 Trade and markets in precapitalist states, in *Economic anthropology*, S. Plattner ed., pp. 78–107. Stanford University Press, Stanford.

1992a Appendix B: Annual tribute in the Codex Mendoza part 2, in *The Codex Mendoza*, F. Berdan and P. Anawalt eds., vol 1, pp. 154–156. University of California Press, Berkeley.

1992b The imperial tribute roll of the *Codex Mendoza*, in *The Codex Mendoza*, F. Berdan and P. Anawalt eds., vol 1, pp. 55–79. University of California Press, Berkeley.

1996 The tributary provinces, in *Aztec imperial strategies*, F. Berdan, R. Blanton, E. Boone, M. Hodge, M. Smith, and E. Umberger eds., pp. 115–135. Dumbarton Oaks Research Library and Collection, Washington.

2006 The technology of ancient Mesoamerican mosaics: An experimental investigation of alternative super glues. (www.famsi.org/index.html.).

2014 *Aztec archaeology and ethnohistory.* Cambridge University Press, Cambridge.

Berdan, Frances, and Patricia Anawalt 1992 *The Codex Mendoza.* 4 volumes, University of California Press, Berkeley.

Berdan, Frances, Edward Stark, and Jeffrey Sahagún 2009 Production and use of orchid adhesives in Aztec Mexico: The domestic context, in *Housework: Craft production and domestic economy in ancient Mesoamerica*, K. Hirth ed., pp. 148–156. Archaeological Publications No 19, American Anthropological Association, Washington D.C.

Beresford, Maurice 1998 *The lost villages of England.* Sutton Publishing Ltd., Stroud.

Berggren, Lars, Nils Hybel, and Annette Landen 2002 *Cogs, cargoes, and commerce: Maritime bulk trade in northern Europe, 1150–1400.* Pontifical Institute of Mediaeval Studies, Toronto.

Bernstein, William 2008 *A splendid exchange: How trade shaped the world.* Atlantic Monthly Press, New York.

Bierhorst, John 1992 *History and Mythology of the Aztecs: The Codex Chimalpopoca.* University of Arizona Press, Tucson.

Bird, James 1958 Billingsgate: A central metropolis market. *The Geographical Journal* 124:464–475.

Bittmann Simons, Bente, and Thelma Sullivan 1978 The pochteca, in *Mesoamerican communication routes and culture contacts*, T. Lee and C. Navarrete eds., pp. 211–218. Papers of the New World Archaeological Foundation, No. 40. Brigham Young University, Provo, Utah.

Blanton, Richard 1978 *Monte Albán: Settlement patterns at the ancient Zapotec capital*. Academic Press, New York.

1983 Factors underlying the origin and evolution of market systems, in *Economic Anthropology: Topics and theories*, S. Ortiz ed., pp. 51–66, University Press of America, Lanham, Maryland.

1996 The Basin of Mexico market system and the growth of empire, in *Aztec imperial strategies*, F. Berdan, R. Blanton, E. Boone, M. Hodge, M. Smith, and E. Umberger eds., pp. 47–84. Dumbarton Oaks Research Library and Collection, Washington.

1998 Comment, *Current Anthropology* 39:463–464.

2013 Cooperation and the moral economy of the marketplace, in *Merchants, markets and exchange in the pre-columbian world*, K. Hirth and J. Pillsbury eds., pp. 23–48. Dumbarton Oaks Research Library and Collection, Washington

Blanton, Richard, and Gary Feinman 1984 The Mesoamerican world system. *American Antiquity* 86:673–682.

Blanton, Richard, and Mary Hodge 1996 Data on market activities and production specializations of tlatoani centers in the Basin of Mexico and areas north of the Basin (excluding Texcoco and Tenochtitlan-Tlatelolco), in *Aztec imperial strategies*, F. Berdan, R. Blanton, E. Boone, M. Hodge, M. Smith, and E. Umberger eds., pp. 243–246. Dumbarton Oaks Research Library and Collection, Washington.

Blanton, Richard, Stephen Kowalewski, Gary Feinman, and Jill Appel 1993 *Ancient Mesoamerica*. Cambridge University Press, New York.

Bohannan, Paul, and George Dalton 1965 *Markets in Africa*. Doubleday, Garden City, New York.

Boone, Elizabeth Hill 1984 *Ritual human sacrifice in Mesoamerica: A conference at Dumbarton Oaks, October 13 and 14, 1979*. Dumbarton Oaks Research Library and Collection, Washington.

2000 *Stories in red and black*. University of Texas Press, Austin.

Borah, Woodrow 1943 *Silk raising in colonial Mexico*. University of California Press, Berkeley and Los Angeles.

Borah, Woodrow, and Sherburne Cook 1958 *Price trends of some basic commodities in Central Mexico, 1531–1570*. University of California Press, Berkeley and Los Angeles.

Bovill, Edward 1970 *The golden trade of the Moors*. Oxford University Press, London

Bradley, Keith 1987 *Slaves and masters in the Roman empire*. Oxford University Press, Oxford.

Brady, Thomas 1991 The rise of the merchant empires, 1400–1700: A European counterpoint, in *The political economy of merchant empires*, T. James ed., pp. 117–160. Cambridge University Press, Cambridge.

Brasswell, Geoffrey 2003 Obsidian exchange spheres, in *The Postclassic Mesoamerican world*, M. Smith and F. Berdan eds., pp. 117–158. University of Utah Press, Salt Lake City.

Braudel, Fernand 1982 *Civilization and capitalism, 15th–18th century: The perspective of the world*. University of California Press, Berkeley.

   1986 *Civilization and capitalism 15th–18th century: The wheels of commerce*. Harper Row, New York.

Bresson, Alain n.d. *Capitalism and the ancient Greek economy*. Cambridge University Press, Cambridge. (in press)

Bromley, Ray, and Richard Symanski 1974 Marketplace trade in Latin America. *Latin American Research Review* 9:3–38.

Bromley, Rosemary, Richard Symanski, and Charles Good 1975 The rationale of periodic markets. *Annals of the Association of American Geographers* 65:530–537.

Brumfiel, Elizabeth 1986 The division of labor at Xico: The chipped stone industry, in *Research in economic anthropology, supplement No. 2. Economic aspects of prehispanic highland Mexico*, B. Isaac ed., pp. 245–279. JAI Press, Greenwich, Connecticut.

   1987 Elite and utilitarian crafts in the Aztec state, in *Specialization, exchange, and complex societies*, E. Brumfiel and T. Earle eds., pp. 102–118. Cambridge University Press, Cambridge.

Bunzel, Ruth 1959 *Chichicastenango*. University of Washington Press, Seattle.

Burger, Richard 2013 In the realm of the Incas: An archaeological reconsideration of household exchange, long-distance trade, and marketplaces in the pre-hispanic central Andes, in *Merchants, markets, and exchange in the pre-columbian world*, K. Hirth and J. Pillsbury eds., pp. 319–334. Dumbarton Oaks Research Library and Collection, Washington D.C.

Burns, Kathryn 1999 *Colonial habits*. Duke University Press, Durham and London.

Callen, Eric 1970 Diet as revealed by coprolites, in *Science in archaeology: A survey of progress and research*, D. Brothwell and E. Higgs eds., pp. 235–243. Basic Books, New York.

Calnek, Edward 1978 El sistema de mercado de Tenochtitlan, in *Economía política e ideología en el México prehispánico*, P. Carrasco and J. Broda eds., pp. 95–114. Editorial Nueva Imagen, México City.

   2001 Tenochtitlán-Tlatelolco (Federal District, Mexico), in *Archaeology of ancient Mexico and Central America*, S. Evans and D. Webster eds., pp. 719–722. Garland Publishing, New York.

Cancian, Frank 1965 *Economics and prestige in a Maya community: The religious cargo system in Zinacantan*. Stanford University Press, Stanford.

   1972 *Change and uncertainly in a peasant economy: The Maya corn farmers of Zinacantan*. Stanford University Press, Stanford.

Carballo, David 2013 The social organization of craft production and interregional exchange at Teotihuacan, in *Merchants, markets, and exchange in the pre-columbian world*, K. Hirth and J. Pillsbury eds., pp. 113–140. Dumbarton Oaks Research Library and Collection, Washington D.C.

Cardos de Méndez, Amalia 1959 El comercio de los Mayas antiguos. *Acta Anthropologica*, 2, number 7.

1975 El comercio de los Mayas antiguos, in *El comercio en el Mexico prehispanico*, M. Acosta Saignes, M. León-Portilla, A. Chapman, and A. C. de Méndez eds., pp.159–268. Instituto Mexicana de Comercio Exterior, Mexico City.

Carmack, Robert 1965 The documentary sources, ecology, and culture history of the prehispanic Quiche Maya of Guatemala. PhD dissertation, Department of Anthropology, University of California, Los Angeles.

Carneiro, Robert 1974 A reappraisal of the role of technology and organization in the origin of civilization. *American Antiquity* 39:179–186.

Carrasco, Davíd, and Scott Sessions 1998 *Daily life of the Aztecs: People of the sun and earth*. The Greenwood Press, Westport, Connecticut.

Carrasco, Pedro 1963 Las tierras de los indios nobles de Tepeaca en el siglo XVI. *Tlalocan* 4:97–119.

1964 Family structure of sixteenth-century Tepoztlan, in *Process and pattern in culture*, R. Manners ed., pp. 185–210. Aldine, Chicago.

1966 Rango de Tecuhtli entre los nahuas tramontanos. *Tlalocan* 5:133–160.

1969 Más documentos sobre Tepeaca. *Tlalocan* 6:1–37.

1970 Carta al rey sobre la ciudad de Cholula en 1593. *Tlalocan* 6:176–192.

1971 Social organization of ancient Mexico, in *Handbook of Middle American Indians*, vol 10, pp. 349–375. University of Texas Press, Austin.

1974 Introducción: La matrícula de Huexotzinco como fuente sociológica, in *Matrícula de Huexotzinco*, H. Prem ed., pp. 1–16. Akademische Druck, Verlagsanstalt Graz, Austria.

1978 La economía del México prehispánico, in *Economía política e ideología en el México prehispánico*, P. Carrasco and J. Broda eds., pp. 13–74. Editorial Nueva Imagen, México City.

1980 Markets and merchants in the Aztec economy. *Journal of the Steward Anthropological Society* 11:249–269.

1981 Comment on Offner. *American Antiquity* 46:62–68.

1999 *The Tenochca empire of ancient Mexico*. University of Oklahoma Press, Norman.

Carrasco, Pedro, and Jesús Monjarás-Ruiz 1976 *Colección de documentos sobre Coyoacan (volumen primero)*: Colección Científica 39. INAH, Mexico City.

1978 *Colección de documentos sobre Coyoacan (volumen segundo)*: Colección Científica 65. INAH, Mexico City.

Cashdan, Elizabeth 1990 *Risk and uncertainty in tribal and peasant economies*. Westview Press, Boulder.

Casson, Lionel 1989 *The periplus maris erythraei*. Princeton University Press, Princeton.

1991 *The ancient mariners*. Princeton University Press, Princeton.

Cato, Marcus Porcius, Marcus Terrentius Varro, and Harrison Boyd Ash 1935 *On Agriculture. [and] on Agriculture*. Heinemann, Portsmouth, NH.

Chakravarti, Ranabir 2000 Nakhudas and nauvittakas: Ship-owning merchants in the west coast of India (c. AD 1000–1500). *Journal of the Economic and Social History of the Orient* 43:34–64.

2005 Introduction, in *Trade in early India*, C. Ranabir ed., pp. 1–101. Oxford University Press, Oxford.

Chandler, Tertius 1987 *Four thousand years of urban growth: An historical census*. The Edwin Mellen Press, Lewiston, New York.

Chang, Ha-Joon 2008 *Bad Samaritans: The myth of free trade and the secret history of capitalism*. Bloomsburg Press, New York.

Chapman, Ann 1957a Port of trade enclaves in Aztec and Maya civilizations, in *Trade and market in the early empires*, K. Polanyi, C. Arensberg, and H. Pearson eds., pp. 114–153. The Free Press, Glencoe, Illinois.

1957b *Puertos de intercambio en Mesoamérica prehispánica*. INAH, Mexico City.

Charlton, Thomas, Deborah Nichols, and Cynthia Otis Charlton 1991 Craft specialization within the Aztec city-state of Otumba, Mexico: The archaeological evidence. *World Archaeology* 23:98–114.

2000a Otumba and its neighbors: Ex oriente lux. *Ancient Mesoamerica* 11:247–265.

2000b The Otumba project: A review and status report, in *The Teotihuacan Valley project final report: The Aztec period occupation of the valley, part 2*, W. Sanders ed., pp. 875–887. Occasional Papers in Anthropology 26. Department of Anthropology, Pennsylvania State University, University Park.

Charlton, Thomas, Cynthia Otis Charlton, Deborah Nichols, and Hector Neff 2008 Aztec Otumba, AD 1200–1600: Patterns of the production, distribution, and consumption of ceramic products, in *Pottery economics in Mesoamerica*, C. Pool and G. Bey eds., pp. 237–266. University of Arizona Press, Tucson.

Chattopadhyaya, Brajadulal 2005 Markets and merchants in early medieval Rajasthan, in *Trade in early India*, R. Chakravarti ed., pp. 282–311. Oxford University Press, Oxford.

Chavero, Alfredo 1892 *Lienzo de Tlaxcala*. Artes de Mexico, Mexico City.

Chayanov, Aleksandr 1966 *The theory of peasant economy*. American Economic Association, Homewood, Illinois.

Cheong, Weng Eang 1997 *The Hong merchants of Canton: Chinese merchants in Sino-Western trade*. Nordic Institute of Asian Studies, Monograph 70. Curzon Press, England.

Chimalpahin Cuauhtlehuanitzin, and Francisco de San Antón Muñón 1965 *Relaciones originales de Chalco Amaquemecan*. Fondo de Cultura Económica, Mexico City.

Chorley, Richard, and Peter Haggett 1967 *Models in geography*. Metheun, London.

Christaller, Walter 1966 *Central places in southern Germany*. Englewood Cliffs, New Jersey.

Christiansen, Mark 2011 Fair and fraudulent Nahuas: A confessional manual's insight into the sixteenth-century market economy of Central Mexico. *Latin American Indian Literatures Journal* 27:111–140.

Clark, Colin, and Margaret Haswell 1967 *The economics of subsistence agriculture*. MacMillan and Co., London.

Clark, John 1986 From mountains to molehills: A critical review of Teotihuacan's obsidian industry, in *Research in economic anthropology, supplement No. 2: Economic aspects of prehispanic highland Mexico*, B. Isaac ed., pp.23–74. JAI Press, Greenwich, Connecticut.

   1987 Politics, prismatic blades, and Mesoamerican civilization, in *The organization of core technology*, J. Johnson and C. Morrow eds., pp. 259–285. Westview Press, Boulder.

   1989 Obsidian: The primary Mesoamerican sources, in *La obsidiana en Mesoamérica*, M. Gaxiola and J. Clark eds., pp. 299–319. Colección Científica 176, INAH, Mexico City.

Clark, John, and Douglas Bryant 1997 A technological typology of prismatic blades and debitage from Ojo de Agua, Chiapas, Mexico. *Ancient Mesoamerica* 8:111–136.

Clark, John, and William Parry 1990 *Craft specialization and cultural complexity: Research in Economic Anthropology*, vol 12, pp. 289–346. JAI Press, Greenwich, Connecticut.

Clavijero, Francisco Javier 1974 *Historia antigua de México*. Purrua, Mexico City.

Cline, Sarah 1993 *The book of tributes: Early sixteenth-century nahuatl censuses from Morelos*. UCLA Latin American Center Publications, Los Angeles.

Cline, Sarah, and Miguel León-Portilla 1984 *The testaments of Culhuacan*. UCLA Latin American Center Publications, Los Angeles.

Codere, Helen 1966 *Fighting with property: A study of Kwakiutl potlatching and warfare 1792–1930*. University of Washington Press, Seattle.

Codex Matritense 1906 *Códice Matritense del Real Palacio*. Fototipia de Hauser y Menet, Madrid.

Coe, Sophie, and Michael Coe 1996 *The true history of chocolate*. Thames and Hudson, New York.

Cohen, Abner 1966 Politics of the Kola trade: Some processes of tribal community formation among migrants in West African towns. *Africa: Journal of the International African Institute* 36:18–36.

   1971 Cultural strategies in the organization of trading diasporas, in *The development of indigenous trade and markets in west Africa*, C. Meillassoux ed., pp. 266–281. Oxford University Press, London.

Collier, Jane 1973 *Law and social change in Zinacantan*. Stanford University Press, Stanford.

Cook, Sherburne 1946 Human sacrifice and warfare as factors in the demography of pre-colonial Mexico. *Human Biology* 18:81–102.

Cook, Sherburne, and Lesley Byrd Simpson 1948 *The population of Central Mexico in the sixteenth century*. Ibero Americana, vol 31, University of California Press, Berkeley.

Cook, Sherburne, and Woodrow Borah 1971–1979 *Essays in population history, Mexico and the Caribbean*. 3 volumes, University of California Press, Berkeley.

Cortés, Hernando 1866 *Cartas de relación de la conquista de México (Cartas y relaciones al emperador Carlos V)*. Edición de Gayangos, París.

   1962 *5 letters of Cortés to the emperor*. W. W. Norton, New York

Costin, Cathy 1991 Craft specialization: Issues in defining, documenting, and explaining the organization of production, in *Archaeological method and theory*, M. Schiffer ed., pp. 1–56. University of Arizona Press, Tucson.

2000 Craft production systems, in *Archaeology at the millennium*, C. Costin and R. Wright eds., pp. 3–16. Archaeological Paper No 8, American Anthropological Association, Washington D.C.

Cox, Nancy 2000 *The complete tradesman: A study of retailing, 1550–1820.* Ashgate Publishing Limited, Hants, England.

Craine, Eugene, and Reginald Reindorp 1970 *The chronicles of Michoacan.* The University of Oklahoma Press, Norman.

Cuddy, Thomas 2008 *Revolutionary economies: What archaeology reveals about the birth of American capitalism.* AltaMira Press, Lanham, Maryland.

Cunow, Heinrich 1926 *Allgemeine Wirtschaftgeschichte: Eine Übersicht über die Wirtschaftsentwicklung von der primitiven Sammelwirtschaft bis zum Hochkapitalismus*, vol 3, JHW Dietz Nochfolger, Berlin.

Curtin, Philip 1984 *Cross-cultural trade in world history.* Cambridge University Press, Cambridge.

Daaku, Kwame Yeboa 1970 *Trade and politics on the Gold Coast 1600–1720.* Clarendon Press, Oxford.

Dale, Stephen Frederic 1994 *Indian merchants and Eurasian trade, 1600–1750.* Cambridge University Press, Cambridge.

Dalton, George 1961 Economic theory and primitive society. *American Anthropologist* 63:1–25.

1965 Primitive money. *American Anthropologist* 67:44–65.

1977 Aboriginal economies in stateless societies, in *Exchange systems in prehistory*, T. Earle and J. Ericson eds., pp. 191–212. Academic Press, New York

D'Altroy, Terrence, and Timothy Earle, 1985 Staple finance, wealth finance, and storage in the Inka political economy. *Current Anthropology* 26:187–206.

Dandamayev, Muhammed 1999 Land use in the Sippar region during the Neo-Babylonian and Achaemenid periods, in *Urbanization and land ownership in the ancient Near East*, M. Hudson and B. Levine eds., pp. 363–389. Bulletin 7, Peabody Museum of Archaeology and Ethnology, Harvard University, Cambridge.

Das Gupta, Ashin 2001a Indian merchants and trade in the Indian Ocean, c. 1500–1750, in *The world of the Indian Ocean merchant, 1500–1800: Collected essays of Ashin Das Gupta*, pp. 59–87. Oxford University Press, Oxford.

2001b Some attitudes among eithteenth-century merchants, in *The world of the Indian Ocean merchant, 1500–1800: Collected essays of Ashin Das Gupta*, pp. 102–109. Oxford University Press, Oxford.

Davies, Susanna 1996 *Adaptable livelihoods.* St. Martin's Press, New York.

Davis, Dorothy 1966 *Fairs, shops, and supermarkets: A history of English shopping.* University of Toronto Press, Toronto.

de Alcalá, Fray Jerónimo 2013 *Relación de Michoacán.* Colegio de Michoacan, Zamora, Michoacan. (Orig 1540)

De Haan, Arjan 1999 Livelihoods and poverty: The role of migration a critical review of the migration literature. *The Journal of Development Studies* 36:1–47.

de las Casas, Fray Bartolomé 1967 *Apologética historia sumaria.* 2 volumes, UNAM and Instituto de Investigaciones Historicas, Mexico City.

De León, Jason 2009 Rethinking the organization of Aztec salt production: A domestic perspective, in *Housework: Craft production and domestic economy in ancient Mesoamerica*, K. Hirth ed., pp. 45–57. Archaeological Publications No 19, American Anthropological Association, Washington D.C.

De Ligt, Luuk 1993 *Fairs and markets in the Roman empire*, J. C. Gieben, Amsterdam.

De Lucia, Kristin 2011 Domestic economies and regional transition: Household production and consumption in Early Postclassic Mexico. PhD dissertation, Department of Anthropology, Northwestern University.

Dercksen, Jan Garrit 1996 *The Old Assyrian copper trade in Anatolia.* Nederlands Historisch-Archaeologisch Instituut, Istanbul.

Díaz del Castillo, Bernal 1956 *The discovery and conquest of Mexico 1517–1521.* Farrar, Straus and Cudahy, New York.

Dibble, Charles 1981 *Codex en cruz.* University of Utah Press, Salt Lake City.
    1988 Molina and Sahagún, in *Smoke and mist: Mesoamerican studies in memory of Thelma*, D. Sullivan, J. Josserand, and K. Dakin eds., pp. 69–76. BAR International Series 402, Oxford.

Dike, Kenneth Onwuka, and Felicia Ekejiuba 1990 *The Aro of south-eastern Nigeria, 1650–1980.* The University Press Limited, Ibadan, Nigeria

Dobbin, Christine 1996 *Asian entrepreneurial minorities: Conjoint communities in the making of a world-economy 1570–1940.* Curzon Press, Surrey, England.

Dobres, Marci-Anne, and John Robb 2000 *Agency in archaeology.* Routledge, London and New York.

Donkin, Robin 1977 Spanish red: An ethnogeographical study of cochineal and the Opuntia cactus. *Transactions of the American Philosophical Society* 67:1–84.

Dreiss, Meredith, and David Brown 1989 Obsidian exchange patterns in Belize, in *Research in Economic Anthropology, supplement 4, Prehistoric Maya economies of Belize*, P. McAnamy and B. Isaac eds., pp. 57–90. JAI Press, Greenwich, Connecticut.

Drennan, Robert 1984a Long-distance movement of goods in the Mesoamerican Formative and Classic. *American Antiquity* 49:27–43.
    1984b Long-distance transport costs in pre-hispanic Mesoamerica. *American Anthropologist* 86:105–112.

Drucker, Philip 1967 The potlatch, in *Tribal and peasant economies*, G. Dalton ed., pp. 481–493. American Museum of Natural History, New York.

Drucker, Philip, and Robert Heizer 1967 *To make my name good: A reexamination of the southern Kwakiutl potlatch.* University of California Press, Berkeley and Los Angeles.

Durán, Diego 1971 *Book of the gods and rites and the ancient calendar.* University of Oklahoma Press, Norman.

1994 *The history of the Indies of New Spain*. University of Oklahoma Press, Norman.

Durand-Forest, Jacqueline 1967 El cacao entre los Aztecas. *Estudios de la Cultural Nahuatl* 9:155–181.

1971 Cambios económicos y moneda entre los Aztecas. *Estudios de la Cultural Nahuatl* 9:105–124.

1994 The Aztec craftsman and the economy, in *Chipping away on earth*, E. Quiñones Keber ed., pp. 173–176. Labyrinthos, Lancaster, California.

Durkheim, Emile 1984 *The division of labor in society*. MacMillan, New York. (Orig 1893)

Dycherhoff, Ursula, and Hanns Prem 1976 La estratificación social en Huexotzinco, in *Estratificación social en la Mesoamérica prehispánica*, P. Carrasco ed., pp. 157–177. INAH, Mexico City.

Dyer, Christopher 2005 *The age of transition? Economy and society in England in the later Middle Ages*. Oxford University Press, Oxford.

Ellickson, Robert, and Charles Thorland 1995 Ancient land law: Mesopotamia, Egypt, Israel. *Chicago-Kent Law Review* 71:321–411.

Epstein, Steven 1991 *Wage labor and guilds in medieval Europe*. University of North Carolina Press, Chapel Hill.

Evans, Susan 1991 Architecture and authority in an Aztec village: Form and function of the tecpan, in *Land and politics in the Valley of Mexico*, H. Harvey ed., pp. 63–92. University of New Mexico Press, Albuquerque.

2004 Aztec palaces and other elite residential architecture, in *Palaces of the ancient New World*, S. Evans and J. Pillsbury eds., pp. 7–58. Dumbarton Oaks Research Library and Collection, Washington D.C.

2007 Precious beauty: The aesthetic and economic value of Aztec gardens, in *Botanical progress, horticultural innovation and culture change*, M. Conan and W. Kress eds., pp. 81–101. Dumbarton Oaks Research Library and Collection, Washington D.C.

2008 Concubines and cloth: Women and weaving in Aztec palaces and colonial Mexico, in *Servants of the dynasty: Palace women in world history*, A. Walthall ed., pp. 215–231. University of California Press, Berkeley.

Evans, Susan, and David Webster 2001 *Archaeology of ancient Mexico and Central America*. Garland Publishing, New York.

Evers, Hans-Dieter 1994 The trader's dilemma: A theory of the social transformation of markets and society, in *The moral economy of trade: Ethnicity and developing markets*, H. Evers and H. Schrader eds., pp. 7–14. Routledge, London and New York.

Fall, Particia, Steven Falconer, and Lee Lines 2002 Agricultural intensification and the secondary products revolution along the Jordan rift. *Human Ecology* 30:445–482.

Fei, Hsiao and Chih-I Chang 1949 *Earthbound China: A study of rural economy in Yunnan*. Routledge & Kegan Paul, London.

Feinman, Gary 1999 Rethinking our assumptions: Economic specialization at the household scale in ancient Ejutla, Oaxaca, Mexico, in *Pottery and people*, J. Skibo and G. Feinman eds., pp. 81–98. University of Utah Press, Salt Lake City.

Feinman, Gary, and Linda Nicholas 1993 Shell-ornament production in Ejutla: Implications for highland-coastal interaction in ancient Oaxaca. *Ancient Mesoamerica* 4:103–119.

2000 Exploring craft production and shell ornament production in Ejutla, Mexico, in *Exploring the past: Readings in archaeology*, J. Bayman and M. Stark eds., pp. 303–314. Carolina Academic Press, Durham.

Feldman, Larry 1976 Words from Molina: Elements of Nahuatlaca culture in sixteenth century central Mexico. *Katunob* 9:24–41.

1978a Inside a Mexica market, in *Mesoamerican communication routes and culture contacts*, T. Lee and C. Navarrete eds., pp. 219–222. Papers of the New World Archaeological Foundation, No. 40. Brigham Young University, Provo, Utah.

1978b Moving merchandise in protohistoric central Quauhtemallan, in *Mesoamerican communication routes and cultural contacts*, T. Lee and C. Navarrete eds., pp. 123–126. Papers of the New World Archaeological Foundation, No. 40. Brigham Young University, Provo, Utah.

1985 *A tumpline economy: Production and distribution systems in sixteenth-century eastern Guatemala*. Labyrinthos, Culver City, California.

Finley, Moses 1959 Was Greek civilization based on slave labour? *Historia: Zeitschrift für Alte Geschichte* 2:145–164.

1985 *The ancient economy*. University of California Press, Berkeley.

Flannery, Kent 1972 The cultural evolution of civilizations. *Annual Review of Ecology and Systematics* 3:399–426.

1976a *The early Mesoamerican village*. Academic Press, New York.

1976b The empirical determination of site catchments: Oaxaca and Tehuacán, in *The early Mesoamerican village*, K. Flannery ed., pp. 103–117. Academic Press, New York.

1999 Process and agency in early state formation. *Cambridge Archaeological Journal* 9:3–21.

Foster, George 1948 The folk economy of rural Mexico with special reference to marketing. *Journal of Marketing* 13:153–162.

Frank, Andre Gunder 1966 *The development of underdevelopment*. New England Free Press, Boston.

1976 *On capitalist underdevelopment*. Oxford University Press, Oxford.

1981 *Crisis in the third world*. Heinemann Educational Publishers, Portsmouth, New Hampshire.

Frayn, Joan 1979 *Subsistence farming in Roman Italy*. Centaur Press, London.

Gage, Thomas 1929 *A new survey of the West Indies, 1648*. Robert McBride and Company, New York. (Orig 1648)

Garibay, Angel 1961 *Vida económica de Tenochtitlan: 1. Pochtecayotl. Informantes de Sahagún 3*, UNAM, Mexico City.

1973 *Teogonía e historia de los Mexicanos: Tres opúsculos del siglo XVI*. Editorial Porrua, Mexico City.

Garraty, Christopher 2010 Investigating market exchange in ancient societies: A theoretical review, in *Archaeological approaches to market exchange in pre-capitalistic societies*, C. Garraty and B. Stark eds., pp. 3–32. University Press of Colorado, Boulder.

Garraty, Christopher, and Barbara Stark 2010 *Archaeological approaches to market exchange in pre-capitalistic societies.* University Press of Colorado, Boulder.

Gasco, Janine, and Barbara Voorhies 1989 The ulitimate tribute: The role of Soconusco as an Aztec tributary, in *Ancient trade and tribute: Economies of the Soconusco region of Mesoamerica*, B. Voorhies ed., pp. 48–94. University of Utah Press, Salt Lake City.

Gasco, Janine, and Frances Berdan 2003 International trade centers, in *The Postclassic Mesoamerican world*, M. Smith and F. Berdan eds., pp. 107–116. University of Utah Press, Salt Lake City.

Gaxiola González, Margarita 2010 Huapalcalco, un santuario-mercado del Epiclásico en la región de Tulancingo, in *Caminos y mercados de México*, J. Long Towell and A. Attolini Lecón eds., pp. 107–219. UNAM and INAH, Mexico.

Geertz, Clifford 1963 *Peddlers and princes: Social change and economic modernization in two Indonesian towns.* University of Chicago Press, Chicago.

Gerhard, Peter 1986 Geografía histórica de la Nueva España, 1519–1821. UNAM, México.

Gibson, Charles 1964 *The Aztecs under Spanish rule.* Stanford University Press, Stanford.

1967 *Tlaxcala in the sixteenth century.* Stanford University Press, Stanford.

Goitein, Shelomo 1963 Letters and documents on the India trade in Medieval times. *Islamic culture* 37:188–205

1967 *A Mediterranean society: The Jewish communities of the Arab world as portrayed in the documents of the Cairo Geniza. vol 1, Economic Foundations.* University of California Press, Berkeley

1973 *Letters of medieval Jewish traders.* Princeton University Press, Princeton.

Goitein, Shelomo, and Mordechai Friedman 2008 *India traders of the Middle ages. Documents from the Cairo Geniza.* Brill, Leiden.

Golas, Peter 1977 Early Ch'ing guilds, in *The city in Late Imperial China*, W. Skinner ed., pp 555–580. Stanford University Press, Stanford.

Good, Catherine 1995 Salt production and commerce in Guerrero, Mexico: An ethnographic contribution to historical reconstruction. *Ancient Mesoamerica* 6:1–13.

Gottfried, Robert 1983 *The black death: Natural and human disaster in medieval Europe.* The Free Press, New York.

Graeber, David 2011a *Debt: The first 5,000 years.* Melville House Publishing, Brooklyn.

2011b *Debt, violence, and impersonal markets: Polanyian meditations.* Cambridge University Press, Cambridge.

Granovetter, Mark 1985 Economic action and social structure: The problem of embeddedness. *The American Journal of Sociology* 91:481–510.

Grassby, Richard 1999 *The idea of capitalism before the industrial revolution.* Rowman and Littlefield Publishers, Lanhama, Massachusetts.

Gregory, Clare 1980 Gifts to men and gifts to god: Gift exchange and capital accumulation in contemporary Papua. *Man* 15:625–652.

1981 A conceptual analysis of a non-capitalist gift economy. *Cambridge Journal of Economics* 5:119–135.

1982 *Gifts and commodities*. Academic Press, New York.

Grief, Avner 1989 Reputation and coalitions in medieval trade: Evidence on the Maghribi traders. *The Journal of Economic History* 49:857–882.

2000 The fundamental problem of exchange. *European review of economic history* 4:251–284.

Gudeman, Stephen 2001 *The anthropology of economy*. Blackwell publishing, Malden, Massachusetts.

Gutiérrez, Gerardo 2013 Negotiating Aztec tributary demands in the tribute record of Tlapa, in *Merchants, markets, and exchange in the pre-columbian world*, K. Hirth and J. Pillsbury eds., pp. 141–167. Dumbarton Oaks Research Library and Collections, Washington D.C.

Gutiérrez, Gerardo, Viola Koenig, and Baltazar Brito 2009a *Códice Humboldt Fragmento 1 (Ms. amer. 1) y Códice Azoyu 2 reverso: Nomina de tributos de Tlapa y su provincia al imperio mexicano*. Centro de Investigaciones e Estudios Superiores en Antropología Social and Stiftung Preussischer Kulturbesitz, Mexico City and Berlin.

2009b *Codice Humboldt Fragmento 1 (Ms. amer. 1) y Codice Azoyu 2 reverso. Nomina de tributos de Tlapa y su provincia al imperio mexicano: Facsimile.* Centro de Investigaciones e Estudios Superiores en Antropología Social and Stiftung Preussischer Kulturbesitz, Mexico City and Berlin.

Habib, Irfan 1982 Non-agricultural production and urban economy, in *The Cambridge economic history of India*, T. Raychaudhuri and I. Habib eds., vol 1, pp. 76–93. Cambridge University Press, Cambridge.

1999 *The agrarian system of Mughal India 1556–1707*. Oxford University Press, Oxford.

Hagstrum, Melissa 2001 Household production in Chaco Canyon. *American Antiquity* 66:47–55.

Halperin, Rhoda 1994 *Cultural economics: Past and present*. University of Texas Press, Austin.

Halstead, Paul 1989 The economy has no surplus: Economic stability and social change among early farming communities of Thessaly, Greece, in *Bad year economics*, P. Halstead and J. O'Shea, eds., pp. 68–80. Cambridge University Press, Cambridge.

Halstead, Paul, and John O'Shea 1989 *Bad year economics*. Cambridge University Press, Cambridge.

Hammond, Norman 1978 Cacao and cobaneros: An overland trade route between the Maya highlands and lowlands, in *Mesoamerican communication routes and cultural contacts*, T. Lee and C. Navarrete eds., pp. 19–25. Papers of the New World Archaeological Foundation, No. 40. Brigham Young University, Provo, Utah.

Harding, Thomas 1967 *Voyagers of the Vitiaz strait*. University of Wasington Press, Seattle.

Harris, Marvin 1959 The economy has no surplus. *American Anthropologist* 61:385–99.

Harvey, Herbert 1984 Aspects of land tenure in ancient Mexico, in *Explorations in ethnohistory: Indians of Central Mexico in the sixteenth century*, H. Harvey and H. Prem eds., pp. 83–102. University of New Mexico Press, New Mexico.

1991 *Land and politics in the Valley of Mexico: A two thousand-year perspective*. University of New Mexico Press, Albuquerque.

Hassig, Ross 1982a Periodic markets in pre-columbian Mexico. *American Antiquity* 47:346–355.

1982b Tenochtitlan: The economic and political reorganization of the urban system. *Comparative Urban Research* 9:39–49.

1985 *Trade, tribute and transportation: The sixteenth-century political economy of the Valley of Mexico*. University of Oklahoma Press, Norman.

1986 One hundred years of servitude: Tlamemes in early New Spain, in *Ethnohistory, Supplement to the Handbook of Middle American Indians*, R. Spores ed., pp. 134–152. University of Texas Press, Austin.

1988 *Aztec warfare: Imperial expansion and political control*. University of Oklahoma Press, Norman.

2001 *Time, history, and belief in Aztec and colonial Mexico*. University of Texas Press, Austin.

Hay, Conran 1978 Kaminaljuyu obsidian: Lithic analysis and the economic organization of a prehistoric Maya chiefdom. PhD dissertation, Pennsylvania State University, University Park, Pennsylvania.

Hayden, Brian 2001 Richman, poorman, beggarman, chief: The dynamics of social inequality, in *Archaeology at the millennium: A sourcebook*, G. Feinman and D. Price eds., pp. 231–272. Kluwer Academic Press, New York.

Heider, Karl 1969 Visiting trade institutions. *American Anthropologist* 71:462–471.

Hernández, Francisco 1959 *Historia natural de Nueva España,* 2 volumes, UNAM, Mexico City.

Hernández Xolocotzi, Efraim 1949 Maize granaries in Mexico. *Botanical Museum Leaflets* 13:153–192.

Herrera de Tordesillas, Antonio 1725–1726 *The general history of the vast continent and islands of America...translated into English by Capt. John Stevens*, 6 volumes, J. Batley, London.

1934–1957 *Historia general de los hechos de los castellanos en las islas I tierra firme del Mar Océano*, 17 volumes, Academia de la Historia, Madrid.

Herrera Meza, Maris del Carmen, and Ethelia Ruíz Medrano 1997 *El códice de Tepeucila: El entintado mundo de la fijeza imaginaria*, INAH, Mexico City.

Herskovits, Melville 1965 *Economic anthropology: The economic life of primitive peoples*. Norton, New York.

Hicks, Frédéric 1974 Dependant labor in prehispanic Mexico. *Estudios de cultura náhuatl* 11:244–266.

1976 Mayeque y calpuleque en el sistema de clases del México antiguo, in *Estratificación social en la Mesoamérica prehispánica*, P. Carrasco ed., pp. 67–77. INAH, Mexico City.

1978 Los calpixque de Nezahualcoyotl. *Estudios de cultura Náhuatl* 13:129–152.

1984 Rotational labor and urban development in prehispanic Tezcoco, in *Explorations in ethnohistory: Indians of Central Mexico in the sixteenth century*, H. Harvey and H. Prem eds., pp. 145–174. University of New Mexico Press, Albuquerque.

1987 First steps toward a market-integrated economy in Aztec Mexico, in *Early State Dynamics*, H. Claessen and P. Van de Velde eds., pp. 91–107. Brill, Leiden.

Hill, Polly 1966 Landlords and brokers: A west African trading system (with a note on Kumasi butchers). *Persée* 6: 349–366.

Hirth, Friedrich 1966 *China and the Roman orient: Researches into their ancient and medieval relations as represented in the old Chinese records*. Paragon, New York. (Orig 1885)

Hirth, Friedrich, and William Woodville Rockhill 1911 *Chau Ju-Jua: His work on the Chinese and Arab trade in the twelfth and thirteenth centures, entitled Chu-fan-chi*. Office of the Imperial Academy of Sciences, St. Petersburg.

Hirth, Kenneth 1993 The household as an analytical unit: Problems in method and theory, in *Household, compound, and residence: Studies of prehispanic domestic units in western Mesoamerica*, R. Santley and K. Hirth eds., pp. 21–36. CRC Press, Boca Raton.

1996 Political economy and archaeology: Perspectives on exchange and production, *Journal of Archaeological Research* 4:203–239.

1998 The distributional approach: A new way to identify market behavior using archaeological data. *Current Anthropology* 39:451–476.

2000 *Ancient urbanism at Xochicalco: The evolution and organization of a prehispanic society. Archaeological research at Xochicalco*, vol 1, The University of Utah Press, Salt Lake City

2003 The altepetl and urban structure in prehispanic Mesoamerica, in *El urbanismo en Mesoamerica*, W. Sanders, G. Mastache, and R. Cobean eds., pp. 57–84. INAH and Pennsylvania State University, Mexico City and University Park.

2006a Market forces or state control: The organization of obsidian production in a civic-ceremonial context, in *Obsidian craft production in ancient Central Mexico*, K. Hirth ed., pp. 179–201. The University of Utah Press, Salt Lake City.

2006b Modeling domestic craft production at Xochicalco, in *Obsidian craft production in ancient Central Mexico*, K. Hirth ed., pp. 275–286. The University of Utah Press, Salt Lake City.

2006c *Obsidian craft production in ancient Central Mexico*. The University of Utah Press, Salt Lake City, Utah.

2008a Incidental urbanism: The structure of the prehispanic city in Central Mexico, in *The ancient city: New perspectives in the Old and New Worlds*, J. Marcus and J. Sabloff eds., pp. 273–297. School of American Research, SAR Publications, Sante Fe, New Mexico.

2008b The economy of supply: Modeling obsidian procurement and craft provisioning at a Central Mexican urban center. *Latin American Antiquity* 19:435–457.

2009a Craft production, household diversification, and domestic economy in prehispanic Mesoamerica, in *Housework: Craft production and domestic economy in ancient Mesoamerica*, K. Hirth ed., pp. 13–32, Archaeological Publications No 19, American Anthropological Association, Washington D.C.

2009b Craft production in the Mesoamerican marketplace. *Ancient Mesoamerica* 20:89–102.

2009c *Housework: Craft production and domestic economy in ancient Mesoamerica*. Archaeological Publications No 19, American Anthropological Association, Washington D.C.

2009d Intermittent crafting and multicrafting at Xochicalco, in *Housework: Craft production and domestic economy in ancient Mesoamerica*, K. Hirth ed., pp. 75–91. Archaeological Publications No 19, American Anthropological Association, Washington D.C.

2010 Finding the mark in the marketplace: The organization, development and archaeological identification of market systems, in *Archaeological approaches to market exchange in pre-capitalistic societies*, C. Garraty and B. Stark eds., pp. 227–247. University Press of Colorado, Boulder.

2012a Markets, merchants, and systems of exchange, in *Oxford handbook on Mesoamerican archaeology*, D. Nichols and C. Pool eds., pp. 639–652. Oxford University Press, Oxford.

2012b Producción azteca de maíz y almacenamiento institucional en la Cuenca de México: Un modelo de descentralización del almacenaje, in *Almacenamiento prehispánico del norte de México al altiplano central*, S. Bortot, D. Michelet, and V. Darras, eds., pp. 179–186. Centro de Extudios Mexicanos y Centroamericanos and Universidad Autónoma de San Luis Potosí, Mexico City and San Luis Potosí.

2013a Economic consumption and domestic economy in Cholula's rural hinterland, Mexico. *Latin American Antiquity* 24:123–148.

2013b The merchant's world: Commercial diversity and the economics of interregional exchange in highland Mesoamerica, in *Merchants, markets and exchange in the pre-columbian world*, K. Hirth and J. Pillsbury eds., pp. 85–112. Dumbarton Oaks Research Library and Collection, Washington D.C.

Hirth, Kenneth, and Deborah Nichols n.d. The structure of Aztec commerce: Markets and merchants, in *Oxford handbook on Aztec archaeology*, D. Nichols and E. Rodriguez-Alegria eds., Oxford University Press, Oxford. (in press)

Hirth, Kenneth, and Joanne Pillsbury 2013 Redistribution and markets in Andean South America. *Current Anthropology* 54:642–647.

Hirth, Kenneth, and Ronald Castanzo 2006 Production for use or exchange: Obsidian consumption at the workshop, household, and regional levels, in *Obsidian craft production in ancient Central Mexico*, K. Hirth ed., pp. 218–240. The University of Utah Press, Salt Lake City.

Hirth, Kenneth, Ann Cyphers, Robert Cobean, Jason De Leon, and Michael Glascock 2013 Early Olmec obsidian trade and economic organization at San Lorenzo. *Journal of Archaeological Science* 40:2784–2798.

Holleran, Claire 2012 *Shopping in ancient Rome: The retail trade in the Late Republic and the Principate*. Oxford University Press, Oxford.

Homans, George C. 1974 *Social behavior: Its elementary forms*. Harcourt Brace Jovanich, New York.

Hopkins, Keith 1978 Economic growth and towns in Classical antiquity, in *Towns in societies*, P. Abrams and E. Wrigley eds., pp. 35–77. Cambridge University Press, Cambridge.

1980 Taxes and trade in the Roman empire (200 BC–AD 400). *The Journal of Roman Studies* 70:101–125.

Horn, Rebecca 1998 Testaments and trade: Interethnic ties among petty traders in Central Mexico (Coyacan, 1550–1620), in *Dead giveaways: Indigenous testaments of colonial Mesoamerica and the Andes*, S. Kellogg and M. Restall eds., pp. 59–83. The University of Utah Press, Salt Lake City.

Horrox, Rosemary 1994 *The black death*. Manchester University Press, Manchester.

Hoselitz, Bert 1955 Generative and parasitic cities. *Economic development and cultural change* 3:278–294.

Hudson, Michael 1996 Privatization: A survey of the unresolved controversies, in *Privatization in the ancient Near East and Classical worlds*, M. Hudson and B. Levine eds., International Scholars on Ancient Near East Economics, vol 1, pp. 1–32. Peabody Museum of Archaeology and Ethnology, Harvard University, Cambridge.

Hudson, Michael, and Baruch Levine 1996 *Privatization in the ancient Near East and Classical worlds*, International Scholars on Ancient Near East Economics, 2 volumes, Peabody Museum of Archaeology and Ethnology, Harvard University, Cambridge.

Hugill, Peter 1993 *World trade since 1431*. The Johns Hopkins University Press, Baltimore and London.

Humphrey, Carolin, and Stephen Hugh-Jones 1992 Introduction: Barter, exchange, and value, in *Barter, exchange and value: An anthropological approach*, C. Humphrey and S. Hugh-Jones, eds., pp. 1–20. Cambridge University Press, Cambridge.

Hunt, Edwin 1994 *The medieval super-companies: A study of the Peruzzi company of Florence*. Cambridge University Press, Cambridge.

Hutson, Scott 2000 Carnival and contestation in the Aztec marketplace. *Dialectical Anthropology* 25:123–149.

Hybel, Nils 2002 Introduction, in *Cogs, cargoes, and commerce: Maritime bulk trade in northern Europe, 1150–1400*, L. Berggren, N. Hybel, and A. Landened eds., pp. x–xvii. Pontifical Institute of Mediaeval Studies, Toronto.

Isaac, Barry 1986 Notes on obsidian, the pochteca, and the position of Tlatelolco in the Aztec empire, in *Economic aspects of prehispanic highland Mexico*, B. Isaac ed., pp. 319–343. JAI Press, Greenwhich, Connecticut.

2013 Discussion, in *Merchants, markets and exchange in the pre-columbian world*, K. Hirth and J. Pillsbury eds., pp. 85–112. Dumbarton Oaks Research Library and Collection, Washington D.C.

Ixtlilxóchitl, Fernando de Alva 1891 *Obras históricas de Fernando de Alva Ixtlilxóchitl*. 2 volumes, Oficina de la Secretaria de Fomento, Mexico City.

1977 *Obras históricas*. 2 volumes, UNAM, Mexico.

Jacobs, Jane 1969 *The economy of cities*. Random House, New York.

Jain, Vardhman 2005 Trading community and merchant corporations, in *Trade in early India*, R. Chakravarti ed., pp. 344–369. Oxford University Press, Oxford.

Jefferys, James 1954 *Retail trading in Britain 1850–1950*. Cambridge University Press, Cambridge.

Johnson, Allen and Timothy Earle 1987 *The evolution of human societies*. Stanford University Press, Stanford.

Jongman, Willem 1988 *The economy and society of Pompeii*. J. C. Gieben, Amsterdam.

Karttunen, Frances 1983 *An analytical dictionary of nahuatl*. The University of Oklahoma Press, Norman.

Karttunen, Frances, and James Lockhart 1976 *Nahuatl in the middle years: Language contact phenomena in texts of the colonial period*. University of California Publications in Linguistics, No. 85, University of California, Berkeley.

Katz, Friedrich 1966 *Situación social y económica de los Aztecas durante los siglos XV y XVI*. Instituto de Investigaciones Históricas, UNAM, Mexico City.

Keen, Benjamin 1994 Editor's introduction, in *Life and labor in ancient Mexico*, by A. Zorita, pp. 1–11. University of Oklahoma Press, Norman.

Kellogg, Susan 1986 Aztec inheritance in sixteenth-century Mexico City: Colonial patterns, pre-hispanic influences. *Ethnohistory* 33:313–330.

Kellogg, Susan, and Matthew Restall 1998 *Dead giveaways: Indigenous testaments of colonial Mesoamerica and the Andes*. University of Utah Press, Salt Lake City.

Keltzer, David 1988 *Ritual, politics and power*. Yale University Press, New Haven.

Kepecs, Susan 1998 The political economy of Chikinchel, Yucatan, Mexico: A diachroinic analysis from the prehispanic era through the age of Spanish administration. PhD dissertation, Department of Anthropology, University of Wisconsin, Madison.

2003 Salt sources and production, in *The Postclassic Mesoamerican world*, M. Smith and F. Berdan eds., pp. 126–130. University of Utah Press, Salt Lake City.

Khachikian, Lvon 1966 The ledger of the merchant Hovannes Joughayetsi. *Journal of the Asiatic Society* 8:153–186.

Kicza, John 1983 *Colonial entrepreneurs: Families and business in Bourbon Mexico City*. University of New Mexico Press, Albuquerque.

Kobayashi, Muhehiro 1993 *Tres estudios sobre el sistema tributario de los mexicas*. CIESAS and Kobe City University, Mexico and Kobe, Japan.

Kohler, Josef 1924 *El derecho de los Aztecas*. Tribunal Superior de Justicia, Mexico City.

Kron, Geoffrey 2012 Food production, in *The Cambridge companion to the Roman economy*, W. Scheidel ed., pp. 156–174. Cambridge University Press, Cambridge.

Kurtz, Donald 1974 Peripheral and transitional markets: The Aztec case. *American Ethnologist* 1:685–705.

La Lone, Darrell 1982 The Inca as a nonmarket economy: Supply in command versus supply and demand, in *Contexts for prehistoric exchange*, J. Ericson and T. Earle eds., pp. 291–316. Academic Press, New York.

Landers, John 2003 *The field and the forge: Population production and power in the pre-industrial west.* Oxford University Press, Oxford

Las Casas, Bartolomé 1877 *Historia de las Indias.* 2 volumes, Imprenta y litografía de I. Paz, Mexico City.

    1967 *Apologética historia sumaria.* UNAM, Mexico City.

Lattimore, Owen 1995 *The desert road to Tukestan.* Kodansha America, New York.

LeClair, Edward, and Harold Schneider 1968 Some further theoretical issues, in *Economic anthropology: Readings in theory and analysis*, E. LeClair and H. Schneider eds., pp. 455–473. Holt, Rinehart and Winston, New York.

Lee-fang Chien, Cecilia 2004 *Salt and the state: An annotated translation of the Songshi salt monopoly treatise.* University of Michigan Press, Ann Arbor.

León-Portilla, Miguel 1962 La institución cultural del comercio prehispánico. *Estudios de la Cultural Nahuatl* 3:23–54.

Levi, Scott Cameron 1994 The Banjaras: Medieval Indian peddlers and military commissariat. Masters thesis, Department of History, University of Wisconsin, Madison.

    2002 *The Indian diaspora in Central Asia and its trade 1550–1900.* Brill, Leiden.

Lewis, Leslie 1976 In Mexico City's shadow: Some aspects of economic activity and social processes in Texcoco, 1570–1620, in *Provinces of early Mexico*, I. Altman and J. Lockhart eds., pp. 125–136. UCLA Latin American Center, Los Angeles.

Lewis, Oscar 1951 *Life in a Mexican village: Tepoztlan restudied.* University of Illinois Press, Urbana.

Littlefield, Alice, and Larry Reynolds 1990 The putting-out system: Transitional form or recurrent feature of capitalist production? *The Social Science Journal* 27:359–372.

Litvak King, Jaime 1971 *Cihuatlán y Tepecoacuilco provincias tributarias de México en el siglo XVI.* UNAM, Mexico City.

Liu, Xinru 1988 *Ancient India and ancient China: Trade and religious exchanges AD 1–600.* Oxford University Press, Delhi.

Lloyd, Peter 1953 Craft organization in Yoruba towns. *Africa* 23:30–44.

Lockhart, James 1992 *The Nahuas after the conquest.* Stanford University Press, Stanford.

Lockhart, James, Frances Berdan, and Arthur Anderson 1986 *The Tlaxcalan actas: A compendium of the records of the Cabildo of Tlaxcala (1545–1627).* University of Utah Press, Salt Lake City.

López Austin, Alfredo 1973 *Hombre-dios: religión y política en el mundo nahuatl.* UNAM, Mexico City.

    1974 The research methodology of Fray Bernardino de Sahagún: The questionnaires, in *Sixteenth century Mexico: The work of Sahagún*, M. Edmonson ed., pp. 111–149. University of New Mexico Press, Albuquerque.

1988 *The human body and ideology: Concepts of the ancient Nahuas.* University of Utah Press, Salt Lake City.

López Corral, Aurelio 2011 Crop subsistence yield variability within Late Postclassic (1325–1521 AD) and early colonial (16th century) indigenous communities in the Tepeaca Region, México. PhD dissertation, Department of Anthropology, Pennsylvania State University, University Park, Pennsylvania.

2013 Agricultura de humedales y su impacto en la economía institucional y de subsistencia en poblaciones posclásicas del valle de Puebla-Tlaxcala. Paper presented at XXXV Coloquio de Antropología e Historia Regionales: El Pasado Tecnológico: Cambio y Persistencia, Colegio de Michoacan, Zamora.

López Corral, Aurelio, and Kenneth Hirth 2012 Terrazguero smallholders and the function of agricultural tribute in sixteenth-century Tepeaca, Mexico. *Mexican Studies/Estudios Mexicanos* 28:73–93.

López de Gómara, Francisco 1966 *Cortés. The life of the conquistador by his secretary.* University of California Press, Berkeley.

Losch, August 1938 The Nature of economic regions. *Southern Economic Journal* 5:71–78.

Lumholtz, Carl 1902 *Unknown Mexico: A record of five years' exploration among the tribes of the western Sierra Madre; In the tierra caliente of Tepic and Jalisco; and among the Tarascos of Michoacan.* Scribner's, New York.

Luna, Gregory 2014 Modeling the Aztec agricultural waterscape of Lake Xochimilco: A GIS analysis of lakebed chinampas and settlement. PhD dissertation, Department of Anthropology, Pennsylvania State University, University Park, Pennsylvania.

Mabry, J. B. and D. A. Cleveland 1996 The relevance of indigenous irrigation: A comparative analysis of sustainability, in *Canals and communities: Small-scale irrigation systems*, J. Mabry ed., pp. 227–260. University of Arizona Press, Tucson.

Macazaga Ordoño, Cesar 1978 *Nombres geográficos de México.* Editorial Innovación, Mexico City.

Mackinder, Halford 1921 L'envol. *Scottish Geographical Magazine* 37:77–79.

MacLeod, Murdo 1980 *Historia socio-economic de la America Central espanola.* Tallers Piedra Santa, Guatemala.

Maldonado, Blanca 2009 Metal for the commoners: Tarascan metallurgical production in domestic contexts, in *Housework: Craft production and domestic economy in ancient Mesoamerica*, K. Hirth ed., pp. 225–238. Archaeological Publications No 19, American Anthropological Association, Washington D.C.

Maldonado Jiménez, Druzo 1990 *Cuauhnáhuac y Huaztepec (Tlahuicas y Xochimilcas en el Morelos prehispánico).* UNAM, Mexico City.

Malinowski, Bronislaw 1922 *Argonauts of the western Pacific.* Routledge and Kegan Paul, London.

Malville, Nancy 1999 Porters of the eastern hills of Nepal: Body size and load weight. *American Journal of Human Biology* 11:1–11.

2001 Long-distance transport of bulk goods in the pre-hispanic American Southwest. *Journal of Anthropological Archaeology* 20:230–243.

Malville, Nancy, William Byrnes, H. Allen Lim, and Ramesh Basnyat 2001 Commercial porters of eastern Nepal: Health status, physical work capacity, and energy expenditure. *American Journal of Human Biology* 13:44–56.

Martin, Janet 1986 *Treasure of the land of darkness: The fur trade and its significance for medieval Russia.* Cambridge University Press, Cambridge.

Martínez, Hildeberto 1984 *Tepeaca en el siglo XVI: Tenencia de la tierra y organización de un señorío.* Ediciones de la Casa Chata, Mexico City.

Marx, Karl 1964 *Pre-capitalist economic formations.* Lawrence and Wishart, London.

Masson, Marilyn, and David Freidel 2013 Wide open spaces: A long view of the importance of Maya market exchange, in *Merchants, markets and exchange in the pre-columbian world*, K. Hirth and J. Pillsbury eds., pp. 201–228. Dumbarton Oaks Research Library and Collection, Washington D.C.

Matrícula de Huexotzinco http://gallica.bnf.fr/ark:/12148/btv1b7200005f/f1 .image

Matos Moctezuma, Eduardo 1988 *The great temple of the Aztecs: Treasures of Tenochtitlan.* Thames and Hudson, New York.

Mauro, Frederic 1993 Merchant communities, 1350–1750, in *The rise of merchant empires: Long-distance trade in the modern world, 1350–1750*, J. Tracy ed., pp. 255–286. Cambridge University Press, Cambridge.

Mauss, Marcel 1990 *The gift.* Routledge, London, England.

Mayer, Enrique 2002 *The articulated peasant. Household economies in the Andes.* Westview Press, Boulder.

McAnany, Patricia 2010 *Ancestral Maya economies in archaeological perspective.* Cambridge University Press, Cambridge.

2013 Artisans, *ikatz*, and statecraft: Provisioning Classic Maya royal courts, in *Merchants, markets, and exchange in the pre-columbian world*, K. Hirth and J. Pillsbury eds., pp. 229–253. Dumbarton Oaks Research Library and Collection, Washington D.C.

McCormick, Michael 2001 *The origins of the European economy: Communications and commerce, A.D. 300–900.* Cambridge University Press, Cambridge.

McEwan, Colin. 2006 *Turquoise mosaics from Mexico.* Duke University Press, Durham.

McKendrick, Neil, John Brewer, and John Plumb 1982 *The birth of a consumer society: The commercialization of eighteenth-century England.* Indiana University Press, Bloomington.

Menard, Russell 1991 Transport costs and long-range trade, 1300–1800: Was there a European "transportation revolution" in the early modern era, in *The political economy of merchant empires*, T. James ed., pp. 228–275. Cambridge University Press, Cambridge.

Mendieta, Fray Geronimo de 1945 *Historia eclesiastica indiana.* 4 volumes, Editorial S Chávez Hayhoe, Mexico City. (Orig 1596)

Messer, Ellen 1989 Seasonality in food systems: An anthropological perspective on household food security, in *Seasonal variability in Third World agriculture*, D. Sahn ed., pp. 151–175. John Hopkins University Press, Baltimore.

Millon, Rene 1973 *Urbanization at Teotihuacán, Mexico, vol 1, The Teotihuacán Map. Part one: Text.* University of Texas Press, Austin.

Milton, Giles 2002 *Samurai William: The Englishman who opened Japan.* Farrar, Straus, and Giroux, New York.

Minc, Leah 2006 Monitoring regional market systems in prehistory: Models, methods, and metrics. *Journal of Anthropological Archaeology* 25:82–116.

2009 Style and substance: Evidence for regionalism within the Aztec market system. *Latin American Antiquity* 20:343–374.

Miner, Horace 1953 *The primitive city of Timbuctoo.* Princeton University Press, Princeton.

Mintz, Sidney 1964 The employment of capital by market women in Haiti, in *Capital, saving, and credit in peasant societies*, R. Firth and B. Yamey eds., pp. 256–286. Aldine Publishing Company, Chicago.

Miranda, José 1952 *El tributo indigena en Nueva Espana durante el siglo XVI.* Colegio de México, Mexico City.

Molina, Fray Alonso de 1977 *Vocabulario en lengua castellana y mexicana y mexicana y castellana.* Editorial Porrua, Mexico city.

1984 *Confesionario mayor en la lengua mexicana y castellana (1569).* Instituto de Investigaciones Filológicas, Instituto de Investigaciones Históricas and Universidad Nacional Autónoma de México, Mexico City. (Orig 1569)

Monaghan, John 1995 *The covenants with earth and rain.* University of Oklahoma Press, Norman.

Monzón, Cristina, Hans Roskamp, and J. Benedict Warren 2009 La memoria de Don Melchor Caltzin (1543): Historia y legitimación en Tzintzuntzan, Michoacan. *Estudios de Historia Novohispana* 40:21–55.

Moore, Karl, and David Lewis 1999 Birth of the multinational: 2000 years of ancient business history from Ashur to *Augustus.* Copenhagen Business School Press, Copenhagan.

Moraley, William. 1743 *The infortunate: The voyage and adventures of William Moraley, an indentured servant.* Penn State Press, University Park.

Morante López, Rubén 2010 Las antiguas rutas comerciales: Un camio por las sierras nahuas de Puebla y Veracruz, in *Caminos y mercados de México*, J. Long Towell and A. Attolini Lecón eds., pp. 107–127. UNAM and INAH, Mexico City.

Morley, Neville 2007 *Trade in classical antiquity.* Cambridge University Press, Cambridge.

Morris-Suzuki, Tessa 1989 *A history of Japanese economic thought.* Routledge, London.

Motolinia, Fray Toribio de Benavente 1950 *Motolinía's history of the indians of new Spain.* The Cortés Society, Berkeley, California. (Orig 1568)

1971 *Memoriales o libro de las cosas de la Nueva España y de los naturales de ella.* Instituto de Investigaciones Históricas, UNAM, Mexico City.

1973 *Historia de los indios de la Nueva España.* Editorial Porrúa, Mexico City.

Muñera Bermudez, Luis Carlos 1985 Un taller de ceramica ritual en la Ciudadela, Teotihuacan. Licenciatura Thesis, ENAH, Mexico City.

Muñoz Carmargo, Diego 1972 *Historia de Tlaxcala.* Biblioteca de Facsimiles Mesicanos, Mexico City.

Murphy, Robert, and Julian Steward 1956 Tappers and trappers: Parallel process in acculturation. *Economic Development and Culture Change* 4:335–355.

Murra, John 1972 El control vertical de un máximo de pisos ecológicos en la economía de las sociedades Andinas, in *Vistas de la provincia de León de Huánuco [1562]*, I. O. de Zuñiga ed., pp. 429–476. Universidad Nacional Hermilio Valdizán, Huánuco, Peru.

  1980 *The economic organization of the Inka state*. JAI Press, Greenwich, Connecticut.

  1985 El archipelago revisited, in *Andean ecology and civilization: An interdisciplinary perspective on Andean ecological complementary*, S. Masuda, I. Shimada, and C. Morris eds., pp. 3–13. Tokyo University Press, Tokyo.

Nash, Manning 1967 The organization of economic life, in *Tribal and peasant economies*, G. Dalton ed., pp. 3–11. The Natural History Press, New York.

Netting, Robert McC. 1981 *Balancing on an Alp: Ecological change and continuity in a Swiss mountain community*. Cambridge University Press, Cambridge.

  1989 Smallholders, householders, freeholders: Why the family farm works well worldwide, in *The household economy: Reconsidering the domestic mode of production*, R. Wilk ed., pp. 221–244. Westview Press, Boulder.

  1990 Population, permanent agriculture and polities: Unpacking the evolutionary portmanteau, in *The evolution of political systems*, S. Upham ed., pp. 21–61. Cambridge University Press, Cambridge.

  1993 *Smallholders, households, farm families, and the ecology of intensive, sustainable agriculture*. Stanford University Press, Stanford.

Netting, Robert, Richard Wilk, and Eric Arnould 1984 Introduction, in *Households: Comparative and historic studies of the domestic group*, R. Netting, R. Wilk, and E. Arnould eds., pp. xiv–xxxviii. University of California Press, Berkeley.

Nichols, Deborah 1994 The organization of provincial craft production and the Aztec city-state Otumba, in *Economies and polities in the Aztec realm*, M. Hodge and M. Smith eds., pp. 175–194. State University of New York and University of Texas Press, Albany and Austin.

  2013 Merchants and merchandise: The archaeology of Aztec commerce at Otumba, Mexico, in *Merchants, trade and exchange in the pre-columbian world*, K. Hirth and J. Pillsbury eds., pp. 49–83. Dumbarton Oaks Library and Research Collection, Washington D.C.

Nichols, Deborah, Elizabeth Brumfiel, Hector Neff, Mary Hodge, Thomas Charlton, and Michael Glascock 2002 Neutrons, markets, cities, and empires: A 1000-year perspective on ceramic production and distribution in the Postclassic Basin of Mexico. *Journal of Anthropological Archaeology* 21:25–82.

Nicholson, Henry 1971 Religion in pre-hispanic Central Mexico, in *Handbook of Middle American Indians*, vol 11, pp. 395–446. University of Texas Press, Austin.

Nissen, Hans Jörg, Peter Damerow, and Robert Englund 1993 *Archaic bookkeeping: Early writing and techniques of economic administration in the ancient Near East*. University of Chicago Press, Chicago.

North, Douglass 1981 *Structure and change in economic history*. W. W. Norton and Company, New York.

    1991 Institutions, transaction costs, and the rise of merchant empires, in *The political economy of merchant empire*, T. James, ed., pp. 22–40. Cambridge University Press, Cambridge.

    1997 Institutions, transaction costs, and the rise of merchant empires, in *The political economy of merchant empires: State power and world trade 1350–1750*, J. Tract ed., pp. 22–40. Cambridge University Press, Cambridge.

O'Mack, Scott 1985 Yacapitztlan: Ethnohistory and ethnicity. Masters thesis, Department of Anthropology, University of Kentucky, Lexington.

Offner, Jerome 1981a On Carrasco's use of theoretical "first principles" *American Antiquity* 46:69–74.

    1981b On the inapplicability of "oriental despotism" and the "Asiatic mode of production" to the Aztecs of Texcoco. *American Antiquity* 46:43–61.

    1983 *Law and politics in Aztec Texcoco*. Cambridge University Press, Cambridge.

Oka, Rahul, and Chapurukha Kusimba 2008 The archaeology of trading systems, part I: Towards a new trade synthesis. *Journal of Archaeological Research* 16:339–395.

Olivera, Mercedes 1984 *Pillis y macehuales: Las formaciones sociales y los modos de producción de Tecali del siglo XII al XVI*. Ediciones de la Casa Chata 6. Centro de Estudios Superiors, INAH, Mexico City.

Orozco y Berra, Manuel 1940 Los comerciantes Aztecas. *Divulgación Histórica* 2:107–110.

Otis Charlton, Cynthia 1993 Obsidian as jewelry: Lapidary production in Aztec Otumba, Mexico. *Ancient Mesoamerica* 4:231–243.

    1994 Plebeians and patricians: Contrasting patterns of production and distribution in the Aztec figurine and lapidary industries, in *Economies and polities in the Aztec realm*, M. Hodge and M. Smith eds., pp. 195–220. Institute for Mesoamerican Studies, State University of New York and University of Texas Press, Albany and Austin.

    2007 Artesanos y barro: Figurillas y alfarería en Otompan, estado de México. *Arqueologia* 14:71–76.

Otis Charlton, Cynthia, Thomas Charlton, and Deborah Nichols 1993 Aztec household-based craft production: Archaeological evidence from the city-state of Otumba, Mexico, in *Prehispanic domestic units in western Mesoamerica: Studies in household, compound, and residence*, R. Santley and K. Hirth eds., pp. 147–172. CRC Press, Boca Raton, Florida.

Ortiz de Montellano, Bernard 1989 The body, ethics and cosmos: Aztec physiology, in *The imagination of matter: Religion and ecology in Mesoamerican traditions*, D. Carrasco ed., pp. 191–209. BAR International Series 515, Oxford.

Ortiz Díaz, Edith 2010 El camino Real de Soconusco: Eje de articulación comercial entre la provincia de Oaxaca y la audiencia de Guatemala en el siglo XVI, in *Caminos y mercados de México*, J. Long Towell and A. Attolini Lecón eds., pp. 241–260. UNAM and INAH, Mexico City.

O'Shea, John 1989 The role of wild resources in small-scale agricultural systems: Tales from the lakes and the plains, in *Bad year economics*, P. Halstead and J. O'Shea, eds., pp. 57–67. Cambridge University Press, Cambridge.

Oviedo y Valdés, Gonzalo Fernádez 1851–1855 *Historia general y natural de las Indias, islas y tierra-firme del mar océano.* J. Amador de los Ríos, Madrid.

Palerm, Ángel 1955 The agricultural basis of urban civilization in Mesoamerica, in *Irrigation civilizations: A comparative study*, J. Steward ed., pp. 28–42. Pan American Union, Washington D.C.

Parker, William 1984 *Europe, America and the wider world.* Cambridge University Press, Cambridge.

Parkins, Helen 1998 Time for change? Shaping the future of the ancient economy, in *Trade, traders and the ancient city*, H. Parkins and C. Smith eds., pp. 1–15. Routledge, London and New York.

Parks, Tim 2005 *Medici money.* Norton and Company, New York.

Parsons, Jeffrey 1976 The role of chinampa agriculture in the food supply of Aztec Tenochtitlan, in *Cultural change and continuity*, C. Cleland ed., pp. 233–258. Academic Press, New York.

1991 Political implications of prehispanic chinampa agriculture in the Valley of Mexico, in *Land and politics in the Valley of Mexico: A two thousand year perspective*, H. Harvey ed., pp. 17–43. University of New Mexico Press, Albuquerque.

1996 Tequesquite and ahuauhtle: Rethinking the prehispanic productivity of Lake Texcoco-Xaltocan-Zumpango, in *Arqueología mesoamericana: Homenaje a William*, T. Sanders, A. Mastache, J. Parsons, R. Santley, and M. C. Serra Puche eds., vol 1, pp. 439–459. INAH, Mexico City.

2001 *Last saltmakers of Nexquipayac, Mexico. An archaeological ethnography.* Anthropological Papers No. 92, Museum of Anthropology, University of Michigan, Ann Arbor.

2008 Beyond Santley and Rose (1979): The role of aquatic resources in the prehispanic economy of the Basin of Mexico. *Journal of Anthropological Research* 64:351–366.

Parsons, Jeffrey, and Mary Parsons 1990 *Maguey utilization in highland Central Mexico: An archaeological ethnography.* Anthropological Papers No. 82. Museum of Anthropology, University of Michigan, Ann Arbor.

Pastrana Cruz, Alejandro 1998 *La explotación azteca de la obsidiana en la Sierra de las Navajas.* Colección Científica No. 383. INAH, Mexico City.

Pearson, M. N. 1988 Brokers in western Indian port cities: Their roles in servicing foreign merchants. *Modern Asian Studies* 22:455–472.

1991 Merchants and states, in *The political economy of merchant empires*, T. James ed., pp. 41–116. Cambridge University Press, Cambridge.

Pegolotti, Francisco Balducci 1936 *La practica della mercatura.* The Mediaeval Academy of America, Cambridge, Massachusetts. (Orig circa 1340)

Pellicani, Luciano 1994 *The genesis of capitalism and the origins of modernity.* Telos Press, New York.

Peñafiel, Antonio 1885 *Catálogo alfabético de los nombres de lugar al idioma "nahuatl."* Secretaria de Fomento, Mexico City.

Percival, John 1976 *The Roman villa.* B. T. Batsford, London

Perelman, Michael 2000 *The invention of capitalism.* Duke University Press, Durham.

Pettinato, Giovanni 1991 *Ebla: A new look at history.* John Hopkins University Press, Baltimore.

Pirenne, Henri 1939 *Mohammed and Charlemagne.* W. W. Norton and Company, New York.

1956 *Medieval cities.* Doubleday and Company, New York.

Plattner, Stuart 1975 The economics of peddling, in *Formal methods in economic anthropology,* S. Plattner ed., pp. 55–76. Publication No. 4, American Anthropological Association, Washington D.C.

1989a Economic behavior in marketplaces, in *Economic anthropology,* S. Plattner ed., pp. 209–221. Stanford University Press, Stanford.

1989b Markets and marketplaces, in *Economic anthropology,* S. Plattner ed., pp. 171–208. Stanford University Press, Stanford.

Polanyi, Karl 1957 The economy as instituted process, in *Trade and market in the early empires,* K. Polanyi, C. Arensberg, and H. Pearson eds., pp. 243–270. The Free Press, Glencoe, Illinois.

Polanyi, Karl, Conran Arensberg, and Harry Pearson 1957 *Trade and market in the early empires.* The Free Press, Glencoe, Illinois.

Pollard, Hellen 1982 Ecological variation and economic exchange in the Tarascan state. *American Ethnologist* 9:250–268.

1987 The political economy of prehispanic Tarascan metallurgy. *American Antiquity* 52:741–752.

2003 Development of the Tarascan core: The Lake Pátzcuaro Basin, in *The Postclassic Mesoamerican world,* M. Smith and F. Berdan eds., pp. 227–237. University of Utah Press, Salt Lake City.

Pomeranz, Kenneth, and Steven Topik 2006 *The world that trade created: Society, culture, and the world economy.* M. E. Sharpe, Armonk and New York.

Pool, Chrisopher 1993 Quest for fire: Fuel costs and pottery manufacture at Matacapan, Veracruz, in *Culture and environment: A fragile coexistence,* R. Jamieson, S. Abonyi, and N. Mirau eds., pp. 395–409. University of Calgary, Calgary.

Pospisil, Leopold 1968 The Kapauku individualistic money economy, in *Economic anthropology,* E. LeClair and H. Schneider eds., pp. 381–394. Holt, Rinehart and Winston, New York.

Postgate, J. Nicholas 2004 *Early Mesopotamia: Society and economy at the dawn of history.* Routledge, London and New York.

Prem, Hanns 1974 *Matrícula de Huexotzinco (Ms mex. 387 der Bibliothèque Nationale Paris)* Akademische Druck -u. Verlagsanstalt, Graz, Austria.

Prem, Hanns, Ursula Dyckerhoff, and Günter Miehlich 1978 *Milpa y hacienda: Tenencia de la tierra indígena y española en la cuenca del Alto Atoyac, Puebla, México, 1520–1650.* Franz Steiner Verlag, Wiesbaden.

Pryor, Frederic 1977 *The origins of the economy.* Academic Press, New York.

Puleston, Dennis 1978 Terracing, raised fields, and tree cropping in the Maya lowlands: A new perspective on the geography of power, in *Pre-hispanic*

Maya agriculture, P. Harrison and B. Turner eds., pp. 225–245. University of Texas Press, Austin.

Radford, R. A. 1968 The economic organization of a P.O.W. camp, in *Economic anthropology*, E. LeClair and H. Schneider eds., pp. 403–414. Holt, Rinehart and Winston, New York.

Rathje, William, David Gregory, and Frederick Wiseman 1978 Trade models and archaeological problems: Classic Maya examples, in *Mesoamerican communication routes and cultural contacts*, T. Lee and C. Navarette eds., pp. 147–175. Papers of the New World Archaeological Foundation, No. 40, Brigham Young University, Provo, Utah.

Ratnagar, Shereen 2004 *Trading encounters from the Euphrates to the Indus in the Bronze age*. Oxford University Press, Oxford.

Rauh, Nicholas 1993 *The sacred bonds of commerce: Religion, economy, and trade society at Hellenistic Roman Delos*. J. C. Gieben, Amsterdam.

Redfield, Robert 1939 Primitive merchants of Guatemala. *Quarterly Journal of Inter-American Relations* 1:42–56.

Reed, C. M. 2003 *Maritime traders in the ancient Greek world*. Cambridge University Press, Cambridge.

Rees, Peter 1975 Origins of colonial transportation in Mexico. *Geographical Review* 65:3:323–334.

Restall, Matthew, Lisa Sousa, and Kevin Terraciano 2005 Exerpt from the Mixtec Codex Sierra, of the community accounts of Santa Catarina Texupa, 1550–1564, in *Mesoamerican voices*, M. Restall, L. Sousa, and K. Terraciano eds., pp. 86–93. Cambridge University Press, Cambridge.

Reyes, García Luís 1997 *Matrícula de tributos o códice Moctezuma*. Akademische Druck- und Verlagsanstalt, Graz, and Fondo de Cultura Económica, Mexico City.

Rice, Prudence 1987 *Pottery analysis*. University of Chicago Press, Chicago.

Robinson, Joan 1960 *An essay on Marxian economics*. Macmillan, London. (Orig 1942)

Rojas, Gabriel de 1927 Descripción de Cholula. *Revista Mexicana de Estúdios Históricos* 1:158–169.

Rojas, José Luis de 1995 *México Tenochtitlan: Economía y sociedad en el siglo XVI*. Fondo de Cultura Económica, Mexico City.

2012 El almacenamiento en el imperio mexica: una necesidad evidente en busca de evidencias, in *Almacenamiento prehispánico del norte de México al altiplano central*, S. Bortot, D. Michelet, and V. Darras eds., pp. 173–178. Laboratorie Archéologie des Amériques, Mexico City.

Rojas Rabiela, Teresa 1983 *La agricultura chinampera: compilación histórica*. UNAM, Mexico City.

1987 *Padrones de Tlaxcala del siglo XVI y padron de nobles de Ocotelolco*. Colección de Documentos 1, CIESAS, Mexico City.

Rossabi, Morris 1993 The "decline" of the central Asian caravan trade, in *The rise of merchant empires: Long-distance trade in the modern world, 1350–1750*, J. Tracy ed., pp. 351–370, Cambridge University Press, Cambridge.

Rounds, Jeffrey 1977 The role of the tecuhtli in ancient Aztec society. *Ethnohistory* 24:343–361.

Roys, Ralph 1939 *The titles of Ebtun*. The Carnegie Institution of Washington, Publicataion No. 505, Washington D.C.

1943 *The Indian background of colonial Yucatan*. The Carnegie Institution of Washington, Publicataion No. 548, Washington D.C.

Rudner, David West 1987 Religious gifting and inland commerce in seventeenth-century South India. *The Journal of Asian Studies* 46:361–379.

Rush, James 1990 *Opium to Java: Revenue farming and Chinese enterprise in colonial Indonesia, 1860–1910*. Cornell University Press, Ithaca.

Sahagún, Fray Bernardino de 1905–1907 *Historia general de las cosas de Nueva España*, F. del Paso y Troncoso ed., *(facsimile edition)*. Real Academía de la Historia, Madrid.

1953 *Florentine Codex, Book 7, The sun, moon, and stars, and the binding of the year*, A. Anderson and C. Dibble eds. and trans., University of Utah Press, Salt Lake City.

1959 *Florentine Codex, Book 9, The merchants*, C. Dibble and A. Anderson eds. and trans., University of Utah Press, Salt Lake City.

1961 *Florentine Codex, Book 10, The people*, C. Dibble and A. Anderson eds. and trans., University of Utah Press, Salt Lake City.

1969 *Florentine Codex, Book 6, Rhetoric and moral philosophy*, C. Dibble and A. Anderson eds. and trans., University of Utah Press, Salt Lake City.

1979a *Florentine Codex, Book 4, The Soothsayers and Book 5, The omens*, C. Dibble and A. Anderson eds. and trans., University of Utah Press, Salt Lake City.

1979b *Florentine Codex, Book 8, Kings and Lords*, A. Anderson and C. Dibble eds. and trans., University of Utah Press, Salt Lake City.

1981a *Florentine Codex, Book 2, the ceremonies*, A. Anderson and C. Dibble eds. and trans., University of Utah Press, Salt Lake City.

1981b *Historia general de las cosas de Nueva España*. 4 volumes, Editorial Porrua, Mexico City.

2008 *Florentine Codex (facsimile edition)*. 3 volumes, Hispanic Research Center, Arizona State University, Tempe.

Sahlins, Marshal 1972 *Stone age economics*, Aldine, Chicago.

Salomon, Frank 1977 Pochteca and mindalá: A comparison of long-distance traders in Ecuador and Mesoamerica. *Journal of the Steward Anthropological Society* 9:231–247.

1987 A north Andean status trader complex under Inka rule. *Ethnohistory* 34:63–77.

Sanders, William 1956 The Central Mexican symbiotic region: A study in pre-historic settlement patterns, in *Prehistoric settlement patterns in the New World*, G. Willey ed., pp. 115–127. Viking Fund Publications in Anthropology 23, Wenner-Gren Foundation for Anthropological Research, New York.

1957 *Tierra y agua: A study of the ecological factors in the development of Mesoamerican civilizations*, Harvard University, Boston.

1962 Cultural ecology of nuclear Mesoamerica. *American Anthropologist* 64: 34–44.

1965 *The cultural ecology of the Teotihuacan Valley*. Pennsylvania State University, University Park.

1970 The population of the Teotihuacan valley, the Basin of Mexico and the central Mexican symbiotic region in the 16th century, in *The natural environment, contemporary occupation and 16th century population of the valley*, W. Sanders, A. Kovar, T. Charlton, and R. Diehl eds., pp. 385–457. Occasional Papers in Anthropology, Pennsylvania State University, University Park.

1976 The agricultural history of the Basin of Mexico, in *The valley of Mexico*, E. Wolf ed., pp. 101–159. University of New Mexico Press, Albuquerque.

2003 The population of Tenochtitlan-Tlatelolco, in *El urbanismo en Mesoamerica*, W. Sanders, G. Mastache, and R. Cobean eds., pp. 203–216. INAH and Pennsylvania State University, Mexico City and University Park.

2008 Tenochtitlan in 1519: A pre-industrial megalopolis, in *The Aztec world*, E. Brumfiel and G. Feinman eds., pp. 67–86 Abrams, New York.

Sanders, William, and Barbara Price 1968 *Mesoamerica: The evolution of a civilization*. Random House, New York.

Sanders, William, and Robert Santley 1983 A tale of three cities: Energetics and urbanization in pre-hispanic central Mexico, in *Prehistoric settlement patterns*, E. Vogt and R. Leventhal eds., pp. 243–291. University of New Mexico Press and the Peabody Museum of Archaeology and Ethnology, Harvard University, Albuquerque and Cambridge.

Sanders, William, and Susan Toby Evans 2001 The Teotihuacan valley and the Temascalapa region during the Aztec period, in *The Aztec period occupation of the valley, part 3, syntheses and general bibliography*, W. Sanders and S. Evans eds., pp. 932–1078. Occasional Papers in Anthropology, Pennsylvania State University, University Park.

Sanders, William, Jeffrey Parsons, and Robert Santley 1979 *The Basin of Mexico: Ecological processes in the evolution of a civilization*. Academic Press, New York.

Sandstrom, Alan 2015 Why pilgrimage: The ethnography and archaeology of journeys to the center. Paper presented at the 80th Annual Meeting of the Society for American Archaeology, San Francisco, California.

Sandstrom, Alan, and Pamela Effrein Sandstrom 1986 *Traditional papermaking and paper cult figures of Mexico*. University of Oklahoma Press, Norman.

Santley, Robert 1984 Obsidian exchange, economic stratification, and the evolution of complex society in the Basin of Mexico, in *Trade and exchange in early Mesoamerica*, K. Hirth ed., pp. 43–86. University of New Mexico, Albuquerque.

Santley, Robert, and Rani Alexander 1992 The political economy of core-periphery systems, in *Resources, power, and interregional interaction*, E. Schortman and P. Urban eds., pp. 23–59. Plenum, New York.

Saville, Marshall 1922 *Turquois mosaic art in ancient Mexico*. Museum of the American Indian, Heye Foundation, New York.

Scheffler, Tim, Kenneth Hirth, and George Hasemann 2012 The El Gigante rockshelter: Preliminary observations on an Early to Late Holocene occupation in southern Honduras. *Latin American Antiquity* 23:597–610.

Scheidel, Walter 2012 Slavery, in *The Cambridge companion to the Roman economy*, W. Scheidel ed., pp. 89–113. Cambridge University Press, Cambridge.

Schmandt-Besserat, Denise 1978 The earliest precursor of writing. *Scientific American* 238: 50–59.

Schneider, Jane 1977 Was there a pre-capitalist world-system? *Peasant Studies* 6:20–29.

Scholes, Frances, and Eleanor Adams 1957 *Información sobre los tributos que los indios pagaban a Moctezuma: Año 1554*. José Porrúa e Hijos, Mexico City.
    1958 *Sobre el modo de tributar los indios de Nueva España a su majestad, 1561–1564*. Documentos para la historia del México colonial, vol V, Editorial Porrúa, Mexico City.

Scholes, Frances, and Ralph Roys 1968 *The Maya Chontal indians of Acalan-Tixchel*. University of Oklahoma Press, Norman.

Schurz, William 1918 Mexico, Peru, and the Manila galleon. *Hispanic American Historical Review* 1:389–402.

Séjourne, Laurette 1976 *Burning water: Thought and religion in ancient Mexico*. Shambhala Publications, Berkeley.

Sen, Sudipta 1998 *Empire of free trade: The East India company and the making of the colonial marketplace*. University of Pennsylvania Press, Philadelphia.

Shaw, Leslie 2012 The elusive Maya marketplace: An archaeological consideration of the evidence. *Journal of Archaeological Research* 20:117–155.

Sheehy, James 1996 Ethnographic analogy and the royal household in 8th century Copan, in *Arqueología Mesoamericana: Homenaje a William Sanders*, A. G. Mastache, J. Parsons, R. Santley, and M. C. Serra Puche eds., vol 2, pp. 253–276. INAH, Mexico City.

Sheets, Payson 1975 Behavioral analysis and the structure of a prehistoric industry. *Current Anthropology* 16:369–391.

Shiba, Yoshinobu 1977 Ningpo and its hinterland, in *The city in Late Imperial China*, W. Skinner ed., pp. 391–439. Stanford University Press, Stanford.

Shimada, Izumi 2007 *Craft production in complex societies: Multicraft and producer perspectives*. University of Utah Press, Salt Lake City.

Siemens, A. H. 1983 Wetland agriculture in pre-hispanic Mesoamerica. *Geographical Review* 73:166–181.

Silver, Harry 1981 Calculating risks: The socioeconomic foundations of aesthetic innovation in an Ashanit carving community. *Ethnology* 20:101–114.

Silver, Morris 1995 *Economic structures of antiquity*. Greenwood Press, Westport, Connecticut.

Silverstein, Jay 2000 A study of the Late Postclassic Aztec-Tarascan frontier in northern Guerrero, Mexico: The Oztuma-Cutzamala project. PhD dissertation, Department of Anthropology, The Pennsylvania State University, University Park.
    2001 Aztec imperialism at Oztuma, Guerrero. *Ancient Mesoamerica* 12:31–48.

Siméon, Remi 1991 *Diccionario de la lengua Náhuatl o Mexicano*. Siglo Veintiuno, Mexico City. (Orig 1885)

Simmel, George 1906 Types of social relationships, in *The sociology of Georg Simmel*, K. Wolf ed., pp. 317–329. The Free Press, New York

Skinner, Elliott 1964 West African economic systems, in *Economic transition in Africa*, M. Herskovits and M. Harwitz eds., pp. 77–97. Northwestern University Press, Evanston.

Skinner, George William 1964 Marketing and social structure in rural China, part 1. *Journal of Asian Studies* 24:3–43.

Sluyter, Andrew 1993 Long-distance staple transport in western Mesoamerica: Insights through quantitative modeling. *Ancient Mesoamerica* 4:193–199.

Smith, Adam 1937 *The wealth of nations*. Modern Library, New York. (Orig 1776)

Smith, Alan 1991 *Creating a world economy: Merchant capital, colonialism and world trade 1400–1824*. Westview Press, Boulder.

Smith, Carol 1974 Economics of marketing systems: Models from economic geography. *Annual Review of Anthropology* 3:167–201.

1976 Regional economic systems: Linking geographical models and socioeconomic problems, in *Regional analysis, vol 1, economic systems*, C. Smith ed., pp. 3–67. Academic Press, New York.

1983 Regional analysis in world-system perspective: A critique of three structural theories of uneven development, in *Economic anthropology: Topics and theories*, S. Ortiz ed., pp. 307–359. University Press of America, Lanham, Maryland.

Smith, Claude Earle 1967 Plant remains, in *The prehistory of the Tehuacan valley*, vol 1, pp. 220–255. University of Texas Press, Austin

1986 Preceramic plant remains from Guilá Naquitz, in *Guilá Naquitz: Archaic foraging and early agriculture in Oaxaca, México*, K. Flannery ed., pp. 265–301. Academic Press, New York.

Smith, Colin 1999 The market place and the market's place in London, c. 1660–1840. PhD dissertation, University College London, London.

Smith, Michael Ernest 1979 The Aztec marketing system and settlement pattern in the Valley of Mexico: A central place analysis. *American Antiquity* 44:110–125.

1992 *Archaeological research at Aztec-period rural sites in Morelos, Mexico: vol 1, Excavations and architecture*. Monographs in Latin American Archaeology, No. 4, University of Pittsburgh, Pittsburgh.

1996 The strategic provinces, in *Aztec imperial strategies*, F. Berdan, R. Blanton, E. Boone, M. Hodge, M. Smith, and E. Umberger eds., pp. 137–150. Dumbarton Oaks Research Library and Collection, Washington D.C.

2003a Economic change in Morelos households, in *The Postclassic Mesoamerican world*, M. Smith and F. Berdan eds., pp. 238–242. University of Utah Press, Salt Lake City.

2003b Key commodities, in *The Postclassic Mesoamerican world*, M. Smith and F. Berdan eds., pp. 117–125. University of Utah Press, Salt Lake City.

2004 The archaeology of ancient state economies. *Annual Review of Anthropology* 33:73–102.

2008 *Aztec city-state capitals*. University Press of Florida, Gainesville.

2010 Regional and local market systems in Aztec-period Morelos, in *Archaeological approaches to market exchange in pre-capitalistic societies*, C. Garraty and B. Stark eds., pp. 161–182. University Press of Colorado, Boulder.

2012a El almacenamiento en la economica azteca: una perspective comparativa, in *Almacenamiento prehispánico del norte de México al altiplano central*, S. Bortot, D. Michelet, and V. Darras eds., pp. 203–220. Laboratorie Archéologie des Amériques, Mexico City.

2012b Graneros y almacenamiento de maíz en Morelos posclásico, in *Almacenamiento prehispánico del norte de México al altiplano central*, S. Bortot, D. Michelet, and V. Darras eds., pp. 159–172. Laboratorie Archéologie des Amériques, Mexico City.

2012c *The Aztecs*. Wiley Blackwell Publishers, Cambridge.

2014 The Aztecs paid taxes, not tribute. *Mexicon* 36:19–22.

n.d. Aztec taxation at the city-state and imperial levels. www.academia.edu/4618310/Aztec_Taxation_at_the_City-State_and_Imperial_Levels_n.d._

Smith, Michael Garfield 1955 *The economy of Hausa communities of Zaria*. Colonial Research Studies No. 16, Colonial Office Social Science Research Council, England.

Smith, Robert 1978 Periodic market-places, periodic marketing and travelling traders, in *Market-place trade: periodic markets, hawkers, and traders in Africa, Asia, and Latin America*, R. Smith ed., pp. 11–25. Centre for Transportation Studies, University of British Columbia, Vancouver.

Souden, David 1978 Rogues, whores and vagabonds? Indentured servant emigrants to North America, and the case of mid seventeenth century Bristol. *Social History* 3: 23–41.

Spielman, Katherine 2002 Feasting, craft specialization, and the ritual mode of production in small-scale societies. *American Anthropologist* 104: 195–207.

Spores, Ronald 1984 *The Mixtecs in ancient and colonial times*. University of Oklahoma Press, Norman.

Stahle, David, J. Villanueva Diaz, Dorian Burnette, J. Paredes, R. Heim, Falco Fye, R. Acuna Soto, Matthew Therrell, Malcolm Cleaveland, and David Stahle. 2011 Major Mesoamerican droughts of the past millennium. *Geophysical Research Letters* 38, No. 5.

Stanish, Charles 2010 Labor taxes, market systems, and urbanization in the prehispanic Andes: A comparative perspective, in *Archaeological approaches to market exchange in ancient societies*, C. Garraty and B. Stark eds., pp. 185–205. University Press of Colorado, Boulder.

Stanish, Charles, and Lawrence Coben 2013 Barter markets in the pre-hispanic Andes, in *Merchants, markets and exchange in the pre-columbian world*, K. Hirth and J. Pillsbury eds., pp. 85–112. Dumbarton Oaks Research Library and Collection, Washington D.C.

Stark, Barbara, and Alanna Osa 2010 Origins and development of Mesoamerican marketplaces: Evidence from south-central Veracruz, Mexico, in *Archaeological approaches to market exchange in ancient societies*, C. Garraty and B. Stark eds., pp. 99–126. University Press of Colorado, Boulder.

Stark, Barbara, and Christopher Garraty 2010 Detecting marketplace exchange in archaeology: A methodological review, in *Archaeological approaches to market exchange in ancient societies*, C. Garraty and B. Stark eds., pp. 33–58. University Press of Colorado, Boulder.

Starr, Chester 1977 *The economic and social growth of early Greece 800–500 BC*. Oxford University Press, New York.

Stein, Burton 1960 The economic function of a medieval south Indian Temple. *The Journal of Asian Studies* 19:163–176.

Steward, Julian 1938 *Basin Plateau aboriginal sociopolitical groups*. Bulletin 120, Bureau of American Ethnology. Washington D.C.

Stinson, Marie 1983 Assarting and poverty in early-fourteenth-century western Yorkshire. *Landscape History* 5:53–67.

Stone, Glenn 1986 *Settlement ecology: The social and spatial organization of Kofyar agriculture*. University of Arizona Press, Tucson.

Strathern, Andrew 2007 *The rope of moka: Big-men and ceremonial exchange in Mount Hagen, New Guinea*. Cambridge University Press, Cambridge.

Sundström, Lars 1974 *The exchange economy of pre-colonial tropical Africa*. St. Martin's Press, New York.

Symanski, Richard, and Michael Webber 1974 Complex periodic market cycles. *Annals of the Association of American Geographers* 64:203–213.

Szewczyk, David 1976 New elements in the society of Tlaxcala 1519–1618, in *Provinces of early Mexico*, I. Altman and J. Lockhart eds., pp. 137–153. UCLA Latin American Center, Los Angeles.

Tacitus, Gaius Cornelius 2006 *Agricola, Germany, and dialogue on orators*. The Hackett Publishing Company, Indianapolis.

Tax, Sol 1953 *Penny capitalism: A Guatemalan Indian community*. Smithsonian Institute of Social Anthropology, Washington D.C.

Tax, Sol, and Robert Hinshaw 1969 *The Maya of the midwestern highlands: Handbook of Middle American Indians*, vol 7, pp. 69–100. University of Texas Press, Austin.

Terraciano, Kevin 2001 *The Mixtecs of colonial Oaxaca: Ñudzahui history, sixteenth through eighteenth centuries*. Stanford University Press, Stanford.

Tezozomoc, Hernando Alvarado 1878 *Crónica Mexicana*. Imprenta y Litografía Paz, Mexico City.

  1980 *Crónica Mexicana*. Editorial Porrua, Mexico City.

Therrell, Matthew, David Stahle, and Rodolfo Acuña Soto 2004 Aztec drought and the "curse of one rabbit." *Bulletin of the American Meterological Society* 85:1263–1272.

Thompson, Edward 1991 *The making of the English working class*. Penguin Books, London.

Thompson, Eric 1949 Canoes and navigation of the Maya and their neighbours. *Journal of the Anthropological Institute of Great Britain and Ireland* 1:69–78.

  1966 Merchant gods of middle America, in *Summa anthropologica en homenaje a Roberto J. Weitlaner*, A. Pompa y Pompa ed., pp. 159–172. INAH, Mexico City.

  1970 *Maya history and religion*. University of Oklahoma Press, Norman.

Torquemada, Juan de 1975 *Monarquia indiana*, 3 volumes, Editorial Porrua, Mexico City

Townsend, Richard 1992 *The Aztecs*. Thames and Hudson, London.

Tozzer, Alfred 1941 *Landa's relación de las cosas de Yucatan*. Vol XVIII, Papers of the Peabody Museum of Archaeology and Ethnology, Harvard University, Cambridge.

Tracy, James 1990 *The rise of merchant empires: Long-distance trade in the early modern world 1350–1750*. Cambridge University Press, Cambridge.

1991 *The political economy of merchant empires: State power and world trade 1350–1750*. Cambridge University Press, Cambridge.

Trigger, Bruce 2003 *Understanding early civilizations*. Cambridge University Press, Cambridge.

Turner, Billie, and Peter Harrison. 1981 Prehistoric raised-field agriculture in the Maya lowlands. *Science* 213: 399–405.

Urcid, Javier 2010 Valued possessions: Materiality and aesthetics in western and southern Mesoamerica, in *Ancient Mexican art at Dumbarton Oaks: Objects in the Bliss collection from central highlands, southwestern highlands, gulf lowlands*, S. Evans ed., pp. 127–220. Dumbarton Oaks Research Library and Collections, Washington D.C.

van Zantwijk, Rudolf 1970 Las organizaciones social-económica y religiosa de los mercaderes gremiales Aztecas. *Boletin de Estúdios Latino-Americanos* 10:1–20.

1985 *The Aztec arrangement*. University of Oklahoma Press, Norman.

Vance, James 1970 *The merchant's world: The geography of wholesaling*. Prentice-Hall, Englewood Cliffs, New Jersey.

Varey, Simon 2000 *The writings of Dr. Francisco Hernández*. Stanford University Press, Stanford.

Vargas Pacheco, Ernesto, and Kimiyo Teramoto Ornelas 1996 Las ruinas arqueológicas de El Tigre. Campeche ¿Itzamkanac? *Mayab* 10:33–45.

Veenhof, Klaas 2003 Trade and politics in ancient Assur. Balancing of public, colonial, and entrepreneurial interests, in *Mercanti e politica nel mondo antico*, C. Zaccagnini ed., pp. 69–118. L'erma di Bretschneider, Rome.

Velázquez Castro, Adrián 2011 El reinado de Axayacatl y la creación del estilo tenochca del trabajo de la concha. *Ancient Mesoamerica* 22:437–448.

Vogt, Evon 1969 *Zinacantan: A Maya community in the highlands of Chiapas*. Belknap Press of Harvard University Press, Harvard,

von Hagen, Victor 1999 *The Aztec and Maya papermakers*. Dover, New York.

Voorhies, Barbara 1989 Whither the king's traders? Reevaluating fifteenth-century Xoconochco as a port of trade, in *Ancient trade and tribute. Economies of the Soconusco region of Mesoamerica*, B. Voorhies ed., pp. 21–47. University of Utah Press, Salt Lake City.

Wallerstein, Immanuel 1976 *The modern world-system*. Academic Press, New York.

1980 *The modem world system II: Mercantilism and the consolidation of the European world economy, 1600–1750*. Academic Press, New York.

Warren, John 1968 Minas de cobre de Michocan, 1533. *Anales del Museo Michoacano* 6:35–52.

Waters, Tony 2007 *The persistence of subsistence agriculture*. Rowman and Littlefield Publishers, Lanham, Maryland.

Weatherford, Jack 1997 *The history of money*. Three Rivers Press, New York.

2004 *Genghis Khan and the making of the modern world*. Random House, New York.

Webber, Michael, and Richard Symanski 1973 Periodic markets: An economic location analysis. *Economic Geography* 49:213–227.

Weber, Max 1946 *From Max Weber: Essays in sociology*, H. Garth and C. Wright Mills eds., Oxford University Press, New York.

1976 *The agrarian society of ancient civilizations*. NLB, London. (Orig 1909)

1992 *The protestant ethic and the spirit of capitalism*. Routledge Press, New York and London. (Orig 1930)

2003 *General economic history*. Dover publications, Mineola, New York. (Orig 1927)

Webster, David n.d. The population of Tikal (among other things). Paper presented at the Tikal and its Neighbors seminar, Meetings of the Mesoamerican Center, Antigua, Guatemala.

Webster, David, and Susan Toby Evans 2013 Mesoamerican civilization, in *The Human Past*, C. Scarre ed., pp. 594–639. Thames and Hudson, New York.

Websters New World Dictionary of the American Language 1968 The Southwestern Company, Nashville.

Wells, Christian, and Karla Davis-Salazar 2007 *Mesoamerican ritual economy*. University of Colorado Press, Boulder.

Wendt, Carl 2009 The scale and structure of bitumen processing in Early Formative Olmec households, in *Housework: Craft production and domestic economy in ancient Mesoamerica*, K. Hirth ed., pp. 33–44. Archaeological Publications No 19, American Anthropological Association, Washington D.C.

Wendt, Carl, and Ann Cyphers 2008 How the Olmec used bitumen in ancient Mesoamerica. *Journal of Anthropological Archaeology* 27:175–191.

Whitmore, Thomas, Billie Lee Turner, D. L. Johnson, R.W. Kates, and T.R. Gottschange 1990 Long-term population change, in *The earth as transformed by human action*, B. Turner, W. Clark, J. Richards, J. Matthews, and W. Meyer eds., pp. 25–40. Cambridge University Press, Cambridge.

Wiessner, Polly 1982 Risk, reciprocity and social influences on !Kung San economics, in *Politics and history in band societies*, E. Leacock and R. Lee eds., pp. 61–84. Cambridge University Press, Cambridge.

Wilk, Richard 1989 *The household economy: Reconsidering the domestic mode of production*. Westview Press, Boulder.

Wilk, Richard, and Robert Netting 1984 Households: Changing forms and functions, in *Households*, R. Netting, R. Wilk and E. Arnould eds., pp. 1–28. University of California Press, Berkeley.

Wilk, Richard, and William Rathje 1982 Household archaeology. *American Behavioral Scientist* 25:617–639.

Williams, Barbara 1994 La producción y el consumo de maíz: un estudio preliminar de Tlanchiuhca, Tepetlaoztoc, in *Agricultura indígena: pasado y presente*, T. Rojas Rabiela ed., pp. 209–226. CIESAS, Mexico City.

Williams, Barbara, and Frederic Hicks 2011 *El Códice Vergara*. UNAM, Mexico City.

Williams, Barbara, and Herbert Harvey 1997 *The Códice de Santa María de Asunción*. University of Utah Press, Salt Lake City.

Williams, Eduardo 1997 Producción de sal en la cuenca de Cuitzeo, Michoacán. *Arqueología Mexicana* 27:66–71.

Williams, Eric 1994 *Capitalism and slavery*. University of North Carolina Press, Chapel Hill.

Winterhalder, Bruce, Flora Lu, and Bram Tucker 1999 Risk-sensitive adaptive tactics: Models and evidence for subsistence studies in biology and anthropology. *Journal of Archaeological Research* 7:301–348.

Wolek, Francis 1995 The managerial principles behind guild craftsmanship. *Journal of Management History* 5:401–413.

Wolf, Eric 1959 *Sons of the shaking earth*. University of Chicago Press, Chicago.

1966 *Peasants*. Prentice-Hall, Englewood Cliffs.

1982 *Europe and the people without history*. University of California Press, Berkeley.

Wonderley, Anthony 1986 Naco, Honduras: some aspects of a late precolumbian community on the eastern Maya frontier, in *The southeast Maya periphery*, P. Urban and E. Schortman eds., pp. 313–337. University of Texas Press, Austin.

Worrall, Simon 2009 Made in China: A sunken ship's 55,000 bowls attest to ancient trade. *National Geographic* 215:112–123

Wrigley, Edward 1978 Parasite or stimulus: The town in a pre-industrial economy, in *Towns in societies*, P. Abrams and E. Wrigley eds., pp. 295–309. Cambridge University Press, Cambridge.

Ximénez, Francisco 1920 *Historia de la conquista de las provinicas de San Vicente de Chiapa y Guatemala*. 3 volumes, C.A. Tipográfica Nacional, Guatemala.

Yoshinobu, Shiba 1970 *Commerce and society in Sung China*. Michigan Abstracts of Chinese and Japanese Works on Chinese History No. 2, University of Michigan, Ann Arbor.

Young, Gary 2001 *Rome's eastern trade: International commerce and imperial policy, 31 BC–AD 305*. Routledge, London and New York.

Zavala, Silvio 1984–1989 *El servicio personal de los indios en la Nueva España*. 4 volumes, El Colegio de Mexico, Mexico City.

Zeder, Melinda 1988 Understanding urban process through the study of specialized subsistence economy in the Near East. *Journal of Anthropological Archaeology* 7:1–55.

Zorita, Alonso de 1994 *Life and labor in ancient Mexico*. University of Oklahoma Press, Norman.

Index

371